THE OXFORD HISTORY OF '

COMPANION S

The extraordinary influence of Scots in the British Empire has long been recognized. As administrators, settlers, temporary residents, professionals, plantation owners, and as military personnel, they were strikingly prominent in North America, the Caribbean, Australasia, South Africa, India, and colonies in South-East Asia and Africa. Throughout these regions they brought to bear distinctive Scottish experience as well as particular educational, economic, cultural, and religious influences. Moreover, the relationship between Scots and the British Empire had a profound effect upon many aspects of Scottish society.

This volume of essays, written by notable scholars in the field, examines the key roles of Scots in central aspects of the Atlantic and imperial economies from the eighteenth to the twentieth centuries, in East India Company rule in India, migration and the preservation of ethnic identities, the environment, the army, missionary and other religious activities, the dispersal of intellectual endeavours, and in the production of a distinctive literature rooted in colonial experience. Making use of recent, innovative research, the chapters demonstrate that an understanding of the profoundly interactive relationship between Scotland and the British Empire is vital both for the understanding of the histories of that country and of many territories of the British Empire.

All scholars and general readers interested in the dispersal of intellectual ideas, key professions, Protestantism, environmental practices, and colonial literature, as well as more traditional approaches to politics, economics, and military recruitment, will find it an essential addition to the historical literature.

John M. MacKenzie has been working on social and cultural aspects of the British Empire for some forty years. He has published on aspects of imperial propaganda, popular culture, the environment, art, and the dispersal of cultural institutions such as museums. He has also been interested in the role of Scots in the British Empire since delivering an inaugural lecture on the subject twenty years ago. He has lived in Canada, southern Africa, England, and Scotland, and has travelled extensively in many of the territories of the former Empire, conducting research and attending conferences. He has appeared on television and radio programmes associated with the British Empire.

T. M. Devine has written or edited over three dozen books on various aspects of the history of the Scottish people at home and abroad since c.1600. He is Fellow of the British Academy and Royal Society of Edinburgh, and an Honorary Member of the Royal Irish Academy. He was appointed OBE for services to Scottish History (2005) and awarded Scotland's supreme academic accolade, the Royal Gold Medal, by HM the Queen on the recommendation of the Royal Society of Edinburgh in 2001. In 2014 Devine was knighted 'for services to the study of Scottish history'.

THE OXFORD HISTORY OF THE BRITISH EMPIRE

Volume I. *The Origins of Empire*
EDITED BY Nicholas Canny

Volume II. *The Eighteenth Century*
EDITED BY P. J. Marshall

Volume III. *The Nineteenth Century*
EDITED BY Andrew Porter

Volume IV. *The Twentieth Century*
EDITED BY Judith M. Brown and Wm. Roger Louis

Volume V. *Historiography*
EDITED BY Robin W. Winks

THE OXFORD HISTORY OF THE BRITISH EMPIRE
COMPANION SERIES

Black Experience and the Empire
Philip D. Morgan and Sean Hawkins

Gender and Empire
Philippa Levine and Wm. Roger Louis

Ireland and the British Empire
Kevin Kenny and Wm. Roger Louis

Missions and Empire
Norman Etherington

Environment and Empire
William Beinart and Lotte Hughes

Australia's Empire
Deryck Schreuder and Stuart Ward

Settlers and Expatriates: Britons over the Seas
Robert Bickers

Migration and Empire
Marjory Harper and Stephen Constantine

THE OXFORD HISTORY OF THE BRITISH EMPIRE

COMPANION SERIES

Wm. Roger Louis, CBE, D. Litt., FBA

*Kerr Professor of English History and Culture, University of Texas, Austin
and Honorary Fellow of St Antony's College, Oxford*

EDITOR-IN-CHIEF

Scotland and the British Empire

EDITED BY

John M. MacKenzie
and
T. M. Devine

OXFORD
UNIVERSITY PRESS

OXFORD

UNIVERSITY PRESS

Great Clarendon Street, Oxford, OX2 6DP,
United Kingdom

Oxford University Press is a department of the University of Oxford.
It furthers the University's objective of excellence in research, scholarship,
and education by publishing worldwide. Oxford is a registered trade mark of
Oxford University Press in the UK and in certain other countries

First published 2011
First published in paperback 2016

Published in the United States of America by Oxford University Press
198 Madison Avenue, New York, NY 10016, United States of America

British Library Cataloguing in Publication Data
Data available

Library of Congress Cataloging in Publication Data
Data available

ISBN 978–0–19–957324–0 (Hbk.)
ISBN 978–0–19–879462–2 (Pbk.)

FOREWORD

The purpose of the five volumes of the Oxford History of the British Empire was to provide a comprehensive survey of the empire from its beginning to end, to explore the meaning of British imperialism for the ruled as well as the rulers, and to study the significance of the British Empire as a theme in world history. The volumes in the Companion Series carry forward this purpose. They pursue themes that could not be covered adequately in the main series while incorporating recent research and providing fresh interpretations of significant topics.

Wm. Roger Louis

CONTENTS

ABBREVIATIONS

ADB	*Australian Dictionary of Biography*
c.i.f.	cost, insurance, freight
DCB	*Dictionary of Canadian Biography*
DNZB	*Dictionary of New Zealand Biography*
DRC	Dutch Reformed Church
EIC	East India Company
f.o.b.	free on board
GDP	gross domestic product
GMS	Glasgow Missionary Society
ICS	Indian Civil Service
JICH	*Journal of Imperial and Commonwealth History*
JISS	*Journal of Irish and Scottish Studies*
LMS	London Missionary Society
Parl. Deb.	*Parliamentary Debates*
RHS	Royal Historical Society
SMS	Scottish Missionary Society
SPG	Society for the Propagation of the Gospel in Foreign Parts
SSPCK	Scottish Society for the Propagation of Christian Knowledge
VOC	Dutch East India Company

CONTRIBUTORS

JOHN M. MACKENZIE is Emeritus Professor of Imperial History at the University of Lancaster and holds honorary professorships at Aberdeen, St Andrews, and Stirling Universities. He is an Honorary Fellow of Edinburgh University and is a Fellow of the Royal Society of Edinburgh. He has been publishing on aspects of the history of the British Empire since the 1970s, his most recent books being *The Scots in South Africa: Ethnicity, Identity, Gender and Race* (2007) and *Museums and Empire: Natural History, Human Cultures and Colonial Identities* (2009). He is the general editor of the Manchester University Press 'Studies in Imperialism' series, which now runs to more than eighty books, and was editor of the journal *Environment and History*, 2000–5. His edited collection *European Empires and the People* was published in 2011.

T. M. DEVINE is Senior Research Professor in History and Director of the Scottish Centre for Diaspora Studies in the University of Edinburgh. He previously held chairs at Aberdeen and Strathclyde Universities. He was appointed OBE for services to Scottish history in 2005 and is a Fellow of the British Academy and the Royal Society of Edinburgh and an Honorary Member of the Royal Irish Academy, the only historian elected to all three of the national academies in the British Isles. In 2001 he was awarded the Royal Gold Medal of the Royal Society of Edinburgh, Scotland's supreme academic accolade, by HM The Queen. Professor Devine's most recent publications include *To the Ends of the Earth: Scotland's Global Diaspora 1750–2010* (2011) and, as co-editor, *Scotland and Poland: Historical Encounters 1500–2010* (2011).

ESTHER BREITENBACH is a Research Fellow in the School of History, Classics, and Archaeology at the University of Edinburgh. She was awarded a Ph.D. in 2005 on the topic of *Empire, Religion and National Identity: Scottish Christian Imperialism in the Nineteenth and Early Twentieth Centuries*. Previously based in Social Policy at the University of Edinburgh, she has written widely on women in contemporary Scotland and on gender equality policies. She was co-editor of *The World is Ill Divided: Women's Work in Scotland in the Nineteenth and Early Twentieth Centuries* (1990), and *Out of Bounds: Women in Scottish Society 1800–1945* (1992), both with Eleanor Gordon. Her most recent publication is *Women and Citizenship in Britain and Ireland in the Twentieth Century* (2010) co-edited with Pat Thane. Her *Empire and Scottish Society: The Impact of Foreign Missions at Home, c.1790 to c.1914* was published in 2009, and she has also published book chapters relating to Scottish missions and empire. She is currently the holder of an ESRC Research Award on 'Empire and Civil Society in 20th Century Scotland'.

CAIRNS CRAIG is Glucksman Professor of Irish and Scottish Studies and Director of the AHRC Centre for Irish and Scottish Studies (2006–2010) at the University of Aberdeen. He was previously Professor of Scottish and Modern Literature at the University of Edinburgh. He is the author of *Yeats, Eliot, Pound and the Politics of Poetry* (1982), *Out of History* (1996), *The Modern Scottish Novel* (1999), *Associationism and the Literary Imagination* (2007), and was general editor of 'The History of Scottish Literature' (4 vols, 1987–9). His *Intending Scotland: Explorations in Scottish Culture since the Enlightenment* was published in 2009.

RICHARD J. FINLAY is Professor of Scottish History at the University of Strathclyde. His most recent book, *Modern Scotland*, was published in 2004. He has published a number of articles relating to Scotland and aspects of British imperialism.

ANGELA MCCARTHY is Professor of Scottish and Irish History and Associate Director of the Centre for Irish and Scottish Studies at the University of Otago, New Zealand, where she teaches courses on Scottish and Irish migrations, and modern Scottish history. She is the author of *Personal Narratives of Irish and Scottish Migration, 1921–65: 'For Spirit and Adventure'* (2007), *Scottishness and Irishness in New Zealand since 1840* (2011), and editor of *A Global Clan: Scottish Migrant Networks and Identities since the Eighteenth Century* (2006), as well as numerous articles on Scottish and Irish migrations.

ANDREW MACKILLOP is a lecturer at the University of Aberdeen. He is the author of *'More Fruitful than the Soil': Army, Empire and the Scottish Highlands 1715–1815* (2000) and co-editor of *Fighting for Identity: Scottish Military Experience c.1550–1900* (2002) and *Military Governors and Imperial Frontiers c.1600–1800* (2003). He has published a number of articles on Scots in Asia and his book *Scotland, Ireland and British Imperialism in Asia, 1695–1813* is due to be published by Manchester University Press in 2012. His essay on the Welsh in the East India Company will be published in a collection on Wales and the British overseas empire in 2011.

PHILIPP RÖSSNER is a lecturer in the Department of History (Social and Economic History) at the University of Leipzig, Germany. He holds a Ph.D. of the University of Edinburgh and is the author of *Scottish Trade in the Wake of Union (1700–1760), The Rise of a Warehouse Economy* (2008), *Scottish Trade with German Ports, 1700–1770: A Study of the North Sea Trades and the Atlantic Economy on Ground Level* (2008), and is co-editor (with Jan De Vries and Markus A. Denzel) of *Small is Beautiful: Interlopers in Early Modern World Trade. The Experience of Smaller Trading Nations and Companies in the Mercantilist Era* (2011).

ANGELA SMITH is Professor Emerita in English Studies, and was a founding member and Director of the Centre of Commonwealth Studies, at the University of Stirling in Scotland. She taught at universities in California, Wales, and Malawi, and held research fellowships in Melbourne and Canberra. Her books include *East African Writing in English* (1989), *Katherine Mansfield and Virginia Woolf: A Public of Two* (1999), and *Katherine Mansfield: A Literary Life* (2000). She has edited, with a critical introduction and notes, Jean Rhys's *Wide Sargasso Sea* for Penguin (1997), and *Katherine Mansfield Selected Stories* for Oxford World's Classics (2002). She was an associate editor of the *Oxford Companion to English Literature* (2009), edited by Dinah Birch.

ACKNOWLEDGEMENTS

All the papers in this collection were discussed in early versions at two symposia at the Scottish Centre for Diaspora Studies, University of Edinburgh, in 2009–10. All the contributors would like to thank Esther Breitenbach for organizing these symposia, as well as the several members of staff of the University of Edinburgh who helped in arranging them. Contributors are most grateful to the various scholars in the audience who commented so helpfully and constructively on the papers. The contributors and editors also had significant input into each other's chapters. In significant respects, this book has indeed been a collaborative venture.

Editors and contributors would also wish to express their gratitude to William Roger Louis and the editors at OUP for commissioning this volume for the Oxford History of the British Empire Companion Series.

1

Introduction

John M. MacKenzie and T. M. Devine

Background

The relationship between Scotland and the English, then British, Empire has been complex, contested, and of long standing. Even during the era of mercantilist and other exclusivist legislation in the seventeenth century, Scots found it possible to penetrate the English Empire as settlers, indentured labourers, and traders. Famously, after 1707, the Scots gained legitimate entry to the newly constituted 'British' Empire and rapidly played a significant role in all its geographical sectors, in the West in the thirteen colonies, Canada, and the Caribbean, and in the East through the East India Company (EIC). In this the Scots were building on a long-standing tradition of trading, sojourning, and settling in the Baltic, in Scandinavia, and in the Low Countries.[1] Sometimes, the Scots also penetrated the overseas territories of continental European countries, as they did in the Cape Colony of the Dutch East India Company (VOC).[2] They were also, of course, central to the 'planting' of Ulster in the seventeenth century, with notable effects upon the British Empire through the migration of the so-called 'Scotch Irish'. This tradition of wandering and settling can be explained by the geographical position of Scotland off the north-west coast of Europe, a country with a strikingly long coastline and many offshore islands, yet with usable, if often dangerous, sea crossings across the Irish and North Seas. The connections with Scandinavia (through the

---

[1] T. C. Smout (ed.), *Scotland and Europe, 1200–1850* (Edinburgh, 1986); idem (ed.), *Scotland and the Sea* (Edinburgh, 1992); Christopher Harvie, *Travelling Scot* (Glendaruel, 1999).

[2] John M. MacKenzie with Nigel R. Dalziel, *The Scots in South Africa: Ethnicity, Identity, Gender and Race 1772–1914* (Manchester, 2007), 29–31. The activities of Scots in imperial territories, both of the English and other European powers, is worthy of more attention that this introduction has space to provide.

Vikings) and with Ireland had served to emphasize these traditions of seafaring, fishing, and trading. Despite their comparatively small population (fewer than one million in the seventeenth century), their own lands were often marginal and poor. Looking outwards to make a living was often a necessity.

In the eighteenth century the comparative ubiquity of the Scots became a source of much comment. Often unpopular in London, they nonetheless had their uses, not least in the military and in key professions (such as medicine,[3] botany, and seafaring), particularly after the spirit of Jacobite rebellion in some parts of the Highlands and Islands had been crushed in 1746. But as contributions to this book demonstrate, they were already important in many of the settler territories of the British Empire in the West, as well as in commercial exploits in the East, well before the later eighteenth century. By the nineteenth, they had developed a remarkably positive reputation as settlers, soldiers,[4] merchant seamen, botanists, foresters, engineers, missionaries, teachers, founders of universities, and not least as bankers, merchants, and creators of companies. All this activity raises many questions about the nature of Scottish society, about the flourishing of its intellectual endeavours in the Enlightenment of the eighteenth century, its curious mix of endemic poverty and striking economic transformation, as well as of its anomalous status as a nation with distinctive institutions (church, law, banking, and education, preserved in the Act of Union of 1707) which nonetheless lacked its own apparatus as a state.[5]

These very conditions help to explain the complexity of the Scottish relationship with the British Empire—and indeed with the rest of the world since emigration, trade, and investment were in no way confined to the empire. The paradox of a successful industrialized society with very high rates of emigration can in part be resolved by the deep social inequalities and chronic mal-distribution of wealth in Scotland. The familiar explanations of famine, destitution, and clearance in the Highlands do not satisfy

---

[3] Brian Lavery, *Shield of Empire: The Royal Navy and Scotland* (Edinburgh, 2007) has material, among much else, on the significance of Scots doctors in the RN.

[4] In this regard, see for example Steve Murdoch and A. Mackillop (eds), *Fighting for Identity: Scottish Military Experience c.1550–1900* (Leiden, 2002); James Miller, *Swords for Hire: The Scottish Mercenary* (Edinburgh, 2007).

[5] For a recent discussion of Scotland and the Union, together with its overseas affiliations and imperial connections, see Allan I. Macinnes, *Union and Empire: The Making of the United Kingdom in 1707* (Cambridge, 2007).

for the decades after *c*.1860 because by then the overwhelming majority of Scottish migrants did not come from regions of economic backwardness but from the Lowland areas of industrial and urban modernity. During the period from the late eighteenth to the early twentieth centuries, at least two million people left Scotland, the majority for the United States, but many for Canada, Australia, New Zealand, and the Cape, with the colonial/dominions proportion rising considerably in the years between the 1890s and the Second World War. But much migration was 'elective', for some of the participants were people who had some modest means—or the younger sons of gentry and professionals—looking for even better opportunities overseas. Scotland was also over-producing graduates from its institutions of higher education (at least four of them throughout this period[6]) and the flow of such people into the educated professions. Moreover, many of Scotland's migrants were in skilled trades which were at a premium in many colonies. Further factors included the manner in which Scotland's industrial revolution both produced a dependence on heavy industries whose fortunes passed through sharp cyclical fluctuations, feeding the emigration stream at times of depression, and also helped to suck in many Irish migrants. Moreover, Scotland had one of the most concentrated patterns of landownership in Europe and the vast majority of Lowland rural dwellers were lease-holding tenants (themselves a small elite) and a great army of landless farm servants living within a social system of great rigidity. Often the only recourse for the ambitious and those who aspired to 'independence' was to leave for the colonies or the USA.

The heavy industries which became such a marked characteristic of the Scottish economy became closely related to imperial trades, both in the supplying of transport systems and infrastructure (like ships, railway engines, engineering associated with harbour works, roads, and so on) and of products (iron, steel, chemicals, jute) vital to the creation of the British world's global capitalist system. It is for all these economic and social reasons that it is far too simplistic to consider the British Celtic fringe (and Scotland in particular) as somehow in a quasi-colonial relationship

---

[6] As well as the three medieval universities, St Andrews, Glasgow, and Aberdeen, Edinburgh was a Reformation foundation. Aberdeen had two colleges, King's and Marischal, which were separate institutions until the nineteenth century. The Andersonian Institution, a university in all but name, was founded in Glasgow in the late eighteenth century and ultimately became the University of Strathclyde.

with the central and dominant English power.[7] 'Victimhood' has always been an inadequate concept when considering the Scottish relationship with the British Empire, even if Sir John Seeley saw the extension of the English state in its adjacent lands and islands as the vital prerequisite for the expansion of English or British power.[8] 'Collaboration' also constitutes an inaccurate way of explaining these processes. Scots and English (also joined by the Welsh and many Irish people) operated in complex forms of partnership in creating the British world system. Elaborate networks of migratory patterns, of economic activity, of professional and missionary endeavour, were established which are only now being subjected to intensive study.

The Historiography of Scotland, the British State, and Empire

At one time, British historians had a tendency to separate domestic from imperial history. This is no longer sustainable. The existence of the British Empire had major effects upon the workings of the metropolitan state, not least in conditioning the relationships among its different ethnicities. It is a striking feature of a modern historiography that the climax of the progressive devolution of the British state between the 1920s and the 1990s has produced a fresh interest in the histories of the various ethnicities of the British and Hibernian Isles. Such devolution started with Irish independence and the accompanying devolution for Northern Ireland, which was checked by the 'troubles' in that 'province' in the later decades of the twentieth century. These produced in turn the abrogation and then a major reworking of such devolved powers, together with the culmination of pressures for devolution for both Scotland and Wales, strikingly coincidental with (though unrelated to) one of the last major acts of 'decolonization' in the British Empire with the handing back of Hong Kong to the Chinese in 1997. The creation of the British–Irish Council in 1998, even if its public profile is low, symbolized a new relationship for the various peoples of the 'Atlantic archipelago', bringing together governments (albeit with varying status at international law) in Dublin and Belfast, Edinburgh and Cardiff, with those of London and also administrations in the Isle of Man,

[7] Michael Hechter, *Internal Colonialism: The Celtic Fringe in British National Development, 1536–1966* (London, 1975).
[8] J. R. Seeley, *The Expansion of England* (London, 1883).

Guernsey, and Jersey.[9] Perhaps it is not surprising that these developments have produced a new and energetic interest among historians in the manner in which these various peoples interacted with the English and with each other, not least through the medium of the British Empire.

In all of this, histories of Ireland have inevitably been in the forefront, at least in some specialized ways. The Irish position within the British state up to the 1920s always seemed to be more 'colonial' that that of any of the other non-English peoples. British politicians invariably saw Ireland as essentially an imperial problem. From the rebellion of 1798 through the Union of 1800 to the controversies respecting 'home rule' between the 1880s and 1914 Ireland's status was discussed in terms of constitutional developments within the British settler colonies, very much in the context of the development of such concepts as 'responsible government'. These fraught debates unquestionably had an influence upon Scotland, not least in the creation of a Scottish Office in 1885 and in the discussions of what was known as 'home rule all round', a concept which placed the component parts of the United Kingdom in a similar position to white settler colonies that were later to be known as the dominions (a status which the British sought for Ireland, but which the Irish ultimately rejected). Thus, in a constitutional sense, there can be little doubt that empire and the British state were closely connected, not least through the Irish question.

Stephen Howe has suggested that work on the Scottish connection with empire has been more extensive in recent years, but this relates mainly to the reciprocal effects upon Scotland itself.[10] It is apparent that, for obvious political reasons, there was a certain amnesia about empire, at least until the Irish state was securely established within the European Union. Nevertheless, from a constitutional point of view, as well as issues such as migration and the relationship between Ireland and other colonial territories, the historiography of Ireland within the British Empire is now well advanced.[11] Although Irish migration has been closely studied for many years, it was mainly in respect of the USA until research spread out towards

---

[9] The Council's website provides valuable information on its foundation, workings and objectives, http://www.british-irishcouncil.org.

[10] Stephen Howe, 'Historiography', in Kevin Kenny (ed.), *Ireland and the British Empire* (Oxford, 2004), 247.

[11] For a survey of recent books on Ireland and empire, see the review essay by Stephen Howe 'Minding the Gaps: New Directions in the Study of Ireland and Empire', *Journal of Imperial and Commonwealth History* (*JICH*), 37.1 (March 2009), 135–49.

British territories in the past three decades. Later, Keith Jeffery's edited *An Irish Empire?* was a pioneering collection of 1996.[12] This was followed by Kevin Kenny's edited volume in the present series *Ireland and the British Empire*.[13] There have, moreover, been studies of the Irish in Canada, Australia, New Zealand, South Africa, India and the Caribbean.[14] There has also been an interest in the bilateral relations of Ireland with other parts of the British Empire, since the example of Ireland was influential in the development of nationalism elsewhere, notably in India.[15] The specific contribution of Irish people to the professions and to particular territories such as India has also become a focus for research.[16]

In some ways, the historiography of Scotland within both the metropolitan state and the British Empire has been less advanced. Yet the literature on Scots overseas is extensive, if for many years unsophisticated. These studies can perhaps be divided into four phases, starting with the first in the nineteenth century, when explorations of Scots abroad were fed into the attempts at a cultural resurgence within Scotland itself. Such works would include J. H. Burton's *The Scot Abroad* of 1864 and W. J. Rattray's

---

[12] Keith Jeffery (ed.), *An Irish Empire? Aspects of Ireland and the British Empire* (Manchester, 1996). One of the co-editors of the present volume was active in commissioning this collection of essays.

[13] Kenny (ed.), *Ireland and the British Empire*.

[14] A selection from a considerable literature might include: D. H. Akenson, *The Irish in Ontario* (Montreal, 1984), Patrick O'Farrell, *The Irish in Australia* (Kensington, NSW, 1986); Cecil J. Houston and William J. Smyth, *Irish Emigration and Canadian Settlement* (Toronto, 1990); D. H. Akenson, *The Irish in South Africa* (Grahamstown, 1991), Donal McCracken, 'Irish Settlement and Identity in South Africa before 1910', *Irish Historical Studies*, 28.110 (1992), 134–49; D. H. Akenson, *If the Irish Ran the World: Montserrat, 1630–1730* (Liverpool, 1997); Michael and Denis Holmes (eds), *Ireland and India* (Dublin, 1997); Brad Patterson (ed.), *The Irish in New Zealand: Historical Contexts and Perspectives* (Wellington, 2002). See also David Fitzpatrick, 'Ireland and the Empire', in Andrew Porter (ed.), *The Oxford History of the British Empire*, iii: *The Nineteenth Century* (Oxford, 1999), 495–521 and Deirdre McMahon, 'Ireland and the British Empire/Commonwealth 1900–1948', in Judith M. Brown and Wm Roger Louis (eds), *The Oxford History of the British Empire*, iv: *the Twentieth Century* (Oxford, 1999), 138–62.

[15] Kate O'Malley, *Ireland, India and Empire: Indo-Irish Radical Connections 1919–64* (Manchester, 2008).

[16] Barrie Crosbie, 'Ireland, Colonial Science and the Geographical Construction of British India, c.1820–1870', *Historical Journal*, 52 (2009), 963–87; idem, *Irish Imperial Networks, Migration, Social Communication and Exchange in Nineteenth-Century India* (Cambridge, 2012). See also Patrick O'Leary, *Servants of the Empire: The Irish in Punjab, 1881–1921* (Manchester, 2011).

monumental four-volume *The Scot in British North America* of 1880.[17] The second phase can be associated with a renewed Scottish nationalism in the twentieth century, when Scottish activities in the British Empire seemed to offer Scots (so far as some nationalists were concerned) the status of a global people worthy of a separate state. The classic works in this phase were Andrew Dewar Gibb's *Scottish Empire* of 1937, together with his *Scotland in Eclipse* (1930) and his *Scotland Resurgent* of 1950.[18] An interest in Scots overseas seemed to go into abeyance between the 1940s and 1960s. This may have been because of the Second World War, the moderate post-war boom for Scotland's heavy industries, and the strength of Unionist politics during that period. But from the 1960s to the 1980s we can identify a third phase, the first entry by professional historians into the study of Scots overseas, but yet to be placed within a truly modern historiography of empire. Gordon Donaldson's *The Scots Overseas* of 1966 was the pioneer and it was followed by a sequence of books on Scots in specific territories of settlement, including G. L. Pearce, *The Scots of New Zealand* of 1976, W. Stanford Reid, *The Scottish Tradition in Canada* of the same year, followed by a number on Australia, David Macmillan's *Scotland and Australia 1788–1850* of 1967 (the same author wrote about the Scots influence on Canada), Malcolm Prentis, *The Scots in Australia* (1983), and Don Watson's *Caledonia Australis* (1984).[19] These sought to identify the significance of Scots in those territories and the contribution they made to the economic and cultural life of the three former dominions.

But little of this work has been integrated into wider issues of imperial history, particularly its central theoretical positions, or with the connection between Scotland and the British state. Radical precursors of studies in the latter field include Michael Hechter's *Internal Colonialism* of 1975 and Tom

---

[17] J. H. Burton, *The Scot Abroad*, 2 vols (London, 1864; reissued in a 2nd edn in 1881); W. J. Rattray, *The Scot in British North America*, 4 vols (Edinburgh, 1880).

[18] Andrew Dewar Gibb, *Scotland in Eclipse* (London, 1930), *Scottish Empire* (London, 1937), *Scotland Resurgent* (Stirling, 1950).

[19] Gordon Donaldson, *The Scots Overseas* (London, 1966); David S. Macmillan, *Scotland and Australia, 1788–1850: Emigration, Commerce and Investment* (Oxford, 1967); G. L. Pearce, *The Scots of New Zealand* (Auckland, 1976); W. S. Reid, *The Scottish Tradition in Canada* (Toronto, 1976); Malcolm D. Prentis, *The Scots in Australia: A Study of New South Wales, Victoria and Queensland, 1788–1900* (Sydney, 1983); Don Watson, *Caledonia Australis: Scottish Highlanders on the Frontier of Australia* (Sydney, 1984). A later popular work was Jim Hewitson, *Far Off in Sunlit Places: Stories of the Scots in Australia and New Zealand* (Edinburgh, 1998).

Nairn's *The Break-up of Britain* of 1977.[20] These were largely polemical accounts of alleged English repression of other ethnicities within Britain, with Nairn's book proposing the imminent decolonization of British ethnic satellites to match the apparent worldwide movement of the time. His book acted as an antidote to Sir Reginald Coupland's appeal in his *Welsh and Scottish Nationalism* of 1954 that Irish independence should *not* lead to the break-up of Britain.[21] These political debates focusing on Britain itself were followed by R. A. Cage's edited collection *The Scots Abroad* of 1985, which began to open up some of the wider imperial issues, suggesting a distinctive contribution by Scots to the British Empire.[22] In the same decade there was a considerable development of migration studies, not least relating to Scotland. This has been perhaps the richest field of all, as well as the most extensive, with work by Marjory Harper, Tom Devine, and Eric Richards among others.[23] Such studies have been set into an extensive historiography of British and European migration and continue to be regularly augmented.[24] Interestingly, in this same period, a sequence of exhibitions in Glasgow and (mainly) in Edinburgh set out to celebrate the role of Scots in some overseas territories.[25] It may be (though this is highly speculative) that this renewed interest was connected with decolonization in the British Empire and with further efforts at instilling fresh vigour into Scottish nationalism.

It was only from the 1990s that further efforts at conceptualization of this relationship between Scotland and the British Empire were attempted. The important question of the relationship between the imperial experience and

---

[20] For Hechter, see n. 7; Tom Nairn, *The Break-up of Britain* (London, 1977).

[21] Sir Reginald Coupland, *Welsh and Scottish Nationalism* (London, 1954).

[22] R. A. Cage (ed.), *The Scots Abroad* (London, 1985).

[23] Marjory Harper, *Emigration from North-East Scotland*, 2 vols (Aberdeen, 1988) and *Adventurers and Exiles: The Great Scottish Exodus* (London, 2003); T. M. Devine (ed.), *Scottish Emigration and Scottish Society* (Edinburgh, 1992); Eric Richards, *The Highland Clearances: People, Landlords and Rural Turmoil* (Edinburgh, 2000) and *Britannia's Children* (London, 2004).

[24] See, for example, the setting of the Scottish example into a wider context in Marjory Harper and Stephen Constantine, *Migration and Empire* (Oxford, 2010).

[25] *Clyde Men of the World*, an exhibition of Archives at Kelvingrove Museum and Art Gallery, November 1979; Helen Smailes, *Scottish Empires: Scots in Pursuit of Hope and Glory* (National Portrait Gallery, Edinburgh, 1981); *Scotland and Africa* (National Library of Scotland, 1982); *The Scots and the Commonwealth* (National Book League Scotland Exhibition, 1986); Alex M. Cain, *The Cornchest for Scotland: Scots in India* (National Library of Scotland, Edinburgh, 1986); *That Land of Exiles: Scots in Australia* (National Library of Scotland, Edinburgh, 1988).

the history of Scotland itself was opened up, virtually for the first time.[26] This was followed by a consideration of the extent to which the British Empire may have failed to become truly 'British', but instead had, for various reasons, helped to ensure the cultural survival of the respective ethnicities of the British metropolitan state.[27] (Recently, an interest in the role of the Welsh in the British Empire has begun to develop, almost for the first time.[28]) The extensive work now available on Scotland was pulled together into a major survey by T. M. Devine in his book *Scotland's Empire, 1600–1815* (2003) and his *To the Ends of the Earth: Scotland's Global Diaspora 1750–2010* (2011).[29] Moreover, whole new areas have been opened up relatively recently, for example respecting Scots and the environment and a distinctively Scottish literature relating to empire.[30] But there is a danger in all this activity and that lies in the possible creation of a new myth, that of Scots 'exceptionalism'.

The Scots: Exceptionalism or Difference?

In the wave of books about the Scots emanating from the 1990s and the early years of the twenty-first century, there were some which seemed to offer titles that were hostages to fortune. Michael Fry's engagingly, if cheekily, titled *The Scottish Empire* of 2001 offered such a vast compendium of Scots and their achievements across the globe that it seemed to imply that Scots migration constituted a diaspora both of major proportions and of a uniquely gifted people.[31] His *'Bold, Independent, Unconquer'd and Free': How the Scots Made America Safe for Liberty, Democracy and Capitalism*

[26] John M. MacKenzie, 'Essay and Reflection: On Scotland and the Empire', *International History Review*, 15.4 (November 1993), 661–880 (based on an inaugural lecture delivered in Lancaster University in May 1992).

[27] John M. MacKenzie, 'Empire and National Identities: The Case of Scotland', *Transactions of the Royal Historical Society*, 6th series, 8 (1998), 215–31.

[28] H. V. Bowen (ed.), *Wales and the British Overseas Empire: Interactions and Influences*, c.1680–1830 (Manchester, 2011).

[29] T. M. Devine, *Scotland's Empire, 1600–1815* (London, 2003); idem, *To the Ends of the Earth: Scotland's Global Diaspora 1750–2010* (London, 2011).

[30] Douglas Mack, *Scottish Literature and the British Empire* (Edinburgh, 2006) and the contribution of Angela Smith in this volume.

[31] Michael Fry, *The Scottish Empire* (Phantassie, 2001). Fry's serious point, that Scots ideas, ideologies, political economy, and philosophy had an enduring intellectual influence upon the British Empire, is, however, an important one, explored in this volume by Cairns Craig.

(2003) appeared to make this more explicit.[32] Arthur Herman, an American with apparently no Scottish connections, had already produced what seemed like an even more outrageous title in 2001: *The Scottish Enlightenment: The Scots' Invention of the Modern World* (the American edition has the even more ambitious sub-title *How Western Europe's Poorest People Invented our World and Everything in it*).[33] If this myth seemed to be ballooning in modern times, it also appeared to be based on nineteenth-century precedents. Andrew Carnegie, himself a somewhat interested party, was said to have remarked that 'America would have been a poor show but for the Scots'.[34] Victorian travellers in the empire, even those who were not themselves Scots, also seemed impressed. The Irish Sir Charles Dilke, who toured the British Empire in 1867, wrote that 'wherever abroad you come across a Scotchman, you invariably find him prosperous and respected'. He also suggested that 'for every Englishman that you meet who has worked himself up from small beginnings, without external aid, you find ten Scotchmen'.[35] The celebrated novelist Anthony Trollope wrote that 'in the colonies those who make money are generally Scotchmen and those who do not are mostly Irishmen'.[36] The academic and political commentator J. A. Froude, touring the empire in the 1880s, also commented on the apparent ubiquity of the Scots and their alleged capacities in developing the empire.[37]

Trollope offers a clue to one explanation for these comments: the English often seemed to extol the Scots in order to denigrate the Irish.[38] Yet Trollope's canard was far from the truth. There is a good deal of evidence to suggest that there were many successful Irish migrants, for example in New Zealand.[39] Another might be the fact that the Scots were ever eager to

---

[32] Michael Fry, *'Bold, Independent, Unconquer'd and Free': How the Scots Made America Safe for Liberty, Democracy and Capitalism* (Ayr, 2003).

[33] Arthur Herman, *The Scottish Enlightenment: The Scots' Invention of the Modern World* (London, 2002).

[34] Quoted in Cage (ed.), *The Scots Abroad*, 80, from David Macrae, *American Presidents and Men I have Met* (Glasgow, 1908), 123.

[35] Sir Charles Wentworth Dilke, *Greater Britain* (London, 1872), 373, 533.

[36] Anthony Trollope, *Australia* (London, 1872), 420.

[37] J. A. Froude, *Oceana or England and her Colonies* (London, 1886), 118.

[38] This started in the eighteenth century. Edward Long did the same thing in his *History of Jamaica* of 1774.

[39] See, for example, Lyndon Fraser, 'Irish Migrants to the West Coast, 1884–1900', *New Zealand Journal of History*, 34.2 (2000), 197–225. See also Angela McCarthy, *Irish Migrants in New Zealand, 1840–1937* (Woodbridge, 2005).

advance themselves. Many were literate or well educated. They published extensively. They were active in the colonial press. They often saw themselves and their fellow countrymen in the spirit of the notorious Scots phrase 'here's tae us; wha's like us?'. A third possibility is that the Scots were more highly skilled than some migrants. Contemporary commentators and modern historians have suggested that this might have been the case.[40] Many Scottish artisans and craftsmen secured good jobs in colonial enterprises, notably the building of infrastructural projects.[41] Other well-educated Scots appeared to dominate a number of professions.[42] Then there is the fraught question of the Scottish Enlightenment, claims about which are more easily asserted than proved. Obviously the Enlightenment was a Europe-wide phenomenon, though its Scottish manifestations were certainly remarkable. It is perhaps possible to chart the intellectual ancestry, as it were, of many colonial figures to dominant Enlightenment thinkers, and this may well have helped in the creation of their visibility in publications and policies throughout the empire and indeed the world.[43] In his chapter, Cairns Craig argues that the Scottish Enlightenment and the intellectual and philosophical diaspora which flowed from it created a global influence as great as any produced by other forms of migration and the dispersal of economic and cultural influences. But the Enlightenment and its effects arose from the exceptional nature of certain aspects of Scottish institutional life, which then sustained intellectual and disciplinary developments that were unique in their configuration. Thus, this is not an exceptionalism built into the DNA, as it were, of the people, but an exceptional range of outcomes produced by an institutional structure which was, by a series of historical accidents, very distinctive.

Thus, in these respects as in a number of others, it would be safer to suggest that Scots were marked by certain key differences from their English and other contemporaries. They were distinguished more by the differences in their

[40] See below, pp. 165–6.

[41] MacKenzie with Dalziel, *Scots in South Africa*, 154. See also Harper and Constantine, *Migration and Empire*, 59 for Aberdeen stonemasons in New South Wales.

[42] For 'intellectual migrants', see the special issue of the *Journal of Scottish Thought*, 1.1 (2007) and Cairns Craig, *Intending Scotland: Explorations in Scottish Culture since the Enlightenment* (Edinburgh, 2009).

[43] Enlightenment ideas even permeated the activities of Scottish Orientalists in India. Avril A. Powell, *Scottish Orientalists and India: The Muir Brothers, Religion, Education and Empire* (Woodbridge, 2010), 109–12, 134–6.

educational, religious, and cultural upbringing than by any alleged exception-alism. There is also good evidence to suggest that the Scots were indeed 'clannish', establishing networks of kin and friendship, associated with specific areas of the country, and assisting in (for example) chain migration, associational culture, and business (though they were not unique in this). Forming such networks was itself a marker of mutual estimations of worth. It was these characteristics that often enabled them (to use what has become something of a cliché of modern scholarship) to 'punch above their weight' in many colonies.

Yet these constant references to Scots and Scotchmen raise the difficult question of what constitutes a Scot. If modern Britain is a country of geographical and cultural, economic, and social pluralism, as well as of considerable regional diversity, then this can equally be said to be true of Scotland. Scotland was perhaps forced into a sense of national identity through its 'auld enemy' the English, not least (if mainly for an elite) through the Declaration of Arbroath of 1320. While the border between England and Scotland has, of course, been mobile, nonetheless some conception of a change of territorial and geographical significance located between the Solway and (variously) the Tyne or Berwick has been lodged in the perceptions of peoples since at least Roman times. But the great diversity of Scotland in its borderlands, 'central belt', east coastal regions, Highlands and Islands has always been apparent. It may be that most people identified with specific areas of Scotland rather than an overall conception of the country down to the last two centuries or so. Yet there is evidence that by the eighteenth century migrants and sojourners (temporary residents in overseas countries) were thinking of themselves as Scots, with specific cultural affiliations that differentiated them from the English and other peoples. Diaries and memoirs of Scots travelling to Argentina in the 1820s certainly make this clear.[44] As has often been noted, in the post-Jacobite period many Scots paradoxically adopted some of the cultural forms of the Highlands and Islands, combining them with the cults of Robert Burns and Sir Walter Scott to form iconic referents that became the definers of Scots throughout the British Empire.[45] As McCarthy shows in this volume, such forms of

[44] Iain A. D. Stewart, *From Caledonia to the Pampas: Two Accounts by Early Scottish Emigrants to the Argentine* (Phantassie, 2000). See also David Rock, 'The British in Argentina', in Robert Bickers (ed.), *Settlers and Expatriates* (Oxford, 2010), 18–44, particularly 19, 24, 29–32.

[45] Murray G. H. Pittock, *Celtic Identity and the British Image* (Manchester, 1999) and also his *Scottish Nationality* (Basingstoke, 2001).

identity were important to migrants both in the act of migration and once settled in new lands.[46]

It may well be that such definers of cultural difference contributed to the myth of exceptionalism. This almost certainly had significant effects both on the ways in which Scots viewed themselves and the manner in which colonial enterprise and activities looped back to Scotland. Scots formed many cultural associations in which they were able to maintain contacts with each other, 'network' in a variety of professional and business ways, as well as create some aspects of social security for their brethren who encountered economic hardship.[47] In these associations (even if only a minority joined them) they often founded magazines in which they extolled the virtues of heroic and iconic fellow countrymen or, in some cases, expressed admiration for members of their own community. There were two critical factors here. First, the Scots were generally a minority surrounded by English, Irish, or other ethnicities, including sometimes indigenous peoples. Their societies and organizations not only offered mutual help and security, but also a sense of belonging and of distinguishing themselves from those around them. The second essential characteristic was that this could only happen where they existed in a particular setting in the numbers necessary for the establishment of a critical mass, sufficient to permit, for example, the founding of a Presbyterian church (although not all Scots were Presbyterians and many Presbyterians were Irish or Scots Irish), a Masonic lodge of the Scottish constitution, or the associations which preserved their ethnicity. Where such critical mass was not present (and this would also be true of other immigrant ethnicities), it was much more likely that they would integrate. The final factor was that their cultural icons, their dress and presentation of the body (in modern scholarly parlance), their adherence to religious forms and to specific modes of music-making, dancing, or recitation, marked them out from the English, who almost always constituted

---

[46] Angela McCarthy's recent book *Scottishness and Irishness in New Zealand since 1840* (Manchester, 2010) brings these issues down to modern times. We should remember that migrants also returned. Marjory's Harper's *Emigrant Homecomings: The Return Movement of Emigrants, 1600–2000* (Manchester, 2005) is the pioneering book in this regard.

[47] Tanja Bueltmann, Andrew Hinson, and Graeme Morton (eds), *Ties of Bluid, Kin and Countrie: Scottish Associational Culture in the Diaspora* (Guelph, 2009); MacKenzie with Dalziel, *Scots in South Africa*, ch. 8; Angela McCarthy (ed.), *A Global Clan: Scottish Migrant Networks and Identities since the Eighteenth Century* (London, 2006). We should also note the importance of civic associational culture within Scotland.

the majority people. English culture, divided as it was into regional variants in any case, simply could not produce the elements of 'performance' which distinguished the Scots. As Harper and Constantine have recently suggested, the English were perhaps 'least assertive of their "national" identity because of their numerical predominance.'[48] All of these issues are examined further in the contributions of McCarthy, Craig, and MacKenzie in this volume, while the recruitment and reputation of their military regiments, together with the distinctive manner in which they identified themselves are considered by Devine.[49] In all of these distinctiveness and difference are the keys. The Scots made differential contributions to the imperial experience and if they were in any way exceptional, it was sometimes in their numbers proportionate to the relative population of the United Kingdom.[50] Even here it is possible to suggest that such disproportionate numbers are related as much to poverty, lack of opportunity, sometimes even domestic failure, as to any sense of alleged exceptional ability.

The Scots Contribution to the British Empire

If the differences exhibited by the Scots can be demonstrated rather more readily than any form of exceptionalism, what did these distinguishing elements contribute to the character of the British Empire, its domination of indigenous peoples, and the creation of its global economic system as well as the cultural characteristics of the British world? The contributors to this book aim to demonstrate some of these 'contributions'. They include a consideration (by Mackillop) of the incidence of Scots in the employ of the EIC in the eighteenth century, when Scots do seem to have been represented in numbers greater than their proportion in the United Kingdom would warrant. In the operations of the EIC, Scots performed a

---

[48] Harper and Constantine, *Migration and Empire*, 347.

[49] On Scots military identity, see Stephen Wood, *The Scottish Soldier* (Edinburgh, 1987); Stuart Allan and Allan Carswell, *The Thin Red Line: War, Empire and Visions of Scotland* (Edinburgh, 2004); Edward M. Spiers, *The Scottish Soldier and Empire, 1854–1902* (Edinburgh, 2006); Murdoch and Mackillop (eds), *Fighting for Identity*; and Heather Streets, *Martial Races: The Military, Race and Masculinity in British Imperial Culture, 1857–1914* (Manchester, 2004).

[50] It has recently been pointed out that in 1931 Scots constituted 17% of the British community in Malaya. This is symbolized by the names of Malayan hill stations: Maxwell's Hill, the Cameron Highlands, and Frazer's Hill. Tim Harper, 'The British Malayans', in Bickers (ed.), *Settlers and Expatriates*, 236 and 253. Hill stations in Ceylon were likened to Scottish Highland resorts, Margaret Jones, '"Permanent Boarders": The British in Ceylon, 1815–1960', ibid. 221–2.

variety of roles, in the military, as administrators, and as traders. They also became noted as 'Orientalists', that is as scholars and commentators who studied and interpreted Indian religions and cultures, deriving from the group of Scots who were active in the entourage of Warren Hastings during his period as the Governor-General of India.[51] This inaugurated a Scottish tradition of studying indigenous peoples, both in the empire and through the development of anthropological theory at home. Perhaps the most notable example of the latter characteristic is Sir James Frazer, with his epic and highly influential work *The Golden Bough: A Study of Magic and Religion* (1890), although a closer study of this phenomenon would require another volume.

Among the other distinctive contributions of Scots to the British Empire would certainly be forms of economic enterprise, examined in this volume by Devine and Rössner for the earlier period and Devine and MacKenzie for the later. The Scots unquestionably produced a striking response to the opportunities of the western trades, notably in tobacco, and to the fiscal-credit arrangements that helped to develop such trades to an extraordinary extent in the eighteenth century, fuelling, for example, the remarkable growth of Glasgow and the emergence of its industrial base, itself closely connected to the empire.[52] Scots were already well known as bankers and they carried their expertise in this field to many colonies. They also developed roles in other aspects of the financial sector, notably in insurance, in institutions adopting forms of 'mutuality' (that is where investors themselves own the company as a collectivity), and in the development of the concept of the unit trust, important in the mobilization of capital from domestic funds and its distribution within the empire. Moreover, Scots were active in the agency houses of empire which managed other businesses and their trades.[53] All of these are examined in greater detail in the contribution of Devine and MacKenzie below, as are the roles of Scots in both

[51] Jane Rendall, 'Scottish Orientalism: From Robertson to James Mill', *Historical Journal*, 25.1 (1982), 43–69; John Riddy, 'Warren Hastings: Scotland's Benefactor?', in Geoffrey Carnall and Colin Nicholson (eds), *The Impeachment of Warren Hastings* (Edinburgh, 1989), 30–57; Powell, *Scottish Orientalists*.

[52] T. M. Devine, *The Tobacco Lords: A Study of the Tobacco Merchants of Glasgow and their Trading Activities, c.1740–1790* (Edinburgh, 1975); T. M. Devine and Gordon Jackson (eds), *Glasgow*, i: *Beginnings to 1830* (Manchester, 1995).

[53] For agency houses in India, see James G. Parker, 'Scottish Enterprise in India, 1750–1914', in Cage (ed.), *The Scots Abroad*.

manufacturing and professions associated with transport, engineering, and other related enterprises.

This readily connects with the manner in which the Scottish educational system, together with aspects of its internal social and economic arrangements, served to produce an intellectual diaspora which influenced educational and other developments throughout the British Empire.[54] It is possible to trace a Scottish intellectual inheritance in almost all the colonies of settlement, in India and elsewhere.[55] We seem to be on particularly secure ground when the Scots influence on the environmental professions is examined. They were certainly highly active in all enterprises connecting with botany, forestry, surveying, geology, and related activities such as palaeontology, museum collecting, and theoretical geography, with such derivatives as geo-politics and town planning. Sometimes studies of indigenous peoples and of the environment were related to missionary activity and here we find another source of difference, rooted in Scottish domestic traditions of the era subsequent to the Reformation and the times of religious troubles that followed it. Scots Presbyterianism was highly schismatic both in the eighteenth and nineteenth centuries and, far from inhibiting the dispersal of Scots religious and educational influences across the world, this may well have contributed to the remarkable evangelizing energies that developed in the Scottish churches by the 1820s. Scots missionaries were often highly educated. Sometimes they were interested in the kind of theorizing about cultures across the globe which emerged from the Enlightenment (even if some of the greatest Enlightenment figures would have been scarcely sympathetic to their aims). But often they were more interested in purely pragmatic forms of evangelization through which they linked home to the wider world—through recruitment, fund-raising, publications, and other aspects of propaganda. These issues are examined in the contributions of Breitenbach, Craig, and MacKenzie.

In all these areas we can identify significant modes of interaction between a Scottish metropole and a colonial periphery. But we must recognize that imperial networks were not made up only of bilateral lines of influence and behaviour, even if those lines operated in unquestionably reciprocal ways.

---

[54] The background to this can be found in George Elder Davie, *The Democratic Intellect: Scotland and her Universities in the Nineteenth Century* (Edinburgh, 1961).

[55] See, for example, Martha McLaren, *British India and British Scotland, 1780–1830* (Akron, Oh., 2001).

The British Empire also produced significantly multilateral connections, among various colonies of settlement, between such territories and India, and also among all of these and the later so-called dependent empire. Scots were active in all these globalizing activities. We can find their distinctive contributions operating, for example, through the Scottish intellectual diaspora, which is comprehensively surveyed in the chapter by Cairns Craig. Scottish philosophers and other intellectuals spread around the globe, occupying chairs in colonial universities and influencing further generations of students. They can also be found in the products of a Scottish literature of empire, through the works of well-travelled figures such as Robert Louis Stevenson and John Buchan, and also through a more modern literature in Canada and New Zealand (most notably) in which authors see themselves as expressing Scottish roots as well as characteristic forms associated with what they regard as an ultimate cultural 'homeland', as well as the 'hostland' in which they find themselves.[56] Excellent examples are the poets Thomas Pringle from the Scottish Borders and Charles Murray from Aberdeenshire. Pringle (a protégé of Sir Walter Scott) was an 1820 settler to the Cape who wrote romantic poetry connecting Scotland and southern Africa and is regarded as the founder of South African poetry in English. Later, Murray, who emigrated to the Transvaal in 1888, became a senior civil servant, and wrote notable poetry which was highly popular in the inter-war years.[57] Thus, we should recognize that Scots sensibilities with regard to global activities and colonial/imperial experiences are formed through academic writing and imaginative literature as well as through their economic, social, religious, and environmental activities. The chapter of Angela Smith is dedicated to this proposition and to the notion that there was something about Scottish literature, not least the complexity of its attitudes towards indigenous peoples, which represents a distinctive approach when compared with its English (in national terms) equivalent.

---

[56] We are grateful to Cairns Craig for this felicitous juxtaposition.

[57] For Pringle, see MacKenzie with Dalziel, *Scots in South Africa*, 48–57 and 67–75 and Angus Calder, 'Thomas Pringle (1789–1834): A Scottish Poet in South Africa', *English in Africa*, 9.1 (1982), 1–28; and for Murray, Jonathan Hyslop, 'Making Scotland in South Africa: Charles Murray, the Transvaal's Aberdeenshire poet', in David Lambert and Alan Lester (eds), *Colonial Lives across the British Empire: Imperial Careering in the Long Nineteenth Century* (Cambridge, 2006), 309–34.

Murray's poem 'The Whistle' was published in Hugh MacDiarmid (ed.), *The Golden Treasury of Scottish Poetry* (London, 1948), 265–8 without any reference to Murray's South African context.

The ambiguity of the word 'English' does indeed raise the issue of the language. Scots generally operated through English and expressed their elements of difference both through their literary manipulation of its characteristics and sometimes through the dialects which they brought to bear upon their multifarious contributions. It was, of course, a language which had been adopted many centuries earlier in some parts of Scotland and Scots also used its distinctive variants, whether expressed as dialects or as the separate Scots language with its own extensive vocabulary. The combination of 'purer' forms of English and of Scots was kept alive, moreover, by the manner in which Robert Burns used both in his poetry, which was, of course, actively recited in all Scottish communities overseas.[58] Gaelic was also exported from Scotland and survived in some places, notably in Canada and in New Zealand, although that survival was always fragile as the generations moved on. Yet even Gaelic has been showing some tendency to revival in these territories, as well as in Scotland. Moreover, certain cultural forms—such as Scots fiddle music—survived in such places as Cape Breton, sometimes to be re-imported to Scotland (where some traditions had become attenuated) in modern times.

If these linguistic and cultural characteristics represented significant fields for interactive endeavour as between Scotland and its wider, dispersed populations, this was equally true of politics. Scottish politicians throughout the empire often saw their contributions as distinctively rooted in their Scots heritage: this would be true, for example, of Canadian prime ministers such as John A. Macdonald and Alexander Mackenzie, Australian colonial premiers like Sir Thomas McIlwraith and Sir Robert Philp (both in Queensland),[59] or the New Zealand prime minister Peter Fraser and, earlier, minister of lands John McKenzie.[60] Andrew Bonar Law, a British prime minister, maintained his links with Canada, where he had been brought up.[61] But so far as domestic Scottish politics were concerned, there can be little doubt that the British Empire was highly instrumental not only in attitudes towards the Union, but also in the jockeying of the various political parties.

---

[58] The new museum at Burns's birthplace in Ayrshire, opened in 2010, has captions in Scots, with English translations of difficult words. *The Scotsman*, 5 November 2010.

[59] See chapter 9 by MacKenzie and Devine below.

[60] Tom Brooking, *Lands for the People? The Highland Clearances and the Colonisation of New Zealand: A Biography of John McKenzie* (Dunedin, 1996).

[61] R. J. Q. Adams, *Bonar Law* (London, 1999).

Richard Finlay examines these reciprocal influences of empire on Scottish politics in three key periods in the nineteenth and twentieth centuries.

Suggestions for Future Research

Andrew Thompson has suggested that:

Of all the peoples of the United Kingdom, it is the Scots' contribution to the British Empire that stands out as disproportionate. They were the first peoples of the British Isles to take on an imperial mentality, and possibly the longest to sustain one. In the spheres of education, engineering, exploration, medicine, commerce, and shipping, the Scots earned a particularly strong reputation for empire building.[62]

Thompson might have added, among many other phenomena, the central role of Orcadians in the Hudson's Bay Company, and therefore in the hunting, fur trading, and exploration of northern Canada; or Scottish participation in the West Indian plantation economy and transatlantic slavery; and the acknowledged vital role of Scots in pastoralism in Canada, Australia, and New Zealand.[63] Certainly, it has been the central contention of this collection of essays to support some aspects at least of Thompson's argument. However, there is unquestionably a need for further research to confirm its truth (or otherwise). For example, we require additional studies of the Scottish contribution to professionalization both within the British state and throughout the empire. The nineteenth century was a period when a professional bourgeoisie took over much of the power and influence formerly exerted by the landed aristocracy and gentry. In the empire of settlement, the bourgeoisie was, in the main, powerful from the start. There can be little doubt that the Scottish universities contributed mightily to the emergence of the professions associated with education, engineering, and medicine, as Thompson suggests, but also many of those connected with the

---

[62] Andrew Thompson, 'Empire and the British State', in Sarah Stockwell (ed.), *The British Empire: Themes and Perspectives* (Oxford, 2008), 51.

[63] E. E. Rich, *Hudson's Bay Company 1670–1870*, 2 vols (London, 1958, 1959); Peter C. Newman, *Company of Adventurers: The Story of the Hudson's Bay Company* (Harmondsworth, 1985); Jenni Calder, *Scots in Canada* (Edinburgh, 2003); Douglas J. Hamilton, *Scotland, the Caribbean and the Atlantic World, 1750–1820* (Manchester, 2005); John M. MacKenzie, 'Scots and Imperial Frontiers', *Journal of Irish and Scottish Studies*, 3.1 (Autumn 2009), 1–17 and MacKenzie, 'Scotland and Empire: Ethnicity, Environment and Identity', in *Northern Scotland*, vol. i of new series (2010), 12–29.

sciences of botany, forestry, entomology, microbiology, hydrology, and others. Did Scots indeed have a disproportionate influence in territories of settlement, in India, and in colonies of the so-called dependent empire? It would be valuable to have more quantitative studies of the numbers of Scots in these professions and the manner in which they may have dominated the professional societies and associations which regulated them in terms of training, admission, ethics, and development. At the moment the case is largely anecdotal, but further numerical (as well as qualitative) studies are required to establish just how significant Scots were in the establishment of universities and other institutions of higher education which, among other things, were important in the expansion of the numbers in these occupations.[64] It may indeed be the case that Scots played their role in many of these professions precisely because they found entry to other aspects of imperial rule problematic.

For example, while Scots were able to penetrate very successfully, often in disproportionate numbers, the administrative cadres of India during the Company period in the eighteenth and early nineteenth centuries, this became more difficult after the Northcote–Trevelyan reforms of 1853. Patronage had favoured the Scots, but the new competitive examination system placed an emphasis on classical studies for which the products of the English public schools and Oxbridge were particularly well prepared. However, the Scottish universities soon responded and an initial dip in Scots ICS entry was swiftly corrected.[65] As John Hargreaves put it, India remained 'the largest oyster in the Victorian graduate's view of the world'.[66] In the twentieth century, however, recruitment policies for the Colonial Office, dominated as they were for many years by the celebrated Ralph Furse, succeeded again in favouring the products of public schools and of the so-called 'golden triangle' of universities (Oxford, Cambridge, and

---

[64] Some information can be found in Tamson Pietsch, 'A Commonwealth of Learning? Academic Networks and the British World, 1890–1914' (Oxford D.Phil., 2009), later published in a revised and extended version as *Empire of Scholars: University, networks and the British academic world, 1850–1937* (Manchester, 2013).

[65] R. D. Anderson, *Education and Opportunity in Victorian Scotland* (Edinburgh, 1983), 324–6. By 1874, 89 out of 741 successful applicants to the ICS were Scots, again a disproportionate number. By the early twentieth century, one Scottish public school (George Watson's) and Aberdeen University seemed to have created a special connection with ICS entry.

[66] John D. Hargreaves, *Academe and Empire: Some Overseas Connections of Aberdeen University 1860–1970* (Aberdeen, 1994), 4. Hargreaves provides abundant evidence of Scots graduate entry to the ICS, to the technical services, and to some areas of the Colonial Service.

London).[67] As Hargreaves put it, 'Only Scots from upper-class families who had by-passed the Scottish educational system were likely to secure Furse's approval.'[68] Moreover, the legal systems of empire (a field often ignored by imperial historians) were dominated by English-trained lawyers, for the obvious reason that it was the English Common Law which formed the basis of most colonial legal administrations (the Roman Dutch Law of the Cape and of Ceylon, Sri Lanka, were the exceptions). Scots, with their separate legal system, often found it difficult to participate in the colonial legal services, unless they were educated in England or, later, in the colonies themselves. Colonial judges, for example, were more likely to be English or Irish than Scots.[69] It may well be, therefore, that Scots had little alternative but to enter the educational, technical, and scientific professions (for which they may indeed have had a predilection in any case) rather than the administrative and legal ones.

There are several additional points to be made here. One is the balance between the non-official character of such professions (such as private practice in medicine, law, accountancy, and other financial occupations) and the extent to which they were dependent upon the state, whether through educational arrangements or by public government appointments. The second relates to the arrival in colonies of professionals employed by the Christian missions, of whom there were a large number (particularly in education and medicine) by the late nineteenth and early twentieth centuries. A third raises questions about those who were not necessarily Scots (or were second or third generation in settlement territories), but who were trained in Scottish universities and therefore carried, to a certain extent at any rate, Scottish ideas and methods with them.

The fourth related issue is the manner in which the professions became a significant source of female employment from the later nineteenth century and developing particularly in the twentieth. Yet again, there is an important distinction here between such professions and those of administration and the law, where the female presence was minimal until the very end of

---

[67] Robert Heussler, *Yesterday's Rulers: The Making of the British Colonial Service* (Syracuse, NY, 1963); Anthony Kirk-Greene, *On Crown Service: A History of HM Colonial and Overseas Civil Services, 1837–1997* (London, 1999); idem, *Britain's Imperial Administrators 1858–1966* (Houndmills, 2000); all deal extensively with the influence of Furse.

[68] Hargreaves, *Academe and Empire*, 21.

[69] Paul Swanepoel, 'Indifferent Justice? A History of the Judges in Kenya and Tanganyika, 1897–1963' (Ph.D., University of Edinburgh, 2010).

empire. To what extent, therefore, were Scots women active in the empire in the professions, such as medicine (both as doctors and as nurses),[70] in education, and scientific services (notably botany and museum work), some of them in missions and some of them in a capacity more connected with public service? Did Scots women appear in disproportionate numbers in these occupations? It is certainly the case that Scottish universities were admitting women and permitting them to graduate ahead of their English counterparts.

These are very often the most visible women because they appear in official records, had careers that were recorded in the press, joined professional associations (where they were admitted), and were active in voluntary societies of one sort or another. Rather less visible, but still amenable to research, were the many women settlers who contributed to colonial life in all sorts of ways, both in the economies and social life of colonial societies, but also through the maintenance of connections with people at home, through correspondence with kith and kin, with professional colleagues, or with church congregations likely to supply funds and other forms of support.[71] Their role in the maintenance of Scottish identity in the colonies, in the many Scottish organizations which promoted Scottish music, dance, or literature, requires to be better understood than it is now. Moreover, women and family were sometimes left at home and this separation of the breadwinners from senior generations, from siblings, or from their own spouses led to the transmission of remittances from colonies into the domestic economy.[72] This must also have been a characteristic of military service in the empire, starting from at least the eighteenth century. Magee and Thompson have begun to lift the veil on the scale and significance of such transfers (once Post Office records became available) in the case of Cornwall and elsewhere in England.[73] We require studies of the parallel

[70] To what extent, for example, is it the case that Scots doctors were particularly notable in spreading concepts of environmental public health, as well as in notions of childcare?

[71] Lesley Orr Macdonald, *A Unique and Glorious Mission: Women and Presbyterianism in Scotland* (Edinburgh, 2000) and Esther Breitenbach, *Empire and Scottish Society: The Impact of Foreign Missions at Home, c.1790–c.1914* (Edinburgh, 2009).

[72] The techniques used in Elizabeth Buettner's *Empire Families: Britons and Late Imperial India* (Oxford, 2004) need to be extended to other territories of empire.

[73] G. B. Magee and A. S. Thompson, 'The Global and Local: Explaining Migrant Remittance Flows in the English-Speaking World, 1880–1914', *Journal of Economic History*, 66.1 (2006), 177–202; G. B. Magee and A. S. Thompson, '"Lines of Credit, Debts of Obligation": Migrant Remittances to Britain, c.1875–1913', *Economic History Review*, 59.3 (2006), 539–77.

phenomenon in the case of Scotland and, if possible, the extent to which this had a significant effect upon the Scots economy.

The macro-economic effects of this micro-economic individual behaviour reminds us that there still has not been a major cost–benefit analysis of the presence of Scotland in both the British state and the British Empire.[74] We do know that the Scottish economy boomed (even if intermittently) as a result of colonial trades, that there were significant transfers on the part of comparatively wealthy individuals into the Scottish economy, notably from India in the late eighteenth and early nineteenth centuries. We know that a major part of the fortunes of individual towns and cities was based upon the imperial connection (for example, jute in Dundee), but we still lack a study which would set out to amalgamate the results of many specialist pieces of research into something approaching such a cost–benefit analysis. We should also take note of the fact that many individual Scots and their companies relocated to London in the recognition that a presence in the metropolitan capital opened doors to further growth and success. In other words, to what extent did the existence of empire and its centre in the south-east of England ensure that some significant economic activity—as well as associated employment—was lost to Scotland?

The other major area where much research waits to be done is in testing some of the significant theories of imperialism against the Scottish experience. It may be argued that many of the studies of Scotland's role in British overseas trade and in other aspects of the imperial history have remained stubbornly semi-detached from the theoretical debates and conceptual models which have energized historical reappraisals of British imperial studies. This may be a characteristic of all historical studies in their early stages, but it is clearly now important to try to link Scotland's experience of empire with some of the grand theories of empire, some of them by no means new. Some of the earliest theories of imperialism, celebrated and denigrated with equal force, have been those of J. A. Hobson and Joseph Schumpeter, both dating from the early twentieth century.[75] The Scottish

---

[74] A British cost–benefit analysis was attempted by Avner Offer, 'Costs and Benefits, Prosperity and Security, 1870–1914', in Porter (ed.), *The Oxford History of the British Empire: The Nineteenth Century*, 690–711.

[75] J. A. Hobson, *Imperialism: A Study* (London, 1902); Joseph Schumpeter, *Imperialism and Social Classes*, trans. Heinz Norden, ed., with an introduction by Paul M. Sweezy (Oxford, 1951; 1st published 1919). See also P. J. Cain, *Hobson and Imperialism: Radicalism, New Liberalism and Finance 1887–1938* (Oxford, 2002).

case offers material against which both can be tested, in respect of specific social classes, investment, jingoism, and the press. In the case of 'imperialism and social classes', we know that Scots aristocrats and gentry were active as governors and in the military. They also led migration schemes (for example, the Earl of Selkirk in Canada, the Leslie Brothers in New South Wales, and Benjamin Moodie at the Cape),[76] but it was surely the Scottish bourgeoisie that was ultimately much more influential in the empire. All this would require a new book, but it is to be hoped that studies will examine these social dimensions in the future.

One of the most important theories of imperialism, now more than fifty years old, has been that relating to free trade and to concepts of 'informal empire', to the notion, associated with the imperial historians Ronald Robinson and Jack Gallagher, that the British sought economic dominance preferably by indirect and informal means and only by actual territorial acquisition if that became essential to their purposes.[77] In many ways, this theory and its alleged practice in the early to mid-nineteenth century was ultimately based upon the dominant ideas of Adam Smith, both on free trade and in respect of his scepticism about empire, and also to the manner in which his ideas progressively took over the citadels of economic policy (and associated legislation and dismantling of the old mercantilist state), the global expansion in trade, and political attitudes in the first half of the nineteenth century. We need to know about the extent to which the orthodoxy of free trade, and therefore its imperial ramifications, was promoted by Scots.

To take another example, how far can the Cain and Hopkins theory of 'gentlemanly capitalism', with its emphasis upon the financial sector and its centre of activity in London, be modified in the light of Scotland's involvement in financial institutions, notably banking, insurance, and investment trusts?[78] Has the notion of a London-centred theory to be

---

[76] For Selkirk, see, *inter alia*, Phillip Buckner (ed.), *Canada and the British Empire* (Oxford, 2008), 62, 144, 188; for the Leslie brothers (George, Patrick, and Walter), Harper and Constantine, *Migration and Empire*, 50, 279; and for Moodie MacKenzie with Dalziel, *Scots in South Africa*, ch. 2.

[77] R. E. Robinson and J. A. Gallagher, 'The Imperialism of Free Trade', *Economic History Review*, 2nd series, 6 (1953).

[78] P. J. Cain and A. G. Hopkins, 'Gentlemanly Capitalism and British Expansion Overseas, 1: The Old Colonial System, 1688–1850', *Economic History Review*, 2nd series, 39 (1986), 504–8; idem, *British Imperialism*, 2 vols: *Innovation and Expansion, 1688–1914; Crisis and Deconstruction, 1914–1990* (Harlow, 1993). For critiques, see A. Porter, '"Gentlemanly Capitalism" and Empire: The British Experience since 1750', *JICH* 18 (1990), 272; R. E. Dumett, 'Exploring the

modified, or indeed seriously challenged, in the face of regional financial activity, both in Scotland and in the English regions, even if they were proportionately less significant in the overall picture? Scots investments in Australian land, for example, were extremely significant.[79] Moreover, the Scots community in London, important from the eighteenth century and clearly instrumental both in establishing connections between Scotland and the empire, as well as offering examples of Scots participants in the London financial, raw material, and other markets requires further analysis. If the 'gentlemanly capitalists' in London and elsewhere constituted significant pressure groups within the British state arguing for specific economic policies, yet another characteristic of the rise of the bourgeoisie was the development of humanitarian lobbies and pressure groups of various sorts. These can be seen to have modified political processes from the time of the anti-slavery agitation in the late eighteenth century onwards. The precise role of Scots in a variety of pressure groups and societies associated with empire requires further investigation. As events surrounding Uganda and the Central Africa Protectorate (later Malawi) in the early 1890s indicate, such pressure groups could produce significant changes in government policies (or alternatively could be used by administrations to explain and justify their actions).[80] If pressure groups are made up of individuals who collectively find influence, so too do we need histories of specific families and areas of the country. Even the grandest theories must be built upon such basic and particularist information.[81] Nicholas Thomas has suggested that we need to understand the

Cain/Hopkins Paradigm: Issues for Debate, Critique and Topics for New Research' in idem (ed.), *Gentlemanly Capitalism and British Imperialism: The New Debate on Empire* (London, 1999). Mackillop also takes up this issue in his chapter below.

[79] For a recent statement of this oft-repeated assertion, see Geoffrey Bolton, 'Money: Trade, Investment, and Economic Nationalism', in Deryck M. Schreuder and Stuart Ward (eds), *Australia's Empire* (Oxford, 2008), 211–31.

[80] In 1890, a Scottish agitation convinced the London government not to sign the Portuguese treaty which had been negotiated by Sir Harry Johnston and which would have given some of the Scottish missionary areas of the British Central Africa Protectorate (Malawi) to Portugal. In 1893, a further agitation set about ensuring that with the collapse of the Imperial British East Africa Company (itself largely a Scottish creation and extensively manned by Scots) Uganda should be incorporated into the British Empire.

[81] A recent example of a history of one family's connections with the British Empire is Stephen Foster, *A Private Empire* (Millers Point, NSW, 2010), an examination of the Macpherson family's connections with pre-Revolutionary America, Australia, India, and South Africa.

local contexts of imperialism ('localising colonialism'), but this is equally true of the so-called 'mother country'.[82]

Further, studies of Scotland (for that matter Ireland, Wales, or parts of England) and empire perhaps need to be reconsidered in the light of the insights provided by the group of scholars known as 'postcolonials'. This group has sought to shift the focus from the dominant peoples of empire to the subordinate, to 'de-centre' imperialism and view these historical processes from the perspective of those whose lands were taken and who were forced into the capitalist system through wage labour. They also regard imperialism as a shared experience between metropole and so-called periphery. In some respects, however, they are merely building on an older school of historians who asserted that there was no such thing as a 'dual economy' in colonies (that is an allegedly progressive 'advanced' economy contrasted with a 'backward' traditional one). Imperial rule had the effect of placing both peoples within the same system, with poverty and dispossession as the structural component of the 'developing' sector.[83] Does this serve to illustrate the irrelevance of breaking down the imperial people into constituent ethnic parts? Or is it possible to find different aspects of exploitation or even of nationalist or ethnically sympathetic responses among them? These are as yet largely unanswered questions. Another suggestion among the postcolonials is that a number of assumptions exist within British imperial history which help to maintain and perpetuate old-style 'national' history.[84] Is there consequently a danger of erecting a new form of national history, that of Scotland, say, in place of that of Britain? Clearly, it is essential that imperialism should be studied in a much more comparative framework than in the past—as between different European imperial powers[85]—but perhaps an

[82] Nicholas Thomas, *Colonialism's Culture: Anthropology, Travel and Government* (Cambridge, 1994), 2–3. See Emma Rothschild, *The Inner Life of Empires: An Eighteenth Century History* (Princeton, NJ, 2011).

[83] G. Arrighi, *The Political Economy of Rhodesia* (The Hague, 1967); G. Arrighi and J. S. Saul, *Essays on the Political Economy of Africa* (New York, 1973).

[84] A. Burton, 'Who Needs the Nation? Interrogating "British" History', in Catherine Hall (ed.), *Cultures of Empire: Colonizers in Britain and the Empire in the Nineteenth and Twentieth Centuries* (Manchester, 2000), 138–42. See also Antoinette Burton (ed.), *After the Imperial Turn: Thinking with and through the Nation* (Durham, NC, 2003); Kathleen Wilson (ed.), *A New Imperial History: Culture, Identity and Modernity in Britain and the Empire, 1660–1940* (Cambridge, 2004); and Philippa Levine and Susan R. Grayzel (eds), *Gender, Labour, War and Empire: Essays on Modern Britain* (London, 2009).

[85] John M. MacKenzie (ed.), *European Empires and the People: Popular Responses to Imperialism in France, Britain, the Netherlands, Belgium, Germany and Italy* (Manchester,

understanding of different ethnic components of this should feed into just such a comparative approach. For example, it has been suggested that we need more comparative studies of Irish, Scottish, and Welsh reactions to England and to the experience of empire.[86] In all these respects, studies of Irish, Scots, Welsh, and English in the British Empire have the capacity to energize imperial history, serving to facilitate its escape from the severely metropolitan (and largely London-centred) focus which has bedevilled such histories for a very long time. Such a 'four nations' approach constitutes one important way forward in the consideration of the relationship between Britain and its empire.[87] It is noticeable that recent volumes in the companion series of the Oxford History of the British Empire have begun to take note of the ethnic diversity of the United Kingdom.[88]

At any rate, the fact is that consideration of aspects of Scotland and Empire must not be conducted in isolation. They only secure real significance by being tied into wider modes of analysis relating to the British Empire where historians have so often formerly taken little or no account of the variety of skills, historic influences, and economic predilections of the different ethnicities of the United Kingdom. We also require a greater understanding of the extent to which the placing of risk capital (and in some cases not so risky in the perception of investors) in the British Empire inhibited domestic investment which might have been of greater benefit to Scotland and Scottish society. Did dividends and other forms of returns outweigh the loss of such capital through export abroad? Such an economic prospectus offers an exceptionally tall order, but still more specialist studies should help in working towards the larger picture.

To shift the focus, we also require more research on Scottish cultural activities, both in the colonies and in Scotland, in preserving the identities of Scottish people as a nation during a period when the Scottish state was in

2011) represents one comparative approach. Another might be through the regions of these various countries.

[86] Howe, 'Historiography', in Kenny (ed.) *Ireland and the British Empire*, 247.

[87] John M. MacKenzie, 'Irish, Scottish, Welsh and English Worlds? A Four-Nation Approach to the History of the British Empire', *History Compass*, 6.5 (2008), 1244–63; idem, 'Irish, Scottish, Welsh and English Worlds? The Historiography of a Four-Nations Approach to the History of the British Empire', in Catherine Hall and Keith McClelland (eds), *Race, Nation and Empire: Making Histories, 1750 to the Present* (Manchester, 2010), 133–53.

[88] Examples are Norman Etherington (ed.), *Missions and Empire* (Oxford, 2005); Buckner (ed.), *Canada and the British Empire*; Shreuder and Ward (eds), *Australia's Empire*; Bickers (ed.), *Settlers and Expatriates*; Harper and Constantine, *Migration and Empire*.

abeyance. Can any further evidence be found to suggest that Scottish (and maybe also Irish and Welsh) identities, far from being amalgamated into an overall sense of Britishness, were actually preserved by the imperial experience? Moreover, is it possible to argue that Scots produced different responses from indigenous peoples throughout the empire (even although this always requires to be modified by a recognition of extensive participation in the violence and brutalities of the relationship)? There seems to be anecdotal evidence that there may be some kind of argument here, but it requires much more empirical underpinning. It certainly seems to be of some significance that some Lowland Scots regarded Highlanders and Islanders as a people at an earlier stage of cultural development, which placed them closer in evolutionary time to the indigenous people among whom many settled. Dr John Philip, the highly influential superintendent of the London Missionary Society in southern Africa in the early nineteenth century, pointed out in his book *Researches in South Africa* that in his view the Celts on the fringes of his home society had only recently come under the influence of modern civilization and that Africans (no doubt through missionary endeavour) could be similarly 'raised up'.[89] This kind of relativist rhetoric can be found in many missionary publications (including those of David Livingstone) in the nineteenth century. Was it related to the 'stadial' theory (the notion of the evolutionary progression of societies from the hunting and gathering through pastoral, agricultural, and commercial stages) of the Scottish Enlightenment?

Coming down to modern times, all this connects with a need for further research on Scotland and the end of empire, the reciprocal effects of the imperial experience upon the Scots. Was nationalism triggered, as Tom Nairn suggested, by decolonization, or can its origins be traced in other ways? Perhaps it is more interesting to discuss why it is that the dissolution of empire produced such a muted reaction in Scotland, given its imperial past. The obvious additional connection is with multi-cultural Scotland. We need more research on black and Asian communities now settled in the country, some of them transforming its built heritage with temples and mosques. To what extent have they come to take on a Scottish identity? How

---

[89] Philip is quoted in Elizabeth Elbourne, 'Religion and the British Empire', in Stockwell (ed.), *British Empire*, 138. See also John MacKenzie, '"Making Black Scotsmen and Scotswomen?" Scottish Missionaries and the Eastern Cape Colony in the Nineteenth Century', in Hilary Carey (ed.), *Empires of Religion* (Houndmills, 2008), 119–20.

far do they blend this with their own ethnic and religious identities, thereby mirroring some of the characteristics of settlers in the empire? For those born in the country or settled in it for some time, does their Scottish context loom larger than the British? Has their experience in Scotland been similar to or different from those of similar communities in England, Wales, or Ireland? These communities are helping to forge a new version of Scotland and their presence is consequently important in all sorts of ways.

To return to the fundamental issues presented in this volume, the influence of Scots and Scotland upon the British Empire, we should remind ourselves that historians should always ask themselves two key questions: Does it matter? And why does it matter? The conclusion of the editors and contributors must surely be that the study of Scots in the British Empire does indeed matter because without them its various colonies and dependencies would have manifested rather different characteristics and produced strikingly alternative results. The Scots, no less than the Irish, the English, and even the Welsh, had a profound effect on many of the countries of the modern world. And that mix of experiences also had a significant effect upon Scotland, though that must be the subject of another book.

Select Bibliography

TANJA BUELTMANN, ANDREW HINSON, and GRAEME MORTON (eds), *Ties of Bluid, Kin and Countrie: Scottish Associational Culture in the Diaspora* (Guelph, 2009).

R. A. CAGE (ed.), *The Scots Abroad* (London, 1985).

T. M. DEVINE (ed.), *Scottish Emigration and Scottish Society* (Edinburgh, 1992).

—— *Scotland's Empire, 1600–1815* (London, 2003).

—— *To the Ends of the Earth: Scotland's Global Diaspora 1750–2010* (London, 2011).

—— 'The Break-up of Britain? Scotland and the End of the Empire' (The Prothero Lecture), *Transactions of the Royal Historical Society*, XVI (2006), 163–80.

MICHAEL FRY, *The Scottish Empire* (Edinburgh, 2001).

MARJORY HARPER, *Adventurers and Exiles: The Great Scottish Exodus* (London, 2003).

—— and Stephen Constantine, *Migration and Empire* (Oxford, 2010).

ANGELA MCCARTHY (ed.), *A Global Clan: Scottish Migrant Networks and Identities since the Eighteenth Century* (London, 2006).

JOHN M. MACKENZIE, 'Empire and National Identity: The Case of Scotland', *Transactions of the Royal Historical Society*, 6th series, 8 (1998), 215–31.

—— with NIGEL R. DALZIEL, *The Scots in South Africa: Ethnicity, Identity, Gender and Race, 1772–1913* (Manchester, 2007).

EMMA ROTHSCHILD, *The Inner Life of Empires: An Eighteenth Century History* (Princeton, NJ, 2011).

2

Scots in the Atlantic Economy, 1600–1800

T. M. Devine and Philipp R. Rössner

Before the Union[1]

One of the first references to America in Scottish records appeared in 1597 when one Robert Lindsay, a ship's pilot, presented the burgh council of Aberdeen with a 'haill universal see kart (chart) of Europe, Affrica and Asaia, and new found landes of America'. He was rewarded with payment of forty Scots merks for his gift.[2] Around that time there was some Scottish interest in the Newfoundland and Greenland fisheries together with occasional references to the odd vessel returning to a Scottish port from the Caribbean and Chesapeake with speculative cargoes of tobacco, sugar, rice, and a few other exotic commodities.[3] But before the 1650s or so, such transatlantic enterprise was fleeting and the few official attempts at Scottish colonization in the Americas, at Nova Scotia in the 1620s and Cape Breton Island later the same decade, ended in failure.[4] One estimate suggests that fewer than 200 Scots had settled in the English colonies before 1640, with a handful of others in New France and New Netherlands.[5]

The collapse of the official ventures was not unexpected. Scotland was in an anomalous position within the United Kingdom at the time. Other European states, such as Portugal, Spain, Sweden, and the Netherlands, were able to pursue aggressive overseas policies because they had central authorities and the naval and military muscle to support expansionist strategies. But after the Union of the Crowns in 1603 Scotland shared a

---

[1] The section on Success in Tobacco was written by Philipp R. Rössner and the rest of this chapter by T. M. Devine.

[2] David Dobson, *Scottish Emigration to Colonial America 1607–1785* (Athens, Ga., 1994), 26.

[3] Eric J. Graham, *A Maritime History of Scotland, 1650–1790* (East Linton, 2002), 37–8.

[4] George Pratt Insh, *Scottish Colonial Schemes, 1620–1686* (Glasgow, 1922).

[5] Dobson, *Scottish Emigration*, 33.

single monarchy with England, and the Scottish Parliament had never managed to secure much influence over foreign policy before James succeeded Elizabeth to the throne of England in that year. An independent Scottish policy therefore disappeared across the border with James after 1603. Not surprisingly, thereafter, monarchy tended to favour England, the senior partner in the dynastic union, when there was a conflict between Scottish and English interests. Charles I's decision to return Nova Scotia to the French in 1632 was a classic instance of this response.[6]

Private enterprise endeavour across the Atlantic was equally constrained, despite the fact that Scotland's position on the north-west periphery of the European continent provided an excellent location for forging American connections, especially since the country had a long ingrained tradition of seafaring and trading. The explanation was simple. Scotland's commercial relationships with northern and central Europe were too entrenched and beneficial. They were unlikely to be easily sacrificed for long-distance trades across the Atlantic, which were much riskier, more costly, and still limited in market size because of the relatively small numbers of European settlers in the Americas by the early seventeenth century.[7] Scottish customs accounts for 1621–3 confirm the point. Nearly two-thirds of imports came from the Netherlands (32 per cent), the Baltic region and north German plain (22 per cent), and France (18 per cent). Goods from England yielded 22 per cent in revenue and all other destinations a mere 6 per cent.[8]

Furthermore, for generations there had been an extensive and well-established Scottish mercantile diaspora in many European ports. By the sixteenth century communities of Scottish traders flourished in Gdańsk, Copenhagen, Elsimore, Malmö, Bruges, Campveere, Dieppe, and Bordeaux, as well as numerous other centres.[9] Perhaps the most remarkable connection was with Poland-Lithuania. As early as 1569, Sir John Skene observed 'ane great multitude' of Scots pedlars in Cracow, while Fynes Morrison in

[6] S. Murdoch and A. Mackillop (eds), *Military Governors and Imperial Frontiers c.1600–1800: A Study of Scotland and Empires* (Leiden, 2003), pp. xxv, xxxi, xxxv.

[7] T. C. Smout, N. C. Landsman, and T. M. Devine, 'Scottish Emigration in the Seventeenth and Eighteenth Centuries', in Nicholas Canny (ed.), *Europeans on the Move* (Oxford, 1994), 77–91; David Ditchburn, *Scotland and Europe*, vol. i (East Linton, 2000).

[8] Keith M. Brown, 'Reformation to Union, 1560–1707', in R. A. Houston and W. W. J. Knox (eds), *The New Penguin History of Scotland* (London, 2001), 204.

[9] S. Murdoch and A. Grosjean (eds), *Scottish Communities Abroad in the Early Modern Period* (Leiden, 2005).

1598 thought the country was swarming with these petty Scottish merchants.[10] Debates in the London Parliament after the Regal Union of 1603
used 'the multiplicities of the Scots in Polonia' as a dreadful example of the
fate which could befall England if the Scots became naturalized subjects.
The conclusion was unambiguous: 'we shall be over-run with them'.[11]
Urban archives in Poland for this period teem with prohibitions against
vagrant Scottish pedlars and itinerant tradesmen and speak of a country
with Scots hucksters on the make who were destabilizing Crown and town
commercial regulations governing fair trade and established business practices.[12] Scots were also prominent as well-established merchants in the
bigger towns.

Quantifying the actual impact of all this is much more difficult. One
Polish scholar has traced the names of over 7,400 male Scots in 420 places
throughout Poland. Overwhelmingly, they were either natives of the east of
Scotland (140 localities have been indicated in that region) or second-
generation migrants. The same researcher was confident that this number
represented only a fraction of those who came to seek their fortune or try to
escape a life of poverty.[13] However, more recent research has tended to
indicate lower numbers than were either suggested at the time or by modern
historical scholarship.[14] Most were pedlars, petty traders, and merchants
rather than soldiers, often plying their business on horseback, selling cheap
goods, into the remotest part of the country. The rural Polish commercial
structure was stagnant, with few towns across the countryside. At the same
time, the Polish aristocracy was marketing the surplus wheat and rye of their
great estates at a time of population increase and urban growth in western
Europe. The potential for gain was immense. Scots merchants moved in
first from Gdańsk along with the Dutch and other nationalities. Credit was
advanced to grain producers, in a manner not unlike the relationship

---

[10] Smout, Landsman, and Devine, 'Scottish Emigration', 80.

[11] A. F. Steuart (ed.), *Papers relating to the Scots in Poland, 1576–1793* (Edinburgh, 1915), p. ix.

[12] T. A. Fischer, *The Scots in Eastern and Western Prussia* (Edinburgh, 1903).

[13] A. Biegánska, 'Note on the Scots in Poland', in T. M. Smout (ed.), *Scotland and Europe 1200–1850*), 157–65. See also 'James Murray, A Scot in the Making of the Polish Navy', *Scottish Slavonic Review*, 3 (1984); and Anna Biegánska, 'In Search of Tolerance: Scottish Catholics and Presbyterians in Poland', *Scottish Slavonic Review*, 17 (1991).

[14] Smout, Landsman, and Devine, 'Scottish Emigration', 82. For most recent estimates of numbers see Steve Murdoch and Esther Mijers, 'Migrant Destinations, 1500–1750', in T. M. Devine and Jenny Wormald (eds), *The Oxford Handbook of Modern Scottish History 1500–2010* (Oxford, 2012) and the references therein.

between Glasgow tobacco lords and Virginian planters which was to develop in the following century. One suggestion (as yet unconfirmed) is that at the peak of the grain trade's prosperity in the early seventeenth century there were over 400 small Scottish settlements in Poland and along the Prussian coast. The success of these ethnic communities was demonstrated by the rise of the twelve 'Scottish Brotherhoods', each organized by an elected committee of 'Elders' drawn from all the Scottish 'colonies'.[15]

Even in the first few decades of the seventeenth century, however, the beginnings of change in Scotland's old external pattern of trade and emigration were becoming apparent. The move to the west was first inspired by the new opportunities for land in the north of Ireland as a consequence of the development of the Ulster plantation. By the 1630s it is reckoned that around 16,000 Scots, mainly from the western Borders, Ayrshire, Lanarkshire, Renfrewshire, and southern Argyll, had settled across the Irish Sea.[16] In one sense, however, the new migrations to Ulster were further factors inhibiting Scottish movement across the Atlantic. But from a longer-term perspective, Ulster also laid the foundations of later transatlantic commercial success. The Plantation was a new consumer market, a few hours' sail from the Clyde burghs and the towns of the Ayrshire coast. Small craft ran a shuttle service across the North Channel with cargoes of farm tools, clothing, and household goods, exactly the kind of commodities later sent in bulk to the American colonies.[17] Ulster commerce was a kind of apprenticeship in colonial trade for the western Scottish ports. This was especially so for Glasgow. Until the 1630s the burgh tax rolls confirm the continued urban dominance of Edinburgh, Aberdeen, Dundee, and Perth. For over three centuries, these had been the great towns of Scotland. However, by 1649 Glasgow had displaced Perth to take fourth place and also moved clearly ahead of both Aberdeen and Dundee by the 1670s. The stimulus of the Ulster market had had a significant influence on the growing importance of the premier burgh in the west, which soon enabled it to exploit further opportunities across the Atlantic.[18]

---

[15] Neal Ascherson, *Stone Voices* (London, 2002), 241–50. See also a series of chapters on seventeenth-century Scottish links with Poland in T. M. Devine and D. Hesse (eds), *Scotland and Poland: Historical Connections, 1500–2000* (Edinburgh, 2011).

[16] M. Perceval-Maxwell, *The Scottish Migration to Ulster in the Reign of James I* (London, 1973), 311–14.

[17] James McGrath, 'The Medieval and Early Modern Burgh', in T. M. Devine and G. Jackson (eds), *Glasgow*, i: *Beginnings to 1830* (Manchester, 1995), 46–7.

[18] T. M. Devine, 'Scotland', in Peter Clark (ed.), *The Cambridge Urban History of Britain*, vol. ii (Cambridge, 2000), 151–66.

These were becoming more plentiful from the 1650s. The free trade provisions during the Cromwellian Union of that decade encouraged some American adventuring, which became even more extensive in subsequent decades.[19] In part, this was because the Scots were being squeezed out of their traditional European markets by the pressures of economic nationalism. The lucrative trade to the Low Countries in coal was adversely affected by prohibitive duties imposed on cargoes shipped to the Spanish Netherlands. The Norway trade was hit by Danish corn tariffs imposed in the 1680s, while commerce to France, in addition to the effect of war, between 1688 and 1699 and again from 1701 to 1715, was inhibited by absolute prohibitions on Scottish fish and woollen cloth.[20] Ironically, a more stable food supply between 1660 and the famines of the 1690s also helped to undermine the connections with the Baltic. Throughout the sixteenth and early seventeenth centuries the great plains of the southern Baltic lands had been Scotland's emergency granary in times of harvest shortage. After c.1660 this relationship withered, partly because there was a run of favourable harvests in the 1670s and 1680s and only one year (1674) of acute shortage before the sudden catastrophes of the 1690s. Yet, in the middle of that decade of crisis, when Scottish merchants desperately searched the international market for scarce grain supplies, they were now more likely to turn to Ireland and England rather than the old sources in the Baltic.[21] Even the Polish migrations went into decline from the 1650s and 1660s, though the reasons for this still await systematic exploration by historians.

Certainly, the demographic pressures in Scotland from the 1660s to the 1680s were less acute than those of earlier times which had encouraged movement to Poland. But preliminary examination of the situation in the Commonwealth of Poland-Lithuania suggests that conditions were now less attractive there for foreign merchants. This was partly because the cycles of wars which began in 1648 and lasted almost without respite until 1717 were mainly fought (1648–67; 1670–4; 1700–17) on Commonwealth territory, with devastating effects on the trade and economy in central Europe. In parallel

---

[19] T. M. Devine, 'The Cromwellian Union and the Scottish Burghs', in John Butt and J. T. Ward (eds), *Scottish Themes: Essays in Honour of Professor S. G. E. Lythe* (Edinburgh, 1976), 1–16.

[20] T. C. Smout, *Scottish Trade on the Eve of Union 1660–1707* (Edinburgh, 1963), 249–50.

[21] Ibid. 165–6.

with this, from the 1650s the Polish-Lithuanian state began a drive towards imposing Catholic religious conformity, which may have made prospects less attractive for Calvinist Scots. Whatever the reason, European destinations seem not now to be as alluring. Migration there had virtually petered out by the early eighteenth century.[22]

On the surface, however, it seemed that any consequent 'swing to the west' would be impeded by English customs regulation. In 1660, a Navigation Act classified Scotland as a 'foreign' nation and directed that three-quarters of the crew of ships trading with English colonies had to be of English nationality. Further extensions to this legislation in 1662, 1663, and 1664 confirmed Scotland's legal exclusion from colonial commerce, even asserting that goods intended for the plantation markets must first pass through an English or Welsh port in an 'English' vessel as prescribed by the initial Act of 1660.[23]

However, Scots adventurers were remarkably adept at circumventing these protectionist barriers, not least because corruption and administrative laxity rendered them very porous. Scottish and English merchants in Whitehaven, Liverpool, Bristol, and London became important points of contact in this strategy. One of the most successful traders in the 1680s was John Dunlop from Glasgow. He developed business interests which stretched from New York to Jamaica. All his passages were made on English vessels and his letters home were delivered from English ports.[24] English front-men in Scottish towns were commonly employed to legitimize direct colonial trading ventures from Scotland itself. The Crown Agent for Customs in Scotland reported that twenty-four vessels were trading to the Americas in defiance of the Navigation Acts, a figure which was not far off the number of vessels working the tobacco trade in its great heyday of the mid-eighteenth century.[25] Scottish settlers and officials in the Chesapeake colonies were also key links in this clandestine relationship. Edward Randolph, Surveyor

---

[22] We are most grateful for comments provided by Professor Robert Frost of the University of Aberdeen on the condition of Poland-Lithuania in the later seventeenth century.

[23] Graham, *Maritime History*, 13–14.

[24] Glasgow City Archives, Dunlop of Garnkirk Papers, D12/4, Correspondence of John Dunlop.

[25] There is an excellent account of late seventeenth-century Scottish clandestine trading in Hamish Fergusson, 'Before Union: Scottish Trade with the American Plantations 1660–1700' (unpublished MA dissertation, University of Edinburgh, 2008).

General of Customs for the American Plantations, explained the techniques used in a report to his London superiors in 1696:

The people on the Eastern Shore of Virginia and Maryland and the Delaware River, Scotsmen and others, have great stocks lying by them to purchase tobacco and prepare a loading ready to put aboard any vessel. The master assists to get the goods ashore before the vessel is entered. The vessel lying in some obscure creek 40 or 50 miles from the Collector's office is presently loaded and sails away undisturbed.[26]

Another favourite ploy was to use Newfoundland as an entrepôt, as it was not formally considered a colony but an integral part of England. This meant that colonial goods could be landed perfectly legally as if at an English port. Thus, vessels carrying sugar, rum, and tobacco sailed ostensibly from American and West Indian ports with papers showing Newfoundland as the destination but then changed course for Scotland as soon as the customs posts and Royal Navy cruisers had been left behind. Scottish merchants also settled into Newfoundland. In 1701, for instance, one official report noted that 'the Scotch have lately settled a factory there [Newfoundland] and send tobacco etc. to Scotland, Holland and other prohibited places'.[27] The Isle of Man became another centre of excellence for Scots smuggling.[28]

If anything, the pickings were even richer and easier in the Caribbean. The later seventeenth century in the West Indies was a golden age of buccaneering, when the lines between legal privateering and illicit activity were often very blurred. Wars between the Dutch and the English in the 1660s and 1670s, and between the English and the French after 1688, minor conflicts between islands and sporadic conquests, all added to the chaos and created a veritable bonanza of opportunity for seafarers with nerve and limited scruple. It was no coincidence that one of the most notorious pirates of the time was Captain William Kidd, from Dundee, who moved from legitimate privateering against the French in both the West Indies and off the African coast to Madagascar, where he launched his infamous criminal career which ended in his judicial execution in London in 1701.

---

[26] T. M. Fortescue (ed.), *Calendar of State Papers, America and the West Indies 1681–1697* (London, 1898–1904), 1696–7, 71.

[27] C. G. Headlam (ed.), *Calendar of State Papers, America and the West Indies, 1701* (London, 1910), 639.

[28] A. I. Macinnes, 'The Treaty of Union: Made in England', in T. M. Devine (ed.), *Scotland and the Union* (Edinburgh, 2008), 55–60.

Three further points can be made about this colourful phase in Scottish transatlantic activity. First, some inconsistency in London policy helped Scots adventurers to become legally established in the very heart of the English empire. In time of war (1664–7, 1672–4, and 1678) the prohibitions of the Navigation Acts were temporarily lifted. On another two occasions royal licences were granted to the Scots to trade. All this diluted for a time the apparently draconian regulations of the Navigation Acts. Second, the Scottish merchant community clearly regarded trade to the Americas as a long-term venture rather than simply a chance to make some quick opportunistic profits. One confirmation of this was the strategy adopted by the Glasgow traders. In 1668 the town bought the estate of Newark and immediately began work on what was called 'Newport Glasgow' (now Port Glasgow) in order to act as a harbour for ocean-going vessels as a ploy to head off potential competition in Atlantic commerce from Dumbarton and the Ayrshire coastal towns. There was also heavy investment in the processing of colonial products. Between 1667 and 1700 four sugar refining factories were built in Glasgow, with the capital coming from merchant families already engaged in the Atlantic trades. The search was also on for oceanic competence in seamanship. The city appointed a Professor of Navigation in 1681, navigation schools opened in 1695 and 1707, and one Captain Davis became a burgess of Glasgow *gratis* 'in respect he is a person qualified to be useful to this burgh in voyages to Africa and America'.[29]

Third, an equally impressive strand at this time was the relevance of the older ties with Europe to the development of the new Atlantic links. Commercial practices and business habits, refined over many generations in the Scottish trading colonies of Rotterdam, Bergen, Gothenburg, Cracow, Warsaw, and a host of other places, were transferred *en bloc* to the Americas. Scottish mercantile communities were now being steadily built up in New York, Boston, Charleston, Jamaica, and Barbados, based on the same family and neighbourhood networks of recruitment as in the old continental centres. Scottish ethnicity was used as a resource to enhance business trust and security in unstable frontier areas where the rule of law and government protection was weak or underdeveloped. Another classic technique inherited in the Americas from the European tradition was to seek out opportunities at the periphery where competition from commercial rivals was less

---

[29] Gordon Jackson, 'Glasgow in Transition, *c*.1660–*c*.1740', in Devine and Jackson (eds), *Glasgow*, 69–72.

intense. It was no coincidence, for instance, that those Scots involved in the Virginia tobacco trade quickly moved into the back country of the Chesapeake, away from the tidewater districts where London interests were already dominant and well entrenched.[30]

This level of commercial activity, in addition to the two Scottish attempts at American colonization in the 1680s in South Carolina (a failure) and East New Jersey (a relative success), helps to place the famous but ill-fated expedition to Darien in context. The plan to establish a Scottish trading post on the Isthmus of Panama did not come out of the blue, even though it was the most ambitious manifestation of Scottish adventuring in the Americas. Indeed, the key influence on the plan, William Paterson, was a Scot who, like many of his fellow countrymen, was very familiar with the Caribbean and nearby lands on the American mainland. As is well known, managerial incompetence, the hostility of Spain, and lack of support from England ensured that the venture collapsed in national humiliation and financial disaster. But the sheer scale of the endeavour and the huge investment it attracted from Scottish society in general confirmed the aspiration of the nation to seek its economic future in the New World.[31] The Union of 1707, with its concession of free access to English colonial markets and guarantees of Royal Navy protection for Scottish trade now gave further impetus to a trend which was already well established before that historic legislation was finally passed.

Success in Tobacco

In and around 1760 Scotland handled about 1 to 2 per cent of total European trade. Yet she was, after England, Europe's second largest purveyor of American tobacco. In the later 1750s Scotland re-exported about 15 million lbs of American tobacco on average per annum to continental Europe. In 1773, when the highest figure ever was recorded in the eighteenth century, 46 million lbs were shipped to continental destinations. At a yearly level of 2 lbs for per capita consumption these figures would have sufficed to supply about eight to twenty-two million Europeans, six to seventeen times the

---

[30] T. M. Devine, *The Tobacco Lords: A Study of the Tobacco Merchants of Glasgow and their Trading Activities, 1740–90* (Edinburgh, 1975), 56–7.

[31] The most recent scholarly study is Douglas Watt, *The Price of Scotland: Darien, Union and the Wealth of Nations* (Edinburgh, 2007).

Scottish population. Tobacco ranged, alongside some other colonial goods, amongst the most significant foreign imports into eighteenth-century Europe. It accounted for up to 40 per cent of Scotland's total imports and exports at the time, most of which was re-exported to the Continent. The Atlantic colonial trades lay at the heart of Scotland's commercial success in the pre-industrial period. And Scotland by the mid-eighteenth century had developed into a formidable northern European tobacco entrepôt. How did this pattern emerge?[32]

Scholars have underlined the geographical advantages of Glasgow over London and the western ports of England, especially the comparatively short and safe passage across the Atlantic to the English tobacco colonies of Virginia and Maryland.[33]

But geography was not the decisive factor because the Scots had no such advantage over London in relation to the European markets of France and Holland, where they sold most of their tobacco imports. Rather the key influence was the effectiveness of the commercial methods of the Glasgow firms. The giant syndicates, such as John Glassford and Co., William Cunningham and Co., and Speirs, Bowman, and Co., who together controlled almost half the trade, established chains of stores in the colonies run by Scots factors and clerks who bought up tobacco from the planters in advance of the arrival of the ships. This significantly reduced turnaround time in colonial ports and hence operating costs. This was an advantage which increased over time.[34]

Through a sophisticated and innovative forward purchasing system, asymmetrical ('colonial') credit relationships were developed, enabling Glaswegian tobacco lords to control both the purchasing price of tobacco in

---

[32] The following draws, unless otherwise indicated, on P. R. Rössner, *Scottish Trade in the Wake of Union (1700–1760): The Rise of Warehouse Economy* (Stuttgart, 2008), chs. 2, 5, and 6, an argument further refined in idem, *Scottish Trade with German Ports: A Sketch of the Atlantic Economy on Ground Level* (Stuttgart, 2008), 61–75, and idem, 'Interloping, Economic Underdevelopment and the State in Eighteenth-Century Northern Europe: How Scotland became a Tobacco Entrepôt', in M. A. Denzel, Jan de Vries, and P. R. Rössner (eds), *Small is Beautiful: Interlopers in Early Modern World Trade. The Experience of Smaller Trading Nations and Companies in the Mercantilist Era* (Stuttgart, 2011).

[33] J. M. Price, 'The Rise of Glasgow in the Chesapeake Tobacco Trade, 1707–1775', *William and Mary Quarterly*, 2 (1954), 179–99, esp. at 187s.; Devine, *Tobacco Lords*; T. M. Devine, *The Scottish Nation: A History 1700–2000* (US edn New York, 1999); idem, *Scotland's Empire, 1600–1815* (London, 2003), ch. 4.

[34] T. M. Devine, 'Industrialisation', in T. M. Devine, C. H. Lee, and G. C. Peden (eds), *The Transformation of Scotland: The Economy since 1700* (Edinburgh, 2005), 34–70 at 53.

America, as well as the prices they charged for the domestic manufactures they sold in return.[35] To this may be added a comparatively well-developed financial infrastructure in the Glasgow area, as well as a wage-rate differential between Scotland and England, as lower wages of a developing economy created a competitive advantage. Furthermore, a lenient customs administration prevailed, at least into the 1730s. Smuggling levels reached a staggering 62 per cent of legal imports in Scotland during the first half of the century.[36] In the long run, however, several other elements need to be added, such as regional specialization of British ports, the need of foreign monopolist buyers such as the French for central places such as Glasgow and Edinburgh for conducting their bulk purchases, and trends towards concentration in business and larger firms.[37] Even then the list would be far from complete, as scholars have also named improvements in shipping procedures and ships' design, improved harbour facilities at the Glasgow outports (Greenock and Port Glasgow), developments in human capital (skills, commercial training), as well as the demise of Whitehaven, the main and only serious rival of Glasgow in the north-west of England, in the American tobacco trades.[38] If one were to sum up and classify these different facets, the list could be grouped according to the following: human and financial capital, natural endowment and physical geography, commercial geography and infrastructure, micro-economics and business techniques, and cash flow (purchasing monopoly of the French, who paid for large consignments of tobacco in cash or short-term bills, which proved a crucial advantage in a business where delays between purchase and final sale were frequent).

One crucial aspect, however, has rather been overlooked in the discussion so far, and this is the administrative framework of Scotland's trade, which changed in 1707. It can be argued that there were certain beneficial technicalities built into the contemporary customs system that facilitated the rise of an entrepôt economy focused on tobacco, which proved

[35] Devine, *Tobacco Lords*, *passim*, esp. 55–68; idem, *The Scottish Nation*, 119–23.

[36] R. C. Nash, 'The English and Scottish Tobacco Trades in the Seventeenth and Eighteenth Centuries: Legal and Illegal Trade', *Economic History Review*, 2nd series, 35 (1982), 354–72, at 363 (table 5 on 364); 368–70.

[37] Price, 'Rise of Glasgow', 185–93; J. M. Price and P. G. E. Clemens, 'A Revolution of Scale in Overseas Trade: British Firms in the Chesapeake Trade, 1675–1775', *Journal of Economic History*, 47.1 (1987), 1–43, at 9; 30–1; 37–8.

[38] A comprehensive survey may be found in Devine, *Scotland's Empire*, ch. 4.

advantageous within a domestic economy that had as yet little else to offer in world markets.

With the Union of the Parliaments in 1707, central parameters of Scottish foreign trading were altered. The main aspects of the Treaty of Union[39] which are supposed to have stimulated Scottish commercial and economic success after 1707 include direct access of Scots traders and ships to the products and markets of the English colonies overseas (mainly for tobacco, sugar, rum, rice, indigo, and coffee) and thus admission to what was Europe's biggest free trade zone at the time. By the same token, full protection by the English navy was granted, as all Scots ships were, as of May Day 1707, to pass as British. But most important, Article VI of the Treaty stipulated that 'all Parts of the united Kingdom, for ever, from and after the Union, shall have the same Allowances, Encouragements, and Draw-backs, and be under the same Prohibitions, Restrictions, and Regulations of Trade, and liable to the same Customs and Duties, and Import and Export. . . .'[40] It can be argued that it was in fact this English customs system, introduced in Scottish ports in 1707, which—alongside the aspects named above—helped to determine the rise of Scotland's Atlantic trades in the eighteenth century.

The new customs system particularly favoured the transit trades, and encouraged re-exports of colonial non-essentials, such as tobacco, somewhat at the expense of domestic exports. It did so mainly in three ways. First, while most imports of foreign commodities into British ports were either free of charge or only very moderately taxed, imports of colonial goods were taxed at prohibitive levels when retained for domestic consumption. Second, the effective level of taxation fell to very insignificant levels if these goods were re-exported again from British ports to continental European destinations. By a generous refund of import duties upon re-export (draw-back, as it was called in contemporary language)—in the case of tobacco after 1723 amounting to 100 per cent—continental European consumers were provided with tobacco and sugar more cheaply than their English or Scots domestic

---

[39] The most recent accounts on the issue of Union include C. A. Whatley with D. Patrick, *The Scots and the Union* (Edinburgh, 2006); A. I. Macinnes, *Union and Empire: The Making of the United Kingdom in 1707* (Cambridge, 2007). See also the two essay collections S. J. Brown and C. A. Whatley (eds), *The Union of 1707: New Dimensions* (Edinburgh, 2008) and *Scottish Historical Review*, 87, Supplement; and T. M. Devine (ed.), *Scotland and the Union 1707–2007* (Edinburgh, 2008).

[40] The Article of Union of 1707, including the amendments as quoted in C. A. Whatley, *Bought and Sold for English Gold? Explaining the Union 1707* (2nd edn East Linton, 2001), 101–3.

counterparts. But third, the imported commodities became liable to very high duties payable immediately upon landing, regardless of whether the commodities were to be retained as domestic imports or were to be re-exported subsequently. Yet, in order to alleviate what easily might have proven a considerable strain upon any firm or merchant's cash reserves, the Crown had devised an ingenious mode of payment. Under the regulation of the 'bonding system' the merchants were given credit on customs duties which could be offset against the subsequent tax rebate applicable upon re-exports. Thus in the Scottish tobacco trades large amounts of highly taxed tobacco could be shipped without a single penny changing hands. A capital-intensive business, where circulating cash was extremely short between the purchase of the tobacco in the Americas and the re-sale in Europe, was thus freed of the need to advance large sums of cash on customs duties at a stage where the merchants or firms might be seriously short of liquid funds. In this way, the new customs regime of 1707 proved the perfect counterpart to a still rather underdeveloped Scottish economy, which, as was the case in most northern European states, had few attractive domestic products to offer on world markets.

As of May Day 1707, English customs (and excise) rates and procedures became applicable in Scotland, with a somewhat surprisingly low number of differing rates and procedures and other exemptions.[41] At that date, the English customs system consisted of the Old Subsidy Inwards and additional duties related to the former, as well as about eighteen recently added (1660–1706) import duties, the Subsidy Outwards, and a few further export duties. Towards the end of the period concerned, more than fifty separate duties were charged, mainly upon import.[42] The switch from the old Scottish customs system to the 'new' English and now British system in

---

[41] Customs rates and manuals, see below, and Rössner, *Scottish Trade in the Wake of Union*, ch. 2. On excise rates, see S. West, *The Exciseman's Pocket Book* (London, 1769) and J. Figgess, *The Excise-Officer's Vade-Mecum...* (London, 1781), 66–70. On the political economy of British taxation, see, for instance, J. Brewer, *The Sinews of Power: War, Money and the English State, 1688–1783* (London, 1989); P. K. O'Brien, 'Inseparable Connections: Trade, Economy, Fiscal State, and the Expansion of Empire, 1688–1815', in P. J. Marshall (ed.), *The Oxford History of the British Empire*, ii: *The Eighteenth Century* (Oxford, 1998), 53–77; R. Harris, 'Government and the Economy', in R. Floud and P. Johnson (eds), *The Cambridge Economic History of Modern Britain*, i: *Industrialisation* (Cambridge, 2004), 204–37.

[42] Exports—which had not been heavily or comprehensively taxed anyway—in compensation were nearly completely freed from duty in 1722/3. A small but admittedly rather insignificant group of domestic exports, such as horses and lead, remained liable to duty, as did a small

1707 therefore represented an enormous increase in average levels of duty for Scotland's commerce. To name but those commodities that dominated Scotland's overseas import trades after 1707, the increase amounted to 825 per cent in the case of tobacco; 222 per cent in sugar's case; 402 per cent in the case of German linens.[43] For the merchants involved, this was already the biggest, and in financial terms most considerable, change for eighteenth-century Scottish commerce, as after 1707 only minor changes in duty were introduced.[44]

Tobacco thus experienced the highest increase of duty in 1707, when its direct importation from the English colonies into Scottish ports became possible.[45] It remained the most heavily taxed import during the subsequent period. In 1755 it paid more than 220 per cent duty, measured in terms of its free on board (f.o.b.) price,[46] when retained for domestic consumption. In tobacco's case three main characteristic techniques came to work, which in the end all had a profound impact on the risks and profitability of colonial trading on Scottish account, as well as the effect of creating and designing, or at least helping to determine, a peculiarly Scottish eighteenth-century trading pattern.

---

number of re-exports, mainly foreign dyestuffs. Rössner, *Scottish Trade in the Wake of Union*, 52–4.

[43] Rössner, *Scottish Trade in the Wake of Union*, ch. 2.

[44] For the period of concern the duties and changes therein may be traced using contemporary manuals composed for customs officers: H. Crouch, *A Complete View of the British Customs . . .*, Part I (London, 1725), Part II (London, 1728; 2nd edn 1731; 3rd edn 1738; 4th edn 1745; 5th edn 1755); S. Baldwin, *A Survey of the British Customs . . .* (London, 1770). Wherever these manuals are lacking, information can be obtained from 'merchants' digests', for instance T. Langham, *The Neat Duties (All Discounts and Abatements deducted of all Merchandize Specify'd in the Book of Rates* (London, 1708; 3rd edn 1715; 7th edn 1754).

[45] As discussed earlier, there had been a lively, yet from the standpoint of English mercantile law illegal, traffic between Scotland and the English tobacco colonies since the 1640s. T. C. Smout, 'The Overseas Trade of Scotland with Particular Reference to the Baltic and Scandinavian Trades 1660–17078' (unpublished Ph.D. thesis, University of Cambridge, 1959), 60–2 and above, 35–7.

[46] A term used in international commerce, meaning that the seller pays for the transportation of goods up to the port of departure. Then the purchaser pays the cost of marine freight transport, insurance, unloading, and transportation from the arrival port to the final destination. If goods are priced in c.i.f. terms (cost, insurance, freight), the seller pays for the cost of transportation, insurance, and unloading the goods at their final destination, i.e. the country where the respective goods are imported. In national accounting terms, especially regarding foreign trade in historical perspective, imports given in c.i.f. terms are more desirable, as they reflect the true cost of imported goods in the importing country more accurately.

First, although effectively between 1707 and 1760 the rates of import duty on tobacco remained unchanged, the commodity was taxed excessively highly, if consumed domestically. As of May Day 1707, Scottish tobacco imports were effectively taxed at 220 per cent of their f.o.b. value. These were levels which the domestic market in Scotland was neither able nor willing to bear, as the spectacular rise in domestic smuggling shows. During the first two or three decades after 1707 it is said that not more than 60 per cent of total tobacco imported into Scottish ports was declared and taxed.[47]

But a second aspect also came into play. The English customs system operated a variety of draw-backs (tax rebates) of customs duties upon re-export, provided that certain criteria were met.[48] Usually draw-backs amounted to only a fraction of sums originally paid. In sugar's case, 78 to 89 per cent of the import duty could be drawn back; in the case of rice, 87 to 90 per cent. German linens drew back 82 to 89 per cent. These were among Scotland's main re-exports.[49] Only tobacco could, after 1723, draw back 100 per cent of duties paid upon import, provided it had been shipped orderly and duty had been paid in cash.[50] By the draw-back scheme one of the heaviest strains upon the merchants' cash reserves, i.e. an import duty of more than 220 per cent of the goods' value, was removed and circulating capital freed accordingly to enormous benefit.

A third aspect, however, needs to be kept in mind. The fact that import duties on tobacco were usually refunded in the end seems to be one of the ironies built into this particular system. After all, if 90 per cent and more of

---

[47] Nash, *Tobacco Trades*, 364, table 5.

[48] These criteria were mainly that the importers, their ships and the ships' crews were deemed British (meaning that at least 75% of the crew had to be of British birth); the commodities had either originated within the British plantations, or were shipped from their point of production directly to Britain without prior re-landing; and the commodities concerned left Britain no later than three years after importation.

[49] These goods were also not as heavily taxed as tobacco. Foreign Muscovado sugar was taxed at 60%. Muscovado sugar from the British plantations still paid about 20% of its nominal value in 1755 current Scottish prices, when retained for domestic use. Rössner, *Scottish Trade in the Wake of Union*, chs 2, 3, 5.

[50] In 1723, by the otherwise unsuccessful 'Excise Bill', the halfpenny on tobacco retained by the Crown was abolished. J. M. Price, 'The Excise Affair Revisited: The Administrative and Colonial Dimensions of a Parliamentary Crisis', reprinted in J. M. Price, *Overseas Trade and Traders: Essays on Some Commercial, Financial and Political Challenges Facing British Atlantic Merchants, 1660–1775* (Aldershot, 1996).

the imported tobacco was re-exported again, which financial gain would accrue to the state from this type of transaction, if the Crown had to refund the duties anyway? It is important to bear in mind that frequently there were no real (i.e. cash) refunds as there had been no payments in cash! In fact, there was an effective method of fund-raising built into the system, by which the Crown raised considerable sums upon interest payments, and merchants were freed from large cash burdens upon import. In something resembling a quid pro quo, the English and after 1707 British customs system permitted parts of the duties due upon import to be 'bonded'. This was a promise to pay a certain amount of cash at a specified later day, plus interest on the principal for the term given in the bond, which might range from six to eighteen months; a bond represented a non-tradable letter of credit issued by the Crown to a merchant upon importation of a certain cargo in lieu of cash payments towards the applicable customs duties. Upon re-export of the cargo under consideration, the sums stated on the bond were 'refunded'.[51]

The implications of all this become clearer if the sums involved are set in relation to contemporary commercial data. In the 1750s for instance, when the Glaswegian tobacco trade was fully developed, larger firms easily imported 100,000 lbs or more in one single ship.[52] A tobacco cargo of 100,000 lbs would in 1755 have been liable to a net duty of £2,292 sterling—in cash.[53] Such amounts were extraordinary and would have strained the cash reserves of most contemporaries, as 'the average individual share in a Glasgow tobacco company in the years before the American War was between £1,000 and £2,000'.[54] Especially in the colonial trades, dependent upon an intrinsically linked import and re-export business, the sums involved in import declarations would in fact have exceeded the liquidity of all but the richest merchants and companies. The incentive to provide bonds in lieu of cash payments is therefore immediately evident. Often it would have arisen out of pure necessity.

[51] E. E. Hoon, *The Organisation of the English Customs System 1696–1789* (2nd edn Newton Abbot, 1968), 256–64.

[52] National Archives of Scotland, E504/28 (Port Glasgow port books), E504/15 (Greenock port books). Price and Clemens, 'Revolution of Scale', 31–3.

[53] Calculated from the works referred to in n. 44 above.

[54] Devine, *Tobacco Lords*, 10 (quote) and ch. 6 for sources of capital and capital requirements in the tobacco trades.

In fact, bonds provided commercial credit or circulating capital assets at low and sometimes no interest to businesses, which could be short of cash reserves. This problem most typically occurred between the purchase of cargoes in the Americas and their sale at auction in Europe a year or two later. The sum of the purchase price, fees, and customs duties could reach into the tens of thousands of pounds sterling in the most extreme cases. Years could pass between the dispatch of a tobacco vessel from Glasgow to a continental port and its final sale. These were periods during which considerable sums of capital were tied up. The risks of defaults and bankruptcies were immense.[55] By providing near-free of charge access to eighteenth-century cash crops in British Atlantic trade by means of the draw-back on sugar, tobacco, coffee, and rice, plus operating a generous credit system with the bonds, the British customs system thus effectively encouraged massive transit trade in these goods. The system partly discouraged domestic consumption of those products that gained more rapidly in importance in Atlantic trade after the 1660s. The home market was accordingly largely supplied using smuggled tobacco. However, in the re-export trades, the incentives towards illegal behaviour were considerably removed, particularly after the grip of the customs was tightened in the 1730s.

As a consequence, Scottish tobacco imports rose from a yearly average around five million lbs in the late 1720s and 1730s to a staggering figure of forty-five million lbs per year in the late 1760s. Given the profits to be made on tobacco, due to access being limited to those in possession of colonies producing the item (Navigation Acts),[56] the choice of procuring the item legally and re-selling it legally to continental Europeans was, if not strictly logical, at least a feasible one in financial terms. It would have been especially feasible if the domestic economy had not much to offer in turn. Export shares for most Scottish domestic industries were indeed low for most of the eighteenth century.[57] In this way, Scotland shared the fate of most continental European economies prior to industrialization, where low average incomes and productivity levels accounted for limited domestic

---

[55] Rössner, *Scottish Trade in the Wake of Union*; Devine, *Tobacco Lords*.

[56] The full set of economic implications and the applicable price mechanism under the English Navigation Acts are summarized in S. L. Engerman, 'Mercantilism and Overseas Trade, 1700–1860', in R. Floud and D. N. McCloskey (eds), *The Economic History of Britain since 1700*, i: *1700–1860* (Cambridge, 2nd edn 1994), 182–204.

[57] T. M. Devine, 'The Modern Economy: Scotland and the Act of Union', in Devine, Lee, and Peden (eds), *Transformation of Scotland*, 13–33.

(and thus overseas) markets, low levels of consumption, and domestic exports.

Whatley has assembled evidence on stagnating or declining export levels in the more important Scottish industries such as linens, woollens, coal, salt, paper, glass, candle and shoe making, brewing, as well as fishing, mainly in the first half of the eighteenth century.[58] This tendency wore on; after the 1750s, Scots salt makers, for instance, sold between 92 and 100 per cent of output in the home market.[59] Only about 2 per cent of Scotland's yearly production of coal was exported between 1755 and 1759.[60] Linen enjoyed an exceptional export-to-output ratio of 20–30 per cent and a similar relation obtained for the share of linen manufactures in total Scottish exports overseas, c.1760.[61] Even though no comprehensive quantitative study on the Scottish economy in the eighteenth century has been produced yet, the available evidence suggests that woollen and linen textiles, cattle and fish, and some cereals in good harvest years were virtually the only commodities produced in Scotland that could be at least partly disposed of in foreign markets.[62] If the comparison with England is drawn, Scotland exported far fewer domestic products (measured against total domestic production or GDP) and far fewer manufactures (measured against total exports) than England, c.1700–60.[63]

But England, Europe's second richest and most developed economy at the time (the Netherlands took the lead), is not a good benchmark in this regard. Evidence from urbanization figures shows that after the 1750s Scotland was well able to catch up in economic terms and undergo an

---

[58] C. A. Whatley, *Scottish Society: Beyond Jacobitism, towards Industrialisation* (Manchester, 2000), ch. 2, especially 65–71.

[59] C. A. Whatley, *The Scottish Salt Industry 1570–1850: An Economic Social History* (Aberdeen, 1987), 50, table 2.1.

[60] Rössner, *Scottish Trade in the Wake of Union*, 211.

[61] Ibid. 213, 224–5.

[62] Ibid., chs 4–6 for further sources on Scotland's domestic economy in the eighteenth century. For a recent synopsis, see essays in Devine, Lee, and Peden (eds), *Transformation of Scotland*.

[63] England: J. Cuenca Esteban, 'The Rising Share of British Industrial Exports in Industrial Output, 1700–1851', *Journal of Economic History*, 57.4 (1997), 879–906, at 882, table 1, 885, fig. 1; S. D. Smith, 'The Market for Manufactures in the Thirteen Continental Colonies, 1698–1776', *Economic History Review*, 2nd series, 51.4 (1998), 676–708, at 683–4. Scotland: Rössner, *Scottish Trade in the Wake of Union*, chs 5, 6 and appendix, table 6–3.

industrial revolution and significant economic growth.[64] But at least prior to the 1770s, the new customs regime introduced in 1707 proved a great stimulus to the re-export of tobacco—a specifically 'Scottish' commodity in eighteenth-century foreign trade, so to speak—which proved somewhat fortuitous within the pre-industrial framework of the domestic economy of limited markets and opportunities.

Slavery and the Slave Trade

By the time the trade was abolished British ships had carried just over an estimated 3.4 million Africans to slavery in the Caribbean and America. Scottish ports played only a very limited direct role in this human transportation. Current estimates suggest twenty-seven voyages from Scotland to Africa and the West Indies between 1707 and 1766 shipping around 4,500 to 5,000 slaves. Future research may increase this number but will probably not change the overall conclusion that direct Scottish participation in the slave trade was relatively minuscule. Scottish merchants had found their primary commercial niche in the importation of tobacco and, in an era of increasing port specialization, Glasgow rose to pre-eminence in this sector, with Bristol, Liverpool, and London the dominant players in the Africa trade.[65]

This is not to say, however, that Scots were inactive in the slave trade by other routes and means. Expatriate Scots were widely engaged through English ports. In Liverpool there were two principal Scottish houses, Samuel McDowal and the Tod brothers, while dozens more were employed as masters and surgeons in slave ships of the city. Robert Gordon from Moray was a principal Bristol slaver with over ten vessels involved in the trade. But most Scottish slave merchants worked through London. Around one in ten of the capital's slave traders have been accounted Scots, a proportion which increased in subsequent decades. Many were active in African waters, partly through their connections with the Company of Merchants Trading to Africa, but also as private traders scouring the east of Sierra Leone and the Gold Coast for human cargoes. One of the most notable ventures came in 1748 when a consortium of five Scots led by

---

[64] T. M. Devine, 'Urbanisation', in T. M. Devine and R. Mitchison (eds), *People and Society in Scotland*, i: *1760–1830* (Edinburgh, 1988), 27–52; Devine, 'Scotland', in Floud and Johnson (eds), *Cambridge Economic History of Modern Britain*, i. 388–416.

[65] Mark Duffill, 'The Africa Trade from the Ports of Scotland 1707–66', *Slavery and Abolition*, 25 (December 2004), 102–22.

Richard Oswald, Augustus Boyd, and Alexander Grant acquired an old slave 'trade castle' on the Sierra Leone River at Bance Island linked to a dozen 'outfactories' or slave-gathering points deep in the interior of East Africa. The enterprise was managed by kinsmen and associates of the principals. Between 1748 and 1784 the firm and its satellites shipped nearly 13,000 slaves across the Atlantic to clients in the Caribbean and the Carolinas.[66]

More important than these connections, however, was that the two major Scottish trades of the eighteenth century, tobacco and sugar importation, depended in the final analysis on slave labour in the plantation economies of the Americas. The scale of the Scottish tobacco trade has been described earlier in this chapter and no further detailed comment is necessary here. It should, nevertheless, be noted how crucial capital and credit from the great Glasgow houses was in facilitating slave purchases by the planter classes in the back country of Virginia and Maryland. The tobacco plantations were geared to satisfying international markets. Yet increasingly cultivation was being managed by planters with little capital in new areas of production. Finance to buy more slaves had to come from outside and the Scottish stores soon became vital sources of credit. The Glasgow traders became the bankers for many parts of the tobacco slave economies. Much of their own capital was mobilized by borrowing on personal and heritable bonds from the moneyed classes of the west of Scotland who, indirectly, therefore, came to have a major stake in slave societies across the Atlantic.[67] By 1778, Glasgow's colonial debts had swollen to an estimated £1.3 million sterling (see table 2.1).

The Scots were also heavily involved in the Caribbean sugar islands. These were different societies from mainland North America. By the end of the eighteenth century, the British colonies alone had over 700,000 black slaves. In Jamaica, the richest and most productive of the British islands, nine out of every ten inhabitants were enslaved, a proportion significantly greater than the 33 per cent found in the American South. The pattern on other islands was broadly similar.[68] The importance of these plantation

---

[66] Gomer Williams, *History of the Liverpool Privateers and Letters of Marque, with an Account of the Liverpool Slave Trade* (London, 1897), 674; David Hancock, 'Scots in the Slave Trade', in Ned C. Landsman (ed.), *Nation and Province in the First British Empire* (London, 2001), 60–93; M. Duffill and E. Graham, 'Scots in the Liverpool Slave Trade', *History Scotland*, March 2008; Devine, *Scotland's Empire*, 245–6.

[67] 'Sources of Capital for the Glasgow Tobacco Trade, c.1740–80', *Business History*, 16 (1974); Devine, *Tobacco Lords*, 58–60.

[68] B. W. Higman, *Plantation Jamaica 1750–1850* (Kingston, 2005), 3.

Table 2.1 Estimates of Glasgow merchant debts in North America 1778

Colony	Value (pounds sterling)
Virginia	719,038
Maryland	155,810
North Carolina	29,924
Undistinguished	401,313
Total	1,306,085

Source: Glasgow City Archives, Speirs Papers, TD 131/10–12, Diary of Alexander Speirs, 2 March 1778.

economies was widely acknowledged by contemporaries. Even Adam Smith, one of the most eminent critics of the colonial system, was impressed: the profits of a sugar estate in the Caribbean, he observed, 'were generally much greater than those of any other cultivation that is known either in Europe or America'.[69] For Edmund Burke in 1757, no places in the world could match the West Indies for the speed with which great fortunes could be made. Modern research has confirmed that the plantation owners and sugar merchants of Jamaica, the Leeward Islands, and Grenada were, on average, the richest citizens in the eighteenth-century empire, with individual wealth and income exceeding those of Europeans in mainland British America by a significant margin.[70] In 1700 the British islands accounted for about 40 per cent of all transatlantic sugar consignments. By 1815 the figure had reached 60 per cent. At the same time, the Caribbean colonies employed, directly or indirectly, half the nation's long-distance shipping, their fixed and movable wealth was reckoned at more than £30 million sterling, duties in West Indian produce accounted for an eighth of Exchequer revenues, and the credit structures linked to these plantation economies were key segments in UK financial markets.

The Scottish connection with the West Indies was multi-layered. Merchants had imported sugar, rum, cotton, and coffee from there before the Union of 1707. But from the mid-eighteenth century, however, and

---

[69] Quoted in J. R. Ward, 'The British West Indies in the Age of Abolition, 1748–1815', in Marshall (ed.), *The Oxford History of the British Empire*, ii: *The Eighteenth Century*, 427.

[70] T. G. Barnard, '"Prodigious Riches": The Wealth of Jamaica before the American Revolution', *Economic History Review*, 54.3 (August 2001), 508.

especially from the 1770s, the West Indies trade became the most dynamic and important sector in Scottish overseas commerce. Indeed, after 1783, and the decline of the direct importation of tobacco with the emergence of the independent United States, it became central. Merchants sought to diversify, partly to British North America, but more crucially and emphatically towards the Caribbean. In addition, the produce of the islands now became strategic factors in early Scottish industrialization as 'sea-island' cotton was landed in increasing volume at the Clyde ports to power the new textile mills of the western Lowlands. The boom in the trade was also given impetus by the demand for 'slave cloth', or rough and cheap linen clothing, which was the specialization of the eastern Lowlands, and the market in the slave plantations for salted herring from the lochs of the Western Highlands. By 1813 the West Indies accounted for no less than 65 per cent of the share of exports from Scotland of British goods.[71]

Scots were also significantly over-represented among plantation owners, professional managers (attorneys), physicians, and overseers on several of the British islands. Contemporaries noticed. Edward Long, the planter-historian of Jamaica, believed the colony was 'greatly indebted to North Britain, as very nearly one third of the inhabitants are either natives of that country or descendants from those who were'.[72] Lady Maria Nugent, some years later in 1801, thought that 'almost all the agents, attorneys, merchants and shopkeepers [of Jamaica], are of that country [Scotland], and really do deserve to thrive in this, they are so industrious'.[73] But Scots were also employed at much lower social levels. It was reported from Antigua in 1787 that 'The negroes are turned out at sunrise, and employed in gangs from twenty to sixty upwards, under the supervision of white overseers, generally poor Scotch lads...subordinate to these overseers are drivers, commonly called dog-drivers who are mostly black or mulatto fellows of the worst disposition.'[74]

Modern research has confirmed the centrality of the Scottish presence in the British Caribbean. During the years 1771–5 Scots accounted for nearly

---

[71] R. H. Campbell, 'The Making of the Industrial City', in Devine and Jackson (eds), *Glasgow*, 184–213.

[72] E. Long, *The History of Jamaica* (London, 1774), ii. 286–7.

[73] *Lady Nugent's Journal of her Residence in Jamaica from 1801 to 1805*, ed. Philip Wright (Kingston, 1966), 29.

[74] John Luffman, *A Brief Account of the Island of Antigua* (London, 1789).

45 per cent of all inventories at death in Jamaica valued above £1,000.[75] Moreover, unlike the American mainland, they were able to establish themselves as plantation and land owners on a huge scale as island after island was conquered from the French during the successive wars of the eighteenth century. When St Kitts was ceded to Britain in 1713, half the lots of 100 acres and above went to Scottish purchasers.[76] Later, after the end of the Seven Years War in 1763, there was a veritable bonanza of land transfers to Scots in Dominica, St Vincent, Grenada, and Tobago in the wake of British victory and the annexation of the islands from France.[77] In Antigua, eleven of the eighteen members of the planter elite were of Scottish origin in 1775.[78]

The professional impact was also enormous. Increasingly, as slave prices rose, many planters became more attracted to breeding new generations from existing 'stock' rather than the buying of 'salt water' blacks directly off the ships from Africa. The new commitment to the health of the slave populations opened up a huge market for Scottish-trained physicians and surgeons.[79] Similarly, B. W. Higman's recent work on Jamaican attorneys has shown how Scots dominated these posts, which were critical to the profitability of the sugar plantations. Absenteeism of Caribbean plantation owners in Britain was common. The unhealthy climate and environment ensured that the successful always went home, leaving their possessions in the hands of managers, the attorneys, whose basic function was to squeeze 'the maximum possible product from the system and the human beings it oppressed'.[80]

The Caribbean connection can, therefore, be regarded as a factor in Scotland's 'great leap forward' of the eighteenth century. The islands provided markets for Scottish linen, raw material for the country's booming

---

[75] R. B. Sheridan, *Sugar and Slavery* (Barbados, 1974), 369.

[76] Graham, *Maritime History*, 37–44.

[77] Sir W. Forbes, *Memories of a Banking House* (London, 1860), 39. In the sale of lands in St Vincent and Dominica in 1765, out of a total of fifty-nine purchases valued at £111, 535, twenty-two of those who acquired estates gave a place of residence in some part of Scotland. However, while most buyers were West India-based, the majority of these had Scottish surnames. See National Archives of Scotland GD/32/38, An Account of all the Lands Sold in the Islands of St. Vincent and Dominica by H.M. Commissioners, 1765. See also T. M. Devine, 'An Eighteenth-Century Business Élite: Glasgow West India Merchants, c.1750–1815', *Scottish Historical Review*, 57.1: 163 (April 1978), 40–67.

[78] Devine, *Scotland's Empire*, 231.

[79] Ibid. 232–3.

[80] Higman, *Plantation Jamaica*, 17, 77, 292.

textile manufacture, and the sojourners who returned home with their profits put much of their capital into Scottish industry and landownership. It was, however, and is, an uncomfortable fact that these riches garnered from the West Indies would not have been possible without the exploitation of untold thousands of black slaves.

Select Bibliography

Bernard Bailyn and Philip D. Morgan (eds), *Strangers within the Realm: Cultural Margins of the First British Empire* (Chapel Hill, NC, 1991).

T. M. Devine, *The Tobacco Lords* (Edinburgh, 1975).

—— *Scotland's Empire 1600–1815* (London, 2003).

—— *To the Ends of the Earth: Scotland's Global Diaspora* (London, 2011).

—— 'Did Slavery Make Scotia Great?', *Britain and the World*, 4.1 (2011).

Douglas Hamilton, *Scotland, the Caribbean and the Atlantic World* (Manchester, 2005).

Alan L. Karras, *Sojourners in the Sun: Scottish Migrants in Jamaica and the Chesapeake 1740–1800* (Ithaca, NY, 1992).

A. I. Macinnes, *Union and Empire: The Making of the United Kingdom in 1707* (Cambridge, 2007).

Jacob M. Price, *France and the Chesapeake* (Ann Arbor, Mich., 1973).

P. R. Rössner, *Scottish Trade in the Wake of Union 1700–1760* (Stuttgart, 2008).

—— 'Interloping, Economic Underdevelopment and the State in Eighteenth-Century Northern Europe: How Scotland became a Tobacco Entrepot after 1707', in Markus A. Denzel, Jan de Vries, and Philipp Robinson Rossner (eds), *Small is Beautiful? Interlopers and Small Trading Nations in the Pre-industrial Period: Proceedings of the XV World Economic History Congress* (Utrecht, 2009).

Emma Rothschild, *The Inner Life of Empires: An Eighteenth Century History* (Princeton, NJ, 2011).

Douglas Watt, *The Price of Scotland: Darien, Union and the Wealth of Nations* (Edinburgh, 2007).

3

Locality, Nation, and Empire

Scots and the Empire in Asia, c.1695–c.1813

Andrew Mackillop

A chapter on Scotland's involvement in the Asian hemisphere of Britain's eighteenth-century empire can serve two distinct but related purposes. First, it can help to address the ongoing lack of detailed research into one of the most significant and enduring but also least understood aspects of the country's multifaceted participation in British expansion. Compared to the wealth of studies on Scottish connections with the Atlantic world, the volume of work on the Scots in Asia is still remarkably small.[1] Beyond an important survey of the networks that facilitated infiltration of the English East India Company (EIC) between 1720 and 1780, and an exploration of the impact of Enlightenment ideas on Scottish governors in India, the subject continues to lack comprehensive coverage.[2] Other aspects of the topic that have received attention include: the socio-economic factors in Scotland prompting individuals to join the EIC;[3] the commercial and social networks

---

[1] O. D. Edwards and G. Shepperson (eds), *Scotland, Europe and the American Revolution* (Edinburgh, 1976); Eric Richards, 'Scotland and the Uses of the Atlantic Empire', in B. Bailyn and Philip D. Morgan (eds), *Strangers within the Realm: Cultural Margins of the First British Empire* (London, 1991), 68–113; Ned C. Landsman (ed.), *Nation and Province in the First British Empire: Scotland and the Americas, 1600–1800* (London, 2001).

[2] M. McLaren, *British India and British Scotland, 1780–1830* (Akron, Oh., 2001); George K. McGilvary, *East India Patronage and the British State: The Scottish Elite and Politics in the Eighteenth Century* (London, 2008).

[3] G. J. Bryant, 'Scots in India in the Eighteenth Century', *Scottish Historical Review*, 64 (1985), 22–41; J. Riddy, 'Warren Hastings: Scotland's Benefactor?', in G. Carnall and C. Nicolson (eds), *The Impeachment of Warren Hastings* (Edinburgh, 1989), 30–57; T. M. Devine, 'Scottish Elites and the Indian Empire, 1700–1815', in T. C. Smout (ed.), *Anglo-Scottish Relations from 1603–1900* (Oxford, 2005), 213–29.

constructed by Scots in Asia;[4] and the seminal contribution of 'Orientalist' scholarship in the Scottish universities to British perceptions of India.[5] Yet given the long-acknowledged profile of Scots in the British East, coverage of the crucial eighteenth-century period remains partial and disconnected. The origins of this historiographical neglect are significant. The methodological focus upon the colonies of permanent settlement at the expense of Scottish sojourning in the East and West Indies speaks volumes about the central role of emigration history in shaping interpretations of Scotland's place within the British Empire.[6]

This highlights the second objective of the chapter; that is, an exploration of the limitations and value of Scottish perspectives on the empire in Asia. Few if any surveys of post-Union Scotland do not now address the question of overseas expansion and the impact this had upon all aspects of the country's society and culture.[7] Yet while the effervescence of research into Scotland's role in the empire is undeniable, the subject remains stubbornly semi-detached from the debates and conceptual models which have energized reappraisals of British imperialism. Why is this?

Part of the problem, ironically, lies in the very real progress that has been made in recovering the role of Scotland and Scots within the empire. As the commissioning of a volume on Scotland for *The Oxford History of the British Empire* series demonstrates, the country's high profile is now widely accepted by those working outside the field of Scottish studies. Indeed, given the

[4] J. G. Parker, 'Scottish Enterprise in India, 1750–1914', in R. A. Cage (ed.), *The Scots Abroad: Labour, Capital, Enterprise, 1750–1914* (London, 1985), 191–219; B. R. Tomlinson, 'From Campsie to Kedgeree: Scottish Enterprise, Asian Trade and the Company Raj', *Modern Asian Studies*, 36 (2002), 769–91; A. Mackillop, 'Europeans, Britons and Scots: Scottish Sojourning Networks and Identities in Asia, c.1700–1815', in A. McCarthy (ed.), *A Global Clan: Scottish Migrant Networks and Identities since the Eighteenth Century* (London, 2006), 19–47.

[5] J. Rendall, 'Scottish Orientalism: From Robertson to James Mill', *Historical Journal*, 25 (1982), 43–65; Bruce P. Lenman, 'The Scottish Enlightenment and Empire in India, 1772–1813', *Indo-British Review: A Journal of History*, 15 (1993), 53–61; D. M. Peers, 'Soldiers, Scholars, and the Scottish Enlightenment: Militarism in Early Nineteenth-Century India', *International History Review*, 16 (1994), 441–6; Stewart J. Brown, 'William Robertson, Early Orientalism and the *Historical Disquisition* on India of 1791', *Scottish Historical Review*, 88 (2009), 289–312.

[6] John Hill Burton, *The Scot Abroad*, vols. i–ii (Edinburgh, 1863), i, p. vii; G. Donaldson, *The Scots Overseas* (London, 1966), 33–45; Michael Fry, *The Scottish Empire* (Edinburgh, 2001), 493.

[7] T. M. Devine, *The Scottish Nation, 1700–2000* (London, 1999), 25–7, 56–61, 105–23; Christopher A. Whatley, *Scottish Society, 1707–1830: Beyond Jacobitism, towards Industrialisation* (Manchester, 2000), 65–7; 109–13; David Allan, *Scotland in the Eighteenth Century* (London, 2002), 165–85.

perennial fear among practitioners of Scottish history that the subject has
little purchase beyond the Tweed, it is telling testimony to the scale of
Scotland's involvement that surveys and specialist studies of British imperialism alike readily admit the country's intense engagement with empire.[8]
Yet the accumulation of evidence has disguised the subtle ways in which the
historiography of Scots and British imperialism has struggled to engage with
theoretical approaches to the empire's character and impact. Be it the
relationship of 'provincial' culture to expansion, the global nature of the
pre-1815 empire, or the advent of the 'new imperial history', the place of
Scotland remains ambiguous.[9] Too often the country is highlighted in an
instrumental fashion to indicate Britain's internal heterogeneity and
the dilution of England's cultural influence upon the wider empire.[10] For
all the recent emphasis on the empire's 'decentred' and co-dependent
nature, the new imperial histories remain intermittent at best when applying their own methods to a society that was widely understood at the time
to represent a distinctive aspect of British expansionism.[11] This observation
should not be seen as special pleading for more attention to Scottish
evidence. The issue is one of consistency of approach and an equally critical
attitude to the empire's diversity whenever it may have existed, be it in the
colonies or the metropolitan provinces of Britain and Ireland. One of the
obvious benefits of remaining sensitive to Scotland's integrated yet anomalous position within the United Kingdom is that such a perspective enables a
re-examination of concepts such as 'metropole' or 'core' and the myriad

---

[8] Geoffrey Barrow, 'Introduction', in Rosalind Mitchison (ed.), *Why Scottish History Matters*
(Edinburgh, 1991), 5–6; D. Armitage, 'Three Concepts of Atlantic History', in D. Armitage and
M. J. Braddick (eds), *The British Atlantic World, 1500–1800* (Basingstoke, 2002), 24–5; T. M.
Devine, *Scotland's Empire, 1600–1815* (London, 2003), *passim*; P. J. Marshall, *The Making and
Unmaking of Empires: Britain, India, and America, c.1750–1783* (Oxford, 2005), 11, 27–8, 31, 35.

[9] K. Wilson, *The Sense of the People: Politics, Culture and Imperialism in England, 1715–1785*
(Cambridge, 1998), 5–25; F. A. Nussbaum, 'Introduction', in idem (ed.), *The Global Eighteenth-
Century* (Baltimore, 2003), 10.

[10] I. Baucom, *Out of Place: Englishness, Empire and the Locations of Identity* (Princeton, 1999),
5–7; K. Kumar, 'Nation and Empire: English and British National Identity in Comparative
Perspective', *Theory and Society*, 29 (2000), 575–90.

[11] Catherine Hall, 'Introduction: Thinking the Postcolonial, Thinking the Empire', in eadem
(ed.), *Cultures of Empire: Colonisers in Britain and the Empire in the Nineteenth and Twentieth
Centuries* (Manchester, 2000), 1–27; eadem, *Civilising Subjects: Metropole and Colony in the
English Imagination, 1830–1867* (Cambridge, 2002), 11 and 22; Kathleen Wilson, 'Introduction;
Histories, Empires, Modernities', in eadem (ed.), *A New Imperial History: Culture, Identity and
Modernity in Britain and the Empire, 1660–1840* (Cambridge, 2004), 13–17.

connections that made the empire a centralizing and yet contingent entity.[12] This is surely one way in which Scottish studies can contribute to wider controversies within imperial history, while simultaneously illustrating the value of Scottish history beyond its traditional constituencies.

But criticism can and should work both ways. Historians of Scotland are equally guilty of ignoring crucial debates on the boundaries and dynamics of British imperialism. Indeed, with one or two exceptions, much of the literature on Scots in the empire can best be described as conceptually underdeveloped. It is tempting to see this lack of engagement as a by-product of the curious way in which theories of the British Empire tend, in the main, to be applied to the post-1815 phases of imperialism.[13] But it remains the case that scholars working on Scotland have not engaged fully with the disputes that do exist, with the exception of Bernard Porter's thesis that the empire had little significant impact on British society.[14] Neither surveys nor specific articles on Scottish subjects have much if anything to say about the influential concept of 'gentlemanly capitalism' and the re-centring of London as the dominant site of imperial activity.[15] The failure to explore fully London's role in shaping Scottish participation overseas is in marked contrast to the enduring concentration upon emigration history. As in so many other respects, the methodology of highlighting Scottish distinctiveness rather than similarities or connections with England has distorted studies of Scotland's place in the empire.[16]

The conspicuous exception to this theory-adverse tradition is John MacKenzie. In first asserting that the empire enhanced metropolitan heterogeneity and reinforced national identities in Scotland, Ireland, and Wales, MacKenzie has been at the forefront of a distinctive challenge to the

---

[12] Elazar Barkan, 'Post-Anti-Colonial Histories: Representing the Other in Imperial Britain', *Journal of British Studies*, 33 (1994), 190; H. V. Bowen, *Elites, Enterprise and the Making of the British Overseas Empire, 1688–1775* (London, 1996), 154–65.

[13] C. A. Bayly, *Imperial Meridian: The British Empire and the World, 1780–1830* (London, 1989), 2.

[14] B. Porter, *The Absent Minded Imperialists: Empire, Society and Culture in Britain* (Oxford, 2004), 147.

[15] A. Porter, '"Gentlemanly Capitalism" and Empire: The British Experience since 1750', *Journal of Imperial and Commonwealth History*, 18 (1990), 272; P. J. Cain and A. G. Hopkins, *British Imperialism: Innovation and Expansion, 1688–1914* (London, 1993), 5–42.

[16] Keith Wrightson, 'Kindred Adjoining Kingdoms: An English Perspective on the Social and Economic History of Early Modern Scotland', in R. A. Houston and I. D. Whyte (eds), *Scottish Society, 1500–1800* (Cambridge, 1989), 250–9.

categories of analysis privileged by the 'new imperial history'.[17] The result
has been doubly beneficial. A compelling argument now exists for greater
sensitivity towards the various component parts of the British–Irish Isles
and their significance within the empire: the converse is that Scottish studies
now have no excuse not to contribute more consistently to general debates
within British imperial studies.

One of the most immediately relevant of these disputes is the suggestion
that a number of assumptions exist within British imperial history which
help to perpetuate old-style 'national' history.[18] It is not necessary to fully
support or completely disagree with this proposition to realize its fundamental
importance to historians working on Scotland's role in the empire. The
implication is unmistakable; far from heralding a new interactive variant
of Scottish historical studies, interest in the imperial dimension merely con-
tributes to the underlying impulse to demarcate Scotland from England.
British imperial studies emerge as a crutch for Scottish national history. It is
a measure of the failure to appreciate general debates that this issue has not
been fully acknowledged in the existing literature on Scotland and the empire.

The relative neglect of the Scottish aspects of eighteenth-century British
expansion in Asia and the lack of engagement with some of the key debates
in British imperial studies form the context for this chapter. The dates of
1695 and 1813 in the title highlight how paying greater attention to the
eastern empire challenges assumptions about the timing of Scottish infiltration of England's empire. The earlier date is associated in Scottish history
with the inauguration of the Company of Scotland trading to Africa and the
Indies; but it was also the year in which the 'old' English East India
Company ensured that the assistance of the City of London and the English
state was quickly denied to the Scots.[19] While Scottish emigration and trade

[17] John M. MacKenzie, 'On Scotland and the Empire', *International History Review*, 15 (1993),
721; idem, 'Empire and National Identities: The Case of Scotland', *Transactions of the Royal
Historical Society*, 6th series, 8 (Cambridge, 1998), 221; John M. MacKenzie with Nigel
R. Dalziel, *The Scots in South Africa: Ethnicity, Identity, Gender and Race, 1772–1914*
(Manchester, 2007), 1–28; John M. MacKenzie, 'Irish, Scottish, Welsh and English Worlds?
A Four Nation Approach to the History of the British Empire', *History Compass*, 6 (2008),
1244–63.
[18] A. Burton, 'Who Needs the Nation? Interrogating "British" History', in Hall (ed.), *Cultures
of Empire*, 138–42.
[19] H. Horwitz, 'The East India Trade: The Politicians and the Constitution: 1689–1702',
Journal of British Studies, 17 (1977), 8–9; Douglas Watt, *The Price of Scotland: Darien, Union
and the Wealth of Nations* (Edinburgh, 2007), 31–45.

to the Atlantic colonies developed rapidly in the 1690s and 1700s, the same period witnessed the country's exclusion from what would become one-half of Britain's global empire.[20] These radically different trajectories were institutionalized rather than effaced by the 1707 Union, which established a distinctive regulatory framework for the eastern empire. Individual Scots might participate in the affairs of the EIC—Scotland, the country, could not.[21] The Anglo-Scottish Union is a largely unnoticed incidence of London's 'gentlemanly capitalism' asserting its authority over 'provincial' interests seeking to circumvent the city's control of the Asia trades.

Even after 1707 this control did not go unchallenged. Indeed, the example of Scotland has lessons for historians of the EIC and for advocates of London's uncontested hegemony over colonial commerce. In the 1710s to 1740s Scottish kin and mercantile networks redeployed established links with Europe to erode the EIC's monopoly. Scots played a major and enduring role in the Swedish East India Company, and used the corporation to exploit routes to Asia which bypassed London's domination of the British East Indies trade.[22] These European-based commercial realignments have implications for how the spatial geography of the empire can be understood. They reveal how the global character of British expansion also facilitated renewed links with Europe.

The chapter's end date refers to the loss of the EIC's trade monopoly with India, a development that finally opened up the eastern empire to Scotland, Ireland (Cork had already gained access to limited aspects of the trade in 1793), and regional England.[23] This chronology reveals how a greater awareness of the distinctive constitutional and economic structures of the empire in Asia challenges the most basic assumptions about when and how Scotland participated within imperialism. While 1707 is usually accepted as the date when the country effected entry into England's

---

[20] Allan I. Macinnes, *A Union for Empire* (Cambridge, 2007), 317, and Chapter 2 above.

[21] A. Mackillop, 'A Union for Empire? Scotland, the English East India Company and the British Union', *Scottish Historical Review*, 83 (2008), 116–34.

[22] Holden Furber, *Rival Empires of Trade in the Orient, 1600–1800* (Oxford, 1976), 217–18; A. Mackillop, 'Accessing Empire: Scotland, Europe, Britain and the Asia Trade, 1695–c.1750', *Itinerario*, 29 (2005), 8–15.

[23] *Acts and statutes, made in a session of Parliament at Dublin, begun the tenth day of January, Anno Domini, 1793*, ch. XXXI, 'An Act for Regulating the Trade of Ireland to and from the East Indies'.

empire, this is not in fact the case. Only in 1813 did Scotland (as opposed to individual Scots) finally obtain unrestricted access to all the major sectors of imperial territory and commerce.[24] The example of Asia underlines how the empire was a remarkably diverse series of colonies and regulatory arrangements which became accessible to Scotland, Ireland (and indeed provincial England and Wales) only over a protracted period of time. Sensitivity to the internal mosaic of the British–Irish isles can help to reaffirm the empire's heterogeneity.

If the example of the eastern empire calls into question the established periodization of Scottish participation, there is at least a consensus on how and when Scots accessed the EIC. The trend has involved pushing back the timing of substantial Scottish involvement to the early decades of the eighteenth century, far earlier than the previous emphasis on the patronage of Warren Hastings in the 1770s and 1780s or the favouritism of Henry Dundas during the 1780s to early 1800s.[25] The new timeline stresses a combination of financial contacts in London and political interests in the Scottish shires and burghs which expedited the placement of Scots from the mid-1720s. John Drummond of Quarrel, an EIC director and Scottish MP, assisted fifty of his countrymen into the Company's civil, maritime, military, and medical branches from 1722 to his death in 1742.[26]

The timing and nature of this development is as significant as the volume of Scots it was able to send to Asia. The emergence of patronage networks that linked Scotland to London and from there to the EIC's outposts is an important example of the powerfully connective character of political, commercial, professional, and sojourning activity within the empire. The nature of such links is an excellent example of how standard categories of geographic and cultural location—London, Scotland, India—can be re-aligned. Far from marking a retrogressive return to a focus on elites or questions of nationality, exploring how Scots first accessed the EIC chimes with the new imperial history's insistence on the need to recapture how the local and global aspects of empire were intertwined and mutually constitutive. Individuals like Drummond also exemplify Cain and Hopkins's

---

[24] Anthony Webster, 'The Political Economy of Trade Liberalization: The East India Company Charter Act of 1813', *Economic History Review*, 43 (1990), 404–19.

[25] Riddy, 'Warren Hastings: Scotland's Benefactor?', 30–50; Michael Fry, *The Dundas Despotism* (Edinburgh, 1992), 112; Devine, *Scotland's Empire*, 260–70.

[26] McGilvary, *East India Patronage*, 49–50.

'gentlemanly capitalist'; but the markedly Scottish nature of his activities and networks also challenges the conceptualization of London as the uncomplicated and singular centre of British expansion.[27] The metropole's central role in the organization of the empire in Asia is clear; but Scottish examples can add nuance by revealing the City's role as a filter or junction point from which personnel and capital from all over provincial Britain were redistributed across Asia.

Care must be taken not to place too much emphasis on prominent patrons such as John Drummond or Henry Dundas, important though these men were. Scots had already begun drifting into the EIC since its inception: for most of the seventeenth century the numbers remained inconsequential and concentrated in limited areas such as medicine. Yet as the Scottish community in London expanded its political, financial, and social contacts, so the number of Scots entering the Company increased. No single point marked the 'start' of Scottish involvement in the English East; the reality is more prosaic and entailed a gradually intensifying drift of individuals into service. One of the eight EIC surgeons' wills registered at the Probate Court of Canterbury in the late 1680s belonged to a Scot, James Brodie from Forres.[28] The directors' minutes demonstrate that Brodie was part of a growing trend; of the six surgeons noted by the directors between 1700 and 1709, two were Scots—Dr Alexander Brown from Kirkcaldy and Alexander Stuart from Aberdeenshire.[29] The high-profile example of Dr William Hamilton of Dalziell, who treated the Mughal emperor Farrukhsiyar in 1717, detracts from the less obvious processes by which the Company's medical service already contained a significant minority Scottish presence by the early 1700s.[30]

Military men too had begun to take up service with the small garrisons that protected the Company's settlements at Calcutta, Madras, Bombay, and the other subsidiary factories.[31] In 1709 Alexander Fullerton from Argyll and

---

[27] A. Mackillop, 'Dundee, London, and the Empire in Asia', in Charles McKean, Bob Harris, and Christopher A. Whatley (eds), *Dundee: Renaissance to Enlightenment* (Dundee, 2009), 160–86.

[28] The National Archives, Kew (TNA), PROB 11/401, 114–15.

[29] National Archives of Scotland (NAS), Kirkness Papers, GD1/49/44: London, 10 March 1699; Oriental and India Office Collections (OIOC), B/49, 319; Glasgow University Library (GUL), Hunter MS 50.T.2.8, 67–177.

[30] OIOC, B/54, 234; Devine, *Scotland's Empire*, 253.

[31] Gerald James Bryant, 'The East India Company and its Army, 1600–1778' (Ph.D., University of London, 1975), 35–7, 328.

Lachlan Mackintosh from Inverness-shire were appointed as lieutenants to the Madras and Bombay factories.[32] These examples underline again how incorporating evidence from the Asian hemisphere of the empire challenges established chronologies in Scottish history. The international conflict most consistently associated with heightened Scottish participation in imperial affairs is the Seven Years War.[33] However, infiltration of the Company's military had begun decades earlier, during a previous war which is far less readily associated with Scotland's increasingly high profile within the empire. The significance of the Spanish War of Succession, not least in determining aspects of the 1707 British Union, is rightly the subject of renewed interest. Less well appreciated is the fact that the end of the war in 1713 created a large pool of half-pay officers who were forced to consider service overseas.[34] In 1720 the EIC's directors received applications from a number of these pensioned military men. Among the three Scots appointed in that year alone was Robert Gordon from Aberdeen, who had served as a surgeon in Flanders. A year later, John Campbell, 2nd Duke of Argyll, a commander during the Spanish War, acted as patron for one of his ex-officers, Donald Christie. In 1723 Argyll and John Dalrymple, 2nd Earl of Stair, another aristocratic veteran, lobbied on behalf of Lieutenant Robert Walker, who was subsequently appointed as an EIC lieutenant.[35]

Be it medical or military professionals, Scottish links to the EIC were firmly established prior to the emergence on the directorate of individuals like Drummond. Although these webs of professional and local affiliation catered as yet for only very small numbers, assessing the importance of these networks in purely numeric terms rather misses the point: Scots had begun infiltrating the EIC at multiple levels and by a wide variety of methods in the years immediately before and after the Union. The parameters of Scottish patronage politics had moved beyond Scotland and had co-located in London prior to 1707. This informal expansion of the country's boundaries ensured that Scotland's upper and middling elites were not at a significant

[32] OIOC, B/49, 411, 452; B/52, 325; Julian James Cotton, *List of Inscriptions on Tombs or Monuments in Madras*, vols. i–iii (Madras, 1905), iii. 17.

[33] L. Colley, *Britons: Forging the Nation, 1707–1832* (London, 1992), 101–32; P. J. Marshall, 'A Nation Defined by Empire, 1755–1776', in A. Grant and K. J. Stringer (eds), *Uniting the Kingdom? The Making of British History* (London, 1995), 209–11.

[34] Christopher Storrs, 'The Union of 1707 and the War of the Spanish Succession', *Scottish Historical Review*, 87 (2008), 31–44.

[35] OIOC, B/55, 488, 512–17; B/56, 347; B/57, 216.

disadvantage in what was to become the increasingly competitive world of EIC patronage politics.[36]

The process of colonizing the Company shifted up a gear in the 1730s and 1740s, an era not normally associated with any dramatic advances in Scotland's role in the empire. Robert Cumming and Charles Foulis acquired command of East Indiamen merchant ships in August 1735 and September 1741 respectively, while co-partnership of the *Winchelsea* enabled Abraham Hume from Berwickshire to appoint Alexander Adair from Stranraer as its captain in 1742.[37] Command of an East Indiaman was a lucrative office and carried with it a range of commercial and patronage privileges.[38] It took only one or two such high-profile postings to enable local and kin networks to intrude into the EIC's merchant marine. In 1740 Cumming used his prerogative to appoint a fellow Scot, Thomas Inglis, as surgeon on his vessel, the *Caesar.* It was precisely this sort of inconspicuous, routine affiliation that facilitated the slow but steady build-up of Scottish personnel. By the end of the 1740s Foulis was a highly respected figure within the shipping interest and in a position to assist the move of Scots into other areas of the corporation, not least the civil service. In December 1749 he, along with Archibald Stirling of Keir, a returned free merchant from Calcutta, supported the application of Robert Erskine, son of John Erskine of Carnock in Fife, MP for Stirlingshire, to be a writer at Bombay.[39]

The combination of political and social influence in the Scottish shires and mercantile and financial connections at East India House facilitated a seamless interaction of localism, London-Scots lobbying, and the centripetal influence of the Company's economy in Asia. Focusing upon these informal, flexible, often ephemeral social connections should not be interpreted as resurrecting a form of Scottish exceptionalism. In deploying such connections Scots differed little, if at all, from other local, regional, and national groups across Britain, Ireland, and Asia. The importance of social networking in shaping professional, gendered, and ethnic identities among

---

[36] P. Lawson, *The East India Company: A History* (London, 1993), 72.

[37] OIOC, Court Minutes, B/63, 413; B/66, 370; B/69, 167; TNA, PROB 11/735, 388–9; PROB 11/744, 135–6.

[38] Huw Bowen, 'Privilege and Profit: The Commanders of East Indiamen as Private Traders, Entrepreneurs, and Smugglers, 1760–1813', *International Journal of Maritime History*, 19 (2007), 43–88.

[39] This information and tabulated figures are drawn from an AHRC-funded database: 'The Scots, Irish and Welsh in Asia, 1695–1813': OIOC, B/65, 597; B/70, 539, 542–3; J/1/1, 53–6.

both colonizers and colonized is widely accepted and is the subject of increasing study.[40] If not exceptional, the development and operation of Scottish networks is still instructive. It is the blurring of locations, social affiliations, and identities that is most striking. The sense of boundaries crossed, connections made, and distinctions between Scotland, England, Fife, London, and India effaced is palpable in the manner in which Erskine moved between and through different geographies, cultures, and modes of affiliation. His experience could stand for the several thousand Scottish sojourners who joined the higher echelons of the EIC's mercantile, military, medical, and maritime service over the course of the century. Viewed in this way, Scottish perspectives need not be about reinventing dominant national narratives under the guise of imperial studies, but about engaging with the new imperial history's injunction to question all forms of boundaries and identities.

What is significant about the infiltration of Scots is not the volume of individuals involved, impressive though the numbers could on occasion be, but rather what the process says about the capacity of networks in the metropolitan provinces to evolve, connect with London and its imperial institutions, and transfer rapidly across the empire's oceanic spaces. In comparison to these developments, too much emphasis has been placed on the percentages of Scots employed, and insufficient rigour applied to the methods for extrapolating the Scottish presence. Figures have been treated in isolation and without reference to the total number of people employed by the Company. The reliance on isolated examples of impressive Scottish percentages in the civil, medical, or military services, combined with the uncritical recycling of unsubstantiated estimates, leaves the impression that a tendency towards Scottish exceptionalism endures still.[41] Historians of the EIC have in turn, quite rightly, questioned the suggestion that the Company came to be numerically dominated by Scots.[42]

---

[40] N. Glaisyer, 'Networking: Trade and Exchange in the Eighteenth-Century British Empire', *Historical Journal*, 47 (2004), 451–75; Alan Lester, 'Imperial Circuits and Networks: Geographies of the British Empire', *History Compass*, 4 (2006), 124–41.

[41] McGilvary, *East India Patronage*, 253; Devine, 'Scottish Elites and the Indian Empire', 214–15; T. M. Devine, 'The Spoils of Empire', in idem (ed.), *Scotland and the Union, 1707–2007* (Edinburgh, 2008), 104–5.

[42] H. V. Bowen, *The Business of Empire: The East India Company and Imperial Britain, 1756–1833* (Cambridge, 2006), 274–6.

The figures which can be verified from the EIC's own records confirm that the Scottish presence was usually above the percentage that might reasonably be expected given the kingdom's relatively small share of Britain and Ireland's total population. But the Scottish profile was, in some areas and at certain periods, not especially excessive. This was the case for much of the eighteenth century with regard to the potentially remunerative civil service. One reason for the constant overestimation of numbers is that the evidence relating to the volume of appointments to the civil service is contradictory. The most detailed records survive in the 'Writers' Applications', which for the 1760s show that there were 345 requests for the writer-ships which initiated a civil service career: Scots acquired 42—exactly 12 per cent. Yet the directors' minutes for the same decade show that the Company sanctioned the appointment of at least 459 individuals—54 of whom were Scots, a slightly lower percentage than the other evidence indicates.[43] Both ratios do, however, point to the conclusion that within two generations of

Table 3.1 East India Company writers, 1806

Total	Region	Education	Social background	Patrons	Presidency
94	Lothians = 6	Unknown = 7	Landed = 7	Non-Scots EIC	Bengal = 13
Scots = 21	Highlands = 3	Edinburgh = 5	Aristocracy = 2	Directors = 10	Madras = 5
(22.3%)	North-East = 3	London = 5	Merchant = 2	Charles Grant = 6	Bombay = 2
	Central = 2	York = 2	Legal = 2	Hugh Inglis = 3	Unknown = 1
	West Central = 2	Fife = 1	Clergy = 2	Simon Fraser = 2	
	West Indies = 2	Aberdeen = 1	West Indian = 2		
	Borders = 1		Govt = 1		
	Northern = 1		RN = 1		
	London = 1		EIC = 1		
			Unknown = 1		

Source: 'The Scots, Irish and Welsh in Asia, 1695–1813': OIOC, J/1/22, fos 1–357.

[43] 'The Scots, Irish and Welsh in Asia, 1695–1813'. The sources are: OIOC, B/75–B/85; J/1/4–5.

1707 Scots were able to acquire some of the most competitive posts anywhere in the empire at roughly the rate that might be expected given the
country's weight of population.[44]

A comparison of the 1760s figures and those in Table 3.1 demonstrates that
the general trend was undoubtedly towards an increasing Scottish profile
within the EIC's administrative elite. But this was neither a linear nor
inevitable development. What emerges is an erratic process of peaks and
troughs, with the influence of Drummond, Hastings, and Dundas combining with a growing number of Scots on the Company directorate to produce
a generally upward trajectory punctuated by phases or years when the
acquisition of posts was less dramatic.[45] Rather than a simple emphasis
on numeric over-representation, the significant lesson to be drawn is the
acute sensitivity and responsiveness of kin, regional, and social networks to
constantly changing conditions in London, the EIC, and in Asia.

In other branches of the British regime the Scottish presence expanded in
an accumulative fashion. Less prestigious than the civil service, free merchant and mariners' licences to trade in the East attracted hundreds of Scots.
By 1789 they constituted a quarter of Madras's 202 free traders, while
Scottish agency houses in Bombay and Calcutta, such as Forbes, Smith,
and Co. and Fairlie, Ferguson, and Co., were among the most powerful
private corporations anywhere in the empire.[46] With approximately 12 per
cent of Britain and Ireland's total population, there is no question that Scots
were noticeably over-represented in a key sector of the evolving colonial
economy in Asia. What is impressive about Scottish penetration of the
eastern empire is its comprehensiveness. Over the last quarter of the century
28 per cent of new East Indiamen commanders were Scots, a percentage
which not only mirrors the better-known rates of participation in the
Company's military but also points to the need for a greater understanding
of the relationship between Scotland's imperial and maritime histories.[47]
During the 1790s no fewer than fifty-one Scots served as East Indiamen
commanders. The regional background of this elite shows a distinct preponderance towards the east coast ports and central counties of Scotland,

---

[44] P. J. Marshall, *East Indian Fortunes: The British in Bengal in the Eighteenth Century*
(Oxford, 1976), 11–15.

[45] 'The Scots, Irish and Welsh in Asia, 1695–1813': OIOC, J/1/1–28.

[46] Parker, 'Scottish Enterprise in India, 1750–1914', 200–5; OIOC, O/5/31, fos 7–11.

[47] Bowen, *The Business of Empire*, 273.

especially Stirlingshire, Fife, Perth, and Angus.[48] Just as Glasgow's geography explains the city's specialization in the Atlantic trades, it is clear that Scotland's network of east coast burghs looked south towards London and from there out into the Asian hemisphere of British expansion.

The large number of Scots in the upper echelons of the merchant marine was testimony to the extent to which the corporation's shipping sector had been infiltrated by an assortment of kin-based groups. These included the likes of Robert Preston, who managed six East Indiamen by 1790, John Cameron of Lundaaray, and the Grahams of Airth.[49] The 'shipping interest' cartels that supplied the EIC with its expensive ocean-going ships are a telling microcosm of the hybridity between London venture capitalism and older concepts of familial-based networks which so characterized the pre-1815 empire. In the 1780s, Robert Preston used his rights as co-partner of the *Southampton* to give command to John Lennox of Antermonie, an experienced captain whose Stirlingshire family had developed a myriad of East India interests. He, along with various siblings, cousins, and nephews, connected financial services in Edinburgh and shipping in London with agency houses in Calcutta and the Canton credit market. This overlapping web of contacts enabled the family to diversify into a mutually supportive set of activities that spanned the full geographic and economic scope of Britain's empire in Asia.[50] John, William, and Alexander Lennox pursued commodity trading with the London and Calcutta agency houses run by their fellow Scots David Scott from Montrose and John Ferguson and William Fairlie from Ayrshire. In 1802 the family successfully tendered for the construction of the East Indiaman the *Lord Melville*; command of the ship was given to Antermonie's son Charles, an example of the hereditary service ethic which so characterized aspects of the EIC's empire.[51]

For the British and Irish middling and impoverished landed families who increasingly perceived the EIC as a means of maintaining or improving their material and social status, the military offered a cheap and

[48] Anthony Farrington, *A Biographical Index of East India Company Maritime Service Officers, 1600–1834* (London, 1999), 1–885; Mackillop, 'Dundee, London, and the Empire in Asia', 172.

[49] NAS, Cameron of Fassifern Papers, GD1/736/52: 21 November 1803: Knightsbridge; National Library of Scotland (NLS), Airth Papers, MS 10872, fos 70–2, 173; NAS, Scott of Raeburn Muniments, GD104/297/2.

[50] Mitchell Library, Glasgow (ML), Lennox of Woodhead Records, T-LX 3/22/3; Tomlinson, 'From Campsie to Kedgeree', 769–91.

[51] ML, Lennox of Woodhead Records, T-LX 3/12/4, 17; T-LX 3/13/, 6, 10, 23–4.

non-competitive point of access. Table 3.2 compares the Scottish, Irish, and Welsh profile within the EIC military personnel shipped to South Asia between 1753 and 1763. Other than in a number of British Army regiments deployed in India during the first phase of occupation from the early 1750s to the mid-1780s, Scots never formed a large element of the European rank and file sent to the East. As is well known, Irish manpower proved a vitally important resource for the EIC's three presidency armies of Bengal, Madras, and Bombay.[52] Table 3.2 also shows that Irish cadets formed an important minority within the ranks of the aspiring officer corps, acquiring a much larger share than the Scots during the 1750s. Scots were far more prominent in the higher echelons, garnering over a quarter of the senior officers' posts during the early stages of the EIC's territorial aggression; this was twice the ratio that might be expected given Scotland's share of Britain and Ireland's population.

A comparison of Tables 3.2 and 3.3 highlights the need for a reassessment of the timing, nature, and consequences of Scottish participation in the Company's military economy. Over the course of the second half of the century the percentage of Scots in the ordinary rank and file remained small, if not negligible, while the share of cadet posts increased, more than doubling from 6.5 per cent to 16 per cent between the 1750s and 1800s. Indeed, the ratio shown in Table 3.3 was below average: 87 of the 377 cadet appointments in 1804–5 (23 per cent) went to Scots.[53] Patterns of Irish involvement took a separate trajectory: having begun with an impressive profile among the cadets, Ireland's role narrowed after the 1780s to that of an exporter of rank-and-file manpower, with a smaller percentage (invariably between 12 and 15 per cent) of the socially and materially remunerative officers' positions.[54] These divergences reveal the radically different capacity of Scotland and Ireland to benefit from expansion in Asia. Scotland sent out a relatively small number of socially well-connected sojourners who stood a far better chance of generating some sort of financial return, either through prize money or military entrepreneurship. Ireland sent out

---

[52] Bryant, 'Scots in India', 23; Thomas Bartlett, 'The Irish Soldier in India, 1750–1947', in Michael Holmes and Denis Holmes (eds), *Ireland and India: Connections, Comparisons, Contrasts*, (Limerick, 1997), 12–28.

[53] 'The Scots, Irish and Welsh in Asia, 1695–1813': OIOC, L/MIL/9/111–20.

[54] P. Cadell, 'Irish Soldiers in India', *Irish Sword*, 1 (1949–53), 75–6; P. E. Razzell, 'Social Origins of Officers in the Indian and British Home Army: 1758–1962', *British Journal of Sociology*, 14 (1963), 250; Bryant, 'Scots in India', 22–41.

Table 3.2 EIC military embarkations, 1753–1763

Total		Scots (%)	Irish (%)	Welsh (%)
Officers	87	22 (25.2%)	14 (14.5%)	0 (0%)
Cadets	290	19 (6.5%)	65 (22.4%)	13 (4.4%)
Rank and file	7,268	618 (8.5%)	889 (12.2%)	170 (2.3%)

Source: 'The Scots, Irish and Welsh in Asia, 1695–1813': OIOC, L/MIL/9/85.

Table 3.3 East India Company cadets, 1803

Total	Region	Social background	Patron	Presidency
502	North-East = 17	Landed = 16	Unknown = 36	Unknown = 24
	Lothians = 16	Unknown = 16	Non-Scots EIC	Bombay = 22
Scots = 80 (15.9%)	Central = 16	Merchant = 15	Directors = 19	Bengal = 18
	West Central = 13	Clergy = 11	William Fullerton	Madras = 16
	Borders = 9	Tenant = 7	Elphinstone = 8	
	Highlands = 9	Army = 5	Charles Grant = 7	
		EIC = 4	Simon Fraser = 4	
		Other professional = 4	John Inglis = 4	
		Govt/burgh = 2	Lord Castlereagh = 2	

Source: 'The Scots, Irish and Welsh in Asia, 1695–1813': OIOC, L/MIL/9/113/Pts 1–3, No. 1–502.

far larger numbers; but the deployment congregated at the lowest echelons of the EIC's European workforce, where the opportunities for survival and financial and social success were drastically reduced. Ireland always retained a far higher demographic presence in the British East than Scotland; but the significant lesson is the fact that the different political, economic, social, and religious characteristics of these two metropolitan provinces profoundly shaped patterns of participation and indeed were reinforced through involvement in British imperialism. Whatever other impact the eastern empire may have had upon Britain and Ireland, it did not include the removal of enduring internal differences between the metropolitan provinces.

Tables 3.1–3.4 outline the general pattern of Scottish involvement in the Company approximately 100 years after the Union. Using the EIC's voluminous records it is possible to recapture many of the social attributes of these Scottish sojourners, as well as the professional networks and webs of regional, national, and oceanic affiliation that shaped their careers and identity.[55] By the 1790s and early 1800s Scots were consistently over-represented with the corporation's various establishments: Table 3.4 con-firms that this was especially the case in the medical service. The social and educational backgrounds in Tables 3.1–3.4 also speak of a remarkably con-sistent engagement with the EIC by a wide range of locales and class interests. Although the country's landed elites obtained a high percentage of posts—another feature of Scottish interaction with Asia which resonates with the notion of the 'gentlemanly capitalist'—so too did scions of the clergy, lawyers, and merchants. Company surgeons in particular hailed from the country's middling orders.

These trends confirm the important observation that the disparity in access to imperial employment experienced by Scotland and Ireland's disenfran-chised but socially aspiring middling orders may have been a key factor behind the sharply differing reactions of both countries to constitutional radicalism in the 1790s.[56] With its large volume of annually replenished posts, the EIC—more so than almost any other sector of the empire—offered a form of imperial 'liberty' in the shape of privileged and honourable employment that compensated for the lack of domestic political status. In this sense, the political impact of the eastern empire extended far beyond the angst which surrounded the limited number of nabobs in Parliament and their suppo-sedly corrosive social and cultural influence.[57]

There is also a geographic aspect to the figures in Tables 3.1–3.4. The capacity of Scotland's political managers or Scots on the EIC directorate to provide for individuals from across the country is striking. Participation was remarkably evenly spread across the various regions, although there was a pronounced tendency for the eastern and central districts to be over-

---

[55] B. S. Cohn, 'Recruitment and Training of British Civil Servants in India, 1600–1800', in R. Braibanti (ed.), *Asian Bureaucratic Systems Emergent from the British Imperial Tradition* (Durham, NC, 1966), 87–101; Mackillop, 'Europeans, Britons & Scots', 37–47.

[56] L. M. Cullen, 'Scotland & Ireland, 1600–1800: Their Role in the Evolution of British Society', in Houston and Whyte (eds), *Scottish Society, 1500–1800*, 231–43.

[57] P. Lawson and Jim Phillips, '"Our Execrable Banditti": Perceptions of Nabobs in Mid-Eighteenth Century Britain', *Albion*, 16 (1984), 225–41; Tillman W. Nechtman, 'Nabobs Revisited: A Cultural History of British Imperialism and the Indian Question in Late-Eighteenth-Century Britain', *History Compass*, 4 (2006), 645–67.

Table 3.4 East India Company assistant surgeons, 1806

Total	Region	Social background	Education	Patron	Presidency
52	North-East = 3	Unknown = 5	Edinburgh	Non-Scots	Bengal = 7
	Central = 3	Clergy = 4	Diploma = 5	EIC Directors = 9	Madras = 5
Scots = 14 (26.9%)	West Central = 3	Medical = 2	East Indiaman	Charles Grant = 2	Unknown = 2
	Highland = 2	Merchant = 2	surgeon = 1	Simon Fraser = 1	
	Lothians = 1	Tenant = 1		Hugh Inglis = 1	
	Borders = 1			Unknown = 1	
	Unknown = 1				

Source: 'The Scots, Irish and Welsh in Asia, 1695–1813': OIOC, L/MIL/9/359, fos. 1–113.

represented. While the eighteenth-century Atlantic empire is associated with the tobacco and sugar economies of the west of Scotland and mass Highland emigration, the eastern empire's influence was less regionally specific but surprisingly pervasive given the small number of people involved. Contrary to the image of the EIC as a closed monopoly, responsive only to a privileged circle of London-based 'gentlemanly capitalists', the corporation was remarkably permeable, open to colonization by personnel and networks from all over Scotland.

Links to London emerge as a key factor in Scotland's infiltration of the British East. Tables 3.1–3.4 confirm that Scots such as David Scott, Charles Grant, William Fullerton Elphinstone, and Hugh Inglis provided a sizeable percentage of offices. Yet many Scots began their career in Asia because friends and kinsmen in the metropolis were connected to a wider circle of directors that was genuinely British in character.[58] An awareness of how

---

[58] J. G. Parker, 'The Directors of the East India Company 1754–1790', vols. i–ii (University of Edinburgh, Ph.D., 1977), i, pp. xiii–xiv.

Scots accessed the eastern empire confirms the importance of networks that connected to the metropolis and that combined local allegiances with British associative culture and an ethos of imperial service.

The balancing act between localism and cosmopolitanism which drew individuals and kin networks into the EIC might suggest that Scottishness was not an especially important dimension of the Scottish experience of Asia. The question of nationality certainly should not be taken as an uncomplicated given or as an overriding factor in determining links with the East Indies. To some extent national categories of analysis have given way to other methods of evaluating the nature and experience of the colonial elite. There is a new emphasis on the central role of social status and the use of imperial service to maintain or recover a family's gentility and cultural respectability. It was these issues, it seems, rather than concerns over Englishness, Scottishness, or Britishness which in the main preoccupied sojourners in Asia.[59] There can be no doubt that notions of British and Scottish nationality were contested and forced into new paradigms by the challenges of geography, society, and race inherent in the establishment of a global empire. The new imperial history's warning against resurrecting outmoded national histories which privilege the experience, anxieties, and cultural constructions of the colonizer ought to loom large at this juncture. But neither should the subject of Scottishness be artificially downplayed or sidelined as an anachronistic topic of more interest to present-day historians than to contemporaries struggling to conceptualize far more pressing issues of race, gender, and 'other-ness'.[60]

Focusing upon the role, if any, of Scottish identities in Asia is in no way to deny the central importance of race, gender, social class, or the acts of cultural representation used to justify Britain's presence in South Asia. However, if the new imperial history is indeed about recovering the role of 'differences' between and within metropolitan and colonial societies, and understanding how these differences shaped and were in turn reshaped by British expansion, then questions of heterogeneity within Britain and its

---

[59] Margot Finn, 'Anglo-Indian Lives in the Later Eighteenth and Early Nineteenth Centuries', *Journal for Eighteenth-Century Studies*, 33 (2010), 54–63.

[60] Edward W. Said, *Culture and Imperialism* (London, 1994), 8–72; idem, *Orientalism* (London, 2003), 7–8, 15–23; Wilson, 'Introduction; Histories, Empires, Modernities', 4; Kathleen Wilson, 'Old Imperialisms and New Imperial Histories: Rethinking the History of the Present', *Radical History Review*, 95 (2006), 212–15.

culture are important.[61] However much possession of an empire may have contested ideas of Englishness, the situation was of an altogether different order of magnitude in Scotland. Empire was central to the intense debates generated over the country's very nature and its future status; empire and union were fused in the consciousness of Scottish society in ways that simply were not the case in England. While the capacity of empire to unite Scotland and England is not in doubt, the nature and extent of the unity so formed is a matter of intense debate.[62] Did the empire erode Scottishness and generate only new forms of Britishness or did it impact upon Scotland in ways that preserved or even enhanced Scottish identity?

Expansion in Asia was in some important respects an Anglo-British rather than British phenomenon. The EIC was after all an 'English' corporation in its formal title and its legal and political structures. The settlements in South Asia, South-East Asia, and China were characterized by remarkable efforts to replicate the municipal, social, professional, and religious norms of England. Physical separation, climate, radically alien social and cultural conditions, and a severe demographic regime which combined high mortality rates with the greatest imbalance between Britons and 'natives' anywhere in the empire rendered futile such efforts to recreate England in Asia. But this did not stop sojourners from trying.[63] Historians of the EIC have noted that Scots in the British East willingly adapted to the markedly Anglicized nature of the Company's empire.[64] This ready acceptance of the corporation's 'Anglo-British' tenor can be seen as an extension overseas of the pronounced Anglophilia of North British culture. Yet the emphasis on the development of Britishness must also allow for the substantial, if informal, forces that sustained various forms of Scottishness in Asia and

---

[61] Linda Colley, 'What is Imperial History Now?', in David Cannadine (ed.), *What is History Now* (Basingstoke, 2002), 144.

[62] Colin Kidd, 'North Britishness and the Nature of Eighteenth-Century British Patriotisms', *Historical Journal*, 39.2 (1996), 361–82; Richard J. Finlay, 'Caledonia or North Britain? Scottish Identity in the Eighteenth Century', in Dauvit Broun, R. J. Finlay, and Michael Lynch (eds), *Image and Identity: The Making and Re-making of Scotland through the Ages* (Edinburgh, 1998), 143–53; Neil Davidson, *The Origins of Scottish Nationhood* (London, 2000), ch. 6.

[63] P. J. Marshall, 'The Whites of British India, 1780–1830: A Failed Colonial Society?', *International History Review*, 16 (1990), 26–44; Durba Ghosh, *Sex and the Family in Colonial India: The Making of Empire* (Cambridge, 2006), 39–47.

[64] P. J. Marshall, 'British Society in India under the East India Company', *Modern Asian Studies*, 31 (1997), 90–1, 101.

which brought the eastern empire back to Scotland in ways that directly affected perceptions of the 'nation'.

By the last quarter of the eighteenth century Scottish society had become self-consciously aware that large numbers of middling and professional Scots were sojourning in Asia. The press began listing examples of Scots travelling to or dying in the East and those who returned home. In the 1740s the *Scots Magazine* noted only four such instances, although these were all high-ranking individuals such as James McRae of Orangefield, the retired Governor of Madras, and Thomas Rigg from Midlothian, the Governor of Benkulen in Sumatra.[65] A generation later, in the 1770s, the magazine recorded the deaths and marriages of fifty-four Scots who were or had been in Asia. The difference was not simply numeric. The coverage ranged from the death of two commanders of the Bombay Army, large numbers of military officers, private traders, and civil servants from all parts of Scotland, to the marriage of returned EIC personnel.[66] The death of Scottish women in India was now noted, and it is telling that the passing in Madras of women such as Anne Hay of Huntington, daughter of a Scottish law lord, was linked to the fact that she was married to another Scot, Captain William Campbell of Succoth, a son of the clerk of the Court of Session.[67] Given that they both came from legal families with similar expectations of gentility, it is hardly surprising that Anne and William married when they met on the voyage to Bombay. Yet in highlighting their nuptials and those of other couples in Asia the Scottish press was intentionally or otherwise assisting in a vital cultural process of incorporating, normalizing, and domesticating the East Indies.

The East Indies quickly became a natural part of the mental geography and world view of thousands of Scots who never even ventured to Asia. Once repackaged as a routine sojourning destination, Britain's eastern territories could be reimaged in non-threatening ways that enabled Scottish culture to address the ambivalence and tensions generated by incorporation into the Union and the empire. In early 1772 one of the leading Edinburgh newspapers published a letter sent back by a Scot from Bengal dated

---

[65] *Scots Magazine*, 5, 6, 8 (Edinburgh, 1743, 1744, 1746), 294, 298, 346, 499; TNA, PROB 11/735, 388–9; PROB 11/763, 351–2.

[66] *Scots Magazine*, 32–41 (Edinburgh, 1770–9), *passim*.

[67] ML, Campbell of Succoth Papers, TD219/8/4: Cape of Good Hope: 29 September 1770; TD219/8/4: Madras, 11 September 1771.

1 November 1771. The missive noted 'that there were 4 Scotch lieutenant colonels, 25 captains, 72 lieutenants, 52 ensigns and 120 cadets, in all 289 men all of the same nation belong[ing] only to the army at Bengal'.[68] Impressive as these officer numbers are—and the figures can be verified from the Bengal Army's annual muster rolls as accurate—it is their cultural usage that is arguably more significant.[69] The manipulation of this and other examples highlight exactly the process, first outlined by John MacKenzie, by which Scottish society used the empire and the role of Scots within it to re-imagine and reconstruct new forms and variants of Scotland. Empire in this instance became a means of generating the 'nation'—but it was not auto-matically a British nation.

The cultural representations and exchanges at work in this example give a fascinating insight into the mutually reinforcing nature of human mobility across the empire with ideas of the 'nation'. Here was a letter written by a Scot in Bengal about the substantial Scottish presence in that part of the world, subsequently publicized in Scotland and then replicated in a letter returned to yet another Scot serving as a Company civil servant. This was a form of Scottishness conceived in Bengal, sent back to Scot-land, absorbed and normalized within that society by means of the press, and then redistributed back to Scots in the empire. The new imperial history is surely right to question the automatic link between empire and interpretations that privilege concepts of the nation; but it must also be recognized that a desire to buttress nation and nationality was a constant preoccupation for English, Welsh, Scots, Irish, and British individuals operating within the empire. As the example of marriage patterns and typical Scottish chauvinism over the prominence of its soldiers demon-strates, empire was quickly dragged into the service of those keen to demonstrate the importance of Scotland within the Union and to the effort of sustaining Britain's status as an imperial power. Whatever else it may have been, eighteenth-century Scotland was in no way a society of absent-minded imperialists.

If Asia was used to re-inscribe ideas of 'the nation' within Scotland itself, local and national variants of Scottishness also emanated outwards into the British East. Scottishness (along with the other nationalities of the British–Irish isles) was one of the official designations used by the EIC to list

[68] ML, Bogle Papers, Box 4: 1772–80; Box 29, London, 17 August 1772.
[69] OIOC, L/MIL/10/131.

soldiers, officers, free merchants, and mariners.[70] The noticeable lack of Britishness in the EIC's Census practice is remarkable and has not attracted detailed study. Whatever bureaucratic ethos determined the use of these labels, the identities of thousands of Scottish, English, Welsh, and Irish sojourners were institutionalized by the corporation's distinctive categorizing of Britain and Ireland's diverse nationalities. This formal use of Scottishness within the EIC's political society was unusual; it was far more common to see local allegiances and informal expressions of Scottish identity operating through the political, commercial, financial, professional, and familial networks that supported sojourners and their associates during their time in the East. Given the severe gender imbalance in the male-dominated EIC settlements, it is worth drawing attention to the way in which women could play a significant role in the development and maintenance of this 'domestic Scottishness'. It was Anne Hay's kin connections rather than those of her new husband which enabled the couple to traverse India from Bombay to Madras in 1771. Her relation, a Hay of Drumelzier, assisted them at an EIC outpost and 'from his connections with Mrs Campbell showed us every civility'.[71] There is a tendency to view such developments as expressions of purely local affiliation; but this example of social networking involved representatives of families from Perthshire, Peebles, and Dunbartonshire associating together thousands of miles away in South Asia. The local could be very powerful, even within a global empire.

The influence of Elizabeth (Betsy) Reid of Colleonard near Banff, who in 1801 married a Madras Army officer, John Orrok from Fife, further exemplifies the ways in which women played a significant role in creating informal versions of household Scottishness. Betsy lay at the heart of a Banff–Fife web that mirrors the circle of contacts utilized by Anne Hay of Huntington. Her marriage into the Orrok family opened up opportunities for her own male relatives. Her father- and uncle-in-law held the rank of lieutenant-colonel and East Indiaman commander, respectively. Through their patronage her brothers William and Thomas gained commissions in the Madras Army and a British regiment in India in 1805 and 1807. Meanwhile, Betsy maintained contact with six other 'Banff folk' serving in the

---

[70] OIOC, L/MIL/9/85; L/MIL/9/90; L/MIL/10/131; L/MIL/11/109; O/5/26; O/5/30.
[71] ML, Campbell of Succoth Papers, TD219/8/4: Madras, 25 March 1771.

Madras presidency and insisted on speaking Scots to her husband at home, who in turn corresponded in Scots with his Banffshire in-laws.[72]

Far more research is needed on the status and experience of women during the era of the Company Raj, be they Scottish, British, or 'native'. What is clear is that women from Scotland developed their own webs of affiliation which, allowing for their lack of professional standing, were similar to that of their male counterparts. Katherine Read, a portrait painter from near Dundee, may have been atypical in having independent financial means; but the subtle mixture of the global and the local that characterized her kin and wider networks was not. Her will, registered at Madras on 29 June 1778, is eloquent evidence of the life of a Scottish woman operating in one of the most testing frontier environments within the empire. Katherine was part of what amounted to a small Angus cooperative in Madras: she was in close contact with her nephew Ensign Alexander Read and David Young, a free merchant from Kirriemuir. Dundonians in London were entrusted with conveying her wealth to an array of family in Scotland, female patrons in London, and a circle of male friends in India. The bulk of her estate—worth £2,100—went to female relatives, although her nephew Alexander received £200 to assist his military career in Madras. While clearly a highly successful individual who was comfortable moving in a wide range of social and geographic circles, the enduring Scottishness of Katherine's identity and those of her closest associates comes across clearly. Apologizing to her brother and uncle, who were to administer her affairs, Katherine noted that 'having before I left England, made a Trust deed in the form of the Scotch law, I refer my executors to it....'[73] Law, family, language, and the imperatives of constructing durable and flexible networks produced patterns of association and mutual reliance which could be strikingly Scottish in character.

Local, Scottish, British, gender, occupational, and racial identities also shaped the ways in which the empire in Asia impacted upon Scotland. John Cochrane of Rochsoles, whose son James served as a writer in Madras in the 1790s, saw race as a hugely complicating factor that could all too easily distract his son from a career designed to secure the family's land and respectability. Any successful return home would be marred by James bringing back 'what yellow sons and daughters.... [he] might have in India'. On

---

[72] *The Letters of John Orrok*, ed. H. Forbes and A. and H. Taylor (Aberdeen, 1927), 3–100.
[73] TNA, PROB 11/1057, 370–1.

the advice of an old friend who had returned to Scotland from EIC service, Rochsoles even attempted to arrange James's marriage to the daughter of a neighbouring laird in Lanarkshire and send the young lady out to Madras. This was 'far better than his [James] getting....a tawny progeny'.[74] Acute and pervasive anxieties over colour and race undoubtedly generated cultur- ally constituted notions of 'whiteness' and Britishness'; but they also com- bined to reinforce pre-existing familial and local identities in Scotland. The question of return could dominate the agendas of individuals and networks in Asia. This is not surprising given that the majority of those who travelled to the East did so in the hope of returning at some stage.[75] Career failure or a combination of alienation from home and acculturation to local conditions meant that in reality many sojourners settled in India permanently. This was especially the case for ordinary soldiers such as Sergeant Alexander Fraser from Inverness, who joined the Bombay Army in 1789. Although he retired in 1807 with a pension, Fraser remained in India.[76] Little is known about such men or the growing number of women who travelled to Asia and ended up, intentionally or otherwise, spending the rest of their lives there. Mortality rates and limited wealth have reduced the surviving archival trace of these sojourners and the lives they made for themselves.[77]

Middling or elite sojourners operated on the assumption that they would acquire sufficient material resources to return to Europe before Asia's climate and diseases killed them. Many failed in this objective, with esti- mates suggesting that 57 per cent of writers appointed to Bengal between 1707 and 1775 died there.[78] One consequence of the well-known mortality rates is an emphasis on the minuscule numbers returning from Asia. It has been calculated that of the 508 individuals appointed to the Bengal presi- dency between 1762 and 1784, 321 died in the East, with only 37 returning to Britain.[79] The numbers will never be known with certainty, but it is clear

---

[74] NAS, Cochrane of Rocholes Papers, GD 1/594/1: Edinburgh, 21 March 1801 and 3 February 1803.

[75] Marshall, 'British Society in India under the East India Company', 89–105.

[76] OIOC, L/MIL/12/109.

[77] Linda Colley, *Captives: Britain, Empire and the World, 1600–1850* (London, 2002), 241–56; Durba Ghosh, 'Decoding the Nameless; Gender, Subjectivity, and Historical Methodologies in Reading the Archives of Colonial India', in Wilson (ed.), *A New Imperial History*, 299–303.

[78] Marshall, *East Indian Fortunes*, 218–19.

[79] J. M. Holzman, *The Nabobs in England: A Study of the Returned Anglo-Indian, 1760–1785* (New York, 1926), 29–30; Michael Edwardes, *The Nabobs at Home* (London, 1991), 28–33.

that the rate of homecoming officials, military officers, and free merchants was statistically insignificant when set against the tens of thousands involved in transatlantic mobility and return emigration.[80] However, the flow of personnel and wealth back from Asia to Scotland was almost certainly larger than has hitherto been realized. It has been argued that as many as 124 individuals returned to Scotland between 1720 and 1780 with middling or large fortunes. The more affluent of these sojourners went on to exert significant influence over the localities in which they settled.[81] While Scotland certainly attracted a considerable number of these elite returnees, care is needed to avoid exaggerating the volume of capital remitted north of the border. Estimates of £500,000 annually by the 1760s or a total of between £34 million and £68 million over the sixty years between 1720 and 1780 are flatly contradicted by the most detailed study of this aspect of the eastern empire.[82] The most informed estimate suggests that the entire British community in Bengal remitted approximately £16,900,000 in the years between 1709 and 1784, with Scots responsible for only a substantial minority percentage of this total. Neither is there supporting evidence in the EIC's accounts or in the remittance activities of Scots in India or China for the larger amounts noted above.[83]

Although the volume of capital returning from the East may well have been far less than some estimates suggest, this does not mean that the connection with Asia was inconsequential. A wide range of financial and legal mechanisms supported a veritable industry in the remittance of monies and estates from India and Canton back to London and then north of the border. The result was a major inflow of imperial wealth that undoubtedly contributed to Scotland's remarkable development between the 1750s and 1820s. There is no need to rely on overblown guesstimates to demonstrate that the empire in Asia had a profound material and financial

[80] T. C. Smout, N. C. Landsman, and T. M. Devine, 'Scottish Emigration in the Early Modern Period', in Nicholas Canny (ed.), *Europeans on the Move: Studies on European Migration* (Oxford, 1994), 90–104; D. J. Hamilton, *Scotland, the Caribbean and the Atlantic World, 1755–1820* (Manchester, 2005) 23.

[81] A. Mackillop, 'The Highlands and the Returning Nabob: Sir Hector Munro of Novar, 1760–1807', in M. Harper (ed.), *Emigrant Homecomings: The Return Movement of Migrants, 1600–2000* (Manchester, 2005), 233–61; McGilvary, *East India Patronage*, 199.

[82] McGilvary, *East India Patronage*, 200; Devine, 'The Spoils of Empire', 106.

[83] Marshall, *East Indian Fortunes*, 229–55; Bowen, *The Business of Empire*, 279–81; OIOC, B/75-B/85.

legacy on Scottish society. A survey of twenty-nine Scottish wills registered in Madras between 1780 and 1789 confirms that the sums of wealth involved could be impressive. Madras was by no means the richest of the three presidencies; yet the wills still record a minimum of £81,640, much of which was used to support families in India or remitted to localities as diverse as Caithness, Inverness, Aberdeenshire, Brechin, Edinburgh, and Selkirk.[84] The wealth of the limited number of nabobs who were fortunate enough to survive was substantially augmented by the capital of those who never returned. Profits seeped into Scotland by a number of different routes, not least through the augmented provision of credit. Mortgages raised overseas and secured on Scottish landed estates occurred on a huge scale: sasine records for Fife show that £132,960 was lent by former EIC servants or individuals still in Asia to various landowners between 1781 and 1813. Fife was not exceptional: evidence from Angus shows that shires far from the metropolis and not normally associated with the empire in Asia could accrue over £150,000 in less than thirty years.[85] These capital flows reveal how London was not the only controlling point which connected landed power and imperial finance.

This flow of imperial wealth confirms the value of using Scottish evidence in the debate over whether or not the empire had a substantive impact upon British society. The dense nexus of human and monetary links with Asia confirms the need to incorporate into the 'gentlemanly capitalism' theory the sophisticated sojourning and remittance economy of eighteenth-century Scotland. In no other part of the UK, except London, was the importance of returning personnel and resources from the East as pervasive. Nabobs intruded into Scottish politics at a rate unmatched elsewhere in Britain or Ireland: 26 per cent of Scottish constituencies in 1790 were held by individuals connected to the EIC. Meanwhile, nabobs bought estates as far afield as St Kilda and Orkney or Kirkcubright and Berwickshire.[86] These circuits of human mobility and capital remittance exemplified Scotland's profound immersion into Britain's imperial world and the depth of inter-

---

[84] 'The Scots, Irish and Welsh in Asia, 1695–1813': OIOC, L/AG/34/29/185–90.

[85] 'The Scots, Irish and Welsh in Asia, 1695–1813': NAS, Register of Seisins, 1781–1820 (Fife), [1–9985]; Mackillop, 'Dundee, London, and the Empire in Asia', 179.

[86] C. H. Philips, *The East India Company, 1784–1834* (Manchester, 1940), 311–12. For estates, see NAS, General Register of Seisins Minute Books, RS62/18-20; Register of Seisins, 1781–1820.

action between localities, the metropolis, and sojourning communities thousands of miles away in Asia.

Awareness of the distinct character of the eastern hemisphere of British expansion advances our understanding of Scotland's place in the empire in two ways. The timing, extent, character, and consequences of the country's links with Asia can be more fully comprehended. It is clear that Scots were already participating in the East Indies trade from the earliest decades of the eighteenth century, with patterns of individualized involvement evident prior to the Union and expanding quickly from the 1720s to the 1760s. By the later decades of the century Scots were without doubt over-represented in the EIC's administrative, mercantile, military, and medical services. There is no need to over-inflate this situation and emphasize the disproportionate incidence of Scots. Even conservative estimates demonstrate that the number and social and geographic backgrounds of those travelling to and back from Asia was remarkably diverse, sustained by a complex, responsive economy of social networks which linked localities all over Scotland to London, Calcutta, Canton, Madras, and Bombay. It is this powerful combination of localism and global mobility that emerges as the striking feature of the Scottish presence in Asia: few other sectors of the empire better illustrate the 'imperial-localism' which historians have attributed to post-Union Scotland.[87]

The example of the empire in Asia also shows the value of linking Scottish perspectives to wider debates within imperial studies, be these about the constitutive influence of empire upon Britain, or the new imperial history's critique of categories of analysis such as 'metropole' or the 'nation'. Studying the Scots should not be about uncritically re-centring the 'nation' at the expense of vitally important issues of race, gender, and deeply entrenched attitudes towards Asian 'difference' held in common by all British and Irish personnel. There is no need for an either/or approach to studying the full range of factors that shaped the cultures and practices of Britain's empire in Asia, or the subsequent consequences of these for the colonizer and colonized. What an awareness of the Scottish dimension can reveal is the amalgamated nature and enduring hybridity of the colonizer, with powerful kin, local, regional, and Scottish identities channelled through London into the EIC and the East. One of the many keys to British hegemony in Asia was an

---

[87] Murray G. H. Pittock, *Scottish Nationality* (Basingstoke, 2001), 81–5.

effective combination of highly networked localism organized under the centripetal influence of the metropolis and formal institutions of the empire such as the Company. That Scottish evidence facilitates such a wider interpretation of the nature of British power leads to a final thought. Clearly, there is much that Scottish history can learn by engaging more consistently with imperial history; but the reverse is equally true. Specialists in British imperial studies too can benefit from efforts to recapture fully Scotland's distinctive and endlessly complex place within Britain's empire.

Acknowledgements

I would like to thank the editors for their helpful comments on an earlier version of this chapter and to acknowledge John MacKenzie's ceaseless advocacy of the need for a Scottish companion volume to the Oxford History of the British Empire series.

Select Bibliography

H. V. Bowen, *The Business of Empire: The East India Company and Imperial Britain, 1756–1833* (Cambridge, 2006).

Stewart J. Brown, 'William Robertson, Early Orientalism and the *Historical Disquisition* on India of 1791', *Scottish Historical Review*, 88 (2009).

J. G. Bryant, 'Scots in India in the Eighteenth Century', *Scottish Historical Review*, 64 (1985).

Antoinette Burton, 'Who Needs the Nation? Interrogating "British" History', in Catherine Hall (ed.), *Cultures of Empire: Colonisers in Britain and the Empire in the Nineteenth and Twentieth Centuries* (Manchester, 2000).

T. M. Devine, 'Scottish Elites and the Indian Empire, 1700–1815', in T. C. Smout (ed.), *Anglo-Scottish Relations from 1603–1900* (Oxford, 2005).

—— *Scotland's Empire, 1600–1815* (London, 2003).

Catherine Hall, 'Introduction: Thinking the Postcolonial, Thinking the Empire', in idem (ed.), *Cultures of Empire: Colonisers in Britain and the Empire in the Nineteenth and Twentieth Centuries* (Manchester, 2000).

Bruce P. Lenman, 'The Scottish Enlightenment and Empire in India, 1772–1813', *Indo-British Review: A Journal of History*, 15 (1993).

George K. McGilvary, *East India Patronage and the British State: The Scottish Elite and Politics in the Eighteenth Century* (London, 2008).

John M. MacKenzie, 'Irish, Scottish, Welsh and English Worlds? A Four Nation Approach to the History of the British Empire', *History Compass*, 6 (2008).

A. Mackillop, 'A Union for Empire? Scotland, the English East India Company and the British Union', *Scottish Historical Review*, 83 (2008).

M. McLaren, *British India and British Scotland, 1780–1830* (Akron, Oh., 2001).

P. J. Marshall, *The Making and Unmaking of Empires: Britain, India, and America, c.1750–1783* (Oxford, 2005).

J. G. Parker, 'Scottish Enterprise in India, 1750–1914', in R. A. Cage (ed.), *The Scots Abroad: Labour, Capital, Enterprise, 1750–1914* (London, 1985).

A. Porter, '"Gentlemanly Capitalism" and Empire: The British Experience since 1750', *Journal of Imperial and Commonwealth History*, 18 (1990).

J. Rendall, 'Scottish Orientalism: From Robertson to James Mill', *Historical Journal*, 25 (1982).

J. Riddy, 'Warren Hastings: Scotland's Benefactor?', in G. Carnall and C. Nicolson (eds), *The Impeachment of Warren Hastings* (Edinburgh, 1989).

B. R. Tomlinson, 'From Campsie to Kedgeree: Scottish Enterprise, Asian Trade and the Company Raj', *Modern Asian Studies*, 36 (2002), 769–91.

Kathleen Wilson, 'Introduction; Histories, Empires, Modernities', in idem (ed.), *A New Imperial History: Culture, Identity and Modernity in Britain and the Empire, 1660–1840* (Cambridge, 2004).

4

Empire of Intellect

The Scottish Enlightenment and Scotland's Intellectual Migrants

Cairns Craig

The 'Scottish Enlightenment' has come to be seen as an unparalleled period of Scottish intellectual achievement and, indeed, as Scotland's major contribution to world history: 'Here I stand at what is called the *Cross of Edinburgh*', one now oft-quoted visitor observed, 'and can, in a few minutes, take fifty men of genius and learning by the hand.'[1] The sources of this efflorescence of Scottish culture have been much debated—primarily between those who see it as a product of the Union of 1707 and of the economic changes that access to empire made possible, and those who see it as a consequence of cultural changes internal to Scottish society and, in particular, to Scottish religion, with the gradual dominance of the 'Moderates' over the more theologically rigid Calvinism that had held sway in the seventeenth century. The date of the Enlightenment's conclusion has been equally a matter of debate, primarily between those who see it as over by the 1790s, crushed by government crackdown on any possible radicalism in the aftermath of the French Revolution, and those who see it continuing into the 1830s, when the departure of Thomas Carlyle for London marks the point at which Edinburgh's literary world acknowledges the ultimate power of the metropolis. Whatever the sources and the endpoints, Scotland's inability to maintain the intellectual quality of its 'Enlightenment' has regularly been attributed to the effects of migration. Especially in the period from the 1960s to the 1980s, when the achievements of the Enlightenment

---

[1] William Smellie, *Literary and Characteristic Lives of Gregory, Kames, Hume, and Smith* (Edinburgh, 1800), 161–2.

began to be trumpeted, nineteenth-century Scotland was presented as empty of significant ideas, a provincial backwater left by the flight of the nation's intellectuals to the richer possibilities of London. This was a key conclusion of David Craig's *Scottish Literature and the Scottish People* in 1961: 'During the nineteenth century the country was emptied of the *majority* of its notable literary talents—men who, if they had stayed, might have thought to mediate their wisdom through the rendering of specifically Scottish experience.'[2] It was a point picked up and elaborated by Tom Nairn in *The Break-up of Britain* (1979): '... in a broad sense there is no doubt what happened: unable, for the structural reasons described, to fulfil the "standard" nineteenth-century function of elaborating a romantic-national culture for their own people, they applied themselves with vigour to the unfortunate southerners. Our former intelligentsia lost its cohesion and unitary function (its nature *as* an elite) and the individual members poured their energies into the authentically "organic community" centred on London.'[3] Eighteenth-century Scotland is the Scotland of a compact intellectual elite with a common agenda at the very forefront of European thought; that 'hot-bed of genius' as Tobias Smollett described it.[4] From this perspective, as Rick Sher has argued, 'The Scottish Enlightenment was firmly grounded in personal relationships among its leading practitioners. It functioned as a constellation of overlapping urban communities of scholars and literary figures who were joined through a multiplicity of common ties of nationality, kinship, religion, occupation, education, patronage, friendship and outlook.'[5] By contrast, nineteenth-century Scotland has been quite literally left behind by its intellectuals—a wasteland of fragmented religious disputes of only parochial relevance,[6] its central

---

[2] David Craig, *Scottish Literature and the Scottish People: Character and Influence* (London, 1961), 276.

[3] Tom Nairn, *The Break-up of Britain: Crisis and Neo-Nationalism* (1979; London, 1981), 124.

[4] Tobias Smollett, *The Expedition of Humphry Clinker*, ed. Angus Ross (1771; Harmondsworth, 1967), 269.

[5] Richard B. Sher, *The Enlightenment & the Book* (Chicago 2006), 147.

[6] The achievements of nineteenth-century Scotland have come increasingly to be asserted: T. M. Devine, in *The Scottish Nation* (London, 1999), notes that the work of William Thomson and William McQuorn Rankine 'made Glasgow Britain's leading centre for applied science and engineering' (295), but to an earlier generation of historians, such as William Ferguson in *Scotland 1689 to the Present*, the achievements of scientists and doctors 'did little to enhance the culture of their country' because 'science stands independent of national context' (Edinburgh, 1968), 319; equally, Devine's list of achievements by nineteenth-century Scottish writers and thinkers—for

event, the Disruption, one that to modern eyes can only seem 'a curious diversion from the cares of a society caught up in a quickening process of industrial change'.[7]

That there was a significant outflow of Scottish intellectuals in the nineteenth century cannot be doubted: from Thomas Carlyle, John Stuart Mill, and John Ruskin in the mid-century to Edward Caird and William Wallace in the Oxford of the 1880s, Scots played key roles in defining 'English' culture, and migrant Scottish writers from Thomas Campbell and Lord Byron at the beginning of the nineteenth century to Lewis Grassic Gibbon (Leslie Mitchell, 1901–35) in the 1930s or James Kennaway in the 1960s made their literary careers in London. The increasing concentration of power and influence in London made this inevitable, but its scale was in part a consequence of the success of Scottish universities from the eighteenth century and through the nineteenth. Because Oxford and Cambridge were open only to Anglicans, the Scottish universities attracted not only students from Scotland but dissenters from England (the Darwins, Charles, his father, and grandfather, were all educated at Edinburgh) and Presbyterians from Ireland, as well as non-Anglicans from the colonies in North America. And because they were relatively inexpensive, with individual courses available for an annual fee, many, like the printer William Smellie (1740–95), founder of the *Encyclopaedia Britannica*, or the gardener John Claudius Loudon (1783–1843), the most influential garden theorist of the first half of the nineteenth century, could acquire elements of an education without taking a full degree. The consequence was that Scotland was producing more graduates than the country could itself support, so that many, whether specialists like those trained in medicine or divinity, or the 'generalists' with their training in philosophy and the arts, had no choice but to make their careers outside Scotland. This outward mobility was given religious confirmation by the founding of the Free Church in 1843, which produced two competing versions of the national Church, each galvanized by a missionary zeal for which 'not Scotland, but the

---

instance, J. M. Barrie, Robert Louis Stevenson, Margaret Oliphant, and J. G. Frazer (*Scottish Nation*, 296–8)—would all have been taken precisely *not* as evidence of Scotland's cultural 'renaissance' but of the loss to Scotland caused by intellectual migration. These changes as to whether migrant intellectuals are or are not to be considered ongoing participants in Scottish culture, and whether science and medicine are part of the cultural infrastructure of the nation, are crucial to how we reconstruct the Scottish past: see my *Intending Scotland*, 55ff.

[7] Michael Lynch, *Scotland: A New History* (London, 1991), 398.

world is the field'.[8] This salvational Scottishness made national heroes of missionaries such as David Livingstone (1813–73) and Mary Slessor (1848–1915), both of whom were to die in Africa,[9] but also shaped the careers of people like Dr Robert Burns (1789–1869), who had established the Glasgow Colonial Society in 1825 to provide ministers for Scottish communities in North America, and himself migrated to lead the Free Church in Canada in the 1840s,[10] and John Dougall (1808–86), originally from Paisley, who successfully established both in Montreal and in New York versions of Hugh Miller's newspaper *The Witness*, which had done so much to promote the evangelical cause in Scotland.[11]

That Scotland was thus deprived of many who would have been among its intellectual leaders, or, at the very least, active participants in its local intellectual community, is beyond doubt, but the distinction between eighteenth- and nineteenth-century Scotlands is not as clear-cut as these accounts would suggest. London was just as attractive to Scots in the eighteenth century as in the nineteenth, as witness the careers of writers such as James Thomson, David Mallet (Malloch), and Tobias Smollett,[12] or doctors such as William Smellie, or James Douglas and William Hunter, all of whom became famous as 'man-midwives';[13] or, indeed, the publishers, such as Andrew Millar or Thomas Cadell, who, as Sher points out, played a key role in the promotion of Scottish authors in London.[14] If London, in the second half of the eighteenth century, was suffering, according to John Wilkes, 'an inundation of Scotchmen, who come up and never go back again',[15] other parts of Europe were also flooded with Scots: David Hume wrote the central work of Scottish Enlightenment philosophy, his *Treatise of*

---

[8] Barbara C. Murison, 'The Disruption and the Colonies of Scottish Settlement', in Stewart J. Brown and Michael Fry (eds), *Scotland in the Age of the Disruption* (Edinburgh, 1993).

[9] Esther Breitenbach, *Empire and Scottish Society: The Impact of Foreign Missions at Home, c.1790 to c.1914* (Edinburgh, 2009), especially ch. 5.

[10] *Dictionary of Canadian Biography*, http://www.biographi.ca,%20Burns,%20Robert.

[11] *Dictionary of Canadian Biography*, http://www.biographi.ca,%20Dougall,%20John.

[12] See Mary Jane Scott, 'James Thomson and the Anglo-Scots', in Andrew Hook (ed.), *The History of Scottish Literature, ii: 1660–1800* (Aberdeen, 1987), 81–101.

[13] See J. Willocks, 'Scottish Man-Midwives in 18th Century London', in Derek A. Dow (ed.), *The Influence of Scottish Medicine: An Historical Assessment of its International Impact* (Carnforth, 1988), 43–62.

[14] Sher, *The Enlightenment & the Book*, ch. 4, 'Forging the London–Edinburgh Publishing Axis'.

[15] *Boswell's Life of Johnson*, ed. George Birkbeck Hill, rev. L. F. Powell, 6 vols (Oxford, 1934–64), 3, 77–8.

Human Nature (1739), not in Scotland but in France, where he resided in the 1730s, and where he seriously considered settling. His biographer, E. C. Mossner, notes that he 'had occasionally thought of taking refuge in France from the persecution of Scotland and the intolerance of England', and came to think seriously about migrating there after the treatment he was accorded in 1763, when he went as secretary to the British ambassador in Paris, 'and was afforded the reception of a hero'.[16] If not a permanent migrant, Hume was certainly a spiritual migrant, in the sense that his work was as at home in French culture as in Scots. And Hume could be at home in France in part because it was home to such a large Scottish migrant community. As Mossner reminds us, 'No Scotsman of the eighteenth century had need to remain long solitary in France, for that kingdom was literally teeming with his fellow-countrymen, many of them exiles along with the royal Stuarts.'[17] While the Stuart court represented a very specific context for Scottish intellectual migration, the tradition of intellectual migration among Scots had been established at least as early as the founding of the Scots College in Paris in 1326 when it became, effectively, the first Scottish university. Subsequent Scots Colleges in France and Germany provided routes by which a variety of Scots, shut out from education for religious or political reasons, could pursue an education and, for some at least, maintain a career as teacher, experimenter, and writer. In the late sixteenth and early seventeenth centuries Scottish Catholics had founded colleges on the Continent in Douai (in the Spanish Netherlands), Rome, and Madrid in order that young men could be educated in the Catholic tradition when the Penal Laws forbade such education in Scotland. At the beginning of the eighteenth century the Scots Benedictine monastery in Regensburg was also designated a college and seminary. The Regensburg monastery was one of three Scottish Benedictine houses in southern Germany—the others were in Würzburg and Erfurt—which were known as *Schottenkloster*, and during the period of the Penal Laws it is estimated that as many as 2,000 Scots were educated at the colleges and *Schottenkloster*.[18] Scottish intellectual exiles could be found in France, Germany, the Netherlands, and as far afield as Russia: John

---

[16] Ernest Campbell Mossner, *The Life of David Hume* (Edinburgh, 1954), 441.

[17] Ibid. 93.

[18] Tom Gordon, 'George Gordon: The Man who Refuted Aristotle', *Journal of Scottish Thought*, 2.1 (2009).

Robison (1739–1805), later Professor of Mathematics at the University of Edinburgh, held the chair of mathematics in St Petersburg in the early 1770s. The tradition of these 'Scots Colleges', educating migrant Scots in Europe, was to be recreated in the 1920s when Patrick Geddes (1854–1932), town planner and ecological theorist, an intellectual migrant who had worked for many years in India and Palestine, returned to Europe to build a new Scots College in Montpellier, and was to be extended by migrant Scots such as poet-essayist Kenneth White, who moved to France in 1968 and became one of that country's leading poets—and a leading theorist of Scottish intellectual migration[19]—in the last quarter of the twentieth century.

One of those eighteenth-century exiles in France, and the first person to welcome Hume to Paris, was Andrew Michael Ramsay (b. 1686, and generally known as 'Chevalier Ramsay'), who lived mostly in France from 1710 till his death in 1743, and whose close connections to the exiled Jacobite court were underlined by the fact that he was briefly tutor to Charles Edward Stuart in Rome. Ramsay wrote a biography of the French thinker Fénelon (sometimes compared to Boswell's of Johnson) and what may be the first Scottish novel, *A New Cyropaedia, or the Travels of Cyrus*, first published in French in 1727. Chevalier Ramsay is interesting, however, because he not only achieved some literary fame in France but left behind an institutional legacy which lasts to this day. It is to Ramsay that the French form of Freemasonry, known as the 'Scottish Rite', can be traced; and, in particular, to an oration made by Ramsay in 1737, in which he claimed that authentic Freemasonry derived originally from the Crusades, and that its aim was a universal enlightenment:

Mankind is not essentially distinguished by tongues spoken, the clothes worn, the lands occupied or the dignities with which it is invested. The world is nothing but a huge republic, of which every nation is a family, every individual a child. Our Society was at the outset established to revive and spread these essential maxims borrowed from the nature of man. We desire to reunite men of enlightened minds, gentle manners and agreeable wit, not only by a love of the fine arts, but, much more, by the grand principles of virtue, science and religion, where the interests of the Fraternity shall become those of the whole human race...[20]

---

[19] Kenneth White, *L'Esprit nomade* (Paris, 1987).
[20] http://www.freemasons-freemasonry.com/ramsay_biography_oration.html.

Ramsay's claim to 'reunite men of enlightened minds' may be the most explicit assertion of the virtues of 'enlightenment' by any eighteenth-century Scot. That it came from the defeated Jacobite tradition, usually seen as the antagonist of 'enlightenment', is indicative of how restricted has been the idea of 'enlightenment' in relation to Scotland. Freemasonry, whose claim to promote 'liberty, equality, fraternity' was to be adopted by the French revolutionaries—as, indeed, they would adopt Fénelon as one of their secular saints, attributing to him a special day in the new calendar—spread rapidly in France after 1737, despite being banned by the authorities. Its roots, however, were in Scottish Jacobitism: the first three Grand Masters of French Masonry were all Jacobite exiles, including Charles Radclyffe, the Earl of Derwentwater, who was to be executed for his part in the 1745 Jacobite Rebellion.[21]

The establishment of Freemasonry in Paris in the 1720s was to have profound implications for European culture, shaping key elements of what we now think of as the 'Enlightenment'.[22] In exactly the same period, Freemasonry was also being established on an apparently different ideological foundation in London, where it was Scottish migrants who were also shaping the emergence of the so-called 'speculative' masonry that replaced the traditional 'operative' masonry of working masons. As David Stevenson has shown, the organization of 'lodges' devoted to passing on the lore of Masonic traditions that claimed to stretch back to ancient times began in Scotland in the 1590s and early 1600s at the court of James VI, and it was a migrant Scot, James Anderson (1679–1739), the son of the secretary of the Lodge in Aberdeen, who drew up the first constitution of the Masonic order for the Grand Lodge of London in 1723.[23] Migrant Scots, whether Presbyterians committed to making their way in England after the Union, or Episcopalians or Catholics exiled in France, took Masonry with them as a tradition that institutionalized their Scottish heritage in their new environments. Anderson's and Ramsay's versions of Masonry might have been significantly different but both emphasize the key role of Scotland in the transmission of Masonic knowledge. Anderson notes that,

---

[21] See Michael Baigent and Richard Leigh, *The Temple and the Lodge* (1989; London, 1998), 253ff.

[22] See Margaret C. Jacob, *The Radical Enlightenment: Pantheists, Freemason and Republicans* (London, 1981).

[23] David Stevenson, *The Origins of Freemasonry: Scotland's Century, 1590–1710* (Cambridge, 1988), 231.

The Kings of SCOTLAND very much encourag'd the *Royal Art*, from the earliest Times down to the *Union* of the Crowns, as appears by the Remains of glorious Buildings in that *ancient* Kingdom, and by the Lodges there kept up without Interruption many hundred Years, the Records and Traditions of which testify the great Respect of those Kings to this honourable Fraternity, who gave always pregnant Evidence of their Love and Loyalty, from whence sprung the old Toast among the *Scots* Masons, *viz.* GOD BLESS THE KING AND THE CRAFT.[24]

Anderson also attributes the development of masonry in England to the influence of the Scots:

Yet the great Care that the SCOTS took of true Masonry, prov'd afterwards very useful to ENGLAND; for the learned and magnanimous Queen ELIZABETH, who encourag'd other Arts, discourag'd this; because, being a *Woman*, she could not be made a *Mason*, . . . But upon her Demise, King JAMES VI. of SCOTLAND succeeding to the Crown of ENGLAND, being a *Mason* King, reviv'd the *English* Lodges; and as he was the *First* King of GREAT BRITAIN, he was also the *First* Prince in the World that recover'd the *Roman* architecture from the Ruins of *Gothic* Ignorance.[25]

Ramsay also presents Scots émigrés in France as the medium for the transmission of ancient knowledge to modern times: when threatened with decay elsewhere, the order, he suggests, 'preserved its splendour amongst those Scotsmen of whom the Kings of France confided during many centuries the safeguard of their royal persons'.[26] That these two traditions of Freemasonry should be formed in the two dominant countries of Europe in the first generation after Scotland's union with England in 1707 is indicative of the way in which Scots responded to the experience both of integration and migration. Michael Fry has suggested that 'Scots seldom severed their connection with home, or with each other: in the Americas, too, they won notoriety for their cliques and mutual self-help',[27] but the examples of Anderson and Ramsay suggest that rather than attempting to preserve Scottish values by isolating themselves from the communities in

[24] Benjamin Franklin edition of *The Constitutions of the Free-Masons* (1734), electronic edition Libraries at University Nebraska-Lincoln, http://digitalcommons.unl.edu/libraryscience/25/, 34.

[25] Ibid. 35.

[26] Martin I. McGregor, 'A Biographical Sketch of Chevalier Andrew Michael Ramsay, including a Full Transcript of his Oration of 1737', http://www.freemasons-freemasonry.com/ramsay_biography_oration.html.

[27] Michael Fry, 'A Commercial Empire', in T. M. Devine and J. R. Young (eds), *Eighteenth Century Scotland: New Perspectives* (East Linton, 1999), 63.

which they moved, they sought to maintain Scottish values by universalizing them, and thereby gaining acceptance for them in their new environments. After 1707 Scotland was a nation which existed only in and through its institutions, and this seems to have made Scots like Anderson and Ramsay sensitive to the significance of institutions as a means of maintaining and transmitting distinctive Scottish values. Their way of 'not losing or fore-swearing their Scottishness', their way of being 'preoccupied with the families, communities and nation they had left behind',[28] was to construct in their places of 'exile' organizations which would continue Scottish tradi-tions precisely by gaining acceptance of them as pathways to universal truth. Just as Masonry itself sought to provide the itinerant mason with a universal fraternity, so Scottish migrants sought to build their national values anew within the fabric of the communities to which they had migrated.

It has become fashionable to think of Scotland's migrants as a 'diaspora', a word whose history in relation to the Jews emphasizes both forced migra-tion and a desire to return to the homeland.[29] Though many Scots were indeed forced into exile by the fluctuations of religious and political con-flicts in the seventeenth and eighteenth centuries, and many more by economic pressures in the nineteenth and twentieth centuries, the ways in which Scots like Ramsay and Anderson went about making themselves *at home* in their hostlands suggests that we need another term than 'diaspora' if we are not to be misled into equating Scottish experience with that of the Jews or the Armenians—and I suggest that we adopt another word of Greek origin to characterize Scottish migration: *xeniteia*. Xeniteian migrants do not arrive in their new territories as victims dreaming of a return to the homeland but as architects who carry with them the plan by which they will rebuild the familiar structures of their homeland in a foreign place.[30]

Masonry, with its emphasis on the mason as geometer and architect, engaged in building a universal enlightenment, is perhaps an appropriate symbol of the xeniteian drive of Scottish migration. Indeed, wherever Scots settled or sojourned in the British Empire, they invariably established

---

[28] Ibid.

[29] See Robin Cohen, *Global Diaspora: An Introduction* (London, 1997), and the criticism of Cohen's categories for defining diaspora in Monika Fludernik (ed.), *Diaspora and Multicultur-alism: Common Traditions and New Developments* (New York, 2003), pp. xivff.

[30] I have adopted this term from Minna Rozen (ed.), *Homelands and Diasporas: Greeks, Jews and their Migration* (London, 2008), 57ff.

Masonic lodges.[31] Moreover, whether they travelled as settlers, as mission-aries, as administrators, or as explorers and scientists, Scots took with them a conception of civilization based on the Reformation commitment to universal education, to the belief that, as Knox put it in *The First Book of Discipline*, 'we think it expedient that in every notable town . . . [there] be erected a college, in which the arts, at least logic and rhetoric, together with the tongues, be read by sufficient masters, for whom honest stipends must be appointed; as also provision for those that are poor, and are not able by themselves, nor by their friends, to be sustained at letters'.[32] The distinctive educational system of Scotland, with its large number of parish schools and its geographically distributed universities, provided the model which Scots set out to replicate wherever they settled. As Sir Robert Falconer (1867–1943), President of the University of Toronto from 1906 till 1932, noted of his nineteenth-century predecessors in Canadian higher education, 'As the social conditions that prevailed in Canada were in many respects much more similar to those of Scotland than of England, the Scottish organization and methods of higher education were adapted to the needs of many portions of the country in the earlier stages of its development.'[33]

Thus, though the Scots had not been numerically significant migrants to North America till the second half of the eighteenth century, among the earliest of American universities were those based on Scottish models: the College of William and Mary was founded in Williamsburg in 1693 and its first President was the Reverend James Blair (1656–1743), an Episcopalian trained at Marischal College, Aberdeen. The curriculum at William and Mary was structured on Scottish lines, foregrounding moral philosophy. The University of Pennsylvania was also built on Scottish foundations—first, on the academy established by Francis Alison (1705–59) in New London, whose curriculum was based on Glasgow University's, with its central teaching texts being the works of Francis Hutcheson, Alison's own teacher at Glasgow; and, second, on the College of Philadelphia, whose first President was William Smith (1727–1803), an Episcopalian who had also studied at Marischal College in Aberdeen and who promoted the Scottish

---

[31] Jessica L. Harland-Jacobs, *Builders of Empire: Freemasonry and British Imperialism 1717–1927* (Chapel Hill, NC, 2007).

[32] *Works of John Knox*, ed. David Laing (Edinburgh, 1895), ii. 183–260, at [10].

[33] Robert Falconer, 'Scottish Influence in the Higher Education of Canada', *Proceedings and Transactions of the Royal Society of Canada*, 3rd series, 21 (1927), section II, 7–20 at 14.

ideal of a broad curriculum of the arts and sciences in a pamphlet which has been described by an American historian as 'the first attempt in America to present systematic analysis of the aims and methods of higher education'.[34] Smith was also involved in the establishment of 'King's College' in New York, which, after the American Revolution, became Columbia University.

The same xeniteian drive towards educational institution-building was equally characteristic of the Scots in Canada, where John Strachan was the inspiration not only of McGill University in Montreal (1821)—which was named after the relative of Strachan's wife Ann Wood McGill, who was encouraged by Strachan to leave his land for an educational establishment—but also of King's College (1843), which became the basis of the University of Toronto. A true xeniteian, Strachan went on to found Trinity College when King's College was absorbed into the University of Toronto in 1849.[35] Other Canadian universities were also Scottish-derived institutions: Dalhousie University was founded by the ninth Earl of Dalhousie (1770–1838) in 1818, and modelled on the University of Edinburgh, where Dalhousie had been a student, though it only became an effective university in the mid-century under the direction of Thomas McCulloch (1776–1843), a graduate of Glasgow University; while Queen's College at Kingston was founded by the Church of Scotland in 1841, and all of its principals and most of its professors were Scottish down to the 1920s.

New Zealand's universities were equally the work of xeniteian Scots: the University of Otago in Dunedin was largely a Scottish institution when it was founded in 1871: the Reverend Thomas Burns (1796–1871), nephew of the poet, who had joined the Free Church in 1843 and arrived in New Zealand in 1848, was its first Chancellor,[36] John Shand, a graduate of King's College Aberdeen, its first Professor of Mathematics and Natural Philosophy, and Duncan MacGregor, another Aberdeen graduate, its first Professor of Mental Science. Among its most influential early appointments was James Gow Black (1835–1914), a classic 'lad o' pairts' from Perthshire who had funded his early education through labouring jobs, and reached

---

[34] Archie Turnbull, 'Scotland and America', in David Daiches, Peter Jones, and Jean Jones (eds), *The Scottish Enlightenment* (Edinburgh, 1986), 140.

[35] *Dictionary of Canadian Biography Online*, http://www.biographi.ca/,%20Strachan,%20John.

[36] Tom Brooking, *Dictionary of New Zealand Biography.*

the University of Edinburgh by way of the Moray House Training College for teachers. Black was to play a key role both in the technologies of the gold fields and in establishing technical education in New Zealand.[37] Similarly, three of the first four professors at the Victoria University of Wellington, founded in 1898, were Scots, as was its first Chancellor, James Hector (1834–1907), from Edinburgh, while the driving force behind its creation was Robert Stout (1844–1930), New Zealand's first premier, originally from Shetland.[38] The need to provide well-trained ministers for Presbyterian congregations in the colonies inspired the establishment of many theological institutions, from the Princeton Theological Seminary in New Jersey, founded in 1812, to Knox College in Toronto, a product in 1844 of the Disruption, and Knox College in Otago, which, in 1909, incorporated an existing seminary founded by Thomas Burns.

Much of this xeniteian endeavour was inspired by religion, and by the struggle between competing religious denominations to provide themselves with an institutional base in the expanding territories of the empire. In their dealings with the 'heathen', missionaries found it necessary to build more than churches and congregations: they had to establish schools and hospitals in order to draw in those they hoped to convert. In Calcutta, Alexander Duff (1806–78) came to see a general education on Scottish lines, including science, philosophy, and the arts, as fundamental to the discrediting of Indian religions, thereby making conversion to Christianity possible. He founded the Scottish Church College in Calcutta in 1830 and his example was followed in 1837 by the Madras Christian College, founded by John Anderson (1805–55) from Galloway, while the Bombay Scottish School was established in 1847. Murray College in Sialkot, Hislop College in Nagpu, and Wilson College, Bombay, were all Church of Scotland foundations. The implicit 'westernization' of India in such schools was to be carried forward by the influence of Lord Dalhousie (1812–60), among whose technological and institutional innovations when he was Governor-General (1848–56) were the founding of India's first three universities.[39] Scots missionaries were also responsible for the establishment of medical

[37] D. V. Fenby, ibid.

[38] Rachel Barrowman, *Victoria University of Wellington 1899–1999: A History* (Wellington, 1999), 11–30; available at the New Zealand Electronic Text Centre.

[39] Fry, *Scottish Empire* (East Lothian, 2002), 207.

colleges and hospitals—as, for instance, at Agra[40]—and it was the medical missionary, in the person of David Livingstone, who was to become the iconic figure of Victorian imperialism. As Daniel MacGowan, an American medical missionary, put it in 1842, 'The physician has access to communities and families in heathen lands as a missionary labourer, where the evangelist is not permitted to enter. He has it in his power at once, to give the distrustful heathen palpable demonstration of the benevolence of his errand.'[41] However much this appealed to the funders in the home country, in places like India and China the medical missionary was in fact being squeezed out by the large numbers of physicians attached to military or naval operations, or to commercial organizations, who extended their income through private practice. William Swan warned the Edinburgh Medical Missionary Society that it would be 'improper to send a Medical Missionary (whose services among the native population must be in general gratuitous) where a private practitioner has established himself, and must live by his profession'.[42] Many of those private practitioners were from Scottish medical schools, since the Scottish universities were producing such large numbers of medical graduates—as many as 10,000 between 1750 and 1850[43]—only a small proportion of whom could possibly obtain posts in the UK, particularly since the major London institutions would employ only those with degrees from the London Royal Colleges. Thus, of the 1,267 doctors appointed to posts in Bengal, Madras, and Bombay between 1767 and 1811, fully 43 per cent (539) had been matriculated at Edinburgh University,[44] and when Patrick Manson, later to play a key role in the discovery of the transmission of malaria, graduated in medicine from Aberdeen in 1866, no fewer than ten of the nineteen who graduated with him left for careers in imperial organizations. This was a high but not an

[40] Dr Matthew Ebenezer, 'Modern Reformed Ecumenism in India', *World Reformed Fellowship*, http://www.wrfnet.org/c/portal/layout?p_l_id=PUB.1.13&p_p_id=62_INSTANCE_XnIU, accessed 15 October 2010 on website of World Reformed Fellowship, http://www.wrfnet.org/web/guest/aboutwrf.

[41] Daniel J. MacGowan, *Claims of the Missionary Enterprise on the Medical Profession* (New York, 1842), 13; quoted in Douglas M. Haynes, *Imperial Medicine: Patrick Manson and the Conquest of Tropical Disease* (Philadelphia, 2001), 22.

[42] Quoted in Haynes, *Imperial Medicine*, 24.

[43] R. H. Girdwood, 'The Influence of Scotland on North American Medicine', in Dow (ed.), *The Influence of Scottish Medicine*, 39.

[44] Lisa Rosner, 'Students and Apprentices: Medical Education at Edinburgh University, 1760–1810' (Ph.D., Johns Hopkins University, 1986), 353.

unusual proportion: John D. Hargreaves calculated that of those graduating from Aberdeen 'about a quarter of arts graduates worked abroad' while 'well over a third of medical graduates did'.[45] The vastly disproportionate numbers of Scottish-trained physicians throughout the empire meant that when new medical schools were required, they were founded on the Scottish model and often by graduates, especially, of Edinburgh: the first medical school in North America, in Philadelphia, was established by a group of American graduates of Edinburgh, which included Benjamin Rush, the only medical signatory to the Declaration of Independence;[46] and Edinburgh graduates were also responsible for the establishment of the medical school at Columbia in New York in 1787, of the medical school attached to McGill University in Montreal in the 1820s, as well as at Dalhousie in the 1840s;[47] the first five appointees at the Sydney medical school were all from Edinburgh,[48] as were the first at Otago.[49] Since the botanic garden was a key adjunct to medical education—the *materia medica* lectures would take place in the garden itself—these medical students took with them an interest in botany that turned many a doctor into a plant hunter—wisteria, gardenia, and poinsettia are all named after graduates of the Edinburgh medical school—and made others, like William Roxburgh in Calcutta, into founders of botanic gardens.[50] Indeed, the heart of the imperial network of botanic gardens at Kew was itself a Scottish foundation, being established by John Stuart, Earl of Bute, in the 1760s and run by Scots through much of its history[51]—Sir David Prain, for instance, who took over as Director at Kew in 1905 after having been superintendent of the Calcutta Botanic Garden, was a graduate of Aberdeen.[52] The same pattern can be seen in the establishment of museums, both in terms of the role of Scottish migrants—such as David Boyle

---

[45] John D. Hargreaves, *Academe and Empire: Some Overseas Connections of Aberdeen University 1860–1970* (Aberdeen, 1994), 7.

[46] Girdwood, 'The Influence of Scotland on North American Medicine', 40.

[47] Ibid. 40–1.

[48] 'The History of the Sydney Medical School', http://sydney.edu.au/medicine/about-the-school/history.php, accessed 12 October 2010.

[49] Sir Charles Hercus and Sir Gordon Bell, *The Otago Medical School under the First Three Deans* (Edinburgh, 1964), 10–13.

[50] See Tim Robinson, *William Roxburgh: The Founding Father of Indian Botany* (Chichester, 2008).

[51] See John MacKenzie's chapter in this volume, and my *Intending Scotland*, ch. 2.

[52] Hargreaves, *Academe and Empire*, 65; Prain had been preceded at Calcutta by another Aberdeen graduate, George King, who held the post from 1871 till 1898, and was succeeded by two more Aberdeen graduates, Andrew Gage and Charles Calder.

in the establishment of the Royal Ontario Museum[53]—and in the provision of models to be emulated: John MacKenzie notes that the 'museums of the Scottish universities were significant' models for Canadian museums, 'as were the Glasgow Normal Schools, civic and mechanics' institutions'.[54]

This worldwide network of interlocking, Scottish-inspired institutions gave mobile and ambitious Scots—and Scots-educated English nonconformists and Irish Presbyterians—a huge advantage in establishing careers outside Scotland. When Patrick Manson began his work on the transmission of disease by mosquitoes, the two experts in the field with whom he corresponded were Thomas S. Cobbold (1828–86), graduate of Edinburgh University (1851) and, for some six years after graduation, curator of the University Anatomical Museum, and Timothy Richard Lewis (1841–86), a graduate of Aberdeen working in the Indian Medical Service. The competition between them to establish the life cycle of filariae (a cause of elephantiasis and other diseases) and then of malarial parasites was played out between China, India, and the London-based medical societies and journals, a competition which was to be closed when Manson began to collaborate with Ronald Ross of the Indian Medical Service, whose empirical work in India would prove conclusively the truth of Manson's hypothesis about the role of the mosquito in the transmission of malaria.[55] Manson, according to his biographer, 'wanted to leave a legacy after spending nearly two decades in China' and 'to this end, he became the chief organizer of the Alice Marble Medical College and the Hong Kong Medical Society, and he served as their Dean and President, respectively'.[56] On his retirement to London, he would found, in 1898, the London School of Tropical Medicine, while Ross, Indian-born and London-educated, but from a Scottish background, would not only win the Nobel prize in 1902 but go on to be Professor of Tropical Medicine at Liverpool and then Director of the Ross Institute and Hospital for Tropical Diseases in London (1926).[57] Without Manson's support, Ross would never have been given the opportunity to make his major scientific discovery; without the Scottish network, they would never have come to work with one another.

---

[53] John M. MacKenzie, *Museums and Empire: Natural History, Human Cultures and Colonial Identities* (Manchester, 2009), 33–40.

[54] Ibid. 39.

[55] Haynes, *Imperial Medicine*, 104–24.

[56] Ibid. 82.

[57] Ibid., chs. 4, 6.

Symptomatic of the way in which this international network of Scottish institutions operated is a note of 1915 from Sir Robert Falconer, President of Toronto University, to his Professor of Political Economy, James Mavor, who had left Scotland for Toronto in 1896:

I have a letter from Professor Seth, who writes as follows:

'I may mention that we have just given the degree of B.Phil to R. M. MacIver, Lecturer in Political Science and Sociology in the University of Aberdeen for an excellent thesis on "Community: a Sociological Study". It is really a large book presented to us in proof, and to be published by Macmillan as soon as the times are more favourable. As there is not much promotion here in this line of work, I think MacIver might be easily induced to cross the Atlantic. He is an Honour graduate (First Class) of Edinburgh and Oxford. I think very highly of him and had him to stay with me for the graduation. I do not know whether you are likely to have any openings of this sort, but I know you like to have names of good men.'

This might be a man worth our keeping in view.

It is probable that by 'Seth' Falconer means James Seth (1860–1925), Professor of Moral Philosophy at Edinburgh, rather than his brother Andrew Seth (1856–1931), Professor of Metaphysics at Edinburgh (later known as Andrew Seth Pringle-Pattison). James had spent several years in North America, first at Dalhousie and then at Brown and Cornell universities, before returning to Edinburgh in the 1890s—though his book on moral philosophy would remain a standard textbook in the USA until the 1920s—and would therefore have understood better the needs of a North American institution. Endorsement by a Seth was sufficient to lead to MacIver's appointment to the Department of Political Economy in Toronto in 1916, despite the fact that he had no formal qualifications in the discipline, having taken a philosophy degree at Edinburgh and written what is essentially a philosophical study of 'community', even if he had delivered lectures on sociology at the University of Aberdeen under the auspices of the Philosophy Department. Sociology was not, however, a part of the Political Economy course at Toronto. MacIver (1882–1970) was to go on to become Head of the Department of Political Science at Toronto in 1925, but was unable to get sociology established in the Toronto curriculum and left, by what he himself describes as a second migration,[58] to become head of department of Economics and

---

[58] Robert Morrison MacIver, *As a Tale that is Told: The Autobiography of R. M. MacIver* (Chicago, 1968), ch. 13, 96.

Sociology at Barnard College, the women's college of Columbia University. Over the next twenty years he became one of the most influential sociologists in America, being elected President of the American Sociological Association in 1940. Despite this, he claimed that his 'books in sociology did not give me anything like the degree of satisfaction I got from my books in political science'.[59] Careers such as MacIver's and Mavor's—Mavor, as his opponents always reminded him, had never graduated from a university but his lectures on political economy to university extension courses in Scotland, and to Patrick Geddes's 'summer schools' in Edinburgh, had been enough to get him appointed as Professor in Toronto—exploited both the generalism of the Scottish tradition and the disciplinary innovations that had been pioneered by their eighteenth-century Scottish predecessors—the development of history as an empirical discipline (Hume, Robertson), of sociology (Adam Ferguson), of political economy (Adam Smith), of literary criticism (Adam Smith, Hugh Blair), and what would turn out, in the nineteenth century, to be the disciplines of psychology (Hume, Reid) and anthropology (Hume, Monboddo). The eclectic combinations which these developments allowed are illustrated by the career of Daniel Wilson, noted for his antiquarian and archaeological researches in Scotland, who was appointed in 1853 as Professor of History and English Literature at Toronto, and turned his hand to literary criticism, with a study of Shakespeare's *Caliban* as a prescient version of evolution, before becoming President of the newly federated University in 1890. A similar 'generalism' is reflected in the appointment in Otago of A. L. H. Dawson, an Aberdeen graduate, as both Professor of English and lecturer in political economy.[60] And the global reach which Scottish networks involved is illustrated by the career of James Hector (1834–1907), who initially trained in medicine at Edinburgh, where he took lectures in botany and zoology and developed an interest in geology. He was selected in 1857 to join John Palliser's expedition to western Canada as both surgeon and geologist. His geological work gained him a fellowship in the Royal Society of Edinburgh and the offer of Director of the Geological Survey of Otago in New Zealand in 1861. As a result of his success in this role, he was made Director of the Geological Survey and Colonial Museum in Wellington, New Zealand, and, subsequently, an Institute for the spread of scientific knowledge which was later to become the Royal Society of New

---

[59] Ibid. 109.   [60] Hargreaves, *Academe and Empire*, 55.

Zealand. He oversaw Museum and Institute for forty years, building up the scientific infrastructure of the country not only through the Institute's published *Transactions* but by establishing the Wellington Botanic Garden, and, as we have seen, becoming Chancellor of Victoria University.[61]

This multitude of Scottish institutions, populated by many migrant Scots, provided the routes by which Scottish ideas could be transmitted across the globe to reshape the intellectual landscape as effectively as the transport of plants was reshaping the physical landscape. In the very period, therefore, when, according to the standard view, Scottish intellectual life was in decline in Scotland, Scottish ideas were achieving a worldwide influence. Even the events which were to bring about the end of the 'First British Empire' were to be the means of consolidating Scottish influence in America and continuing what might best be described as Scotland's spiritual empire in the United States. In pre-Revolutionary Philadelphia, William Smith, Provost of the Academy and College of Pennsylvania, was also 'grand chaplain' to the St John's Lodge in Philadelphia, one of whose members— and later Grand Master of the Philadelphia Lodges—was Benjamin Franklin. Franklin's partner in his printing business was David Hall, recommended by London-based Scottish publisher William Strahan, with whom Hall continued to work closely, acting as the Scottish publisher's American agent. Among Strahan's titles were Adam Smith's *Wealth of Nations* (1776), William Robertson's *The History of America* (1777), and Hugh Blair's *Lectures on Rhetoric and Belles Lettres* (1783), all titles which would become standard texts in North American universities in the following half-century. It was Franklin who encouraged Benjamin Rush to study medicine in Edinburgh (thereby helping establish the Philadelphia medical school) and Rush was to become Smith's personal physician. Hall was printer of the membership lists and regulations of the St Andrew's Society of Philadelphia, founded in 1747, of which William Smith became a member in 1754. Like the Freemasons, the St Andrew's Society had been established as a fraternal benevolent society, and its members included many Scottish sea captains trading between Scotland, the West Indies, and North America, as well as Philadelphia-based Scots such as Robert Smith, born in Dalkeith, and designer, in 1754, of the tower of the Christ Church building at the

---

[61] R. K. Dell, 'James Hector', *Dictionary of New Zealand Biography*, http://www.dnzb.govt.nz/ DNZB.

junction of 2nd and Market Streets.[62] Five members of the St Andrew's
Society of Philadelphia were signatories to the Declaration of Independence—James Wilson, George Ross, Philip Livingston, John Witherspoon,
and Thomas McKean[63]—all of whom would have been known to William
Smith, and Smith's fellow Freemasons, Benjamin Franklin, Benjamin Rush,
and Thomas Jefferson (as well, it is believed, as Witherspoon and McKean)
were also signatories. This nexus of Scottish educational, institutional, and
societal connections was, according to Gary Wills, to lead to the ideas of
eighteenth-century Scottish thinkers having a profound influence in shaping the new institutions of the United States. The Declaration of Independence itself was, according to Wills, fundamentally influenced by Jefferson's
understanding of the philosophies of Hutcheson and Reid, as conveyed by
William Small, his tutor at William and Mary. Of Small (1734–75), an
Aberdeen graduate, Jefferson wrote that 'it was my good fortune, and
what possibly fixed the destinies of my life, that Dr William Small of
Scotland was then Professor of Mathematics, a man profound in all
the usual branches of science, with the happy talent of communication,
correct and gentlemanly manners, and an enlarged and liberal mind'.[64]
Small provided Jefferson with a direct link to Scotland's eighteenth-century
intelligentsia:

Reid's important text [*Inquiry into the Human Mind*] might well have been on
Jefferson's list of select books even without this connection [to Small]; but the
gossip of Aberdeen, relayed to him by his principal witness to intellectual life
abroad, must have made him greet the book with special interest when it was
published in 1764 (the year Small returned to Aberdeen). In the same way,
Jefferson felt a personal connection with Small's classmate, James Macpherson—enough to embolden him to write Macpherson's brother in Edinburgh,
asking for copies of original Ossian manuscripts (*Papers*, 1:96, 100–2). Jefferson
had met that brother, Charles, in Virginia, and James Macpherson himself had
visited America in 1764–66, on business for the central colonial administration.[65]

---

[62] The St Andrew's Society of Philadelphia, http://www.standrewsociety.org/index2.htm,
accessed 15 October 2010.
[63] Ibid.
[64] Quoted in Turnbull, 'Scotland and America', 139, from Thomas Jefferson, *Autobiography*.
[65] Garry Wills, *Inventing America: Jefferson's Declaration of Independence* (New York, 1978),
183.

Though Scots—even prominent Jacobite supporters like Flora MacDon-ald—were largely loyalist during the American Revolution, Scottish ideas helped the creators of the new state define the nature of their project and the institutions by which it should be governed. James Wilson, who was, along with James Madison, the principal architect of the Federal Constitution in 1787, had been a student at St Andrews and formed his political principles on the philosophy of Thomas Reid: 'This philosophy', he wrote, 'will teach us that first principles are in themselves apparent; that to make nothing self-evident is to take away all possibility of knowing anything; that without first principles there be neither reason nor reasoning...Consequently, all sound reasoning must rest ultimately on the principles of common sense.'[66] Madison, in turn, was one of the first graduates of John Witherspoon's tenure as President at the College of New Jersey: Witherspoon (1723–94), originally from Haddington, educated at Edinburgh, and an evangelical minister opposed to the 'Moderates', who then dominated the Church in Scotland, arrived in New Jersey in 1768—in part at the invitation of Benja-min Rush, who had met him in Scotland. Witherspoon built the College of New Jersey into the leading university of the post-Revolutionary period, making moral philosophy—the moral philosophy of Hutcheson and Reid—into the central discipline for the training of future leaders of the new society. Witherspoon's own manual of moral philosophy was to be adopted widely and paved the way for the centrality of the ideas of Hutcheson, Reid, and, later, Dugald Stewart in American colleges. Jefferson, who had met Dugald Stewart in Paris in 1788, much later wrote to congratulate him on his *Philosophy of the Human Mind* having 'become the text book of most of our colleges and academies'.[67] By the mid-nineteenth century, Scottish common sense had been taken up and developed by American thinkers such as Francis Wayland (1796–1865) and Noah Porter (1811–92), and had brought about what one historian of American philosophy described as 'a significant revolution in the very idea of what constitutes philosophy as well as instruction',[68] and inspiring enough textbooks to stock a decent-sized library.[69] The influence of Scottish rhetoric was just as pronounced:

[66] J. R. McCluskey, *The Works of James Wilson* (Cambridge, Mass., 1967), i. 213.

[67] International Association for Scottish Philosophy, 'Scottish Philosophy in North America', http://www.scottishphilosophy.org/scottishphilosophyinnorthamerica.html.

[68] Herbert W. Schneider, *A History of American Philosophy* (New York, 1946), 238.

[69] See ibid. 233–45, and Gladys Bryson, 'The Emergence of the Social Sciences from Moral Philosophy', *International Journal of Ethics*, 42 (April 1932), 304–23.

Blair's *Lectures on Rhetoric and Belles Lettres* (1783) was taken up as a text at Yale as early as 1785 and at Harvard in 1799,[70] and Andrew Hook lists its use at Rhode Island College, Columbia, Pennsylvania, North Carolina, Middlebury, Amherst, Hamilton, and Wesleyan.[71] Meanwhile, at Harvard, Daniel Tyrrel Channing, appointed to the Boylston Chair of Rhetoric and Oratory in 1819, applied the theories of Smith and Blair in using literary criticism as a key component in a general education.[72] It would appear that since Scottish ideas were embedded in the founding documents of the United States, their development in the institutions of higher education was fundamental to the new society's self-understanding.

The history of Princeton illustrates the scope and longevity of this Scottish philosophical empire, since Witherspoon's influence would be reinforced in the nineteenth century by the presidency of James McCosh, who arrived exactly a hundred years after Witherspoon in 1868. McCosh (1811–94) was born in Ayrshire, educated at Edinburgh University, and subsequently became Professor of Logic at Queen's in Belfast. Like Witherspoon he was of the evangelical wing of the Scottish Church but found his métier in raising funds for the rebuilding of a college that had been devastated in the Civil War. His success as an administrator was matched by his influence as a philosopher, as much in his homeland as in his hostland, since his major work was an account of *The Scottish Philosophy*, published in 1875, which both outlined the national history of philosophy in Scotland and proposed the Scottish tradition as the basis for a new and properly American philosophy:

I am represented as being of the Scottish school of philosophy. I am not ashamed of my country, certainly not of my country's philosophy. I was trained in it. I adhere to it in one important principle: I believe that the truths of mental philosophy are to be discovered by a careful observation and induction of what passes in the mind. Not that our observation and induction gives them their authority; they have their authority in themselves; but it is thus we discover them ... So I call my philosophy Realism, and by help of a few obvious distinctions I hope to establish it. America has as yet no special philosophy of its own.

---

[70] Winifred Bryan Horner, 'Introduction', in Lynne Lewis Gaillet (ed.), *Scottish Rhetoric and its Influences* (Mawah, NJ, 1998), 3.

[71] Andrew Hook, *Scotland and America: A Study of Cultural Relations 1750–1835* (Glasgow, 1975), 76.

[72] Franklin E. Court, 'Scottish Literary Teaching in North America', in Robert Crawford (ed.), *The Scottish Invention of English Literature* (Cambridge, 1998), 153.

I long to see it have such. This must be taken directly from the study of the mind, and not from Germany or any other source. My ambition is to aid a little in the foundation of an American philosophy which, as a philosophy of facts, will be found to be consistent with a sound theology.[73]

For over a century Princeton was to be a beacon for how Scottish thought could provide a basis for the enlightenment of American civil society, and even in the early part of the twentieth century, two successive heads of the Philosophy Department were migrant Scots—Norman Kemp Smith (1872–1958) and Archibald Allan Bowman (1883–1936).

Scottish philosophy was no less important in the rest of the settler empire. In Canada, the curriculum at Queen's in Kingston in the 1850s and 1860s, under James George, a graduate of St Andrews, was based on the *Physiology of the Human Mind* and *Lectures on the Philosophy of the Human Mind* by Thomas Brown (1778–1820), Dugald Stewart's successor at Edinburgh, while the curriculum devised by John Clark Murray, who was appointed to McGill in 1872, involved the reading in second year of volume i of Dugald Stewart's *Outlines*, in the third year of volume ii, while in the fourth year they studied Murray's own *Outlines of Sir William Hamilton's Philosophy*.[74] At Dalhousie, too, the emphasis was on Reid, Stewart, and Hamilton. According to A. B. McKillop, the 'decades of the 1850s and 1860s marked the peak of the influence of the Scottish Common Sense philosophy upon the Anglo-Canadian mind. Virtually all professors of philosophy at English-speaking universities had been educated within the Common Sense tradition. Textbooks based on the Scottish philosophy continued to be used, university examination on the thought of the founders of the school continued to be given, at one institution as late as 1890.'[75] The success of 'common sense' in such societies lay in its ability to combine a traditional belief in God with an equally strong commitment to the advancements of science, and, in addition, to combine a commitment to human beings as fundamentally social creatures with a belief in a very personal relationship to God. A notion of progressive history which gave purpose to the building of a new society was thus linked to a natural theology in which God was revealing himself

---

[73] James McCosh, 'Incidents of my Life in Three Countries', typescript, Princeton University Library, Mudd LD4605.M3 A3, 183–4.

[74] A. B. McKillop, *A Disciplined Intelligence: Critical Inquiry and Canadian Thought in the Victorian Era* (Montreal, 1979), 33.

[75] Ibid. 52–3.

progressively through the extension of scientific knowledge. As Daniel Wilson urged in his President's address to the Canadian Institute in 1860, the researcher is involved 'in that glorious advancement of knowledge by which God, who has revealed himself in his world, is making ever new revelations of himself in his works; and having made known to us Him who is the wisdom and power of God, through whom we have the assurance of life and immortality in the gospel of his grace, is anew, in the great volume of nature, adding evidence of man's immortality by revelations of the inexhaustible wonders of that creation...'[76] When the high tide of the influence of common sense had passed—largely under the impact of the Darwinian challenge to its natural theology—the high tide of Scottish influence had not passed, for common sense was replaced by the evolutionary spirituality of the Scottish Idealists, especially the brothers Caird, Edward (1835–1908), Professor at Glasgow and Oxford, and John (1820–98), Professor of Divinity and then Principal at Glasgow University. When, to previous supporters like Clark Murray, it became clear that 'Reid's thinking never represents the speculative toil of a philosophic intellect, but merely the refined opinions of ordinary intelligence',[77] it was to Edward Caird's development of Kant and Hegel that appeal was made as the real foundation for a modern philosophy. That philosophy was to find its voice in Canada through the work of John Watson (1847–1939), Caird's student from the University of Glasgow, who arrived at Queen's, Kingston, in 1872 and who was to become the presiding influence in Canadian intellectual life till the First World War. He returned to Scotland to give the Gifford lectures of 1910–12, which were published as the two-volume *Interpretation of Religious Experience* (1912).[78]

In Australia, on the other hand, philosophy only became established in time to adopt Scottish Idealism, where, at Sydney University, the Challis Chair in Mental and Moral Philosophy was held from 1890 to 1921 by Francis Anderson (1858–1941), another product of Caird's Glasgow. Caird's successor in Glasgow, Henry Jones (1852–1922), visited Sydney in 1910, to deliver lectures on 'Idealism as a Practical Creed', and was hosted by Sydney Scots who included Mungo Maccallum, Professor of Modern Literature since

---

[76] 'President's address', *Canadian Journal*, series 2, 6 (March 1860), 120; quoted in McKillop, *A Disciplined Intelligence*, 95.

[77] J. Clark Murray, 'The Scottish Philosophy', *Macmillan's Magazine*, 39 (December 1876), 121.

[78] Elizabeth A. Trott, 'John Watson', *The Canadian Encyclopedia*, http://www.thecanadianencyclopedia.com CE&Params=A1ARTA0008483, accessed 20 October 2010.

1886, and Alexander Mackie, the first Principal of Sydney Teachers' College in 1906 and Professor of Education in 1910.[79] Philosophy at Sydney was to be transformed, however, by a second Anderson, John Anderson (1893–1962), who arrived to replace the first in the Challis Chair in 1927. A student of Jones's at Glasgow and briefly a member of Edinburgh University philosophy department, Anderson established himself as the dominant figure of Australian philosophy, whose influence was exerted primarily through his contributions to the *Australasian Journal of Psychology and Philosophy* which, according to Anthony Quinton, 'became almost the house organ of the Andersonian school'.[80] Anderson rejected the 'idealism' of his Glasgow teachers and adopted a radical realism which insisted that there was no difference in kinds of knowledge and 'that all knowledge involves observation of matter of fact'.[81] Anderson became a heroic figure to many of his students for his support of workers' rights (he was aligned with, though not a member of, the Communist Party) and for his resistance to University attempts to limit debate on political matters. His appointments were generally of former students who worked within his own conception of philosophy, so that 'Sydney philosophy' came to be identified with Anderson's methodology and to be identified—as opposed to the more Eurocentric or USocentric Melbourne—with a distinctively Australian contribution to modern philosophy, one which was carried forward by students of Anderson such as J. A. Passmore, J. D. Mackie (who took Andersonian ideas to Otago in New Zealand), Eugene Kamenka, and David Armstrong.

The impact of Scottish philosophy, Scottish medicine, Scottish political economy, and Scottish writing was to be amplified by the successes of Scottish publishing. The *Encyclopaedia Britannica*, initially edited by printer and autodidact William Smellie (1740–95), and rapidly escalating from three volumes of 2,659 pages in the 1771 first edition to over 16,000 pages by the fourth edition in 1810,[82] brought together the interests of Scottish

---

[79] Brian Kennedy, *A Passion to Oppose: John Anderson, Philosopher* (Melbourne, 1995), 74. Jones's lectures were published as *Idealism as a Practical Creed: Being the Lectures on Philosophy and Modern Life Delivered before the University of Sydney* (Glasgow, 1909).

[80] Anthony Quinton, 'Foreword', A. J. Baker, *Australian Realism: The Systematic Philosophy of John Anderson* (Cambridge, 1986), p. xi.

[81] Ibid. 19.

[82] David Finkelstein, 'Nineteenth-Century Literary Production', in Susan Manning (ed.), *The Edinburgh History of Scottish Literature, ii: Enlightenment, Britain and Empire* (Edinburgh, 2007), 199–200.

eighteenth-century thinkers and, as the most prominent of them passed
into history, inscribed their lives and writings into its pages, thus giving
them a prominence they would not have been granted by an encyclopaedia
published in London. *Britannica*'s success in establishing itself as the foremost resource for those in search of information meant that, throughout
the nineteenth century—which saw seven further editions—it was able to
command as contributors the most original and advanced thinkers of the
time. Walter Scott contributed to the fourth edition (on drama, romance,
and chivalry) and James Clerk Maxwell was scientific adviser for the ninth
edition. Indeed, it was in the pages of the ninth edition of the *Encyclopaedia
Britannica* that many of the new disciplines stemming from eighteenth-
century Scottish thought would come to assert their independent status:
Clerk Maxwell's own article on 'Atom' announced the advent of a new
physics of energy; John Nicol's 'American Literature' was the first acknowledgement of a separate national literature in North America; James Ward's
much-lauded article on 'Psychology' decisively separated psychology from
philosophy; and J. G. Frazer's analysis of totems and taboos was to set the
course of anthropology (and some psychology) for a generation. William
Robertson Smith was the major editor of the ninth edition, and his article
on the 'Bible' had been sufficiently challenging to the Free Church of which
he was a minister that he was put on trial for heresy and ousted from his
professorship in the Free Church College in Aberdeen. *Britannica*'s international reputation and availability in libraries throughout the empire consolidated the influence of Scottish thought precisely by offering it not
specifically as Scottish but as 'universal truth'.

The influence of *Britannica* was to be reinforced by the impact of the two
most influential English-language journals of the nineteenth century, the
Edinburgh Review, founded in 1802, and *Blackwood's Edinburgh Magazine*,
founded in 1815. *Edinburgh Review* was to set the model for periodical
publishing for nearly a century and, as David Finkelstein has suggested,
'drew for initial inspiration on longstanding eighteenth-century traditions
of Scottish debate on philosophy, politics, economics, evolution and revolution, while consistently upholding the superiority of the Scottish educational and legal systems'.[83] Scotland's intellectual traditions were both
demonstrated and advanced by the reviews in the *Edinburgh Review*—

---

[83] Ibid. 202–3.

followed subsequently by a host of imitators, from London-based Scottish publisher John Murray's *Quarterly Review* (1809), eventually edited by Walter Scott's son-in-law and biographer John Gibson Lockhart, and the *North American Review* founded in Boston in 1815, to *Frazer's Magazine* (1830), which published Thomas Carlyle's *Sartor Resartus* in 1833, and *Macmillan's Magazine* (1859), edited for its first decade by David Masson, then Professor of English Literature at University College, London, and, from 1865, at Edinburgh University. These magazines were not only standard reading matter throughout the empire and across the English-speaking world—pirated editions of *Edinburgh Review* were published in major American cities[84]—but the vehicles through which the new disciplines developing from the works of eighteenth-century Scottish thinkers were promoted to an international public: thus the pioneering work on rhetoric by Adam Smith and Hugh Blair in the 1740s and 1750s became the foundation of the new style of literary criticism promoted in the *Edinburgh Review* by Francis Jeffrey (1773–1850), while the political economy of Smith and Hume was carried forward in the same journal by its economics editor John Ramsay McCulloch (1789–1864).[85] It has been estimated that at their peak the two Edinburgh journals each had an international readership of over 100,000,[86] and that in the 1820s the *Edinburgh Review* was selling 4,000 copies per issue in North America, as much as any American publication.[87]

The Scottish journals and their London and imperial imitators mirrored the idea of the culture of generalism which had been embedded in the Scottish university system, and provided Scottish authors with an international audience. They both promoted and benefited from the success of Burns and Scott, whose international reputations transformed Scotland into a place which resonated with literary associations,[88] and provided European and American publishers not only with the opportunity to sell translations and pirated editions of the works of Scottish authors but to encourage imitations by local writers—Fenimore Cooper was immediately hailed as

---

[84] Hook, *Scotland and America*, 94; Joanne Shattock, 'Reviews and Monthlies', in Bill Bell (ed.), *History of the Book in Scotland, iii: Ambitions and Industry 1800–1880* (Edinburgh, 2007), 347.

[85] A review of his work in the *North American Review* in 1827 noted that 'the basis of his work is the "Wealth of Nations", which he often quotes verbatim for several pages', *North American Review*, 24–5, accessed at http://digital.library.cornell.edu/n/nora/nora.html, Issue 56, 113.

[86] Shattock, 'Reviews and Monthlies', in Bell (ed.), *History of the Book in Scotland*, iii. 347.

[87] Hook, *Scotland and America*, 94.

[88] Ibid., ch. 5.

the 'American Scott' on the publication of *The Spy* in 1821 and William Kirby as the 'Scott of Canada' for his *The Golden Dog*, 1877.[89] Scots vernacular became a familiar part of the educated reading public's literary resources throughout the anglophone world, as celebrations of Burns's centenary in 1869 demonstrated, when no fewer than twenty-five celebratory events were held in Ontario, with two major dinners in Toronto, and when the Bard's birthday was marked in Bombay as fulsomely as in his native land.[90]

The international scope of these Scottish connections and the insistent demand for Scottish materials—Sir James Mackintosh, Scottish judge in Bombay, wrote to his wife, shortly after her departure for Britain, that he had 'read since my separation from you, the 28th and 29th numbers of the *Edinburgh Review*'[91]—meant that Scottish publishers came increasingly to be concerned with satisfying the demands of imperial audiences. In 1843 John Murray initiated a series under the title of 'Colonial and Home Library' designed to sell reprints of their back catalogue in India. The venture failed, but the idea was to be taken up by another London-based Scottish publishing house, that founded by the brothers Daniel and Alexander Macmillan in 1843. By the 1860s they had begun to develop a substantial Indian customer base for educational and recreational reading, and in the 1870s began to publish a series designed specifically for an anglophone Indian public, both primers in English style—P. C. Sircar's *Books of Reading*, containing literary selections and commentaries, sold over five million copies—and cheap editions of novels and travel books which were sometimes published in India before they were published in the UK. According to Priya Joshi, by 1901 'over 80 per cent of Macmillan's total foreign sales came from the Indian market, exceeding even the sales from the firm's New York branch'.[92] Macmillan was able to establish a dominant position in the Indian market for many years, despite competition from a wide range of other

[89] Fiona A. Black, 'Bookseller to the World', in Bell (ed.), *History of the Book in Scotland*, iii. 450.

[90] Canadian details from Nancy Luno, 'Happy 250th Birthday Robbie Burns', at http://www. heritagetoronto.org/news/story/2009/01/22/happy-250th-birthday-robbie-burns, accessed 20 October 2010; see James Ballantine (ed.), *Chronicle of the Hundredth Birthday of Robert Burns* (Edinburgh, 1859).

[91] Robert James Mackintosh (ed.), *Memoirs of the Life of the Right Honourable Sir James Mackintosh*, 2 vols (London, 1835), ii. 23.

[92] Priya Joshi, 'Trading Places: The Novel, the Colonial Library, and India', in Abhijit Gupta and Swapan Chakravorty (eds), *Print Areas: Book History in India* (Delhi, 2004), 17–64 at 42.

British publishers. Although not especially committed to Scottish authors, Macmillan's provided an effective route by which popular Scottish authors such as William Black reached imperial audiences.

If Macmillan's operation in India was run from London to suit the needs of the Orient, in Australia the firm of Angus and Robertson played exactly the opposite role, encouraging local talent and developing a self-consciously 'national' literature. Robertson had been trained in Glasgow in the James Maclehose company, and applied in Sydney the techniques which had given Maclehose such a strong base in its home territory. Their books were largely by Australian writers or on Australian topics and they remained the major developer of Australian writers from their foundation in the 1880s until the later 1980s, when it was taken over by HarperCollins, itself the product of a takeover of a once powerful Scottish company by an American rival.[93]

In *Blackwood's Magazine* for July 1819, an editorial 'On the Proposed National Monument at Edinburgh' reflected on the nature of the relations between Scotland, England, and Ireland, which had been brought into the Union in 1801. 'It is indispensible', it argued

that each nation should preserve the remembrance of its own distinct origin, and look to the glory of *its own people*, with an anxious and peculiar care. It is quite right that the Scotch should glory with their aged sovereign in the name of Britain: and that, when considered with reference to foreign states, Britain should exhibit an united whole, intent only upon upholding and extending the glory of that empire which her united forces have formed. But it is equally indisputable that her ancient metropolis should not degenerate into a provincial town; and that an independent nation, once the rival of England, should remember, with pride, the peculiar glories by which her people have been distinguished. Without this, the whole good effects of the rivalry of the two nations will be entirely lost, and the genius of her different people, in place of emulating and improving each other, will be drawn into the centre where all that is original and characteristic will be lost ...[94]

A 'National Monument' would contribute to maintaining Scottish distinctiveness: while London, *Blackwood's* acknowledged,

---

[93] Martyn Lyons and John Arnold (eds), *A History of the Book in Australia: A National Culture in a Colonised Market* (St Lucia, Queensland, 2001), ch. 3. 'Publishers and Editors: Angus & Robertson, 1888–1945'.

[94] *Blackwood's Edinburgh Magazine*, 5.28 (July 1819), 379.

must always eclipse this city in all that depends on wealth, power and fashionable elegance, nature has given to it the means of establishing a superiority of a higher kind. The matchless beauty of its situation, the superb cliffs by which it is surrounded...have given to Edinburgh the means of becoming the most *beautiful* town that exists in the world...And thus while London is the Rome of the empire...Edinburgh might become another Athens in which the arts and sciences flourished, under the shade of her ancient fame, and established a dominion over the minds of men more permanent than even that which the Roman arms were able to effect.[95]

Traditional accounts of Scotland in the nineteenth century, and, indeed, the failed project of the National Monument itself—'Scotland's Disgrace'—might seem to suggest that the writer's worst fears of provincialization had been realized but, on the other hand, the power across the globe of institutions founded on Scottish models, and the influence of Scottish ideas and Scottish writings in so many different territories, might, by the end of the nineteenth century, have suggested that the country had indeed established 'a dominion over the minds of men' at least as effective as the military and political power which kept the empire together. Building on its great eighteenth-century achievements, Scotland's 'empire of intellect' had given the nation a truly global significance.

And yet, none of the Scottish intellectuals holding chairs in universities from British Columbia to Otago, even in disciplines like English literature, political economy, sociology, or psychology, which had distinct roots in Scotland's eighteenth-century thought, would have thought of themselves as the inheritors of a 'Scottish Enlightenment'—for the simple reason that no such concept existed. There is no mention of 'Enlightenment' in James McCosh's account of Scottish philosophy in 1875 and none in *Scottish Philosophy in its National Development* by Henry Laurie (1837–1922), published in 1902, when Laurie had already been Professor of Mental and Moral Philosophy at Melbourne for over fifteen years. McCosh's failure to identify what has now become so universally acknowledged—Scotland's 'Enlightenment'—should lead us to question the historical model which sees a 'Scottish Enlightenment' culture flowing forth from Scotland to reshape cultures elsewhere in a haemorrhage which leaves the homeland enfeebled. In philosophy itself, so often taken to be the centrepiece of Scottish cultural distinction, McCosh's account of the national past is written from a

---

[95] Ibid. 385.

xeniteian perspective and with a xeniteian ambition. A Scottish past is being constructed to fit with the values and ideals of some, at least, of the country's migrants in their new homelands. For McCosh, the tradition of Scottish philosophy was the tradition of resistance to Hume and his atheistic scepticism, and it was precisely Hume's openness to French values which produced such a corrupt and corrupting philosophy:

With these predilections, France was the country which had most attractions to him, but was at the same time the most unfortunate country he could have gone to, and the middle of the eighteenth century the most unfortunate period for visiting it. In philosophy, the age had outgrown Descartes and Malebranche, Arnauld and Pascal, and the grave and eminent thinkers of the previous century, and was embracing the most superficial parts of Locke's philosophy... in religion he saw around him, among the great mass of the people, a very corrupted and degenerate form of Christianity, while, among the educated classes, infidelity was privately cherished, and was ready to burst out.[96]

It is indicative of the tendency of Hume's philosophy, according to McCosh, that he 'uttered no protest' against French immorality: 'he has left behind no condemnation of the morality of France, while he was fond of making sly and contemptuous allusions to the manifestations of religious zeal in his own country.'[97] McCosh's account of Scottish philosophy was designed to demonstrate both the falsity of Hume's philosophy—a task he undertook more extensively in his book *The Agnosticism of Hume and Huxley* (1884)— and its dangers for an America just entering on the business of constructing a national philosophy: his 'realism' was designed to prove that 'Agnosticism never can become the creed of the great body of any people'[98] and to point the way forward to a religiously empowered philosophy.

When McCosh's version of Scottish philosophy came to be overthrown it was, significantly, by a philosopher appointed to the very institution, Princeton, which McCosh had done so much to put at the forefront of American intellectual life. Only a decade after McCosh's death, in 1906, Norman Smith (later, after his marriage, Norman Kemp Smith) was appointed to the Princeton philosophy department. Kemp Smith, a St Andrews graduate,

---

[96] James McCosh, *The Scottish Philosophy: Biographical, Expository, Critical from Hutcheson to Hamilton* (London, 1875), 115.

[97] Ibid. 122.

[98] James McCosh, *The Agnosticism of Hume and Huxley, with a Notice of the Scottish School* (New York, 1884), 55.

had, the year before, published in the journal *Mind* (another Scottish institution which carried Scottish ideas across the empire, founded by Alexander Bain of the University of Aberdeen[99]) two essays in which he argued for a view of Hume very different from McCosh's: Kemp Smith's Hume was not the sceptic whom McCosh needed to cast out but rather a thinker who held a 'purely naturalistic conception of human nature', one in which 'the thorough subordination of reason to feeling and instinct is the determining factor'.[100] This Hume would no longer be the atheistic antagonist he had been taken to be by Reid and Beattie, or the 'subjective idealist' of the Kantian tradition, for whom 'nothing exists but subjective mental states':[101]

Only when we have recognized the important functions which Hume ascribes to feeling and instinct, and the highly complex emotions and propensities which he is willing to regard as ultimate and unanalysable, are we in a position to do justice to his new, and very original, conception of the nature and conditions of experience. Hume may, indeed, be regarded, even more truly than Kant, as the father of all those subsequent philosophies that are based on an opposition between thought and feeling, truth and validity, actuality and worth.[102]

This new Hume is no longer the outsider to Scottish philosophy that he was for McCosh, and when Kemp Smith returned to Scotland in 1919 and took up his work on Hume again, he completed Hume's re-integration into the Scottish tradition by demonstrating, in his *The Philosophy of David Hume*, not finally published till 1941, how Hume's central conceptions were built on the work of Francis Hutcheson. That integration of Hume into the Scottish tradition made it possible to envisage Hume, a leader of European 'enlightenment', as a participant in a distinct 'Scottish Enlightenment', a conceptual framework which achieved institutional embodiment not in Scotland but at Cambridge in the 1960s, in Duncan Forbes's course on 'Hume, Smith and the Scottish Enlightenment'.[103]

---

[99] *Mind* was founded in 1876 by Alexander Bain, who had been appointed in 1860 to the new post of Professor of Logic and English Literature at the University of Aberdeen.

[100] Norman Smith, 'The Naturalism of Hume (1)', *Mind*, NS 54 (April 1905), 11.

[101] Ibid.

[102] Norman Smith, 'The Naturalism of Hume (2)', *Mind*, NS 55 (July 1905), 346.

[103] For an account of Forbes's course see John Robertson, 'Scotland's Contribution to the Enlightenment', http://www.history.ac.uk/resources/e-seminars/robertson-paper.

The very notion of the Scottish Enlightenment, in other words, is a product of Scottish migration. It was not in Scotland that the concept of the Scottish Enlightenment first began to circulate but in North America, where, as McCosh had predicted, the works of the Scottish school were studied as the foundation of America's own social and political sciences. It was the interest in the Scottish origins of North American ideas that produced W. C. Lehmann's *Adam Ferguson and Modern Sociology*, published in 1930, and Gladys Bryson's *Man and Society: The Scottish Enquiry of the Eighteenth Century*, which appeared in 1945. The interest of both these writers was in establishing that 'social scientists of the twentieth century may properly regard them [eighteenth-century Scottish thinkers] as fore-runners in the effort in which we are engaged',[104] and, therefore, as defining influences on the development of contemporary social science. That emphasis continues to underlie recent American studies of the Scottish Enlightenment, such as Arthur Herman's *The Scottish Enlightenment: The Scots' Invention of the Modern World* (2002) and Sher's *The Enlightenment & the Book* (2006). But the 'Scottish Enlightenment' did not send out its intellectuals to populate the world—rather, Scottish ideas swept around the world and returned to remake Scotland's past into an Enlighten-ment[105]—in the process sidelining that other Scotland, the 'romantic' Scot-land of Macpherson's Ossian, of Burns, and of the Waverley novels, which had itself been sustained in large measure by the commitment to it of Scotland's migrants. The Scottish Enlightenment was not an origin but an outcome, an outcome of the long, sustained interaction of Scotland and its cultural empire; an outcome of the reinterpretation, re-creation, and in-novation by generations of Scots and Scots-educated intellectuals who thought and rethought the systems of ideas which they had inherited, producing new philosophies—like the 'realism' of John Anderson, itself clearly related to Kemp Smith's re-reading of Hume—and new approaches to the natural world—like the environmentalism of John Muir in California, developed from the sustained botanic interests of the Scottish medical schools—and new technologies—like Alexander Graham Bell's telephone, the outcome of a commitment to producing a universal alphabet capable of

---

[104] Gladys Bryson, *Man and Society: The Scottish Enquiry of the Eighteenth Century* (Prince-ton, 1945), 11.

[105] See Jerry Evensky, *Adam Smith's Moral Philosophy: A Historical and Contemporary Perspective on Markets, Law, Ethics and Culture* (Cambridge, 2005), 245ff.

defining all possible human sounds.[106] And far from being an intellectual wasteland, nineteenth-century Scotland was itself the effective breeder of new disciplines only foreshadowed by its 'Enlightenment' predecessors— the evolutionary theories of Charles Lyell and Robert Chambers (on which Darwin was to build), the empirical psychology of Alexander Bain (on which John Stuart Mill and William James were to build), the thermodynamics of Lord Kelvin (on which much of the technology of the mature phase of the industrial revolution was based), the theory of electricity and magnetism of Clerk Maxwell (on which Einstein was to build), the anthropology of Robertson Smith and J. G. Frazer (on which Durkheim and Freud were to build), the idealist philosophy of Edward Caird (out of which would come the distinctive 'personalist' philosophies of Scotland's major modern thinkers, Andrew Seth, John Macmurray, and R. D. Laing), and the city planning of Patrick Geddes (introducing conceptions of urban ecology by which his American follower Lewis Mumford was to shape the debate about the nature and value of the modern city). It was the power of this global empire of intellect which was to make the concept of a Scottish Enlightenment, as its source and point of origin, possible, even if many of those who promoted the idea of the Scottish Enlightenment did so precisely to sever eighteenth-century Scotland, the Scotland of the first British empire, from its nineteenth-century fulfilment, the Scotland of a cultural and spiritual empire whose boundaries were even greater than the most widely dispersed empire in history.

Select Bibliography

Michael Baigent, and Richard Leigh, *The Temple and the Lodge* (1989; London, 1998).

A. J. Baker, *Australian Realism: The Systematic Philosophy of John Anderson* (Cambridge, 1986).

Bill Bell (ed.), *History of the Book in Scotland*, iii: *Ambitions and Industry 1800–1880* (Edinburgh, 2007).

Esther Breitenbach, *Empire and Scottish Society: The Impact of Foreign Missions at Home, c.1790 to c.1914* (Edinburgh, 2009).

Gladys Bryson, *Man and Society: The Scottish Enquiry of the Eighteenth Century* (Princeton, 1945).

T. M. Devine, *Scotland's Empire, 1600–1815* (London, 2003).

---

[106] Bell's father, Melville Bell, published *Visible Speech: The Science of Universal Alphabetics* in 1867; see Edwin S. Grosvenor and Morgan Wesson, *Alexander Graham Bell: The Life and Times of the Man Who Invented the Telephone* (New York, 1997), 23ff.

Derek A. Dow (ed.), *The Influence of Scottish Medicine: An Historical Assessment of its International Impact* (Carnforth, 1988).

Michael Fry, *Scottish Empire* (East Lothian, 2007).

Abhijit Gupta and Swapan Chakravorty, *Print Areas: Book History in India* (Delhi, 2004).

John D. Hargreaves, *Academe and Empire: Some Overseas Connections of Aberdeen University 1860–1970* (Aberdeen, 1994).

Andrew Hook, *Scotland and America: A Study of Cultural Relations 1750–1835* (Glasgow, 1975).

Martyn Lyons and John Arnold (eds), *A History of the Book in Australia: A National Culture in a Colonised Market* (St Lucia, Queensland, 2001).

James McCosh, *The Scottish Philosophy: Biographical, Expository, Critical from Hutcheson to Hamilton* (London, 1875).

John M. MacKenzie, *Museums and Empire: Natural History, Human Cultures and Colonial Identities* (Manchester, 2009).

A. B. McKillop, *A Disciplined Intelligence: Critical Inquiry and Canadian Thought in the Victorian Era* (Montreal, 1979).

Ernest Campbell Mossner, *The Life of David Hume* (Edinburgh, 1954).

Richard B. Sher, *The Enlightenment & the Book* (Chicago, 2006).

Garry Wills, *Inventing America: Jefferson's Declaration of Independence* (New York, 1978).

5

Scottish Migrant Ethnic Identities in the British Empire since the Nineteenth Century

Angela McCarthy

Emigration is a key element in the history of Scotland and the British Empire, and features prominently in other works in this series. Such contributions have provided broad overviews of migrant flows, with particular attention given to categories of migrants including women, children, administrators, missionaries, soldiers, and convicts; migrant recruitment including various policies, schemes, and emigration associations; as well as immigration controls.[1] These areas of interest also feature in a lucid and wide-ranging overview of emigration contained in a new thematic volume on empire.[2] A key theme of this research, apart from mapping emigration patterns, is to explore the empire as a 'field of opportunity' for migrants.[3] Unsurprisingly, these works focus predominantly on the areas of formal empire, those territories of white settlement. Explanations for the scholarly neglect of the migrant experience in the tropical colonies and informal

---

[1] Stephen Constantine, 'Migrants and Settlers', in Judith M. Brown and Wm Roger Louis (eds), *The Oxford History of the British Empire*, iv: *The Twentieth Century* (Oxford, 1999), 163–87; Marjory Harper, 'British Migration and the Peopling of the Empire', in Andrew Porter (ed.), *The Oxford History of the British Empire*, iii: *The Nineteenth Century* (Oxford, 1999); A. James Hammerton, 'Gender and Migration', in Philippa Levine (ed.), *Gender and Empire* (Oxford, 2004), 156–80; Kevin Kenny, 'The Irish in the Empire', in idem (ed.), *Ireland and the British Empire* (Oxford, 2004), 90–122; Marjory Harper, 'Rhetoric and Reality: British Migration to Canada, 1867–1967', in Phillip Buckner (ed.), *Canada and the British Empire* (Oxford, 2008), 160–80; Eric Richards, 'Migrations: The Career of British White Australia', in Deryck M. Schreuder and Stuart Ward (eds), *Australia's Empire* (Oxford, 2008), 163–85; Marjory Harper and Stephen Constantine, *Migration and Empire* (Oxford, 2010).

[2] Kent Fedorowich, 'The British Empire on the Move, 1760–1914', in Sarah Stockwell (ed.), *The British Empire: Themes and Perspectives* (Oxford, 2008), 63–100.

[3] Wm Roger Louis, 'Introduction', in Brown and Louis (eds), *The Oxford History of the British Empire*, iv. 12.

empire include the difficulties for scholars of working in another language, the small numbers of migrants found outside of formal empire, and the complexity in discerning the ethnic origins of such settlers, who were frequently lumped together as 'British' or 'English'. Teasing out the numbers of Scots involved in emigration and their destinations therefore forms the first brief section of this chapter. It then moves to consider a manifestly neglected aspect in overviews of empire: that of migrant ethnic identities. This is a needed task, for even when the subject of migrant identities has received extended treatment in collected histories of the British Empire, the emphasis is typically on the transition to the new homeland identities or Britishness.[4] But how was Scottishness maintained and perceived? In adopting ethnic identities as an analytical category, issues of representativeness and distinctiveness are critical. The chapter therefore adopts a comparative context incorporating, first, diverse ethnic groups and, second, various destinations (including the United States) to acknowledge the non-imperial movement of Scots.

Overview: Numbers and Destinations

Between 1815 and 1930, central and western Europe experienced unprecedented mobility, with approximately 60 million people leaving for overseas shores. Among the largest flows were 11.4 million from Britain, 9.9 million from Italy, 7.3 million from Ireland, and 5.0 million from Austria-Hungary.[5] Scotland's contribution to the outflow to non-European destinations between 1825 and 1914 was around 2 million, while a further 1.25 million left in the period after 1914.[6] While numerically Scotland was a minor player in the outflow, per head of population the loss of people was significant, with Scotland regularly placed third in a league table of European countries experiencing substantial emigration. Ireland consistently topped the table through the nineteenth century before being surpassed by Italy in the early twentieth century. By the time of the inter-war period, however, Scotland led this emigration league

[4] Ged Martin and Benjamin E. Kline, 'British Emigration and New Identities', in P. J. Marshall (ed.), *The Cambridge Illustrated History of the British Empire* (Cambridge, 1996), 254–79; Stuart Ward, 'Imperial Identities Abroad', in Stockwell (ed.), *The British Empire*, 219–43.

[5] Dudley Baines, *Emigration from Europe, 1815–1930* (Basingstoke, 1991), table 2, 9.

[6] Marjory Harper, *Adventurers and Exiles: The Great Scottish Exodus* (London, 2003), 3; R. J. Finlay, *Modern Scotland, 1914–2000* (London, 2004), 302.

table.[7] Importantly, the movement of Scots (and several other ethnic groups) was built upon centuries of mobility, but peaked in the nineteenth and twentieth centuries, an era of mass emigration.

Statistics for estimating Scottish emigration are notoriously slippery, for they fail to determine by birthplace those leaving Scottish ports. Given the influx of Irish migrants into Scotland, many departures might be Irish. Analysis of passenger registers at origin and destination similarly provide some insight into numbers, though problems surrounding their use include place of origin sometimes being recorded as the last place of residence, rather than birthplace. Nevertheless, the available statistics reveal that between 1815 and 1950 just over one million people ventured from Scotland to the United States, almost 800,000 to Canada, and just under 420,000 to Australasia.[8] England was also an attractive option, with around 600,000 Scots moving there between 1830 and 1914.[9]

The appeal of certain destinations for Scots, however, varied over time, and resembled the broader flow out of Britain and Ireland.[10] Most migrants moved to Canada in the period before 1847, between 1910 and 1914, and after the First World War.[11] How many Scots strategically entered Canada to gain access to the United States, however, is unknown. Australia and New Zealand were also periodically important, particularly during the gold rushes in the mid-nineteenth century and assisted migration from 1870 to 1885, while South Africa became more alluring towards the later nineteenth century.[12]

There are no available figures to ascertain the overall numbers of Scots choosing South Africa and the colonies of non-white settlement, but analysis of Census data, albeit a snapshot in time, provides some insight into the origins of migrants abroad. In 1911, a recorded 37,138 Scots were in South Africa, with Scottish males almost double that of their female counterparts.

---

[7] Baines, *Emigration from Europe*, 9–10.

[8] N. H. Carrier and J. R. Jeffrey, *External Migration: A Study of the Available Statistics, 1815–1850* (London, 1953), table D/F/G(I), 95–6.

[9] Harper, *Adventurers and Exiles*, 13.

[10] Gary B. Magee and Andrew S. Thompson, *Empire and Globalisation: Networks of People, Goods and Capital in the British World, c.1850–1914* (Cambridge, 2010), 169.

[11] Marjory Harper, 'Exiles or Entrepreneurs? Snapshots of the Scots in Canada', in Peter E. Rider and Heather McNabb (eds), *A Kingdom of the Mind: How the Scots Helped Make Canada* (Montreal, 2006), 22.

[12] Michael Flinn (ed.), *Scottish Population History from the 17th Century to the 1930s* (Cambridge, 1977), 450–1.

English migrants were more substantial, comprising around 130,000, while Irish migrants were around 15,000.[13] Unlike other areas of white settlement in which migrants swiftly outnumbered indigenous populations, British, Irish, and Dutch ethnicities in South Africa were a minority. Scots in Argentina, meanwhile, were among the 4,000 Scots and English found there in 1865.[14] As with other parts of Latin America, and in contrast to formal parts of empire, the population was predominantly Spanish or Portuguese.

The Census data for the key destinations in formal empire to which Scots gravitated are likewise illuminating (see Appendix 5.1). Significant numbers were returned in the Canadian Census and although the Scots-born were minimal in respect of the total population (3.4 per cent in 1871), they supplied a substantial share of the foreign-born (peaking at just over 21 per cent that same year). There, until 1911 (at which point they exceeded the Irish-born), Scots were outnumbered by both those born in England and Ireland. Australia provides a similar story, although there the Scottish surpassing of the Irish did not occur until 1921. New Zealand, on the other hand, is an arresting contrast. Although the numbers of Scots-born there were less substantial than those moving elsewhere, their share of the *total* population was striking (hovering between 10 and 16 per cent for most of the nineteenth century). The Scots-born in New Zealand also consistently outnumbered the flow from Ireland. This representation and their perceived influence resoundingly suggests that 'New Zealand is *the* neo-Scotland.'[15] By way of contrast, although Scots were present in the United States in substantial numbers, their percentage as part of the foreign-born (less than 3 per cent) and total population (less than 1 per cent) was minimal.

Identities

Throughout the imperial and non-imperial destinations to which they gravitated, Scots expressed their ethnic identities in various ways, including 'the founding of Caledonian societies, the building of memorials, the

---

[13] John M. MacKenzie with Nigel R. Dalziel, *The Scots in South Africa: Ethnicity, Identity Gender and Race, 1772–1914* (Manchester, 2007), 161.

[14] Manuel A. Fernandez, 'The Scots in Latin America: A Survey', in R. A. Cage (ed.), *The Scots Abroad: Labour, Capital, Enterprise, 1750–1914* (London, 1985), 222.

[15] James Belich, *Paradise Reforged: A History of the New Zealanders: From the 1880s to the Year 2000* (Auckland, 2001), 221.

erection of statues...and the organization of Highland games and pipe band competitions'.[16] Although alert to these components, scholars generally focus either on one particular aspect, such as ethnic societies, or fleetingly mention such elements without sustained analysis.[17] The remainder of this chapter attempts a broader survey, governed by two main approaches: public and group expressions of Scottishness, as revealed in various forms of associational culture; and in personal testimonies, two avenues which contradict the assumption that Scots assimilated widely throughout the empire.[18] It therefore engages with established historiographical preoccupations surrounding associational culture, but also provides a new emphasis on personal articulations of Scottishness. This central objective is important for, while Scottish associational culture was critical for some, it alone cannot shape our understanding of ethnic identities, Scottish or otherwise. Indeed, given that most Scottish migrants did not join a Scottish association, it was their personal sense of Scottishness which overshadowed their ethnic affiliations. The second main objective is to highlight similarities and differences pertaining to Scottishness throughout Empire by adopting a comparative methodology along geographic and ethnic lines.

In addressing these issues, a definition of ethnic identity is required. A useful formulation is that devised by Anthony D. Smith, which contains six main aspects of an ethnic identity: a collective proper name; myth of common ancestry; shared historical memories; one or more elements of a common culture; an association with a specific homeland; and a sense of solidarity. National identity, by contrast, is tied to political ideas of the homeland, involving legal rights.[19] This chapter's approach to ethnic identities also incorporates the aspects that outsiders *and* insiders perceived as distinctive of Scottish ethnicities, for as sociologist David McCrone indicates, 'Perhaps too much attention is paid to the identity labels that people

---

[16] John M. MacKenzie, 'Essay and Reflection: On Scotland and the Empire', *International History Review*, 15.4 (1993), 737.

[17] Exceptions include Leigh S. L. Straw, *A Semblance of Scotland: Scottish Identity in Colonial Western Australia* (Glasgow, 2006), and Angela McCarthy, *Scottishness and Irishness in New Zealand since 1840* (Manchester, 2011).

[18] This point is made in Cliff Cumming, 'Scottish National Identity in an Australian Colony', *Scottish Historical Review*, 72.1: 193 (1993), 22.

[19] Anthony D. Smith, *National Identity* (London, 1991), 21, 9, 14.

are "forced" to wear, and not enough on how they select and actively present themselves to others.'[20]

ASSOCIATIONAL CULTURE

The linking of Scots with Presbyterianism is long-standing and is reinforced in studies of Scottish identity in the homeland, in which Presbyterianism, like law and education, was seen as a key pillar for the survival of Scottishness after the Union of 1707, though some scholars, citing divisions within Presbyterianism, challenge this interpretation.[21] Within studies of Scottish emigration this equation between Scottishness and Presbyterianism arises most especially in surveys of settlements organized by church ministers, such as those of Norman MacLeod at Waipu, New Zealand, and John Dunmore Lang in New South Wales, Australia. Yet such an association is long assumed, rather than tested. Indeed, throughout empire not all Scots were Presbyterians and not all Presbyterians were Scots.[22] While their religious beliefs were important and the role of ministers and missionaries critical, the sense in which individuals linked faith and ethnicity or the extent to which ministers professed a sense of Scottish identity to their parishioners is a neglected theme. Indeed, it is suggested that the Presbyterian Church in Toronto, being a transplanted institution, had no need to foster Scottishness.[23] In New Zealand, meanwhile, self-conscious Scottishness only increased in the Presbyterian Church after 1900.[24] Welsh identity, by contrast, was connected to nonconformity throughout their diaspora, while Irish-Catholic migrants were routinely reminded of the linkage of their ethnicity and religious belief. 'Blot from an Irishman's heart the traditional love that links him to the spot where he first saw the light and you pluck from his soul the seeds of his Catholic faith', remarked one

[20] David McCrone, 'Who Do You Say You Are? Making Sense of National Identities in Modern Britain', *Ethnicities*, 2.3 (2002), 316.

[21] See Esther Breitenbach, *Empire and Scottish Society: The Impact of Foreign Missions at Home, c.1790 to c.1914* (Edinburgh, 2009), 19.

[22] R. MacLean, 'The Highland Catholic Tradition in Canada', in W. Stanford Reid (ed.), *The Scottish Tradition in Canada* (Toronto, 1976), 93–117.

[23] Andrew Hinson, 'A Hub of Community: The Presbyterian Church in Toronto and its Role among the City's Scots', in Tanja Bueltmann, Andrew Hinson, and Graeme Morton (eds), *Ties of Bluid, Kin and Countrie: Scottish Associational Culture in the Diaspora* (Markham, Ontario, 2009), 128.

[24] Jessie M. Annabell, '"Caledonia, Stern and Wild": Scottish Identity in Wanganui and Rangitikei, 1880–1918' (MA, Massey University, 1995), 53.

commentator from New Zealand in 1885.[25] Yet the Irish diaspora, comprising a majority of Catholics, was fragmented by its religious cleavages, provoking conflict as to what Irishness meant. Admittedly, Scotland also had its religious divisions, most notoriously the Disruption of the Church of Scotland in 1843, but such events tended not to disrupt an overarching sense of Scottish identity.

Belief in a supreme being was the only requirement for membership of Freemasonry in the homelands and throughout empire. Yet, while histories of each national lodge exist in the homelands, there is little consideration of their ethnic dimensions. Furthermore, the most recent exploration of Masonry in the empire depicts it as a unified British organization, in which 'supranational identities' rather than ethnic ones are emphasized.[26] A study of Scottish, Irish, and English Masonic lodges in Otago, New Zealand, reveals otherwise. There, national origins of Masonic lodges were evident through their suffix EC, SC, or IC (English Constitution, Scottish Constitution, and Irish Constitution), and the name of the lodge. Scots, for example, had the St Andrew and Kilwinning lodges, the Irish had St Patrick, and the English St George and St John. Scottish lodges, however, were the most ethnically inclined, as evident in their use of sprigs of heather, the replacement of traditional Lodge uniform 'colours' with tartan, and the incorporation of Scottish literature, especially Robert Burns, into their formal rituals. English lodges were seemingly without this ethnic dimension, while Irish Protestants played down their Irishness. Despite such differences, the lodges embraced universal goals of benevolence, attended each other's meetings, and practised open membership.[27] Whether these findings are replicated elsewhere in empire awaits verification.

Consideration of Scottish ethnic societies both resembles and differs from investigations of Freemasonry. On the one hand, a flourishing literature examines Burns Clubs, Caledonian Societies, St Andrew's Societies, and a range of Scottish local and regional clubs worldwide, pointing to their distinctive features. On the other hand, there is an assumption that these societies were part of a larger expression of imperial and British identities

[25] William Jones, 'Welsh Identities in Colonial Ballarat', *Journal of Australian Studies*, 25.68 (2001), 41; *New Zealand Freeman's Journal*, 7 August 1885, 11.

[26] Jessica L. Harland-Jacobs, *Builders of Empire: Freemasonry and British Imperialism, 1717–1927* (Chapel Hill, NC, 2007).

[27] Kim Sullivan, 'Lessons of the Lodge: Pioneering Freemasons & Cultural Transition in Colonial New Zealand' (BA Hons essay, University of Otago, 2005), 16, 20, 21–2, 23–4, 27–9.

globally. Yet Scottish societies did not simply emerge in areas of empire, for they were similarly prolific in non-imperial destinations. Nor did they arise in a vacuum. Other ethnic groups likewise utilized associational culture to further their settlement abroad. Distinctively, however, Scottish ethnic organizations were not only cultural in many spheres, but, unlike many other ethnicities which encountered discrimination, were a positive rather than a defensive and political construct. Furthermore, comparative analysis of Scottish ethnic societies suggests that they were limited in their transnational endeavours, if transnationalism is defined as the multiple ties and interactions linking people or institutions across the borders of nation-states.[28] Scottish associations in Canada and Australia were particularly lacklustre in this respect, and although more global contact is evident from New Zealand, even then communication was limited to 'spontaneous, one-off exchanges of good-will letters'.[29]

Contrasts are also discernible when examining the objectives of Scottish ethnic societies, typically characterized by charitable and/or cultural motivations. In Canada, for instance, St Andrew's Societies were predominantly philanthropic, while Caledonian societies, Gaelic societies, and Burns Clubs were literary and/or cultural in their aims.[30] The chiefly charitable dimension to Scottish associations in Canada, it has been suggested, was not just a measure to aid Scots in distress but was a way to control new members and guard the image of the Society presented to the wider public.[31] Again, Scots were not unique in this respect, with mutual aid societies serving to support other ethnic groups, including Germans and Italians.[32] An alternative situation arose in New Zealand and Australia, where philanthropic ethnic

---

[28] Nina Glick Schiller, Linda Basch, and Cristina Blanc-Szanton, 'Transnationalism: A New Analytic Framework for Understanding Migration', in eaedem (eds), *Towards a Transnational Perspective on Migration: Race, Class, Ethnicity and Nationalism Reconsidered* (New York, 1992), 1–24.

[29] Kim Sullivan, 'Scots by Association: Scottish Diasporic Identities and Ethnic Association-ism from the 1800s to the Present' (Ph.D. thesis, University of Otago, 2010).

[30] Shannon O'Connor, '"Nowhere in Canada is St. Andrew's Day Celebrated with Greater Loyalty and Enthusiasm": Scottish Associational Culture in Toronto, *c*.1836–1914', in Bueltmann, Hinson, and Morton (eds), *Ties of Bluid*, 106, 107; Gillian I. Leitch, 'Scottish Identity and British Loyalty in Early-Nineteenth-Century Montreal', in Rider and McNabb (eds), *A Kingdom of the Mind*, 218–20.

[31] Leitch, 'Scottish Identity and British Loyalty', 218–20.

[32] Kathleen Neils Conzen, 'Germans', and Humbert S. Neilli, 'Italians', in Stephan Thern-strom (ed.), *Harvard Encyclopedia of American Ethnic Groups* (Cambridge, Mass., 1980), 416, 552.

societies were rare. Instead, sport and entertainment were to the fore in Scottish associational life, perhaps due to the later settlement of Australasia, whereas more hardships were encountered in the earlier settled Canada.[33]

Motivations to join ethnic societies varied among individuals and included sociability, personal advancement, minimization of risk, ethnic activities, friendship, business opportunities, and patronage.[34] Intellectual stimulation, social well-being, and conviviality characterized the motives of those joining Scottish societies in north-east England, while in South Africa practical objectives were fundamental, with newcomers provided with housing and employment, widows given financial assistance, and children's education supported. Business contacts proved important, ensuring that the Society was 'more than just an opportunity for tartan socialisation'.[35] In India, where celebrations of St Andrew's Day were seen as a forum in which high-ranking Scots could connect with other elites, professional connections were emphasized.[36] Globally, some Scottish societies from the mid-twentieth century onwards might have formed to enable migrants to interact with one another, at a time when some long-established societies were composed predominantly of the multigenerational descent group.[37] Generally, however, descendants of Scots were seemingly less inclined to join such ethnic clubs.[38]

Indeed, striking differences according to class, gender, and ethnicity are evident among the membership of these ethnic societies. Those participating in the celebration of St Andrew's Day in late imperial India, for instance, were predominantly male elites, while in Toronto membership of the St Andrew's Society was confined to Scotsmen or their descendants.

---

[33] Kim Sullivan, 'Scottish Associational Culture in Early Victoria, Australia: An Antipodean Reading of a Global Phenomenon', in Bueltmann, Hinson, and Morton (eds), *Ties of Bluid*, 162.

[34] Tanja Bueltmann, 'Ethnic Identity, Sporting Caledonia and Respectability: Scottish Associational Life in New Zealand to 1910', in Bueltmann, Hinson, and Morton (eds), *Ties of Bluid*, 171, 174, 179.

[35] John A. Burnett, '"Department of Help for Skint Scotsmen!" Associationalism among Scots Migrants in the North East of England, *c*.1859–1939', in Bueltmann, Hinson, and Morton (eds), *Ties of Bluid*, 222–3; MacKenzie with Dalziel, *Scots in South Africa*, 242, 247.

[36] Elizabeth Buettner, 'Haggis in the Raj: Private and Public Celebrations of Scottishness in Late Imperial India', *Scottish Historical Review*, 81.2 (2002), 231.

[37] Rowland Berthoff, 'Under the Kilt: Variations on the Scottish–American Ground', *Journal of American Ethnic History*, 1.2 (1982), 14.

[38] Rowland Tappan Berthoff, *British Immigrants in Industrial America, 1790–1950* (New York, 1953), 210.

A similar rule initially characterized that same society in Hull, though its membership criteria altered through the twentieth century with spouses, those of Scottish descent, and associated members all eventually eligible to join. Similar changes characterized the Sunderland Burns Club.[39] Greater inclusiveness was found in Caledonian societies and Burns Clubs in New Zealand, with both permitting Scots and non-Scots to join. New Zealand's Gaelic Society, by contrast, excluded non-Scots and even some Scots, restricting membership to the Highland-born who spoke Gaelic. Yet the Gaelic Society was progressive in other respects, with both it and the Dunedin Burns Club incorporating female members in the late nineteenth century.[40] In Toronto, meanwhile, the St Andrew's Society, formed in 1836, failed to admit female members until 1978–9.[41]

Membership restrictions inevitably raise the question as to how many participated in such organizations. Alas, few investigations of Scottish associations posit membership data, hindered partly by poor or non-existent membership rolls. Seemingly easier to establish is the proliferation of Scottish societies. Nevertheless, we do know a recorded 387 members belonged in 1892 to the Burns Club in Dunedin, New Zealand, when around 120 Scottish societies throughout New Zealand catered to a Scots-born population of almost 52,000. In London in 1900, meanwhile, 28 clubs served 4,000–5,000 members, while in the mid-1950s, 463 members of Hull's Scots-born population in 1961 of 3,373 belonged to the Society of St Andrew.[42]

The composition of these societies inevitably influenced the ethnic identities they professed. In some cases, scholars have argued for the coexistence of British and Scottish identities. Evidence for such claims of Britishness, however, rest largely on the presence of representatives from other ethnic groups at St Andrew's Day dinners and toasts offered to connect Scotland to

---

[39] O'Connor, '"Nowhere in Canada"', 102; Angela McCarthy, 'The Scots' Society of St Andrew, Hull, 1910–2001: Immigrant, Ethnic and Transnational Association', *Immigrants and Minorities*, 25.3 (November 2007), 215–16; Burnett, '"Department of Help for Skint Scotsmen"', 223.

[40] Bueltmann, 'Ethnic Identity', 176, 173, 177.

[41] O'Connor, '"Nowhere in Canada"', 102.

[42] *Census 1961 England and Wales County Report Yorkshire and East Riding* (London, 1964), table 8. Although not all members of the Society were Scots-born, the figure establishes that a maximum of 14% of Scots-born in Hull were members: McCarthy, 'The Scots' Society of St Andrew'.

the larger British Empire.[43] More widespread, by contrast, was the way in which aspects of Scottish ethnic identities were expressed. In some cases, such as the Sons of Scotland in Canada, a deliberate Scottish identity was demonstrated through clan-like structures, nomenclature, and a martial ethos.[44] In New Zealand both the Gaelic and Burns societies emphasized symbolism, iconography, and emblematic displays of identity.[45] The material culture of Scottishness was similarly to the forefront on the day with celebrations in India marked by Scottish flags, thistles, heather, haggis, military bands, reels, and bagpipes.[46] So too was the Scottishness of the Society of St Andrew in Hull prominent in its symbolic dimension at major events incorporating the display of tartan, the St Andrew's cross, and Lion Rampant. Burns Suppers were also held in which 'Burns's chair, draped in tartan, and containing its history and Burns's portrait, graced the stage'.[47]

Indeed, the cult of Robert Burns is a striking example of associational culture throughout the Scottish diaspora, with the poet representing an imperial British icon, with clubs formed, anniversary dinners held, and statues erected. While Canada contains 9 statues, the United States 15, and Australia 8, New Zealand boasts just 2. As with Caledonian societies in many destinations, Burns Clubs were generally open in their membership criteria to all ethnicities, which facilitated the dissemination of aspects of Scottishness throughout the Empire. Scottish literature was likewise well served throughout empire by Walter Scott, who is credited for the appropriation of Highland culture into a broad Scottish identity.

Scottish writers appeared in another vehicle of Scottish associational culture in empire: that of ethnic periodicals, frequently published to highlight the activities of ethnic societies. The *Scottish Canadian* emerged in 1890, the *South African Scot* in 1905, and in Australia the *Scot at Hame an' Abroad* ran from 1902 to 1919. Appearing between 1912 and 1933 was the *New Zealand Scot*, later named the *Scottish New Zealander* (1925–6) and then the *New Zealand Scotsman & Caledonian* (1927–33). Even earlier was the appearance of a Scottish ethnic press in the United States, including the

---

[43] Catherine Bourbeau, 'The St. Andrew's Society of Montreal: Philanthropy and Power', in Bueltmann, Hinson, and Morton (eds), *Ties of Bluid*, 70; Leitch, 'Scottish Identity and British Loyalty', 215, 217–18; O'Connor, '"Nowhere in Canada"', 108.

[44] O'Connor, '"Nowhere in Canada"', 107.

[45] Bueltmann, 'Ethnic Identity', 177.

[46] Buettner, 'Haggis in the Raj', 225–7.

[47] McCarthy, 'The Scots' Society of St Andrew', 225.

Scottish-American Journal (running from 1857 until 1919 and catering to around 15,000 subscribers), the *Scotsman* (1869–86), and the *Boston Scotsman* (1906–14).[48] While these titles largely appeared just before the peak (1900–30) of the foreign-language ethnic press in the United States, a time of transition from an immigrant to ethnic press, the Scottish ethnic press seemingly shared the inevitable decline of other publications.[49]

More so than the ethnic societies whose activities they promoted, Scottish ethnic periodicals demonstrate a transnational ethos. They not only included articles on Scottish heroes, famous Scots abroad, and obituaries of notable Scots, but published letters from Scotland and reported on a range of global events. Such activities were picked up and circulated to Scottish societies worldwide by the journal *Scotia*, the official periodical of the St Andrew's Society established in Edinburgh in 1907. Despite the earlier foundations of its global affiliates, this homeland society was acknowledged as the 'mother' association.[50] Yet despite these diasporic links, Scottish societies and periodicals remained principally cultural from their inception, whereas homeland politics characterized the press and clubs formed by some other ethnic groups.[51] Furthermore, unlike the ethnic periodicals of groups such as the Italians, Germans, and Welsh, those of the Scots were written in English.[52]

Evidence from throughout the empire suggests that some Scottish ethnic societies retained their appeal, despite a declining and increasingly elderly membership. In Toronto and Melbourne, for instance, the Scots-born dominated the St Andrews and Caledonian Societies, while 40 per cent of Otago's Caledonians in the early twenty-first century possessed no Scottish heritage, seemingly reflecting the inclusiveness of that society's open membership since its formation.[53] Ethnic societies similarly endured in the United States, although the heartland of Scottish-America swung to the south and west, primarily due to the mushrooming formation of clan

---

[48] Berthoff, *British Immigrants*, 163.

[49] Sally M. Miller, 'Introduction', in eadem (ed.), *The Ethnic Press in the United States: A Historical Analysis and Handbook* (Westport, Conn., 1987), p. xvii; Berthoff, *British Immigrants*, 210.

[50] Sullivan, 'Scots by Association', ch. 7.

[51] Conzen, 'Germans', 416; McCarthy, *Scottishness and Irishness*, ch. 5.

[52] Conzen, 'Germans', Neilli, 'Italians', and Rowland Berthoff, 'Welsh', in Thernstrom (ed.), *Harvard Encyclopedia*, 420, 553, 1016.

[53] Sullivan, 'Scots by Association', ch. 8.

societies after 1950.[54] While most clan societies were generated in the new lands, some received impetus from Scotland, such as Clan MacLeod, which blossomed as a consequence of Dame Flora MacLeod's world tour in the mid-twentieth century.[55] Clan societies embraced the cultural ethos of other Scottish societies, as evident from the Clan Mackay Society of New Zealand, formed in Wellington in 1937: 'These socials provide a grand opportunity for clansfolk to meet together, and to contribute towards the maintaining in this country of Scottish sentiment and culture.'[56] Yet they differed by having a strong genealogical focus. This is evident from the proposed constitution of the Shetland Society in New Zealand which, in 1995, sought fellowship with people interested in Shetland in order to foster interest in the traditions and activities of the Shetland past, and promote interest in family history and ancestry.[57]

Scottish clans are likewise well-known for their return visits to the homeland, including several trips organized by the Order of Scottish Clans in America throughout the 1920s and 1930s.[58] This 'roots tourism' continues to this day, with those of Scottish descent returning to localities central to Scottish history or to visit graves or ruined home-steads of ancestors.[59] Moreover, the 250th anniversary in 2009 of Robert Burns's birth sparked a massive Homecoming, comprising more than 400 events, including The Gathering at Edinburgh in July, the largest congre-gation of Scottish clans in more than 200 years.[60] Such gatherings drive the global heritage movement, including in the American South, where the popularity of a Scottish legacy is connected to a southern regional identity by drawing on parallel mythologies. By claiming Scottish origins, southern Scots assert that their identity is a continuous tradition from Scotland, rather than deriving from the Civil War.[61] Both in the USA and

---

[54] Berthoff, 'Under the Kilt', 14, 20, 22.

[55] Ibid. 20; James Hunter, *Scottish Exodus: Travels among a Worldwide Clan* (Edinburgh, 2007), 296.

[56] Clan Mackay Society of New Zealand Minute Book, 31 July 1949, HC (Hocken Collections), Misc-Ms-1433.

[57] Shetland Society, HC, 97-095-1.

[58] Angela McCarthy, *Personal Narratives of Irish and Scottish Migration, 1921–65: 'For spirit and adventure'* (Manchester, 2007), 204–5.

[59] Paul Basu, *Highland Homecomings: Genealogy and Heritage Tourism in the Scottish Dias-pora* (Abingdon, 2007).

[60] http://www.homecomingscotland2009.com/the-year-in-review/july.html.

[61] Celeste Ray, *Highland Heritage: Scottish Americans in the American South* (Chapel Hill, NC, 2001).

throughout empire, a vital feature of the heritage movement is the Highland or Caledonian Games, in which key events include throwing the hammer, putting the stone, tossing the caber, pole vaulting, long jump, tug of war, and foot races. Yet worldwide, from the outset, 'the gatherings transcended Scottish ethnicity'.[62]

Apart from the games pursued at heritage events, sport is another feature of the British Empire which illuminates aspects of Scottish ethnic identities. Yet studies of sport in nation-states have typically downplayed a focus on ethnicity, stressing local and gender identities instead.[63] Part of the difficulty may arise from complications surrounding which sports are perceived to be 'ethnic' in the homeland. In Scotland, for instance, no game is considered to be a truly national sport, although golf, despite its uncertain origins and myth of egalitarianism, is claimed as Scottish, as is curling.[64] Globalizing tendencies, however, make sports like golf seem less distinctively Scottish.[65] Nevertheless, golf, shinty, and curling were transported throughout empire and, whether appropriated or discarded, were perceived as further expressions of Scottish ethnic identity around the world.

The adoption by Scots of sports like 'fitba' was replicated throughout empire as seemingly Scottish events and symbols were appropriated by other communities. Elements of the Sons of Scotland, for instance, fed into a Canadian national identity.[66] In South Africa, the Afrikaner community adopted Scottish symbols, perhaps 'as a means of striking some kind of cultural blow against the English and Anglicisation'.[67] This appropriation of Scottish ethnic symbols figured in dress. In India, the Highland dress was adopted by some Indian regiments and was seen as demonstrating symbolic unity in the empire. In New Zealand, kilts were initially 'a visible fabric of colonisation as Maori traded land for blankets' before being appropriated by schoolgirls, leaving the Scottish national dress to enjoy 'a status far beyond its appeal to or impact on one ethnic

[62] Berthoff, 'Under the Kilt', 8.

[63] Charlotte Macdonald, 'Ways of Belonging: Sporting Spaces in New Zealand History', in Giselle Byrnes (ed.), *The New Oxford History of New Zealand* (South Melbourne, 2009), 270.

[64] Alan Bairner, *Sport, Nationalism, and Globalization: European and North American Perspectives* (Albany, NY, 2001), 62.

[65] Ibid. 67.

[66] Bourbeau, 'The St. Andrew's Society of Montreal', 77.

[67] MacKenzie with Dalziel, *Scots in South Africa*, 241.

grouping'.[68] The appropriation of Scottish symbols by other organizations, especially piping and drumming bands, is also striking and distinctive.

PERSONAL EXPRESSIONS OF ETHNIC IDENTITIES

Focusing on Scots and non-Scots who elected to participate in public and group expressions of ethnic identities through associations, sport, religion, and heritage provides a limited view of Scottish ethnic identities, as not all Scots chose this style of expression. An alternative approach is to examine the values, feelings, ideas, and emotions of individuals, the so-called internal states of mind, to further the exploration of identity.[69] In other words, ethnicity and ethnic identities are about ethnic and cultural essences, as well as processes (practices) and relationships (interactions).[70] Important here is the recognition that 'neither the practice of ethnic culture nor participation in ethnic organizations were essential to being and feeling ethnic'.[71] Yet by contrast with explorations of public and group expressions of ethnic identities, there is minimal investigation of personal Scottish identities within the diaspora. As such, the remaining discussion turns to focus on recent original research in one destination—New Zealand—supplemented by work on Australia.[72] The former is an intriguing locale for analysis, as historians have long connected a British identity to New Zealand, termed the 'Britain of the South', with its inhabitants considered 'Better Britons'. The analysis that follows focuses on those elements discerned as explicitly Scottish and considers when, how, and why Scots identified themselves, and were identified by others, in ethnic terms. Admittedly, not all Scots necessarily felt or articulated a sense of Scottishness, but at least this avenue provides an alternative insight into expressions of Scottish ethnic identity

[68] Heather Streets, *Martial Races: The Military, Race and Masculinity in British Imperial Culture, 1857–1914* (Manchester, 2004), 73, 142; Katie Pickles, 'Kilts as Costumes: Identity, Resistance and Tradition', in Bronwyn Labrum, Fiona McKergow, and Stephanie Gibson (eds), *Looking Flash: Clothing in Aotearoa New Zealand* (Auckland, 2007), 43, 58.

[69] Angela McCarthy (ed.), *A Global Clan: Scottish Migrant Networks and Identities since the Eighteenth Century* (London, 2006).

[70] See Colin Kidd, *British Identities before Nationalism: Ethnicity and Nationhood in the Atlantic World, 1600–1800* (Cambridge, 1999), 5.

[71] Herbert J. Gans, 'Symbolic Ethnicity: The Future of Ethnic Groups and Cultures in America', *Ethnic and Racial Studies*, 2.1 (1979), 14.

[72] New Zealand examples are taken from McCarthy, *Scottishness and Irishness*.

beyond associational culture. Again, contrasts are made, this time with the Irish, to consider the distinctiveness of Scottish ethnic identities.

It is asserted that through empire Scottish migrants 'discovered themselves to be Scots rather than Aberdonians or Glaswegians or peoples from the Borders. Scots, in a sense, discovered the concept of Scotland while overseas.'[73] Yet utilization of migrant personal testimonies—private letters, shipboard journals, and diaries—demonstrates that Scottishness was both an overarching identity and one that was inextricably linked to regional, county, and local identities. So, as well as national, Highland, Lowland, and Island affiliations, emphasis was also given to county origins and particular places of origin. An overarching expression of being Scottish did not then counteract other elements of ethnic identities. Moreover, there is a sense in which these interlocking identities were evident at the outset of migration, captured most vividly in shipboard journals. Commenting on a crew member on the *Matoaka* in 1864, for instance, Peter Thomson revealed 'the Cook turned out, to be "a gude Scot" (a native of Auld reekie, born in the Fishmarket Close.)'.[74] Whether or not a broad sense of Scottishness was similarly felt prior to departure, and by those who remained at home, is an avenue of research requiring investigation.

Ongoing reference to national as well as regional, county, and local identities continued after settlement, with such commentary documenting the emotional and practical support given to other Scots. Sometimes these were broad connections, as John Deans informed more than a decade after his arrival in New Zealand of another Scot expected to arrive soon in the colony: 'I will be glad to do anything I can for him, should he do so, as a countryman.'[75] For some, then, simply being Scottish without the existence of more intimate prior association was sufficient and presumably reduced the perceived differences between migrants from the same country but from different regions and classes. Others drew on more specific intimate connections, such as James Campbell, who reported from Matakana in 1863 on

---

[73] John MacKenzie, 'The British World and the Complexities of Anglicisation: The Scots in Southern Africa in the Nineteenth Century', in Kate Darian-Smith, Patricia Grimshaw, and Stuart Macintyre (eds), *Britishness Abroad: Transnational Movements and Imperial Cultures* (Melbourne, 2007), 111.

[74] Shipboard journal of Peter Thomson, 17 December 1864, Christchurch City Libraries, Arch 796.

[75] John Deans to his father, 10 December 1853, in John Deans, *Pioneers of Canterbury: Deans Letters, 1840–1854* (Dunedin, 1937), 264.

'a little reunion of Saltcoats friends and we had many a talk over old times about Saltcoats'.[76] Scottishness was similarly influential in the work environment at Swan River in Western Australia, with Scots preferring to employ their fellow ethnics, work with them, and authorize them to tend to their affairs. Although regional origins were important in such connections, their overarching Scottishness as much as local ties bound them together.[77] Such networking similarly characterized the Irish in New Zealand and elsewhere, although a recent study of Irish settlement on the west coast asserts that religion, family, class, and locality were more important than ethnicity in sustaining informal social networks.[78]

The regional differences of Scots were likewise strikingly apparent, with the most clearly demarcated area being the Highlands. Divisions between Highlanders arising from social status, class, and geographic origins, however, are generally missing in studies of empire where, as in the homeland, they were represented as 'internally cohesive'.[79] Islanders were equally identified as a distinct group, but so too were contrasts made between the west and east of Scotland: 'Things are entirely different in almost every respect in the West Highlands and Islands from what they are in Aberdeenshire. There is a different race, a different language, and labour on an entirely different footing.'[80] Geographical divides also characterized the regional differences of Irish migrants, with the northernmost province mainly referred to as 'the North of Ireland'. County identities and local connections were likewise articulated.

Language and accent emerge as conspicuous features of Scottish ethnic identities. Mention of Scottish Gaelic appears readily in documents composed in English, particularly in reference to examples of large groups of Gaelic-speaking Scots arriving in New Zealand, and by clubs such as the Gaelic Society, which encouraged maintenance of the language. The most

---

[76] Alexander Campbell (Matakana) to James, 23 March 1863, 96–7, Auckland War Memorial Museum Library (AWMML), MS 50.

[77] Straw, *A Semblance of Scotland*, ch. 3, 103.

[78] Enda Delaney and Donald M. MacRaild (eds), *Irish Migration, Networks and Ethnic Identities since 1750* (London, 2007); Lyndon Fraser, *Castles of Gold: A History of New Zealand's West Coast Irish* (Dunedin, 2007), 156.

[79] See Charles W. J. Withers, *Urban Highlanders: Highland–Lowland Migration and Urban Gaelic Culture, 1700–1900* (East Linton, 1998), 237, 15.

[80] *Appendices to the Journals of the House of Representatives*, 1873, D2 38, Enclosure 3 in No. 36, Revd P. Barclay to Dr Featherston, 10 January 1873.

common reference to the Gaelic language in New Zealand was in connection with Highlanders. According to Isabella Bonthron, travelling in 1863 on the *Helenslee*, 'A great many of the passengers come from the Highlands and Gaelic is much spoken on board.'[81] By contrast, Irish Gaelic appears less frequently, possibly because Irish-speaking settlements have not received the same emphasis as Scottish Gaelic settlements and because the Irish language at home was retreating north and west 'away from the main economic centers and into the sea and oblivion'.[82] A similar dynamic surrounds the use of Ulster Scots (or Ullans), though extensive examination of records emanating from Ulster societies worldwide might throw light on this. For instance, according to the Ulster Society of Otago in 1958, 'members spent a happy hour or so recalling and exchanging Ulster sayings, phrases and words. These recollections stimulated the memory and the quaint idioms of the Ulster speech set a few minds thinking long.'[83]

If Gaelic has attracted some attention in studies of the Scots abroad, the Scots language has generated little investigation. This neglect is not simply the result of a focus on Gaelic-speaking migrants, but also a reflection of the comparative disregard the Scots language has received in Scotland. Yet, as with Highland migrants, language was an important element of the ethnic identification of some Lowland Scots. While the Gaelic language and kilts are often associated with the Highlands, developments in the nineteenth century saw the appropriation by Lowlanders of Highland symbols. It is no surprise, then, that Mae Palmer, writing to her parents at Paisley during a stopover in Perth, Australia, on the way to New Zealand in 1951, described how 'The boys were wearing their kilts of course, and various scotch people stopped to speak to us and wish us luck. One rather wealthy looking woman, kissed me goodbye and said she was thrilled to see the boys and hear the scotch tongue again.'[84] While positive commentary was levied at the use of the Scots language in this case, other remarks were less favourable. According to Scots woman Jessie Campbell in 1843 from Wanganui, 'The broad Scotch

---

[81] Shipboard journal of Isabella Bonthron, 1863, Otago Settlers Museum (OSM), Co11-1 5.

[82] Daniel Nettle and Suzanne Romaine, *The Extinction of the World's Languages* (New York, 2000), 136.

[83] Ulster Society of Otago Inc. Minute Book, 7 August 1958, HC, AG-239-2 167.

[84] Mae Palmer, *At the Bows Looking Forward: The Voyage to NZ by the Palmer Family in 1951, on Board the SS Atlantis, as Described by Mae Palmer in Letters to her Parents in Paisley, Scotland* (London, 1998), 24 May 1951.

sounds so horrid where most of our own society is English and all speak so well.'[85]

A Scottish accent, meanwhile, attracted less attention, although Scots considered it at times to be a hindrance. Harold Armstrong, who moved to New Zealand from Selkirk in 1963, explained: 'The fact that I personally had a strong Scottish accent and my wife a liberal Northumbrian droll [*drawl*] combined with her original London accent was most confusing for the local residents many never having met overseas people until then.' His eldest child, meanwhile, 'was mocked when she started school because of her slight Scottish accent'.[86] This was also the case with Irish migrants, though their accent was occasionally connected to particular counties or regions of origin. The greatest contrast between the two accents, however, relates to attempts to phonetically reproduce an Irish accent, which had several functions, including humour and discrimination. Cartoons, manuscripts, and cinema all contained instances of an Irish brogue.

Material tokens visibly representing Scottishness include dancing and music (particularly the pipes), festivals (especially New Year celebrations), dress (bonnets, kilt, and tartan), and food and drink (particularly whisky, haggis, oatmeal, and porridge). Indeed, Scottish migrants in New Zealand shared a preoccupation with their distinctive fare and material culture, as exhibited by Gaels in Quebec and their counterparts voyaging to Australia.[87] As evident in the voyages Scots made to Australia between 1821 and 1897, porridge, Glengarry bonnets, tartan, Scotch reels, and anniversaries such as New Year were all articulated. Importantly, 'their degree of national self-awareness remained largely constant'.[88] Such elements, then, were generally equated to the entire ethnic group, rather than distinct regions. By contrast with the Scots, less evidence exists of these material aspects of Irishness in New Zealand, with St Patrick's Day and the 'Glorious Twelfth' being exceptions. Irish food rarely received mention, perhaps endorsing assessments

---

[85] Jessie Campbell (Wanganui) to Isabella, 9 March 1843, 16, Alexander Turnbull Library (ATL), qMS-0369.

[86] Harold Armstrong, Ministry of Culture and Heritage, British Assisted Immigrant Questionnaires, 007.

[87] Margaret Bennett, *Oatmeal and the Catechism: Scottish Gaelic Settlers in Quebec* (Edinburgh, 2003); Malcolm Prentis, 'Haggis on the High Seas: Shipboard Experiences of Scottish Emigrants to Australia, 1821–1897', *Australian Historical Studies*, 36.124 (2004), 299.

[88] Prentis, 'Haggis on the High Seas', 299–302, 311.

that the Famine and lack of distinctive food meant an absence of connection between foodways and identity.[89]

Personal Scottish identity was apparent in other spheres, including songs; drink; reading; return trips; and naming homes, landholdings, public houses, and animals after Scottish connections. Missionary literature echoed these aspects.[90] The naming of landscape was linked to broader ideas about colonization and ownership; as such, Scots 'possessed the land by naming it'.[91] In South Africa, such markers of identity seemingly appealed to Afrikaners as a reaction against English and Anglicization and enabled Scots to sympathize with Afrikaners. But efforts to ensure familiarity, such as the naming of the landscape, should not detract from the knowledge that such naming was a symbol of possession by whites and dispossession of blacks.[92] Studies have indicated, however, that Scots were not alone in these practices, with Irish, English, and Welsh settlers similarly adopting naming practices. In other words, 'British migrants as a whole expressed their own cultural identities publicly in similar ways as Scottish migrants.'[93] Perhaps, but the evidence arising from Western Australia fails to endorse this conclusion, for seemingly distinctive aspects of Scottishness stand out. Scottish names given to horses, for instance, were more nationalistic than other ethnicities, while Scottish clothing was distinctive, with tartan and Glengarries. Some Highland Scots expressed pleasure at encountering those speaking Gaelic.[94] Is there similar evidence that clothing and language conveyed the ethnic identities of English migrants?

Certain alleged national characteristics, including martial valour, entrepreneurial dynamism, missionary endeavour, and administrative talent, were conveyed through empire as distinctly Scottish.[95] Yet while national characteristics, encompassing general values and beliefs, such as family,

---

[89] Hasia R. Diner, *Hungering for America: Italian, Irish, and Jewish Foodways in the Age of Migration* (Cambridge, 2001), 97, 112, 145; Panikos Panayi, *Spicing up Britain: The Multicultural History of British Food* (London, 2008), 43.

[90] Breitenbach, *Empire and Scottish Society*, ch. 6.

[91] Straw, *A Semblance of Scotland*, 112. For a discussion of Scots defining themselves in environmental terms, see John M. MacKenzie, 'Scotland and Empire: Ethnicity, Environment and Identity', *Northern Scotland*, 1 (2010), 12–29.

[92] MacKenzie with Dalziel, *Scots in South Africa*, 240–1, 152.

[93] Straw, *A Semblance of Scotland*, 113–15, 196.

[94] Ibid. 115, 122, 136.

[95] Richard Finlay, 'The Rise and Fall of Popular Imperialism in Scotland, 1850–1950', *Scottish Geographical Magazine*, 113.1 (1997), 13.

education, hard work, and loyalty to God and country, are often pinpointed as being confined to a particular ethnic group, such values are universal. Indeed, 'Researchers who concentrate or study one ethnic group at a time do not see how widespread and common such values are.'[96] Other characteristics, such as perceived Scottish grimness, Puritanism, and canniness, can also be queried.[97] Yet, intriguingly, Scots engaged readily with these alleged national traits. As John McNab, a native of Stirling, wrote at sea in 1881: 'I had never met either of the gentlemen before, but perhaps with some of the proverbial clannishness of the race we fell a-talking as if we were the oldest of friends'.[98] While Scots were not alone in being labelled with national characteristics, specific traits became more readily linked to them.

A range of characteristics were also attributed to Maori by Scottish migrants in New Zealand, an important consideration given that 'No experience defines the collective mentality of a people more sharply than contact with other peoples.'[99] Yet within the broader historiography of Scottish migration and identity, little work examines their contact with indigenous cultures, though there are studies of particular components of the Scottish migrant group—Highlanders—engaging with indigenous peoples in Australia and Canada, often highlighting violence and brutality or parallel experiences of cross-cultural encounters.[100] Yet not all encounters represented exploitation on the part of migrants. Preliminary indications from new research in New Zealand, for instance, suggest that the Scots and the Irish, more so than the English, married Maori women, with Maori fathers attempting to secure sound economic futures for their daughters.[101]

Teasing out these ethnic engagements is important since, where studies of migrant impressions of indigenous groups exist, there is a failure to

[96] Mary C. Waters, *Ethnic Options: Choosing Identities in America* (Berkeley, 1990), 134, 138.

[97] Tom Brooking, 'Sharing out the Haggis: The Special Scottish Contribution to New Zealand History', in Tom Brooking and Jennie Coleman (eds), *The Heather and the Fern: Scottish Migration and New Zealand Settlement* (Dunedin, 2003), 49. See also McCarthy, *Scottishness and Irishness*, ch. 6.

[98] Shipboard journal of John McNab, 5 December 1881, OSM, C150 17.

[99] David Fitzpatrick, ' "That beloved country, that no place else resembles": Connotations of Irishness in Irish-Australasian Letters, 1841–1915', *Irish Historical Studies*, 27.108 (1991), 330.

[100] See, for instance, Don Watson, *Caledonia Australis: Scottish Highlanders on the Frontier of Australia* (1984; Sydney, 1997), esp. chs 4 and 8; Colin G. Calloway, *White People, Indians, and Highlanders: Tribal Peoples and Colonial Encounters in Scotland and America* (Oxford, 2008).

[101] Angela Wanhalla, *Matters of the Heart: A History of Interracial Marriage in New Zealand* (Auckland, 2013), p. 74 and ch. 1.

differentiate the views held by diverse ethnicities. Typical in this respect is work on views towards Maori which asserts that 'the average colonist assumed that he had to deal with an inferior and savage people' and that 'Sweeping condemnations of their characters and habits were to be found in the private correspondence and published writings of settlers who had barely stepped off their ships.'[102] Analysis of the personal testimonies of Scottish migrants, by contrast, reveals a more nuanced picture, with impressions of Maori ranging widely and varying according to place, time, and the occupation of the migrant. Scots reported favourably on the assistance Maori provided them and demonstrated curiosity and admiration towards the country's indigenous population. Maori were considered both harmless and rebellious, as well as described physically in flattering and unflattering terms. While other ethnic groups presumably mirrored such diverse impressions, Scots (and Irish) observations were seemingly distinctive in the alleged affinities they perceived with Maori. As Alexander Campbell ventured in 1868, 'Love of country reigns in a Maori as well as a Scotchman'.[103] David Kennedy likewise drew similarities between the Scots and the Maori in the 1870s at Wellington: 'Their store of tradition, fable, poetry, proverb, and song is endless. They are undoubtedly the Scotchmen of savages.'[104] The vexed issue of Scottish impressions of Maori being influenced by their experience of colonialism remains problematic. While some evidence of Scottish similarities with Maori exist, it is difficult to determine whether this arose from experiences of colonialism, recognition of similar customs, or something else altogether.

Maori, meanwhile, saw the Scots in New Zealand as a separate people, with Matiaha Tiramorehu and Tame Haereroa expressing displeasure in 1856 'with all the men of Scotland'.[105] The Maori-language newspaper *Te Pipiwharauroa* was also alert to differences between ethnic groups from the British Isles, informing its readers in 1900 that 'this name, English, applies only to the people of England, not Scotland or Ireland'.[106] Maori,

---

[102] Angela Ballara, *Proud to be White? A Survey of Pakeha Prejudice in New Zealand* (Auckland, 1986), 14–15.

[103] Alexander Campbell (Matakana) to his father, 25 November 1868, AWMML, MS 50 222.

[104] David Kennedy Junior, *Kennedy's Colonial Travel: A Narrative of a Four Years' Tour through Australasia, New Zealand, Canada, &c* (London, 1876), 211.

[105] Otago Settlers Museum. I am grateful to Seán Brosnahan for this reference.

[106] I am grateful to Lachlan Paterson for this reference. See his examination of Maori-language newspapers in *Colonial Discourses: Niupepa Māori, 1855–1863* (Dunedin, 2006).

then, with their own distinctive sub-groupings, displayed some awareness of cultural dissimilarity between the various migrant groups that arrived in New Zealand, and the investigation of Maori-language sources and interviews with Maori may further illuminate this.

Scottish attitudes towards Aborigines in Australia, by contrast, are seen as confirmation that Scots demonstrated an overarching British assumption of cultural superiority and desire to civilize, perhaps reflecting the hierarchy of indigenous peoples in which Australian Aborigines were placed at the bottom.[107] Britishness is likewise seen as evident among Scots in their interaction with other ethnicities, use of the term North Britain, and support for causes such as the Indian Mutiny.[108] These conclusions are not entirely convincing, however. While examples exist of Scots reinforcing their Scottishness, there is no similar evidence that they articulated their identity as a British one. In New Zealand, this issue of dual allegiance is also problematic, being assumed rather than tested. Indeed, analysis of the personal testimonies of the Scots conveys little explicit sense of Britishness. Other sources, such as the ethnic press and poetry, are similarly devoid of British sentiment except in references to war, visits by royalty, and discussion of the British Empire. This echoes J. M. Bumsted's findings for the Scots in Canada, where he noted 'the paucity of the use of the term "British" to refer to customs, culture or the nationality of one's friends and neighbours'.[109] Likewise, Esther Breitenbach's 'analysis of discourses of identity in missionary literature makes clear not only that a Scottish identity was privileged over a British identity, but also that these articulations of identity were differentiated in both function and meaning'.[110] Such studies corroborate John MacKenzie's contention that the British Empire, rather than 'creating an overall national identity [Britishness] ... enabled the sub-nationalism of the United Kingdom to survive and flourish'.[111] Studies of the Irish similarly reveal that 'There is considerable

---

[107] Straw, *A Semblance of Scotland*, 188; Andrew Armitage, *Comparing the Policy of Aboriginal Assimilation: Australia, Canada, and New Zealand* (Vancouver, 1995), 194.

[108] Straw, *A Semblance of Scotland*, 175–87.

[109] J. M. Bumsted, 'Scottishness and Britishness in Canada, 1790–1914', in Marjory Harper and Michael E. Vance (eds.), *Myth, Migration and the Making of Memory: Scotia and Nova Scotia, c.1700–1990* (Halifax, 1999), 102.

[110] Breitenbach, *Empire and Scottish Society*, 182.

[111] John MacKenzie, 'Empire and National Identities: The Case of Scotland', *Transactions RHS*, 6th series, 8 (1998), 230.

evidence to suggest that New Zealand's Protestants adhered to Irish and Ulster identities, rather than the undifferentiated "British" outlook'.[112] These findings have resonance for studies of British identities in the homeland. There, according to one scholar, 'a powerful sense of being Scottish has gone hand in hand with a powerful sense of being British for centuries'.[113] Yet, as Richard Finlay points out for the eighteenth century, the survival of the Scottish language, vibrancy of Presbyterianism, and popular culture are indicative of visions of Scottish and regional identity being untouched by notions of Britishness.[114] Instead, he asserts, it was only with the experience of the Second World War that a 'more homogenous sense of British identity' was cemented.[115]

Conclusion

Aspects of organized Scottish ethnic identities remained central in the lives of some Scots and their descendants and comprised a number of outlets including the Church, ethnic societies, sport, and music. Scottish associational culture was also part of a broader range of non-ethnic associationism pervading empire incorporating Masonry, oddfellows, mutual aid, and benevolent societies. While social and sporting clubs were more important in the non-dominion colonies, like ethnic societies they had a key focus on sociability, and while they facilitated economic connections and marital matches they were largely attended by middle- to high-status company officials and merchants. Examining all forms of associational culture is therefore important for historians of empire, as it was one form of practical adjustment to a new life abroad. A key point about Scottish associational culture, however, is its diversity not only internally, but also between countries of settlement, an important point for those historians who view the British Empire as an undifferentiated mass.

---

[112] Alasdair Galbraith, 'The Invisible Irish? Re-discovering the Irish Protestant Tradition in Colonial New Zealand', in Lyndon Fraser (ed.), *A Distant Shore: Irish Migration and New Zealand Settlement* (Dunedin, 2000), 47–8.

[113] T. C. Smout, 'Perspectives on the Scottish Identity', *Scottish Affairs*, 6 (1994), 112.

[114] Richard Finlay, 'Caledonia or North Britain? Scottish Identity in the Eighteenth Century', in Dauvit Broun, R. J. Finlay, and Michael Lynch (eds), *Image and Identity: The Making and Re-making of Scotland through the Ages* (Edinburgh, 1998), 151.

[115] Finlay, 'The Rise and Fall of Popular Imperialism', 20.

Examining Scottish ethnic identities also re-situates the self-governing colonies or dominions at the heart of imperial history. Certainly, other areas of empire such as the tropical colonies and 'informal empire' were important for the Scots, but in sheer numbers Scots penetrated the settlement colonies to a significant degree. It is also important to avoid losing sight of the non-imperial penetration of Scots and their ethnic identities, as reference to the United States demonstrates. Meanwhile, exploring Scottish (rather than, for instance, Highland) interactions with indigenous peoples provides a more nuanced understanding of migrant–indigenous relations, rather than a persistent focus on the expropriation of native peoples, or claims that a shared experience of dispossession generated empathy. Additionally, in its exploration of ethnic societies the chapter provides a salutary warning for those tempted to view associational culture as comprising multiple connections in a transnational context. Instead, Scottish associations were more inclined to focus on the local and the homeland, than on engagement with similar societies around the globe.

Inevitably, examining Scottish ethnic identities raises the issue of Scottish distinctiveness. Certainly Scots were not the only ethnic group throughout empire to form associations or articulate personal elements of their ethnic identities. Yet by examining their ethnic identities in a comparative context, it becomes clear that the Scots were distinct in many respects. Compared with many other ethnic groups, for instance, their associations were more likely to be cultural than political and established in a positive rather than defensive climate. And, unlike many foreign-language periodicals, the Scottish ethnic press was in English. Moreover, Scottish dress, food and drink, dancing and music, and language and accent were all distinctive. And, despite concerns over national characteristics, certain traits also accompanied the Scots abroad, especially the perception of their frugality and canniness. Particularly intriguing, however, is whether the Scots and Irish were more likely to pursue, either exploitatively or intimately, encounters with indigenous peoples and why. A further glaring gap relates to the ethnic identities held by the multigenerational descent group: to what extent were these articulated and reinvented?

Likewise looming at the heart of this enterprise is the issue of representativeness. It has, for instance, been claimed that Scottish associational culture was the preserve of the elites. New research, however, indicates that such associations were more representative rather than elitist, as previously assumed, though gender clearly remains an issue here. Admittedly, not all Scots participated in Scottish associational culture, just as not all individual Scots held to a personal sense of their ethnic identities. And even among those who did, ethnic identities are situational. In other words, 'we do not routinely proceed through our day perceiving everything through the self-conscious prism of our ethnicity'.[116] Admittedly, the use of personal testimonies is problematic, for such sources are not necessarily representative of migrants or of those who wrote. Nevertheless, it enables incorporation of the insights of women and illuminates aspects of identities that might otherwise be missing. In the long run, such testimonies are more representative than a focus on elites, officials, and public figures, and offer unparalleled insight into such topics as ethnic identities.

Select Bibliography

Tom Brooking and Jennie Coleman (eds), *The Heather and the Fern: Scottish Migration and New Zealand Settlement* (Dunedin, 2003).

Tanja Bueltmann, Andrew Hinson, and Graeme Morton (eds), *Ties of Bluid, Kin and Countrie: Scottish Associational Culture in the Diaspora* (Markham, Ontario, 2009).

T. M. Devine, *To The Ends of the Earth: Scotland's Global Diaspora 1750–2010* (London, 2011).

Marjory Harper, *Adventurers and Exiles: The Great Scottish Exodus* (London, 2003).

—— and Michael E. Vance (eds), *Myth, Migration and the Making of Memory: Scotia and Nova Scotia, c.1700–1990* (Halifax, 1999).

Angela McCarthy (ed.), *A Global Clan: Scottish Migrant Networks and Identities since the Eighteenth Century* (London, 2006).

—— *Personal Narratives of Irish and Scottish Migration: 'For Spirit and Adventure'* (Manchester, 2007).

—— *Scottishness and Irishness in New Zealand since 1840* (Manchester, 2011).

John M. MacKenzie with Nigel R. Dalziel, *The Scots in South Africa: Ethnicity, Identity, Gender and Race, 1772–1914* (Manchester, 2007).

Peter E. Rider and Heather McNabb (eds), *A Kingdom of the Mind: How the Scots Helped Make Canada* (Montreal, 2006).

Leigh S. L. Straw, *A Semblance of Scotland: Scottish Identity in Colonial Western Australia* (Glasgow, 2006).

---

[116] John Downing and Charles Husband, *Representing 'Race': Racisms, Ethnicities, and Media* (London, 2005), 18.

Appendix 5.1 *Scots as a Percentage of the Total Population and Foreign-Born Population in New Zealand, Australia, Canada, and the United States*

New Zealand, 1858–1971

Census year	Number	% total pop	% of foreign
1858	7,976	13.4	19.6
1861	15,534	15.7	21.8
1864	30,940	18.0	23.6
1867	34,826	15.9	22.5
1871	36,871	14.4	22.6
1874	38,431	12.8	21.7
1878	47,949	11.6	20.0
1881	52,753	10.8	19.8
1886	54,810	9.5	19.7
1891	51,916	8.3	20.0
1896	50,435	7.2	19.3
1901	47,858	6.2	18.6
1906	47,767	5.4	16.9
1911	51,709	5.1	16.9
1916	51,951	4.7	17.0
1921	51,654	4.2	16.5
1936	54,188	3.7	18.4
1945	43,818	2.8	17.5
1951	44,049	2.3	16.5
1956	46,399	2.1	14.9
1961	47,078	1.9	16.9
1966	49,937	1.9	15.3
1971	47,508	1.7	11.4

Source: Figures calculated from *New Zealand Population Census*.

Australia, 1891–1981

Census year	Number	% total pop	% of foreign
1891	123,818	3.9	12.3
1901	101,753	2.7	11.9
1911	93,083	2.1	12.3
1921	108,756	2.0	13.0
1933	132,489	2.0	14.7
1947	102,998	1.4	13.8
1954	123,634	1.4	9.6
1961	132,811	1.3	7.5
1966	152,275	1.3	7.1
1971	159,292	1.2	6.2
1976	151,882	1.1	5.6
1981	151,629	1.0	5.0

Source: Figures calculated from Department of Immigration, *Australian Immigration: Consolidated Statistics. No. 4* (Canberra, 1970), 12–13, and Department of Immigration and Ethnic Affairs, *Australian Immigration: Consolidated Statistics. No. 13* (Canberra, 1983), 12–13.

Canada, 1871–1961

Census year	Number	% total pop	% of foreign
1871	125,450	3.4	21.1
1881	115,062	2.7	19.1
1891	107,594	2.2	16.7
1901	83,631	1.6	12.0
1911	169,391	2.4	10.7
1921	226,481	2.6	11.6
1931	279,765	2.7	12.1
1941	234,824	2.0	11.6
1951	226,343	1.6	11.0
1961	244,052	1.3	8.6

Source: http://www.statcan.gc.ca/pub/11–516-x/sectiona/4147436-eng.htm#1 [table A2–14; table A297–326].

United States, 1850–1950

Census year	Number	% total pop	% of foreign
1850	70,550	0.3	3.1
1860	108,518	0.3	2.6
1870	140,835	0.4	2.5
1880	170,136	0.3	2.5
1890	242,231	0.4	2.6
1900	233,524	0.3	2.3
1910	261,076	0.3	1.9
1920	254,570	0.2	1.8
1930	354,323	0.3	2.5
1940	279,321	0.2	2.4
1950	244,200	0.2	2.4

Source: Figures calculated from Rowland Tappan Berthoff, *British Immigrants in Industrial America, 1790–1950* (New York, 1953), table 2, 7.

6

Scots and the Environment of Empire

John M. MacKenzie

In recent years, the Scots' relationship with the environment of imperial territories has emerged as a separate study. Already a considerable historiography has developed, one promoting the notion that Scots, for whatever reasons, had a distinctive approach to the environments of colonies.[1] This chapter will consider why this should be so. Does it represent yet another of the myths of the Scots when transplanted overseas, albeit a myth which, like most myths, encapsulates important kernels of truth? Does it have something to do with the diverse character of Scottish environments and the manner of human interactions with them? Or can we find explanations in the social organization of Scotland in relation to its varied ecologies, as well as central aspects of its civil society? And when it comes to imperial frontiers, is it the case that Scots were capable of coping with marginal lands (in both spatial and qualitative senses) because they themselves often (but by no means exclusively) came from marginal regions of Scotland? In short, to what extent does the capacity of the Scots to interact with, and in some cases successfully respond to, exotic environments lie embedded in the nature of Scotland itself, in its religious and ethical traditions, or in its intellectual and educational attainments?

---

[1] Richard Grove was the pioneer in recognizing distinctive contributions by Scots. Richard H. Grove, 'Scottish Missionaries, Evangelical Discourses and the Origins of Conservation Thinking in Southern Africa, 1820–1900', *Journal of Southern African Studies*, 15 (1989), 163–87; idem, *Green Imperialism: Colonial Expansion, Tropical Island Edens and the Origins of Environmentalism, 1600–1860* (Cambridge 1995), *passim*. See also John M. MacKenzie, *Empires of Nature and the Nature of Empires: Imperialism, Scotland and the Environment* (East Linton, 1997); idem, 'Scots and Imperial Frontiers', *Journal of Irish and Scottish Studies* (*JISS*), 3.1 (2009), 1–17; and idem, 'Scotland and Empire: Ethnicity, Environment and Identity', *Northern Scotland*, NS 1 (2010), 12–29. See also some of the articles in the same issue which bore the title 'Exceptional Peoples? Irish and Scots on the Frontier'.

The Scottish relationship with alien and distant environments does, however, start with a great failure. It is apparent that many of the causes of the disaster of the Darien scheme of the late seventeenth century were rooted in both the promoters' and the aspirant colonists' combination of ignorance and misunderstanding of the Central American environment which they were intending to colonize, although (as argued in Chapter 2) Darien was in many respects unrepresentative of Scottish trading ambitions of the period. The signal and damaging extinction of that over-ambitious adventure lay in lack of knowledge of the climate, the ecological conditions, and the anthropology of the region. Scots who survived deaths from disease or starvation fled elsewhere in the hemisphere. Their compatriots, after all, were already beginning to flourish both in the North American continent (though at this stage their numbers were relatively slight) and in Caribbean islands. Although the Caribbean itself represented a considerable gulf in environmental conditions compared with Scotland, still the relatively settled arrangements of those islands meant that adaptation was possible, particularly when the hard labour there was largely performed by slaves. Darien offered a fatal combination of extreme characteristics, as far from those of Scotland as could be conceived, with lack of experience, the absence of both indigenous labour and any hint of prior settlement. This was a territory too far, in every sense.

Yet the disasters of Darien were a prelude to dramatic shifts in the political tectonic plates of the British Isles. The Union of 1707 was in some respects an outcome of failure, but largely laid the conditions for success, if success (perhaps controversially) be judged as Scots' demographic expansion across the world. The year 1707 was not, however, the single and sudden stimulus to these phenomena. There were many precedents from the late Middle Ages, with a firm foundation of emigration and travel established in the seventeenth century. Union certainly provided a spur for the development of Scottish characteristics, not least in the environmental field, that were seen to be both distinctive and relatively effective in coping with the outer regions of colonies with very different ecologies. Intellectual traditions also developed in Scotland which may to a certain extent have helped with this capacity to respond to alien and exotic conditions. After all, the 'stadial' theories of several thinkers of the Scottish Enlightenment (that is the capacity of peoples to pass through economic phases from hunting and gathering to pastoralism, on to agriculture, and to urban commercial enterprise) were rooted in notions of human responses to environments. Moreover, Scottish thinkers formed connections with their European colleagues,

speculating on apparent environmental phenomena which had been observed since the seventeenth century. Among these was 'desiccation theory',
the notion that specific locations can lose their rainfall (often apparent on
oceanic islands), particularly if their forest cover is removed.[2] These connections were much debated in the eighteenth century and have remained
controversial until modern times. Such ideas did not, however, float in a
vacuum. They were part of the rapidly developing botanical and arboreal
studies of the period, studies in which Scots seemed to excel. There were a
number of reasons for the emergence of Scotland as a location for this
ferment of environmental ideas.

One lay in Scotland's claim to be a major centre of medical training,
a position held within the British Isles until at least the middle of the
nineteenth century.[3] Scottish medical training was adopted and adapted
from European models, particularly that of Leiden in the Netherlands.
Human medicine was deeply embedded within botanical conditions and
their possibilities. Thus medicine and natural pharmacologies were closely
entwined, something which was to ensure that Scottish-trained doctors were
always environmentally aware, both of the botanies of regions in which they
established themselves, but also, as we shall see, in the forest conditions of
colonial territories. Medical students were trained in the dissection, analysis,
and categorization of plants at the Edinburgh Physic Garden, founded in
1670. One of the most celebrated of such teachers of *materia medica* was
Dr John Hope (1725–86), Professor of Botany in Edinburgh 1761–86.[4] Scotland indeed (its only rival being Ireland) over-produced medical men and
became the principal supplier of doctors to the East India Company, to the
British navy and military, and to many other institutions and territories of
the British Empire. The record is full of Scottish doctors whose botanical
and other interests led them to widen their studies within the natural labora-
tories of colonial territories. This would ultimately lead to the development
of environmental concepts of public health and to the specific study of
tropical medicine rooted in the origins of micro-biology which unveiled the
relationships among human health, animal diseases, and the entomological,

[2] Grove, *Green Imperialism*.

[3] Between 1750 and 1850, 70% of all doctors qualifying in the United Kingdom were trained in
Scotland.

[4] Hope's name has been given to a new building at the Edinburgh Royal Botanic Gardens,
opened in July 2010.

zoological, hydrographic, and other natural conditions of colonial territories, though most of this occurred only in the later nineteenth century.

Scottish missionaries were often also doctors, if in some cases trained in relatively rudimentary ways. Their preparations for mission work through a combination of theological and medical studies were rooted in the notion, emerging in the nineteenth century, that conversions could be made through works as well as through faith, and through the characterization of Christ as 'the healer of the world'. Missionaries tended to bring together concepts of natural theology with a conviction that medical training gave them the opportunity to demonstrate the superiority of both the Christian faith and the civilized values which it had supposedly engendered. As it happened, this also ensured that notable Scots medical divines, such as David Livingstone and James Stewart, could also become students of the environment of Africa, making observations which infused their published works, notably Livingstone's best-selling *Missionary Travels and Researches in South Africa* of 1857.[5] Livingstone intended his researches to be scientific as well as theological and anthropological and his hero-worshipping reception in Britain before his Zambesi expedition was partly based on that scientific reputation.[6] Livingstone was also fascinated by gardens as a marker of civilization and even planted one on an island above the Victoria Falls as a sign that a civilized presence had manifested itself there.[7]

This leads naturally to the second Scottish characteristic that emerged in this period, though once again with its roots in the seventeenth century. It is that Scots became celebrated gardeners. This has been charted in some detail by Cairns Craig, among others. Craig has argued that Scots gardeners strongly influenced developments in England and in France.[8] Why it should be so is on the face of it strange. Scotland does not seem to present the most

---

[5] John M. MacKenzie, 'Missionaries, Science and the Environment in Nineteenth-Century Africa', in Andrew Porter (ed.), *The Imperial Horizons of British Protestant Missions, 1880–1914* (Grand Rapids, Mich., 2003), 106–30.

[6] This point is missed by Lawrence Dritsas in his *Zambesi: David Livingstone and Expeditionary Science in Africa* (London, 2010). Revd William Monk (ed.), *Dr. Livingstone's Cambridge Lectures* (London, 1858), which includes material on Livingstone's scientific attainments.

[7] David Livingstone, *Missionary Travels and Researches in South Africa* (London, 1857), 113, 524. Livingstone valued the garden of his father-in-law Robert Moffat at Kuruman, and many missionaries followed him in seeing the garden as emblematic of a Christian state of grace. MacKenzie, 'Missionaries, Science and the Environment', 109–11.

[8] Cairns Craig, *Intending Scotland: Explorations in Scottish Culture since the Enlightenment* (Edinburgh, 2009), 23–36.

sympathetic environment for the establishment of notable gardens. Relatively harsh winters and variable sunshine seemed to militate against the comparative ease of gardening to be encountered, for example, in the Mediterranean world. But difficulty can, of course, be itself a spur. Luxuriance and apparently easy conditions may well reduce the need for effort. Perhaps this teeters on the edge of environmental determinism, so it may be safer to suggest that the Scottish gardening tradition also emerged from botanical fascinations, from institutions—such as the universities—with botanic gardens regarded as essential to their studies, from connections with European equivalents, from the ready availability of stone for the building of walled gardens, and also from the social conditions of Scotland. Great landowners, owners of castles and country houses, were often the protagonists of garden design and layout. This was a matter of fashion, of aesthetic ambition, of social standing, as well as of intellectual interest. Many of the gardeners and plant hunters who travelled in exotic regions emerged from this combination of backgrounds. They were often practical gardeners trained in horticulture on great estates or in the university botanical and physic gardens, notably those of Aberdeen and Edinburgh. Scottish gardeners made their appearance in England and on the continent of Europe. They also became key figures at Kew Gardens or in the Chelsea Physic Garden in London.[9] It is not surprising therefore that they soon made their presence felt within the British Empire.

Indeed, strikingly negative conditions had helped to stimulate Scottish interests in forestry. Deforestation had reached dangerous levels in seventeenth-century Scotland, with possibly a mere 5 per cent of the country forested, one of the lowest ratios in Europe.[10] This was a considerable weakness in respect of house construction, shipbuilding, packaging, and furniture-making. Moreover, the need to import timber had damaging implications for debt, credit, and balance of payments issues and certainly focused interest on the need for afforestation. Even the 'improving acts' of the pre-1707 Parliament sought to push planting forward. Thus, landowners realized the profit that could be secured from tree-planting and great estates became active in this field, not least because it helped to provide economic

---

[9] Richard Drayton, *Nature's Government: Science, Imperial Britain and the 'Improvement' of the World* (New Haven, 2000).

[10] T. C. Smout, 'Woodland History before 1850', in idem (ed.), *Scotland since Prehistory: Natural Change and Human Impact* (Aberdeen, 1993), 41. See also Hugh Cheape, 'Woodlands on the Clanranald Estates: A Case Study', ibid. 50–63.

value for otherwise relatively unproductive land. Thus tree-planting, notably of exotica, became a passion in the eighteenth century, pursued by major
landowners like the dukes of Atholl and Argyll or the earls of Moray and
Fife. Such landowners were greatly helped by the rights and privileges and
considerable security of tenure that they had secured through legislation
in the late seventeenth and eighteenth centuries. This enabled economic,
aesthetic, and scientific interests to merge, helped by the fact that in Scotland many of the estate officials (chamberlains, factors, ground officers)
were university educated and would have been influenced by Enlightenment
thought and teaching.[11] Moreover, since this was also the period when exotic
species were being imported from Europe, later from North America and
elsewhere in the world, such planting became a laboratory for the marrying
of the new trees to Scottish soils, hill conditions, and water availability.
To achieve this, landowners required foresters capable of studying and capi-
talizing upon the characteristics of the various new types of trees coming in
from abroad. By the later eighteenth century, such expertise in forestry, largely
unmatched in England, was beginning to emerge as a Scottish speciality,
once again based on practical needs and training, rather than on any more
formal institutional studies, which came later. In addition to this development of forest skills, by the late eighteenth century Scotland came to be
regarded internationally as an advanced centre of agronomy and a source of
farm servants, some of whom were exceptionally skilled and literate.

If gardening and forestry often developed from purely practical needs,
intellectual interests in the environment certainly emerged from Scottish
Enlightenment thought. Among these were proto-anthropological ideas
and concepts of climatic and environmental determinism, notions which
were to be partly influential in the development of scientific racism in the
nineteenth century. These were not by any means confined to Scotland, but
Scots were certainly among the leaders in the emergence of such thinking.
Moreover, by the end of the eighteenth century, a number of other traditions had developed in Scotland. The need to ensure that rebellion against
the British Protestant state was a thing of the past after 1746 led to efforts at
the mapping of the country, at the creation of infrastructures, including

---

[11] T. M. Devine, *The Transformation of Rural Scotland: Social Change and the Agrarian
Economy, 1660–1815* (Edinburgh, 1994), 64–5. For the intellectual background, see Richard
Saville, 'Intellectual Capital in Pre-1707 Scotland', in Stewart J. Brown and Christopher Whatley
(eds), *Union of 1707: New Dimensions* (Edinburgh, 2008), 45–60.

roads and bridges, and the requirement to understand populations and their conditions. These military requirements quickly passed into more peaceable developments. Scotland's rivers constituted major barriers to travel and to commerce such that by the late eighteenth and early nineteenth centuries a notable tradition of bridge-building had developed. The emergence of increasingly sophisticated techniques would ultimately prove valuable in the creation of viaducts for canals, for the construction of railway lines and more usable roads. Once again, there was no Scottish monopoly here, of course, but Scots engineers became celebrated throughout the British Isles and later in the empire.

Engineers and builders necessarily became acquainted with the geology of the regions through which communications were driven, particularly essential because of the need for blasting, for an understanding of the character of foundations, and for the properties of stone used in building. Through such practical concerns, they became aware of the complex, localized, and perhaps ancient character of the geology of the country. They had, for example, unrivalled opportunities to examine the fossils that came out of their quarrying and other activities. There was a significant intellectual input here too. Scots geologists, such as Charles Lyell, were not the first to begin to doubt the creation of the world on a biblical time-scale, but they did offer increasing evidence of the impossibility of the extraordinary compression required by a divine creationist approach. The researches of Lyell, himself an estate owner at Kinnordy in Angus, were to have a profound effect upon Charles Darwin while he was still travelling on his great voyage of scientific discovery on the *Beagle*.[12] Scottish engineers and geologists, out of all proportion to the numbers of Scots relative to the population of the British, became exceptionally prominent throughout the British Empire. While geology became a significant pursuit of both practical men and gentlemen scholars, so did natural history studies. This became a cross-class fascination throughout Britain, particularly fostered by such bodies as Mechanics' Institutes (founded in Glasgow) and natural history societies.[13] At the very least, Scotland was not behind-hand in the intellectual, aristocratic, and later popular pursuit of natural history.

[12] Janet Browne, *Charles Darwin: Voyaging* (London, 1995), 186. There are many references to Lyell in *On the Origin of Species*.

[13] Material on the relationship between Mechanics' Institutes and natural history study can be found in Saul Dubow, *A Commonwealth of Knowledge: Science, Sensibility and White South Africa 1820–2000* (Oxford, 2006); and also John M. MacKenzie, *Museums and Empire: Natural History, Human Cultures and Settler Identities* (Manchester, 2009), *passim*.

Scots also became interested in what may be described as enumeration exercises, deeply rooted in the environments of the country. The Statistical Accounts of Scotland, begun in the late eighteenth and much developed in the early nineteenth centuries, stimulated local studies, not least by ministers of religion everywhere.[14] Parish ministers were inevitably seen as having both the required intellectual skills and the geographical spread throughout the parishes, and therefore the opportunities to compile lists of populations, resources, agricultural and industrial activities, and the commercial relationships that grew from these. Thus there developed a tradition of enumerating people, their customs, as well as agricultural and industrial products, infrastructural provision and felt needs, as well as commercial relationships with wider domestic and international markets. Once again, such efforts at statistical understanding—and the sense that here was something new and striking, perhaps a further marker of the operations of civilized systems—were to have significant effects on techniques of imperial rule. If Scotland was a land of many different regions and landscapes, of varied geologies and contrasting environmental conditions, of inland and coastal communities, of great estates and sometimes flourishing towns, then an understanding of these complexities might form the foundation for similar studies within the empire.

We must now put some empirical flesh onto the bones of these apparently influential characteristics of Scotland's domestic condition. When turning to specific phenomena rooted in this background, we should note the influence of Scots upon imperial environments through their roles in the environmental professions, the significance of Christian missions, and the manner in which settlers responded to and coped with (or in some cases failed to cope with[15]) overseas environments. In the latter case, this is closely bound up with the relationships between Scots and indigenous peoples.

Scots and the Environmental Professions

The profession of plant collecting (for purposes of transfer) began in the seventeenth century and was greatly extended in the eighteenth and

---

[14] A useful analysis of the Statistical Accounts of Scotland can be found in Charles W. J. Withers, *Geography, Science and National Identity: Scotland since 1520* (Cambridge, 2001), ch. 4 and 244–7. See also idem, *Geography and Science in Britain, 1831–1939: A Study of the British Association for the Advancement of Science* (Manchester, 2010).

[15] In some places, for example in south-west Ontario, Scots found the land to be too wet; in others, parts of Australia for instance, it was too dry.

nineteenth. Its practitioners were closely bound up with the processes of the exchange of plants among continents, searching for suitable or ideal environments in which they could be established. This process took several different forms. Plants were transferred from Britain to colonies of settlement as part of 'acclimatization' processes, born of a desire to recreate aesthetic familiarity with plants from home. Other plants and trees were transferred between colonies because they were perceived to be useful in certain conditions. The dispersal of the eucalyptus and the wattle are important here. Yet other transfers involved important economic crops, such as tea, coffee, cinchona, and rubber, among others, often through the agency of Kew Gardens. Thus, seeds as well as migrants scattered across the world, creating a complex botanical interaction between homeland and new 'hostland'.[16] As just one example, many Scottish plants (and animals) can be found in New Zealand. But this was a two-way flow, with many plants transferred to Britain, both to botanical gardens so that their properties could be studied, and also to great estates for both economic (at least that was the hope) and aesthetic reasons. These activities modified the environment of Scotland while also promoting knowledge of imperial territories. Moreover, as we shall see, these activities were closely bound up with the Scottish interest in forestry.

Scots were key figures, both in the first and second empires, in the exchange of plants across the globe. The university and private gardens of Scotland were connected with the expanding periphery of the British Empire through Kew Gardens in Richmond. Kew was founded by the keen plant collector John Stuart, Lord Bute (1713–92), George III's prime minister, in 1762–3. Bute's ambition was to create a royal botanic garden to emulate the Chelsea Physic Garden, which then held the largest collection of plants in Britain. The latter was run by Philip Miller (1691–1771), a Scot whose *Gardener's Dictionary* and *Gardener's Kalendar* (1731) were the bibles of eighteenth-century gardening. Bute's new garden at Kew therefore began by employing one of Miller's gardeners, another Scot, William Aiton (1731–93), from Hamilton. The Scottish tradition was continued by Aiton's son, William Townsend Aiton (1766–1849), succeeded in turn by William Jackson Hooker (1785–1865) and his son Joseph Dalton Hooker (1817–1911). Although the Hookers were not Scots, they were steeped in the Scottish botanical

---

[16] I am grateful to Cairns Craig for this phrase and for some of the material that appears in this section.

tradition, the father as Professor of Botany at Glasgow University and founder of the Glasgow Botanic Garden, the son wholly educated in Scotland. These figures were to be at the centre of the networks that would connect Scotland to imperial botanical exploits.

The great scientific entrepreneur of the age Sir Joseph Banks (1743–1820) became the unofficial director of Kew from the 1760s until his death and ensured that royal patronage and funds continued to flow in aid of the garden's many projects.[17] Moreover, when Banks wanted information about new plants he would send his assistant to visit Lee and Kennedy's Vineyard Nursery in Hammersmith, which was the prime developer of plants for British gardeners. James Lee (1715–95) from Selkirk, and his business partner Lewis Kennedy (1721–83), also a Scot, dominated the introduction of new plants into Britain in the eighteenth century, and the only competition to their Vineyard Nursery was from the Veitch family nurseries, founded by John Veitch (1752–1839), originally from Jedburgh, which came to dominate the London plant trade in the nineteenth century.[18] When Banks wanted to organize plant-hunting expeditions he would often select people from the ranks of Lee's gardeners, many of whom were Scots. 'So well does the Seriousness of a Scotch Education fit the mind of a Scotsman to the habits of industry, attention and frugality', Banks wrote, 'that they rarely abandon them at any time of life and I may say never while they are young.'[19] Thus it was Banks who selected the Aberdonian Francis Masson (1741–1805) for an expedition to the Cape, Thomas Blaikie (1750–1838) to prospect in the Alps,[20] and Robert Brown (1773–1858) as botanist on the Flinders expedition to Australia in 1802–5. Brown went on to become one of the most distinguished botanists in Britain, partly as a result of his expertise in microscopy. Another protégé of Banks was John Claudius Loudon (1783–1843), one of the most influential gardeners of the early nineteenth century. Born in Cambuslang, Loudon produced the *Gardener's Magazine* and various encyclopedias on gardening.

---

[17] Craig, *Intending Scotland*, 29.

[18] For Scottish gardeners, see Forbes W. Robertson, *Early Scottish Gardeners and their Plants 1650–1750* (East Linton, 2000), 201ff.

[19] Quoted in Patricia Taylor, *Thomas Blaikie: The 'Capability Brown' of France* (East Linton, 2001), 19, from H. C. Cameron, *Sir Joseph Banks* (London, 1966), 100 n. 52.

[20] Blaikie later introduced into French gardening the style that became known as the *jardin anglais*.

As a result of all these influences, Scots appear prominently in all lists of plant hunters of the eighteenth and nineteenth centuries, certainly constituting a higher proportion than the relative population of Scotland to the rest of the British Isles.[21] Their activities reflect the capacity of empire to soak up expertise, often derived from the over-production of professionals and skilled workers in Scotland. Moreover, plant hunters invariably supplied other forms of environmental, anthropological, and even strategic information. They were important field workers in promoting the 'knowledge is power' syndrome. There was also, particularly in the earlier period, a transnational dimension to this. Banks's nominee Francis Masson and another Scottish gardener, William Paterson, were two important plant hunters at the Cape, still under Dutch control, which has one of the most diverse concentrations of flora in the world.[22] Masson arrived at the Cape in 1772 having travelled on the *Resolution*, Captain James Cook's ship on his second expedition. He remained at the Cape for two-and-a-half years, travelling far into the interior and returning to Kew with some 400 specimens, including pelargoniums and strelitzia. He returned to the Cape in 1785 and maintained an extensive international correspondence, for example with the celebrated Swedes Thunberg and Linnaeus, helping to develop Kew's significance as a centre of excellence. His journeys and collections provided him with an eminence remarkable for a figure of such humble origins.

Paterson shared these lowly origins, for he was a gardener associated with the Angus estate of Glamis before moving on to the Chelsea Physic Garden, where the Director Philip Miller was notorious for employing his fellow Scots.[23] His journeys at the Cape, beginning in 1774, were funded by the Countess of Strathmore, enabling him to travel even further north than Masson, making four plant collecting trips over a period of almost three years. But the Dutch became suspicious of Masson and Paterson, considering them to be spies for the British, operating under the disguise of plant collecting, and banned them from visiting areas of the coast. Whether or not

---

[21] For popular accounts, see Charles Lyte, *The Plant Hunters* (London, 1983); Mary Gribbin and John Gribbin, *The Flower Hunters* (Oxford, 2008). See also Ann Lindsay, *Seeds of Blood and Beauty: Scottish Plant Explorers* (Edinburgh, 2008). None of these sources offers any explanation for the prominence of Scots.

[22] John M. MacKenzie with Nigel R. Dalziel, *The Scots in South Africa: Ethnicity, Identity, Gender and Race* (Manchester, 2007), 310–35.

[23] Ibid.

these accusations of spying had any basis in truth, it is certainly the case that the British already had a good deal of information about the interior when they first took the Cape in 1795, for both Masson and Paterson published extensively on their travels, in 1776 and 1789, covering many fields as well as botany.[24] Plant-hunting could indeed have its strategic uses. It could also be important in imperial surveying. Allan Cunningham, of Scottish extraction on his father's side, also worked for William Aiton and, with James Bowie, set off on plant-hunting expeditions in 1814, first to Brazil and then moving on to the Cape, where Bowie remained, and Australia, where Cunningham worked with the Surveyor-General of New South Wales. Cunningham conducted a number of expeditions in both Australia and New Zealand.[25]

Scots were also important in the founding of botanic gardens throughout the British Empire. The first such garden, on the island of St Vincent, was founded by General Robert Melville (1723–1809), a graduate of both Glasgow and Edinburgh universities.

Robert Kyd (1746–93), from Forfar, proposed that the East India Company should found a botanic garden at Calcutta (Kolkata), initially to provide the navy with teak timber. It was duly established in 1787, and after Kyd's death William Roxburgh, from Ayrshire, was appointed his successor. Roxburgh turned it into one of the most important plant transmission centres in the world, documented in his work *Flora Indica*, published in 1820. He also identified the properties of jute, which were to become so important in the economy of Dundee. Roxburgh's assistant and successor was Francis Buchanan, a student of John Hope in Edinburgh, who had made pioneering surveys of Chittagong (in 1798) and north Bengal (from 1807 to 1813), while Robert Wight (1796–1872), from Edinburgh and another of Hope's students, took charge of the botanic garden at Madras in 1823 and brought back to Britain over 3,000 species of Indian plants.[26] Yet another Scot, James Anderson, was influential in the botanic garden in Bombay (Mumbai), and many other lesser-known Scots botanists were active in the botanic gardens of the sub-continent.[27] Indeed, Scots botanists remained significant in Calcutta until well into the twentieth century, with the garden there becoming 'an

[24] Masson's accounts of his travels were published in the *Philosophical Transactions of the Royal Society* of 1776. Lieutenant William Paterson, *A Narrative of Four Journeys into the Country of the Hottentots and of Caffraria in the Years 1777–1778–1779* (London, 1789).

[25] Lyte, *Plant Hunters*, 36–46.

[26] Tim Robertson, *William Roxburgh: The Father of Indian Botany* (Chichester, 2008).

[27] MacKenzie, *Empires of Nature*, 67.

Aberdeen monopoly': graduates George King (Superintendent 1871–98), Sir David Prain (1898–1905), Andrew Gage (1905–1923), and finally Charles Calder succeeding each other in the post.[28]

The reach of the Scots botanical network also extended into Ireland, where Ninian Niven (1799–1879) was appointed curator of the botanic gardens in Dublin in 1834. Other Scots, such as David Moore (1808–79), who had worked in Dundee and Edinburgh, and James Townsend Mackay (1775–1872) from Kirkcaldy, were influential in Irish gardens, while Moore's brother Charles (1820–1905) held the post of Superintendent of the botanic gardens in Sydney, New South Wales, for forty-eight years and turned them into a major centre for scientific research and means of public education. One of the founders of this garden was Charles Fraser (1792–1831) from Blair Atholl in Perthshire, who had arrived in Australia in 1816 as a soldier guarding convicts. Richard Cunningham (1793–1835) and his brother Allan (1791–1839) were superintendents of the garden between 1833 and 1839, both dying in office. James Kidd, a gardener from Fife, who arrived in New South Wales as a convict in 1830, helped to maintain the fortunes of the Sydney gardens until Moore became the dominant figure. James Hector (1834–1907), born in Edinburgh and a medical graduate of its university, better known as a geologist, established the botanic garden in Wellington, New Zealand, in 1865, while John Davidson, trained in Aberdeen, established Canada's oldest surviving botanic garden in British Columbia in 1916.[29]

Plant hunters were also active in regions of 'informal empire', contributing to the diverse flora of British gardens and those of the colonies. China was pulled into this orbit from the 1840s, when Robert Fortune was sent there by the Horticultural Society of London. Fortune was from Berwickshire and trained with a local nurseryman before moving on to the Royal Botanic Gardens in Edinburgh, later to the Horticultural Society gardens, then in Chiswick. As we have seen, this was a well-trodden progression from Scotland to London and on to the wider world. Fortune was in China until 1845 (and also made a trip to the Philippines).[30] He returned to Britain in 1845 with a considerable array of plants, later returning to China and to Japan. Fortune's activities in the Far East were later matched by those of

---

[28] John D. Hargreaves, *Academe and Empire: Some Overseas Connections of Aberdeen University, 1860–1970* (Aberdeen, 1994), 65.

[29] MacKenzie, *Museums and Empire*, 70.

[30] Lyte, *Plant Hunters*, 62–79.

George Forrest from Falkirk.[31] He became a gardener almost by accident, but was trained at the Royal Botanic Garden in Edinburgh. Between 1903 and his death in 1932, he made a number of expeditions in remote corners of China, notably in north-west Yunnan and south-east Tibet, in a region where the ecology was dominated by the presence of three rivers, the Yangtze, the Salween, and the Mekong, enjoying a rich and diverse flora. Forrest was also regarded with great suspicion and was caught up in warfare occasioned by the 1905 Younghusband expedition to Tibet and by the conflicts of Chinese warlords. However much plant hunters claimed their activities were peaceable, this was seldom the perception of those people among whom they travelled. The plants these collectors brought back were to become economically significant in the sales of plantsmen and nurseries, not only in Britain, but through re-export to many parts of the British Empire.

Botany, of course, embraced larger plants like trees as well as shrubs and flowers. David Douglas, born at the very end of the eighteenth century, was a classic instance of a youth from a rural area, Scone in Perthshire, who became fascinated with the natural world, and later apprenticed on a great estate, in this case that of the Earl of Mansfield at his birthplace.[32] He moved on to the botanic garden in Glasgow, and was then chosen by the London Horticultural Society to collect in North America. His expeditions began in 1824, starting out in British Columbia and later moving on to the states of Washington and Oregon to the south. He returned to Britain in 1827 with a considerable collection of plants, having accomplished journeys of several thousand miles. He returned to America in 1829 and is particularly remembered for his introductions of a number of tree species, notably the Douglas fir and the sitka spruce—both significant in Scottish tree-planting—but he died prematurely in an accident in Hawaii in 1834.

It was indeed in the field of forestry that Scots were particularly to make their mark in the nineteenth century. Jan Oosthoek has shown how important the emergence of estate forestry in Scotland was to the development of Indian forestry, where the British turned to German, French, and Scottish expertise.[33] Indian forest departments were in turn to become

---

[31] Brenda MacLean, *George Forrest: Plant Hunter* (Edinburgh, 2004).

[32] Ann Lindsay Mitchell and Syd House, *David Douglas: Explorer and Botanist* (London, 1999).

[33] Jan Oosthoek, 'The Scottish Forestry Tradition and the Development of Forestry in India', *JISS*, 3.1 (2009), 61–74.

highly influential in the foundation of forestry departments throughout the world.[34] Scottish estate owners in Argyll, Perthshire, and on the Moray coast developed techniques for establishing new plantations of conifers, whereas in Europe there was a tendency to concentrate on extending established forests. Much of this knowledge was filtered through the Royal Botanic Garden in Edinburgh. By the mid-nineteenth century Scottish forestry expertise and the link between medicine and botany were fusing in India. Alexander Gibson (1800–67) from Stracathro in Angus was an East India Company surgeon, educated in Edinburgh, who began to note the denuding of forests in parts of India such as the Deccan and corresponded with Sir Joseph Hooker, Director of Kew, on the subject. Between 1838 and 1847 he was Superintendent of the important Dapuri garden at Poona in Bombay. Later, he was instrumental in the founding of the Bombay Forest Department and was its Conservator of Forests 1847–60.

Gibson worked with another Scottish doctor, Hugh Cleghorn from Fife, who was educated at Edinburgh and St Andrews and worked in the medical service of Madras. Like Gibson, he began to press for the foundation of forestry departments in the various presidencies. In 1852, he presented a report on the destruction of Indian forests, and this in turn influenced a memorandum on forests issued by the Governor-General, the Earl of Dalhousie, whose estate was at Brechin in Angus. Further input was made by John McClelland, the Superintendent of Forests in Burma, where there were highly significant economic forest resources. From 1852 Cleghorn was Professor of Botany and *Materia Medica* at the Madras Medical College and he published *Forests and Gardens of South India* in 1861. In 1860 he had brought cinchona plants from Kew to India, thereby helping to develop the cinchona plantations of the Ootacamund area of Madras. In 1855 he organized the Madras Forest Department and became its Conservator of Forests in the following year. He was soon advising on forest policy in the Punjab and Bengal and supported the establishment of an all-India Forest Department. He became its Inspector General in 1864. After retiring to Scotland, he was instrumental in the founding of a lectureship in forestry at Edinburgh University. There is no evidence that either Gibson or Cleghorn was involved in estate forestry in Scotland, but they (like Lord

[34] Gregory A. Barton, *Empire Forestry and the Origins of Environmentalism* (Cambridge, 2002).

Dalhousie) must have been aware of developments there through their many botanical contacts.

John Croumbie Brown was a botanist and a Presbyterian minister. Like Livingstone, he must have found ways of combining his interests into a natural theology. Between 1853 and 1862 he was lecturer in botany at Aberdeen University before being appointed colonial botanist at the Cape in succession to the Austrian Ludwig Pappe.[35] But whereas Gibson and Cleghorn worked within an autocratic imperial system, albeit with some conflicting policy objctives, Brown had to negotiate the difficulties of working in a colony where settlers exerted a great deal of influence and, after 1872, operated so-called responsible government. Brown set out to create forestry reserves and sustainability at the Cape, but he fell foul of settler commercial interests and his post was abolished in 1866. He returned to Britain and published an extraordinary number of books, repeatedly issuing propaganda for forestry studies. In 1866, he gave evidence to a parliamentary committee investigating the possibility of establishing a national school of forestry and stressed that 'Scotchmen can be most efficiently, and at the least expense, trained up so as to manage our Colonial forests advantageously'.[36] He clearly had no doubts that this was a notable ethnic specialism of his fellow countrymen.

Another such specialism seems to have been geology, together with the related fields of surveying and engineering. Each of these was concerned with the evaluation of landscapes, both on the surface and below. Geological understanding was a necessary prerequisite for effective surveying, while the engineering of railway lines, roads, mountain passes, and river bridges required knowledge of the geology of the region.

Hence these three are often found being practised by the same individuals, particularly in the pioneering days of the search for environmental dominance and control. Few were university trained in the initial stages, although some developed their expertise through work in the military. A few examples serve to underline the significance of Scots in these fields in the nineteenth century. In the pioneering years, they often developed their expertise on the ground, rather than from formal training. Several were

---

[35] MacKenzie, *Empires of Nature*, 70–1.

[36] Brown quoted himself in John Croumbie Brown, *Management of Crown Forests at the Cape of Good Hope under the Old Regime and the New* (Edinburgh, 1887), p. iii.

of the same generation, born in the 1790s, and therefore contemporaries of Charles Lyell, who was revered by all of them.

Sir Thomas Livingstone Mitchell, though of humble origins in Grangemouth, received some education at Edinburgh University, but poverty drove him to join the army in 1811.[37] He served in the Peninsular War and was singled out for his expertise in creating topographical intelligence and compiling maps of the battlefields of that campaign. In 1827 he went to New South Wales as the Assistant Surveyor General, succeeding to the senior post in 1828. In 1829 he also became responsible for roads and bridges in the colony. As well as working on road routes north and south from Sydney, he began to lead a series of expeditions into distant parts of the colony, mainly conducted during the 1830s. He also travelled to the far west into what was later to become the separate territory of Victoria, optimistically describing lands suitable for settling and pastoralism. Although he sometimes used Scottish place names, he has a reputation for being sympathetic to Aborigines, travelled with them, and maintained many of their topographical names. His work inevitably led him into the fields of geology and palaeontology and he is credited with starting to uncover the great fossil riches of Australia. He was regarded, particularly by governors, as an extremely difficult man to work with, but this may well have enhanced his reputation among the colonists.

Andrew Geddes Bain from Thurso was originally a saddler, but became a self-taught geologist, surveyor, and engineer.[38] He emigrated to the Cape in 1816, opened a saddlery at Graaff Reinet on the frontier, and became a hunter and trader. He made a number of significant ivory hunting expeditions and was caught up in frontier wars. Somehow this led him into surveying and he supervised the construction of the Van Ryneveld pass near Graaff Reinet in 1832 and of a military road on the Eastern Cape. This gave him the expertise which underpinned his surveying of some of the most spectacular passes in the Cape, still used as major road routes today. He became a keen geologist and like all members of that profession developed an interest in fossil collecting and archaeology. Despite his lack of formal training, Bain is regarded as the founder of geology in South Africa. Similarly, William Logan became the founder of the Canadian geological

---

[37] D. W. A. Baker, 'Mitchell, Sir Thomas Livingstone (1792–1855)', *Australian Dictionary of Biography* (*ADB*), vol. ii (Melbourne, 1967), 238–42.

[38] MacKenzie with Dalziel, *Scots in South Africa*, 208–11.

survey, initially of Upper and Lower Canada, in 1842.[39] Logan was born of
Scots parents in Montreal, was educated partially in Edinburgh, and trained
as a mining engineer in Britain. A man of considerable energies, he was
noted for collecting large quantities of data and had already compiled
meticulous geological maps of south Wales, arising from his work in coal
mines there. Logan set out to ensure that the geological survey was placed
on a permanent footing and was also ambitious to establish a natural
history museum to help to reveal the significance of its work to the colonial
public.

The origins of New Zealand geological exploration were almost entirely in
the hands of German-speaking and Scottish geologists. After initial work by
Ferdinand von Hochstetter and Julius Haast, the dominant figure was James
Hector, who became proficient in geological surveying while exploring in
western Canada in the 1850s.[40] He had been recommended to this expedition
by Sir Roderick Murchison of Easter Ross, the noted geologist and president
of the Royal Geographical Society. The same patron later recommended him
to direct the Otago geological survey, where he accomplished some significant field work, pursuing a policy of examining, with his assistants, all
natural phenomena in the areas surveyed. The government of New Zealand
soon recognized Hector as the leading scientist in the colony and he was
summoned to Wellington in 1865 to direct the Geological Survey and create a
museum. As well as designing the botanic garden there, he founded the New
Zealand Institute, a scientific association with branches in all the major cities
and towns which published annual *Transactions*. Yet a less well-educated
Scot, Alexander McKay, is often credited as the father of New Zealand
geology, since he remained in the field and was prolific in fossil collecting
and in developing both geological and zoological theories—not least in
respect of the extinct Moa. He was born in Kirkcudbrightshire and claimed
to have learned his geology while out in the fields minding cattle.[41] He
emigrated to New Zealand at the age of 22 and was quickly caught up
in geological surveying, working closely with Hector. Modern geologists
regard much of his work as having stood the test of time. He clashed with

[39] MacKenzie, *Museums and Empire*, 29–36; C. Gordon Winder, 'Sir William Edmond Logan',
Dictionary of Canadian Biography (*DCB*), vol. x (1871–80) (Toronto, 2000).

[40] MacKenzie, *Museums and Empire*, ch. 9; R. K. Dell, 'Hector, James 1834–1907', *Dictionary of
New Zealand Biography* (*DNZB*), updated 22 June 2007.

[41] Roger Cooper, 'McKay, Alexander 1841–1917', *DNZB*, updated 22 June 2007.

the German geologist and museum founder in Christchurch, Sir Julius von Haast (as he became), and enjoyed sending his rival up in satirical Scots poetry, which Haast, lacking a sense of humour, did not appreciate.[42]

All of these were regarded as heroic pioneering figures, but there were, of course, many other Scots geologists around the empire. They often filled the chairs of geology in newly founded colonial universities. But many figures were practical men, lacking in formal training, following in the tradition of the remarkable Hugh Miller of Cromarty.

Can this apparent dominance of Scots be explained in terms of the striking geology of Scotland itself, with its ancient formations and great range of deposits, or of the developing taste in walking, climbing, and natural history study and collecting in the period? Or perhaps an explanation can be found in the role of Scots in the military, with their adoption of environmental and topographical roles, as with Mitchell. Moreover, Lyell and Murchison were the two dominant geologists of the age, with Lyell's *Principles of Geology* (3 vols, 1830–3) unquestionably having a very considerable influence on all his geological contemporaries, while Murchison, who has been described as the 'architect of imperial science', was, as we have seen, powerful in nominating Scots to posts within the empire, just as Kew and the Chelsea Physic Garden had been launch pads for botanical careers in the eighteenth century.[43]

Moreover, Scots were famously prominent in railway construction and engineering works like bridge- and harbour-building. One notable example is Canada's most celebrated surveyor and railway engineer, Sir Sandford Fleming from Kirkcaldy, who worked on both the Intercontinental railway to connect the Maritime provinces and the Canadian Pacific to British Columbia.[44] Interestingly, he insisted on the use of stone and iron in bridge-building when cheaper timber was preferred by the companies. He invented the concept of time zones and became an avid transatlantic operator in many scientific and environmental fields. It has also been argued that Scots emigrants were often more highly skilled than other migrants.[45]

---

[42] MacKenzie, *Museums and Empire*, 217–18, 221. Hector also did not get on with Haast.

[43] Robert A. Stafford, *Scientist of Empire: Sir Roderick Murchison, Scientific Exploration and Victorian Imperialism* (Cambridge, 1989), the title of ch. 8. Murchison's father had amassed a fortune as a surgeon in the East India Company in the eighteenth century.

[44] Clark Blaise, *Time Lord: Sir Sandford Fleming an the Creation of Standard Time* (London, 2000); Mario Creet, 'Sir Sandford Fleming', *DCB*, vol. xiv (1911–20) (Toronto, 2000).

[45] Jim McAloon, 'Scots in the Colonial Economy', in Tom Brooking and Jennie Coleman (eds.), *The Heather and the Fern* (Dunedin, 2003), 101.

A good example of this is that there was a demand for Scots stonemasons throughout the British Empire, with major recruitment taking place in Aberdeenshire and elsewhere. The railway and harbour works of South Africa were famously the domain of Scots, which caused some disaffection among other artisans who were displaced. For example, when Scots masons were introduced to the Durban harbour works, English masons complained that they required a 'Mac' before their names in order to get jobs.[46] It is clear that stone masonry skills were at a premium in a country which had such a long stone construction tradition in its built environment. Engineers followed in the tradition of the great pioneering engineers of the late eighteenth and early nineteenth century. James Rennie, Thomas Telford, John Smeaton, and the Stephenson family (Smeaton and the Stephensons of Scots extraction, but mainly associated with England) were the most celebrated engineers upon whose work the foundations of modern engineering were built. It has also been suggested that Scottish engineers were over-represented in this profession in New Zealand, though precise figures are hard to come by.[47]

Other professional fields in which Scots maintained a particularly high profile, again out of proportion to their numbers in the population, were those associated with the merchant marine, and we should not forget that this was also essentially an environmental phenomenon. Scots captains were prominent in the eighteenth-century vessels of the East India Company. From the days of steam, Scots captains and marine engineers seem to have been almost ubiquitous, certainly disproportionately to their population in the United Kingdom. With its long coastlines, navigable rivers, and multiple harbours, Scotland bred a seafaring people, first sailing the North and Irish Seas and the Baltic, later the wider oceans to North America, the Caribbean, and the East. In the nineteenth century, the fishing industry grew considerably and its vessels became increasingly sophisticated, requiring extensive crews. Moreover, as the Clyde became one of the most significant shipbuilding rivers in the world, shipping companies associated with its yards regularly sourced crew, as well as navigation and engineering officers, in Scotland. Additionally, the work of William Thomson, Lord Kelvin (Northern Irish-born, but associated throughout his life with Glasgow), on electro-magnetism

[46] MacKenzie with Dalziel, *Scots in South Africa*, 154.
[47] Tom Brooking, 'Sharing out the Haggis: The Special Scottish Contribution to New Zealand History', in Brooking and Coleman (eds), *Heather and the Fern*, 51.

was vital for the development of submarine cables and the science of tele-graphic communication throughout the world.[48]

Rudyard Kipling's celebrated poem 'McAndrew's Hymn' of 1894 symbol-izes this in striking ways. It is a monologue in which a ship's engineer, McAndrew, reminisces about his life at sea and on land.[49] The effect is to extol the virtues of the Scots engineer, while also characterizing him as a slightly priggish Calvinist, aware of his sinful goings on (as he viewed them in retrospect) in the red light districts of faraway ports. McAndrew sees his beloved steam as being yet another expression of God's grace, offering up its own beauty and a form of salvation in its elemental power. In the course of discovering this, McAndrew has sailed the seven seas and Kipling makes him allude to his origins in Glasgow, to his encounters with typhoons and storms, his explorations of Gay Street, Hong Kong, and Grant Road, Bombay, and the many places he has seen on his journeys, from Ushant to the Barrier Reef, Cape Town to Wellington, Java to the Torres Strait, Kerguelen (a rock in the Indian Ocean) to Borneo. He pleads for 'a man like Robbie Burns' 'to sing the Song o' Steam', and although Kipling was modelling his device upon Robert Browning, some of the rhythms have hints of Burns about them. McAndrew also offers a fascinating characterization of the tropics. They contain 'new fruit, new smells, new air', but provide an excuse for the sailor's consolations in distant ports. Even the stars seemed 'lasceevious' and 'The Deil was lurking there'. As well as these seductive characteristics, the tropics were full of fascinating objects, like shells and parakeets, walking sticks of bamboo and 'blowfish stuffed and dried', which McAndrew loved to collect. Here was an encounter with distant places with their own climatic and environmental characteristics, which could also be expressed in sexual opportunity, in ports, peoples, and products.

Scots Missionaries and the Environment

If Scots migrants were often highly skilled, it is also the case that Scots missionaries were invariably better educated than their English nonconformist

---

[48] Crosbie Smith and M. Norton Wise, *Energy and Empire: A Biographical Study of Lord Kelvin* (Cambridge, 1989).

[49] The companion poem, 'Mary Gloster', is a monologue by Sir Anthony Gloster, whose nationality is not revealed, but was probably English. But the significant thing is that he goes into partnership with a Scot called McCulloch and they move their foundry to the Clyde to be close to the burgeoning shipbuilding industry.

counterparts. As we have seen, the combination of theological and medical training was not uncommon.

Moreover, Scots missions often employed skilled artisans, generally committed Christians, for some of the practical work at their distant stations. These mission stations were often land extensive, particularly in Africa, and in many respects took on the appearance of the Scottish estate.[50] The church, the school, and sometimes the post office stood in for the great house. Land was divided up into a residential area of missionaries, teachers, perhaps nurses, as well as villages for adherents. There were wooded areas where tree-planting took place, and often sections for experimental gardens (including the testing of economic crops), pasture, and agriculture, depending on the nature of soils and water availability. A sawmill and a brick works often underpinned the building and development of the mission. The villages sometimes had long gardens behind each house, very much following the Scots model. The ambition was invariably to try to build in stone, if possible, replacing traditional African huts with what were seen as more permanent and durable dwellings. For Dr John Philip, the Scots London Missionary Society Superintendent at the Cape, conversion to stone was a key marker of civilization,[51] while the Revd William Ritchie Thomson considered the Gwali mission to look like a 'little Scotch village', black faces apart.[52] Scots missionaries also promoted technical education, partly basing their system on what they had learnt from German Moravians, and schools and medical treatment were usually seen as essential parts of their socially interventionist approach.[53]

Although David Livingstone never settled long enough to be a truly successful missionary, judged in terms of numbers of conversions, he did act as a model for many. His works, particularly *Missionary Travels*, were avidly read by his successors. His exploratory activities seemed to many to demonstrate his scientific and environmental credentials. He always claimed that he had developed his natural history interests as a boy in the Clyde Valley and his early writings were full of observations of the climatic, hydrographic, botanical, geological, and other aspects of Africa. Many missionary memoirs relating to the late nineteenth and early twentieth

---

[50] MacKenzie, 'Missionaries, Science and the Environment', 116–20.

[51] MacKenzie with Dalziel, *Scots in South Africa*, 102.

[52] John M. MacKenzie, 'Making Black Scotsmen and Scotswomen? Scottish Missionaries and the Eastern Cape Colony in the Nineteenth Century', in Hilary M. Carey (ed.), *Empires of Religion* (London, 2008), 119.

[53] Ibid. 113–36.

centuries followed this model. Missions were successful in direct proportion to the soils and topography, settlement patterns, and climate (not least in respect of health) that they enjoyed, for adherents not only required productive land, but also access to markets. The most notable stations fulfilled these requirements and missionaries, after many hesitant and mistaken starts, became adept at assessing what was needed. But a more significant quasi-theological spin was given to this. The mission came to be seen as an enclave of civilization, a place where nature was brought into a state of grace through being tamed and controlled. The mission was often contrasted with the wild and 'unconverted' landscape that surrounded it.

Missionaries, particularly in the early days of their activity, were also invariably hunters. Killing animals either for ivory to fund operations or for meat to feed followers and adherents was important to the successful mission. Livingstone himself had been involved in hunting ivory to pay for his travels (though he had doubts about the sacrifice of African elephants). Other missionaries similarly followed the practices of many other early settlers. (In Asia, however, they often settled in more urban environments where different sets of conditions applied, including population densities and disease problems.) Indeed, Scots were invariably leading figures in the exploitation of the animal resource throughout the British Empire. Rural Scotland, after all, was a hunting society. All landowners inevitably hunted and the stag and grouse shoots of Scotland employed large numbers as gamekeepers, stalkers, and angling ghillies. The Revd James Stewart, the son of a farmer in Perthshire, who became one of the most powerful—and autocratic— missionaries of the Eastern Cape frontier, saw the combination of the Bible and the gun as crucial to the keys to both salvation and the understanding and dominance of the environment that was central to missionaries' ambitions.[54]

Explorers, Settlers, and the Environment

It was not only missionaries who hunted, of course. Scots were heavily involved in the fur trades of North America, sometimes hunting themselves, but more often working as 'factors' buying pelts from indigenous and Métis (mixed race) hunters. Many of the factors employed by the Hudson's Bay Company were recruited in Orkney (where the Hudson's Bay Company ships always called to replenish water supplies on their route from London

---

[54] James Wells, *Stewart of Lovedale: The Life of James Stewart DD, MD* (London, 1909), 6.

to the North Atlantic crossing), and the bleak environment of the northern isles must have helped to prepare these migrants for the harsh rigours of the Canadian north. In more salubrious climes, wherever British, including Scottish, settlers went in the empire, at least to rural areas, they were always relieved that they had escaped the tight social and legal controls on access to game that operated in Britain.[55] This seemed to represent one of the freedoms of the colonial lifestyle. Moreover, some of the most notable hunter-explorers in Africa were Scots, including Roualeyn Gordon Cumming, Mungo Murray, and Denis Lyell, among others.[56] In these activities, as in others, Scots tended to publish accounts of their exploits, which perhaps helped to give them a higher profile. Moreover, they soon became caught up in conservation ideas at the end of the nineteenth, and beginning of the twentieth centuries. The classic example of this is James Stevenson-Hamilton, who came from a minor landed family in Lanarkshire. As a military man he was a noted hunter who transformed himself into one of the pioneers of the conservation movement, founding the Sabi reserve, later the Kruger National Park, in what was then the Transvaal in South Africa.[57]

John Muir, from Dunbar had, of course, preceded Stevenson-Hamilton as the iconic conservationist in the United States, securing a statutory foundation for the celebrated national parks of California in 1899. He became an example to many others. In New Zealand three Scots migrants, John McKenzie, James Glenny Wilson, and Thomas Noble Mackenzie, were highly active in environmental matters, spanning pastoralism, land redistribution, conservation, and forestry.[58] Scots were not necessarily the most prominent people in environmental matters in New Zealand, though they have always been significant in the record.[59] But in the territories of

---

[55] Among many references to such freedoms, see James Hunter, *Scottish Exodus: Travels among a Worldwide Clan* (Edinburgh, 2007), 77 and Brooking, 'Sharing out the Haggis', 61.

[56] John M. MacKenzie, *The Empire of Nature: Hunting, Conservation and British Imperialism* (Manchester, 1988).

[57] Jane Carruthers, *The Kruger National Park: A Social and Political History* (Pietermaritzburg, 1995), and eadem, *Wildlife and Warfare: The Life of James Stevenson-Hamilton* (Pietermaritzburg, 2001).

[58] Tom Brooking, *Lands for the People: The Highland Clearances and the Colonisation of New Zealand: A Biography of John McKenzie* (Dunedin, 1996); idem, 'Wilson, James Glenny, 1849–1929', *DNZB*, updated June 2007; idem, 'Mackenzie, Thomas Noble, 1853–1930', *DNZB*, updated June 2007.

[59] Tom Brooking, '"Green Scots and Golden Irish": The Environmental Impact of Scottish and Irish Settlers in New Zealand—Some Preliminary Ruminations', *JISS* 3.1 (2009), 41–60.

settlement in general, the prominence of Scots in, for example, pastoralism seems unanswerable, for they were important in this sector in New Zealand, Canada, Australia, and elsewhere. When 'squatters' moved from New South Wales westwards into what became Victoria, notably the region west of Port Phillip (Melbourne), it has been established that some 40 per cent of those seeking new opportunities there were Scots.[60] Elsewhere, it is known that a group of men from Perthshire made a considerable fortune draining the land on the western edge of Christchurch in Canterbury, New Zealand. They had, apparently, derived their experience from working for an improving landlord who had drained land near Muthill in their home county.[61] In such ways were skills profitably transferred to colonial settings. Indeed, Scots were often in the vanguard of adapting new graduate expertise to colonial environments. An example is the 'special relationship' between Aberdeen University and Ceylon. It has been suggested that between 1840 and 1875, up to one-half of the white plantation managers on the island came from Scotland[62] and, as the relevant studies developed later in the century, many of their successors came to have qualifications in agriculture and chemistry—useful in soil science—while many university entrants from Ceylon, both white and indigenous, came to specialize in medicine and botany.[63]

Moreover, the reputation of Scots in the nineteenth century was that they were particularly capable of coping with marginal lands. This reputation was in some respects promoted by themselves, but neutral observers also considered them to be ideal colonists on frontiers and on low-value lands. In the 1820 settlement on the Eastern Cape, Scots were regarded as ideal settlers. They constituted only about 10 per cent of the total settlement, but the Governor sent them to the north and west of the territory to be settled (a classic 'planting' the frontier project, designed as a buffer against the Nguni peoples of the region). It was as though he was mirroring the ethnic geography of Britain itself. Thomas Pringle, settler, journalist, educator, and poet, protégé of Sir Walter Scott, saw the Scots as ideal for this purpose,

---

[60] Lindsay Proudfoot and Dianne Hall, 'Imagining the Frontier: Environment, Memory and Settlement—Narratives from Victoria (Australia), 1850–1890', *JISS* 3.1 (2009), 19–39, particularly 21.

[61] McAloon, 'Scots in the Colonial Economy', 92.

[62] Ranald C. Michie, 'Aberdeen and Ceylon: Economic Links in the Nineteenth Century', *Northern Scotland*, 4 (1981), 69, 82.

[63] Hargreaves, *Academe and Empire*, 67–73.

familiar as they were with hills and poor land.[64] The Scots were also seen as having an affinity with the Boers, both learning environmental lessons and securing appropriate seeds from them.[65] In 1823 an anonymous letter-writer to the *Morning Chronicle* in London suggested that only Scots, and especially Highlanders, should be sent to the frontier, since they were best equipped for such regions.[66] Pringle and his party were from the Borders, but that letter-writer was perpetuating the usual Highland myth. Moreover, testimony recorded in the MacLeod clan history has offered additional examples of shepherds who claimed that only they could cope with Australian bush or the high Mackenzie country of the South Island of New Zealand, often surviving after the allegedly soft English had left.[67] If nothing else, such testimony offers evidence of a grand conceit which may well have had some basis in truth. It also encapsulates records of hardship and perhaps of a willingness to accept second best. But it must be remembered that not all Scots rural settlers came from disadvantaged regions of the Highlands or Islands: many came from the richer agricultural land of the Lothians, Strathmore, and Aberdeenshire and were displaced because of farm rationalization, land improvement, and new agricultural technologies. They were not the victims of marginality, but of the opportunities on good land to develop new labour-saving techniques.

What can be said is that wherever Scots came from, and wherever they settled—in colonies with highly diverse environments, in rural, urban, or small-town settings—they seem to have maintained a strong attachment to places of origin.[68] Many exile letters reveal this nostalgia for the Scottish environments they had left. This may well be true of all migrants, but many literate Scots seem to have been determined to maintain these connections. They also achieved this through using familiar names for homes, farms, streets, towns wherever they went. Again there is nothing unique in this, but

---

[64] Thomas Pringle, *Some Account of the Present State of the English Settlers in Albany, South Africa* (London, 1824), and idem, *African Sketches* (London, 1834).

[65] William Beinart, *The Rise of Conservation in South Africa: Settlers, Livestock and the Environment 1770–1950* (Oxford, 2003), 89.

[66] Letter of J.H.R. to the *Morning Chronicle*, 12 July 1823, quoted in Pringle, *Some Account of the Present State of the English Settlers*, 108.

[67] Hunter, *Scottish Exodus*, 276–7.

[68] Examples can be found in Angela McCarthy (ed.), *A Global Clan: Scottish Migrant Networks and Identities since the Eighteenth Century* (London, 2006) and eadem, *Personal Narratives of Irish and Scottish Migration, 1921–65: 'For spirit and adventure'* (Manchester, 2007).

Scots naming, a form of taming and reframing a new landscape, seems extraordinary prevalent throughout the territories of settlement. Thus, the identities of emigrant and sojourning Scots overseas were invariably rooted in forms of environmental nostalgia.[69] Scotland was always characterized as a land of hills, straths, burns, and rivers. It was a land with a distinctive natural history, with sports like stalking, shooting, and angling prominently associated with it. It also had urban landscapes and built environments which Scots sometimes sought to recreate in the colonies.[70] But, as Proudfoot and Hall have shown, wealthy colonial landowners could build in sub-Scottish baronial or in classic colonial styles (often more suited to the climate) as their taste took them.[71] Migrants also founded many Scottish societies (often invoking homeland landscapes) and they instituted Highland games, sports which have a strongly environmental element.[72] Moreover, they constantly invoked images of home by claiming similarities in landscape (sometimes to our eyes unlikely) wherever they went.[73]

If these Scots affinities often seem paradoxical, we can also note a very mixed picture in respect of the Scots' relationship with indigenous peoples. Scots were just as brutal, and sometimes more so, in the violent conditions of colonial frontiers. They enthusiastically participated in violent and destructive colonial campaigns in North America, South Africa, Australia, and New Zealand. They were notorious slave holders in the American South and in the Caribbean. If they played a role in the development of conservationist ideas, they can also be identified as classic settler destroyers of the environment. Trees not only stand in the way of agriculture, but are also eminently exploitable for building and for engineering works like railway construction. Many settlers, though by no means all, hated trees if they stood in the way of

---

[69] MacKenzie, 'Scotland and Empire: Ethnicity, Environment, Identity'.

[70] A number of examples have been identified by Marjory Harper, *Adventurers and Exiles: The Great Scottish Exodus* (London, 2003), 372 and Tom Brooking in 'Weaving the Tartan into the Flax', in McCarthy (ed.), *A Global Clan*, 194 and in 'Sharing out the Haggis', in Brooking and Coleman (eds), *Heather and the Fern*, 57.

[71] Proudfoot and Hall, 'Imagining the Frontier', 34–8.

[72] Tanja Bueltmann, Andrew Hinson, and Graeme Morton (eds), *Ties of Bluid, Kin and Countrie: Scottish Associational Culture in the Diaspora* (Guelph, 2009).

[73] Just as a few examples, Lady Aberdeen considered parts of Canada to be like Scotland; Anthony Trollope said the same of New Zealand; missionaries likewise in Nyasaland/Malawi; as did John Buchan of Natal. James Hunter discovered the same phenomenon when researching his history of migrants of the Clan MacLeod, *Scottish Exodus*, 33.

settlement.[74] They therefore subjected the landscape to considerable vio-lence and, in doing so, destroyed environments which indigenous peoples had previously lived in and exploited. Yet Scots also developed a reputation for forming close relationships with local peoples, learning from them, and exploiting their environmental knowledge.

There are a number of examples of such alleged sympathies. The Orcadi-an John Rae survived the Canadian Arctic much better than well-financed naval expeditions because he used Inuit techniques and associated with them in the quest for survival. Scots fur traders acknowledged 'country wives' and were respectful of First Nations peoples, not least because of their successful control of the environment. Scots in New Zealand were prepared to acquire environmental knowledge and agricultural techniques from the Maori.[75] Some Scots there were good linguists and became notable ethno-graphical collectors.[76] They were also active in such activities in Asia and elsewhere. Scots missionaries at the Cape developed connections with the frontier Nguni, sometimes sympathizing with their predicament in facing settler violence.[77] Nevertheless, they were inevitably caught up in frontier warfare. David Livingstone offers a good deal of evidence of sympathetic understanding with Africans in his efforts to study the environments (not always successfully) of southern and Central Africa.[78]

The final important question is 'Does any of this matter?' Scots were 'boosters' of themselves as well as of towns and lands. They were invariably literate, and many published books and articles about their exploits. Some, at least, of the myths were self-generated. But there is evidence that contem-poraries of different ethnicities did regard them as bringing particular skills, capacities, and interests to the environments of colonial territories, however different those might be. Moreover, there is little doubt that Scots were major contributors to the 'environmental professions', both on land and at sea, even if precise proportionate figures are not always easy to come by. They brought some distinctive characteristics to the activities of missionaries and of settlers and they left their mark in naming places and landscapes, in the

[74] Brian S. Osborn, 'The Iconography of Nationhood in Canadian Art', in Denis Cosgrove and Stephen Daniel (eds), *The Iconography of Landscape* (Cambridge, 1988), 165; Douglas Davies, 'The Evocative Symbolism of Trees', ibid. 32–42.

[75] Brooking, '"Green Scots and Golden Irish"', 52.

[76] MacKenzie, *Museums and Empire*, ch. 8.

[77] MacKenzie with Dalziel, *Scots in South Africa*, 107 and 116–17.

[78] Livingstone, *Missionary Travels and Researches*, passim.

infrastructures of imperial territories, and the built environment of cities and towns.[79] What these relationships do suggest is that the peoples of the British and Hibernian Isles do have to be disaggregated into the 'four nations', Irish, English, Scottish, and Welsh, in order to understand fully the various educational attainments, skills, and interests, some of them lying deep in longer-standing cultural traditions, that were brought to bear on the British Empire. Finally, the Scots' medical, scientific, and environmental record associated with empire tends to confirm Craig's view that the notion that Scotland experienced a long decline in the nineteenth and twentieth centuries from the glories of the Enlightenment has been overdrawn.[80]

Select Bibliography

William Beinart, *The Rise of Conservation in South Africa: Settlers, Livestock and the Environment* (Oxford, 2003).

Cairns Craig, *Intending Scotland: Explorations in Scottish Culture since the Enlightenment* (Edinburgh, 2009).

Richard Drayton, *Nature's Government: Science, Imperial Britain and the 'Improvement' of the World* (New Haven, 2000).

Richard H. Grove, *Green Imperialism: Colonial Expansion, Tropical Island Edens and the Origins of Environmentalism 1600–1860* (Cambridge, 1995).

——'Scottish Missionaries, Evangelical Discourses and the Origins of Conservation Thinking in Southern Africa, 1820–1900', *Journal of Southern African Studies*, 15 (1989), 163–87.

Ann Lindsay, *Seeds of Blood and Beauty: Scottish Plant Explorers* (Edinburgh, 2008).

John M. MacKenzie, *Empires of Nature and the Nature of Empires: Imperialism, Scotland and the Environment* (East Linton, 1997).

——*Museums and Empire: Natural History, Human Cultures and Colonial Identities* (Manchester, 2009).

——'Scotland and Imperial Frontiers', *Journal of Irish and Scottish Studies*, 3.1 (2009), 1–17.

——'Scotland and Empire: Ethnicity, Environment and Identity', *Northern Scotland*, NS 1 (2010), 12–29.

Charles W. J. Withers, *Geography, Science and National Identity: Scotland since 1520* (Cambridge, 2001).

---

[79] In the twentieth century, Patrick Geddes became the most celebrated of imperial town planners. He claimed to have developed his interests in the setting of town and region, their social contexts, and the relationship of gardens to towns from his upbringing in Perth, Scotland. Helen Meller, *Patrick Geddes: Social Evolutionist and Town Planner* (London, 1990), 5 and 24–5.

[80] Craig, *Intending Scotland*.

7

Soldiers of Empire, 1750–1914

T. M. Devine

The Martial Highlands

Some battles can change the course of human history. Among these, the defeat of Napoleonic France at Waterloo in 1815 must stand as an epoch-making event. Seven times between 1689 and 1815 Britain and France had fought each other in successive wars for global dominance. The allied victory at Waterloo then settled the conflict for the rest of the nineteenth century. Britain became Europe's most powerful state and the foundations for further massive territorial expansion of its empire across the world were securely laid.

The collapse of France inevitably brought about in its train nationwide celebrations. A year after Waterloo, Scotland's capital welcomed back one of the Scottish regiments which had fought at the decisive battle. In March 1816, the 42nd regiment, to become known as the Black Watch, entered Edinburgh to joyful acclaim from the citizenry. As they marched towards the city, the *Caledonian Mercury* reported that 'nothing could exceed the enthusiasm with which these gallant veterans were welcomed in every town and village through which their route lay'. In Edinburgh itself there were unprecedented scenes:

House tops and windows were also crowded with spectators, and as they passed along the streets, amidst the ringing of bells, acclamations of thousands, their red and white plumes, tattered colours and glittering bayonets, were all that could be seen of these heroes, except by the few who were fortunate in obtaining elevated situations. The scene, viewed from the windows and house tops, was the most extraordinary ever witnessed in this city. The crowds were wedged together across the whole breadth of the street, and extended in length as far as the eye could reach; and this motley throng appeared to move like a solid body slowly along till the gallant Highlanders were safely lodged in the Castle.[1]

---

[1] *Caledonian Mercury*, 21 March 1816.

Public acknowledgement and appreciation for the troops of a victorious army were nothing new. What was remarkable about this triumphant return of the Black Watch was the acclaim given to a Highland regiment, and this a mere two generations after the failure of the '45 rising. The praise for the Gael as hero-warrior representing the ancient martial traditions of the Scottish nation was now unambiguous. A poem published to celebrate the event was entitled 'Caledonia's Welcome to the Gallant 42nd'. In its first stanza, the author proclaimed: 'All hail to the land of the moor and the mountain' from where had come the warriors who had shattered the myth of Napoleonic invincibility. Not only were the Highlanders represented as true and brave Scots but they were also worthy of high praise from 'Britons who will sing "Gallant heroes for ever"'.[2] Elsewhere in the Scottish press, other Highland regiments, such as the 93rd, 92nd, and 79th, attracted glowing tributes from all quarters.[3] The previous year, the kilted battalions had taken pride of place in the allied march of triumph into Paris.

The age-old Lowland perception of Gaeldom as a benighted region of primitives and savages which had spawned a succession of rebellions against the state between 1689 and 1746 had been transformed. Now the Highlands were eulogized as a land of heroes. In the famous song of the time 'The Garb of Old Gaul', the courage of the Highland soldier was incorporated into a Scottish tradition of valour stretching back through the ages. It was deeply significant in this respect that Walter Scott's first novel and run-away best-seller, *Waverley*, was published in 1814, the year before Waterloo. The book is regarded as a landmark text in the military rehabilitation of the Highlanders and their metamorphosis from faithless rebels into imperial warriors.[4] Scott portrayed their lack of achievement in the '45 as the result of misplaced loyalty to a romantic, though hopeless cause, not because of any intrinsic barbarity or savagery. In truth, this capacity for loyal allegiance, coupled with the legendary fighting abilities of the clans, could be of enormous value if employed in the service of the British state. Scott was, however, writing at the end of an earlier process of rehabilitation which had been ongoing during the wars for empire of the second half of the eighteenth century.

---

[2] Ibid.

[3] Ibid., 29 June 1815; 23 March 1816; *Glasgow Herald*, 30 June 1815; 10 July 1815; 28 July 1815; 13 November 1815.

[4] Robert Clyde, *From Rebel to Hero: The Image of the Highlander 1745–1830* (East Linton, 1995), 186.

In the tradition of the Highland regiments of the British Army, 1740 is a seminal date. In that year, the six Independent Companies created by General Wade to police or 'watch' the disaffected Jacobite areas of the Highlands were embodied as the 43rd of Foot. The new regiment then became the 42nd of Foot, the 'Gallant Forty-Twa', in 1749, but became even more celebrated in fame, song, and story as the Black Watch, 'Am Freiceadan Dubh', the name given because of its characteristic dark colours of tartan which set these Highland troops apart from the 'Saighdearan Dearg', the 'Red Soldiers', of the rest of the regular army. The early years of service were not auspicious. In March, 1743 the regiment was sent to England, the intention being to transport it from there to Flanders. Discontent spread among the rank and file at being forced to leave the Highlands. This soon changed to anger and alienation when the rumour spread that they were to be shipped to the dreaded West Indies, known as the graveyard of the ordinary soldier. One-hundred-and-twenty men mutinied and deserted. Three were condemned to death and executed. The rest were then dispersed among other regiments, many of them ending up in the Caribbean and Georgia. In time, however, the reorganized Black Watch served with great distinction in the War of the Austrian Succession, the Seven Years War, and subsequent imperial conflicts. In 1758 it was decided to honour the corps with the title 'Royal Highland Regiment' and to raise a second battalion.

But Highland soldiers were no strangers to imperial warfare before 1740. By 1745 the Scots Brigade in Holland had risen to over 5,000 men, and it was common for cadres there to move back and forth between the Low Countries and service in the British Army. Highland officers served in the expedition led in 1740 to the West Indies under the command of Lord Charles Cathcart. From the 1720s, too, East India Company (EIC) military posts were being offered through the influence of the EIC Director and Scottish financier John Drummond of Quarrell to Jacobite families in Perthshire and Ross-shire to counter disaffection. Long before the concept of the 'Highland regiments', decked out in tartans and kilt, became popular, the clan gentry were sending their sons into Lowland and English regiments. Even the first systematic use of Highland troops on the colonial frontier pre-dated by a few years the foundation of the Black Watch. Clansmen from the central and northern Highlands were recruited to Georgia by Scottish imperial officials in the 1730s, where they formed a defensive barrier against the incursion of Spanish forces on the bitterly contested frontier territories.[5]

[5] W. C. Cooper, *The Story of Georgia* (New York, 1938), i. 1.

But boom time for the Highland regiments as such only really started after the defeat of the '45 rebellion and, in particular, during the Seven Years War, the American War of Independence, and, most crucially of all, during the long years of conflict with France after 1793. Six regiments of the line were mobilized between 1753 and 1783, including Fraser's and Montgomery's regiments. A further ten were recruited during the American War. Around 12,000 men were involved during the Seven Years War, almost the same size as the Highland army of the biggest Jacobite uprising in 1715 and more than twice the level of the forces of Prince Charles Edward Stuart in the '45. It was indeed a great irony that, after the death of clanship, Gaeldom became even more militarized than in the recent past. By the French Revolutionary and Napoleonic Wars the number of recruits was unprecedented. The most recent careful estimate suggests totals ranging from 37,000 to 48,000 men in regular, fencible, and volunteer units. This is quite an extraordinary figure, given that the population of the Highlands was around 250,000 to 300,000 during the second half of the eighteenth century.[6] The region had now become the most intensely recruited region of the United Kingdom. Scotland had the highest density of those famous retired veterans, the Chelsea Pensioners, within the British islands, and the Highland counties had the largest proportion of all.[7]

In some areas, recruitment reached unparalleled levels. Between the years 1793 and 1805, 3,680 men were under arms from the Skye estates of Lord Macdonald, MacLeod of MacLeod, and MacLeod of Raasay. From 1792 to 1837 the numbers included no fewer than 21 lieutenant-generals or major-generals, 48 lieutenant-colonels, 600 other officers, and 120 pipers.[8] The west coast parish of Gairloch in 1799 was nearly stripped of its menfolk. A survey for the Lord Lieutenant of Ross-shire concluded that the parish now mainly consisted of children, women, and old men, so intensive had the recruitment of young men become. One other calculation suggests that on the vast territories of the Earl of Breadalbane which straddled Argyllshire and Perthshire, as many as three farm tenancies out of every five had

---

[6] These estimates are by Andrew Mackillop. See his *'More Fruitful than the Soil'. Army, Empire and the Scottish Highlands, 1715–1815* (Edinburgh, 2000), 236.

[7] Ibid. 150.

[8] S. E. M. Carpenter, 'Patterns of Recruitment of the Highland Regiments of the British Army, 1756 to 1815' (unpublished M.Litt. thesis, University of St. Andrews, 1977), 75.

experienced some level of recruitment in the 1790s.[9] Fort George at
Ardersier, east of Inverness, the most formidable bastion fortress in Europe,
built to control the clans after Culloden, quickly developed a different
function. By the time of the American War after 1775 it had become 'the
great drill square', where the Highland levies were trained for overseas duties.[10]
Clanship had mutated into imperial service. The Gaels now pioneered a role
in the British military, which was later to be assumed by conquered peoples
of the empire with a martial tradition, such as the Ghurkas, Sikhs, and
Pathans.

Why the Highlands should supply so many soldiers for the British
Army for much of the second half of the eighteenth century is an
intriguing question. After all, Gaeldom was portrayed in the 1740s as the
very heartland of treachery, the region which had spawned the rebellion
in 1745 which came close to overthrowing the Protestant succession itself.
Loyal Whigs responded hysterically. 'Scoto-Brittanicus' depicted Highlanders as being beyond the pale of civilization. Charles Edward Stuart
had landed in the most remote and wild recesses of the kingdom 'amidst
dens of barbarous and lawless ruffians' and 'a crew of ungrateful villains,
savages and traitors'.[11] The Young Pretender was the agent of Popery,
the 'limb of Antichrist', and his clansmen 'a Hellish Band of Highland
Thieves'.[12] With enormous relief, Presbyterian Scotland celebrated the
happy deliverance at Culloden from these pernicious forces of darkness.
The *Glasgow Journal*, for instance, brought out a special large-print edition
in honour of Cumberland's comprehensive victory and also to record 'the
great rejoicings that have been known' in the city.[13] The forces of the Crown
then took a terrible revenge, unleashing a reign of terror throughout the
disaffected areas of the north and west.[14]

Yet a mere few years after Culloden, the British state started to deploy
Highlanders as a military spearhead of imperial expansion. Not only that,
but these former rebels were to be regimented in distinctive concentrated
units, permitted to wear the banned Highland dress, and encouraged to

---

[9] Mackillop, *'More Fruitful than the Soil'*, 115.

[10] Bruce Lenman, *The Jacobite Clans of the Great Glen 1650–1784* (London, 1984), 212.

[11] Quoted in W. Donaldson, *The Jacobite Song* (Aberdeen, 1988), 46.

[12] Ibid.

[13] *Glasgow Journal*, 28 April 1746.

[14] Geoffrey Plant, *Rebellion and Savagery: The Jacobite Risings of 1745 and the British Empire*
(Philadelphia, 2006).

develop their own particular *esprit de corps*. These were privileges not
afforded the Irish (who vastly outnumbered the Scottish Gaels in the service
of empire) or the Lowland battalions. In fact, the martial value of the
Highlander was already being recognized some time before the Young
Pretender landed in the Hebrides at the beginning of his ill-fated adventure.
Just before the '45, prominent Whig politicians in the Highlands, such as
Duncan Forbes of Culloden and the Duke of Argyll, had suggested raising
regiments among the Jacobite clans. Military posts in the British Army for
the clan gentry would, it was argued, help to cure disaffection. The appointment of a new prime minister, William Pitt, in 1756 signalled a more overt
commitment to 'a blue water policy', which preferred colonial expansion to
European commitments. A fresh and reliable military supply was now vital,
not least because of the outbreak of the Seven Years War with France, a
conflict which more than any other was to be fought in the colonial theatre.
The catastrophic defeat inflicted by the French and their Indian allies
on General Edward Braddock on the Monongahela River in Maryland,
with the loss of two-thirds of his command killed or wounded, concentrated
Pitt's mind. The 'Great War for Empire' was going very badly and the prime
minister was also known for his resolute opposition to the use of foreign
mercenaries. The only alternative was to expand domestic supply. By early
1757 two additional Highland battalions were sanctioned, commanded by
Simon Fraser, son of the executed Jacobite Lord Lovat, and Archibald
Montgomery, later Earl of Eglinton. By the end of the war, ten more
Highland regiments had been created. They were the first of many which
served during the long American Revolutionary and Napoleonic campaigns.
In 1766, Pitt looked back on his policy in a famous speech:

I sought for merit wherever it was to be found; it is my boast that I was the first
minister who looked for it and found it in the mountains of the north. I called it
forth and drew into your service a hardy and intrepid race of men, who, when left
by your jealousy, became a prey to the artifice of your enemies, and had gone nigh
to have overturned the state in the war before the last. These men in the last war
were brought to combat on your side; they served with fidelity, as they fought
with valour and conquered for you in every part of the world.[15]

A sea-change had taken place in government attitudes. In part, this was
because the destruction of the Jacobite threat was now recognized to be

---

[15] Quoted in Carpenter, 'Patterns of Recruitment', 33.

so complete. The Highlands, unlike Ireland, were no longer an internal menace, and mass recruitment to the Crown forces could therefore proceed. At the same time, however, all of the ingrained fear of disaffection took time to dissipate. The solution was not to allow Highland troops to linger long in Scotland after training but to have them dispatched overseas with all speed. Thus it was that the Highlanders became perforce the crack troops of imperial warfare, with wide experience in North America, the West Indies, and India, encountering long and arduous tours of duty lasting for several years. In the view of Lord Barrington, they should even be enlisted for life to prevent battle-hardened veterans causing trouble at home.[16] The perception of the '45 was also relevant. The Highlanders first impressed themselves on the British state as warriors, and formidable ones at that. The terrifying charge and slashing broadswords which routed Cope's regulars at Prestonpans were not easily forgotten. Even in the carnage of Culloden, the following year, the rebel army had performed with remarkable courage and an almost suicidal tenacity.

Over time the myth hardened and developed. It was argued that the Jacobite soldiers had followed the wrong cause but they had done so only at the behest of their chiefs. Throughout they had displayed not only heroism in battle but undying loyalty. In such best-selling publications as *Young Juba or the History of the Young Chevalier* and *Ascanius or the Young Adventurer* attention was focused on the story of the 'Prince and the Heather', when the Young Pretender was never betrayed by his followers, despite the high price on his head. The Crown assumed that all these virtues were founded on the ethic of clanship, the martial society which had long disappeared from the rest of Britain. For this reason, the government wished to keep Highlanders together in 'Highland regiments' under their 'natural' leaders. Fraser's Highlanders (the 71st of Foot) had no fewer than six chiefs of clans among its officers, as well as many clan gentry. Ironically, while the state was bent on destroying clanship as a threat to the state, it was also at the same time committed to reinforcing clan allegiances through regimental recruitment. The intriguing feature was that the clan ethos was already dying rapidly by the 1750s, through a cycle of inevitable decline, which was soon to be accelerated in the later eighteenth century by commercialization of estates and clearance of people. But the state hardly doubted that the Highlander

---

[16] Lenman, *Jacobite Clans*, 190.

was nonetheless a natural warrior, not least because landowners seeking to establish family regiments constantly milked the glamorous image of clanship in order to gain a favourable response from their political paymasters.

And so, the foundation had been laid for a spectacular expansion of Highland recruitment between 1775 and 1783 and, then, on an even more colossal scale, in the years 1793 to 1815. The higher echelons of the British military were increasingly convinced by German military concepts which stressed that the people of mountainous areas were especially suited to the martial life. David Stewart of Garth's *Sketches of the Character, Manners and Present State of the Highlands of Scotland, with Details of the Military Service of the Highland Regiments*, first published in 1822, was the most influential text on the Highland soldier of the period. Stewart contended that 'nature' had honed the qualities of the perfect warrior:

Nursed in poverty he acquired a hardihood which enabled him to sustain severe privations. As the simplicity of his life gave vigour to his body, so it fortified his mind. Possessing a frame and constitution thus hardened he was taught to consider courage as the most honourable virtue, cowardice the most disgraceful failing.[17]

Enlightenment thought further fortified the legend. The 'stage' theory of the development of human civilization, propounded by such Scottish intellectuals as Adam Ferguson and John Miller, fitted perfectly with the stereotype of the Highlander as a soldier. The region was seen to be still located in the feudal period, where militarism was a way of life. Ferguson, for instance, argued that the Gaels were not interested in the 'commercial arts', but were rather by their very nature disposed to making war.[18] The parallel notion soon also became popular that the Highlander could be easily spared from ordinary manual labour for military activity because the regional economy was so underdeveloped compared to other more advanced areas of the British Isles.[19]

There can be little doubt that in the early years of formation the Highland battalions had a strong sense of identity based on their distinctive dress, language, common heritage, and culture and often on the same name. Imperial war was a godsend for the *Daoine-Uaisle*, the clan gentries, whose status on many Highland estates was being steadily undermined by rising rentals and the breaking up of holdings to create crofting townships. The army became an

---

[17] (new edn Inverness, 1885), 288.

[18] Mackillop, '*More Fruitful than the Soil*', 216–17.

[19] Clyde, *From Rebel to Hero*, 161.

escape route for many members of this class from the irresistible forces of agrarian modernization. In this period, they virtually became a professional military class of full-pay and half-pay officers who only returned to farming in the years between wars. Their traditional leadership role and influence on the localities where their regiments recruited must have been a factor of significance in enhancing *esprit de corps*. Indeed, the bond between the native Highlander and his officer does seem to have been much closer than the relationship between English soldiers and their superiors.[20]

Yet any intimate connection between the clans and the regiments was at best superficial. This was hardly surprising since recruitment boomed at the very time when the Highlands were being transformed from tribalism to capitalism. The mania for raising family regiments fits well into the prevailing context of rampant commercialism. Landowners were military entrepreneurs, rather than patriarchal chieftains. They harvested the population of their estates for the army to make money, in the same way as they established sheep walks, cattle ranches, and kelp shores. But such profiteering had to be done behind the façade of clan loyalties and martial enthusiasms because it was these very attributes which gave the Highlands a competitive brand in the military labour market. Even sophisticated and experienced politicians like Henry Dundas were taken in. During the Napoleonic Wars he exuded praise for the clansmen and their 'chiefs', enthusiastically approved of the great scheme to embody even more of them in 1797, and applauded the Highland warriors for their hostility to the pernicious 'levelling and dangerous principles' of the urban radicals of the time.[21]

Successful recruitment could provide many benefits for the Highland elites. Raising a regiment furnished commissions for a magnate's own kinsmen and associates, but also conferred influence and patronage in the neighbourhood among other impoverished minor gentry who desperately sought officerships and the secure incomes and pensions which came with them. Local power and standing were increased, and military service also consolidated connections with government. The rewards could be substantial. Sir James Grant, whose estates were heavily encumbered, achieved a sinecure worth £3,000 a year and the lord lieutenancy of Inverness in 1794. Mackenzie of Seaforth who, like most Highland landowners, had financial difficulties, did even better.

---

[20] Stephen Brumwell, *Redcoats: The British Soldier and War in the Americas 1755–1763* (Cambridge, 2002), 281–2.

[21] J. E. Cookson, *The British Armed Nation 1793–1815* (Oxford, 1997), 137–8.

In quick succession he became Lord Lieutenant of Ross in 1794, Lord Seaforth in the English peerage in the same year, and, in 1800, Governor of Barbados. But there were also more direct and equally lucrative benefits to recruitment. Allocating lands to soldiers could provide an estate with more regular rentals than were likely from the small tenantry, whose payments were notoriously volatile because of harvest failures and market fluctuations. Soldiers had a secure income, not only when on active service but also at a lower level, through their small pensions when they retired. There is evidence that several proprietors showed a clear preference for such 'military' tenants as a result of this advantage.[22]

There was also on the estates an assumed expectation that men were obliged to serve. When this was in doubt, systematic coercion was employed. Estate records teem with examples. Alexander Macdonnel of Glengarry ordered his agent to 'warn out' a list of small tenants from his Knoydart property, they 'having refused to serve me'. Similarly, MacLean of Lochbuie on the island of Mull threatened to remove seventy-one tenants, cottars, and their families in 1795 because they had not provided sons for service. On several estates, the tradition of 'land for sons' was widespread. In the Lord Macdonald papers relating to his extensive lands in Skye, a document is headed 'List of Tenants who have been promised Lands and an exchange of lands for their sons'.[23] These contracts were often very specific, indicating the length of leases and the tenurial arrangements as a result of sons traded for land. In the long run, however, they generated angry controversy. Many recruits did not return home, but lay buried in foreign graves partly through death in battle or, more likely, from disease. To the families, therefore, their holdings had often been acquired quite literally through the blood of their kinfolk. When these obligations were ended, for whatever cause, the people felt a sense of gross breach of trust. Recruitment was of immense profit to the landed classes of the Highlands. But its consequences often brought down great opprobrium on their hapless successors and gave a special emotional edge to the contentious saga of the Highland Clearances.[24]

---

[22] Ibid. 132–3.

[23] Eric Richards, *A History of the Highland Clearances: Agrarian Change and the Evictions, 1746–1886* (London, 1982), 152–3.

[24] T. M. Devine, 'Social Responses to Agrarian Improvement: The Highland and Lowland Clearances in Scotland', in R. A. Houston and I. D. Whyte (eds), *Scottish Society, 1500–1800* (Cambridge, 1989), 160–1.

Origins of Celebrity

The storming of Quebec, in 1759, the defeat of Napoleon's army in Egypt in 1801 (which shattered the myth of French invincibility on land), and the signal achievements in the Peninsular War, at Quatre Bras, and, finally, at Waterloo, all combined to celebrate the legend of the valorous Highlander. But behind the façade of glorious triumph all was not as it seemed. Clearance and emigration in the north of Scotland made recruitment to the regiments increasingly more challenging. As early as the 1770s, some struggled to make up numbers and by the end of the eighteenth century 'the well had run dry'.[25] When the 79th or Cameron Highlanders were reconstituted in 1798, after their rank and file was decimated by disease, the battalion comprised more non-Scots than Scots.[26] Even the most prestigious formations were forced to extend the geographical range of their recruitment. It was reckoned that at least a third of the Black Watch who fought at Waterloo were drawn from the Scottish Lowlands, the Borders, and even England.[27] The spectacular expansion of the levies drawn mainly from the indigenous Gaelic population had come to an end as early as 1800. The manpower resources of the Highlands were virtually exhausted by over-recruitment, death in battle, discharges, and natural attrition.

In addition, the popular belief that the Gael was a natural warrior was in large part mythical. As has been already noted, there is abundant evidence of the systematic use of coercion of the tenantry to make up numbers in the family regiments. When a battalion of the 78th Seaforth Highlanders was raised, a kinsman of its colonel, Sir George Mackenzie, concluded in his *General View of the Agriculture of the Counties of Ross and Cromarty* (1813) that the young recruits had joined in order to save their parents being turned out of their farms.[28] Hostility to the hazards of army life, low pay (no more than that of a casual labourer), and many years spent far from home was as common in some parts of the Highlands as among the population in general.

---

[25] Hew Strachan, 'Scotland's Military Identity', *Scottish Historical Review*, 85.2: 220 (October 2006), 324.

[26] Bruce Lenman, *The Jacobite Clans of the Great Glen 1650–1784* (Aberdeen, 1995), 207, 211–16.

[27] Carpenter, 'Patterns of Recruitment', 103–4.

[28] Sir George S. Mackenzie, *General View of the Agriculture of the Counties of Ross and Cromarty* (London, 1813), 298.

Thus, in the parish of Blair Atholl, in Perthshire, in the 1790s it was said that '... many had learned to despise a soldier's pay and hate a life of servitude'.[29] Even in poorer counties, such as Ross-shire, one observer argued that by 1813 'it was notorious that the inhabitants have now a strong aversion to a military life'.[30]

It seemed then that at the very pinnacle of their glory the future of the Highland regiments was in serious doubt. In 1809 the problems of recruitment became so acute that the kilt was abandoned in five regiments, leaving only a further five whose social composition merited the wearing of the famous Highland dress. These were the only survivors by 1815 from the total of fifty-nine regular and fencible units which had been raised between 1740 and 1800.[31] Scotland as a whole had contributed disproportionately to the armies which fought Napoleon, but in subsequent decades recruiting fell dramatically. In 1830, when Scots had 10 per cent of the UK population, they made up 13 per cent of the army. By 1870 this had fallen to 8 per cent, and to 7.6 per cent in 1913.[32] In the 1850s, senior army officers continued to complain that not enough Scots, far less Gaels, could be found for the 'kilted regiments'.[33] By the end of the nineteenth century, some observers denounced them as 'cultural forgeries' since they were more likely to recruit from the poorer working classes of the towns and cities than the Highland crofts and glens of the past.[34] Not only did the British Army contract in size in the decades of peace after 1815, but the number of Highland formations declined even more dramatically. At the beginning of Victoria's reign they represented a minute part of the armed forces, with a mere five units surviving demobilization after the end of the Napoleonic Wars: the 42nd (Royal Highland Regiment. The Black Watch), the 78th (Ross-shire Buffs), the 79th (Cameron Highlanders), the 92nd (Gordon Highlanders), and the 93rd (Sutherland Highlanders).[35] Nonetheless, in

---

[29] Quoted in Leah Leneman, *Living in Atholl 1685–1785* (Edinburgh, 1986), 140.

[30] Mackenzie, *General View*, 298.

[31] A. Mackillop, 'For King, Country and Regiment? Motive and Identity within Highland Soldiering 1746–1815', in S. Murdoch and A. Mackillop (eds), *Fighting for Identity: Scottish Military Experience c.1550–1900* (Leiden, 2002), 198–200.

[32] H. J. Hanham, 'Religion and Nationality in the Mid-Victorian Society', in M. R. D. Food (ed.), *War and Society* (London, 1973), 163–6.

[33] Diana Henderson, *Highland Soldier: A Social Study of the Highland Regiments 1820–1920* (Edinburgh, 1989), 25, 38.

[34] Heather Streets, 'Identity in the Highland Regiments in the Nineteenth Century: Soldier, Region, Nation', in Murdoch and Mackillop (eds), *Fighting for Identity*, 222.

[35] Edward M. Spiers, *The Scottish Soldier and Empire, 1854–1902* (Edinburgh, 2006), 3.

the Victorian era they not only managed to maintain their traditional fame and public profile but, if anything, became even more celebrated as national icons of Scotland in the second half of the nineteenth century.

One historian noted how Highlanders were 'the most feted of all Victorian soldiers' while another refers to 'the Victorian cult of the Highlander'. The regiments, out of all proportion to their actual numbers in the British Army, attracted much the lion's share of publicity in contemporary art, advertising, the press, and reports from the front, much to the envy and jealous pride of other units, which often performed just as gallantly in action.[36] Gradually, indeed, Scottish military activity in general became 'Highlandized'. The climax of this process came in 1881, when Scottish Lowland regiments were outfitted with Highland doublets and tartan trews, although some units had already been maintaining pipers in Highland dress for some decades before that.[37] The cult even spread overseas to the Scottish diaspora. Local, part-time volunteer defence forces in Canada, Australia, New Zealand, and South Africa from the 1860s included 'Scottish regiments', clad in kilt, tartan, and uniforms modelled on those of their illustrious parents. In at least one instance, that of the Queensland Scottish in the 1880s, the Australian unit wore uniforms recycled from those cast off by the Gordon Highlanders at home.[38] During the Great War, these formations spawned countless additional battalions, each with a Highland designation. Hardly surprisingly, therefore, to this day, all countries of the Commonwealth boast their own military pipe bands.

Why then, in the words of one authority, did Scottish Highland regiments become 'without question the most popular and celebrated units in the British army' in the course of the nineteenth century?[39] Some argue it came about because of royal patronage and, in particular, was a reflection of the renowned Scotophilia of Queen Victoria. The Highland enthusiasm of the monarchy had in fact begun in the later eighteenth century under her royal ancestors, and was celebrated with much pageantry in the 'plaided panorama' of George IV's famous visit to Edinburgh, not least because of

---

[36] Heather Streets, *Martial Races: The Military, Race and Masculinity in British Imperial Culture 1857–1914* (Manchester, 2004), 180; John M. MacKenzie (ed.), *Popular Imperialism and the Military 1850–1950* (Manchester, 1992), p. vii.

[37] Stuart Allan and Allan Carswell, *The Thin Red Line: War, Empire and Visions of Scotland* (Edinburgh, n.d.), 30.

[38] Ibid.

[39] Streets, 'Identity in the Highland Regiments', 213.

Major-General David Stewart of Garth's (formerly of the Black Watch) influence on the ceremonial costume during that series of events.[40] But Victoria's royal impact was even greater. From her first visit to the Highlands in 1842 she developed a long love affair with the region and its people. As part of this, the Queen took a special interest in 'her' Highland regiments. She decorated Scottish soldiers at Balmoral and, in 1873, bestowed a royal title on the 79th (which thereafter became known as the 79th Queen's Own Cameron Highlanders). She regularly presented regimental colours to other kilted battalions during her annual visits to her Scottish castle.[41] The prestige and status which followed such royal approval doubtless enhanced regimental profiles. But this alone does not explain their remarkable celebrity and social standing. The lens needs also to be widened considerably to take into account the general changes which affected soldiering in Victorian society and then to offer an explanation why Highland soldiers in particular were able to gain from this transformation.

Public esteem for the army and its role in colonial warfare rose dramatically in the Victorian era and especially after c.1870. 'The rapacious and licentious' soldiery came to have a wholly different image in British popular culture.[42] The Crimean War was a key turning point in this process, as it generated unparalleled public sympathy for the hardships suffered before Sebastopol and chronicled in emotive detail in the press, especially in the famous reports in *The Times* by William Howard Russell.[43] Soldiers came to be seen as victims who were badly led by incompetent commanders. The patient fatalism of the men was also depicted as proof of their 'high feelings' and even 'their piety and religion'.[44] The fact that a soldier might also be a good Christian had enormous appeal for the respectable church-going middle classes. This response helped to lay the foundations for the growth of Christian militarism, which in due course gave rise to the Salvation Army, the Boys' Brigade, and other organizations with a quasi-paramilitary identity.

The Indian Rising (Mutiny) of 1857 further confirmed this favourable image. The notorious massacre of British women and children at Kanpur on

[40] John Prebble, *The King's Jaunt* (London, 1988).

[41] Richard J. Finlay, 'Queen Victoria and the Cult of Scottish Monarchy', in Edward J. Cowan and Richard J. Finlay (eds), *Scottish History: The Flower of the Past* (Edinburgh, 2002), 209–24.

[42] John M. MacKenzie, 'Introduction', in idem (ed.), *Popular Imperialism and the Military*, 1.

[43] Olive Anderson, 'The Growth of Christian Militarism in Mid-Victorian Britain', *English Historical Review*, 86.338 (1971), 46–50.

[44] Ibid.

15 July 1857 and the siege of the garrison at Lucknow, which threatened another human catastrophe, generated unprecedented interest at home. The alleged depravity and inhumanity of the rebellious sepoys was contrasted with the righteous vengeance and the heroic deeds of the British solders who valiantly came to the rescue of defenceless civilians.[45]

Underpinning the extraordinary public impact of the Rebellion was the revolutionary expansion of the print media, which ensured that even conflicts at the remote ends of empire were now reported at length to a mass audience at home. By 1841 the delivery of news from India took a month instead of the eight weeks and over of just a few years previously. During the 1850s, the various taxes on newspapers were abolished, leading to huge increases in circulation of the provincial press and the development of weekly papers specifically designed in price and content for a working-class readership.[46]

There was also plenty of copy available for the vast new army of foreign correspondents. With the exception of the Crimean War, all the conflicts in which Britain was involved were colonial, fought in such faraway places as the African bush, the North-West frontier in India, Afghanistan, and the Sudan: 'between 1815 and 1914 there was scarcely a year when the British were not fighting a campaign, however small, somewhere in the world'.[47] But this fact in itself guaranteed a huge and interested reading public. These wars not only had the attraction of the exotic, but were also usually reported as a conflict between civilization and savagery, morality and barbarity, with the British soldier as the heroic incarnation of righteousness, victorious over evil and primitive enemies.

The Highland regiments were soon to be at the heart of this triumphal progress. The roll call of their battle honours stretched from the Alma and Balaclava in the Crimean War to Lucknow, Tel-el-Kebir, Dargai, and Al-Bara on the frontiers of empire. A legend of martial invincibility was generated which not even their disastrous reverses at Majuba Hill and Magersfontein during the South African War could erase. It was said that the mere appearance of kilted soldiers urged on by the skirl of the pipes struck terror into the enemy. Their fame was magnified in the reports of war correspondents and

---

[45] Streets, *Martial Races*, 35–42.

[46] Allan Lee, *The Origins of the Popular Press 1855–1914* (London, 1976); Lucy Brown, *Victorian News and Newspapers* (Oxford, 1985), 27, 31.

[47] MacKenzie, 'Introduction', 3.

by war artists, sculptors, novelists, and composers who delighted in the 'sartorial splendour of kilt and tartan'. One of the most successful battle-painters of the Victorian era, Lady Elizabeth Butler, memorably remarked that 'these splendid troops are so essentially pictorial'.[48] They stood out from the khaki-clad ranks of the rest of the army and, of course, the pipes and drums enabled a distinctive musical dimension. Officers of the regiments were also determined self-publicists, penning copy from the front for news-papers at home and in retirement writing memoirs and histories of the campaigns in which they had fought during their careers. As Alexander Somerville famously remarked in the 1840s in his *Autobiography of a Working Man*: 'it was the *writing* quite as much as the *fighting* of the Scotch regiments which distinguished them'.[49]

Indeed, much of the publicity which the Highland soldier attracted verged on overt propaganda. The news sent back to the press was carefully focused and sanitized. There was little mention in the dispatches of the fate of prisoners in the aftermath of the relief of Kanpur during the Indian Mutiny or what one scholar has described during the same period as the various acts of brutality against sepoys and civilians 'and have even now yet to be fully measured in terms of human life and property'.[50] Victories were also often easily won against opposition which lacked modern weaponry and organization. At least fifteen war correspondents were present at the Anglo-Egyptian battle at Omdurman in the Sudan against the forces of the Mahdi, which numbered possibly 53,000 men. Before noon on 24 August 1898 this great host had been annihilated, leaving some 10,800 corpses on the battlefield and a further 16,000 wounded. The Anglo-Egyptians lost a mere forty-eight officers and men.[51] Carnage on this scale, which was not untyp-ical of colonial campaigns, gave the impression to readers at home of war as sport in which British forces would always triumph with minimal loss, even against seemingly overwhelming odds. The South African War, fought against a much better-armed enemy, deploying 'modern' and superior tactics, brought a reality check. Sir George Younghusband explained the poor showing of the troops, including Highland units, thus:

[48] Quoted in Spiers, *Scottish Soldier*, 14.
[49] Alexander Somerville, *The Autobiography of a Working Man* (London, 1848), 188.
[50] Streets, *Martial Races*, 39.
[51] Spiers, *Scottish Soldier*, 144.

The British public, fed by sensational newspapers, were chiefly to blame for this low standard. Easy victories, against ill-armed though brave adversaries, where the enemy lost thousands, and we counted our casualties by tens, or at most hundreds, became to be thought the normal proportion in the wars we waged.[52]

Towards the Great War

Scottish history of whatever period is incomprehensible without an understanding of war and the martial tradition. For better or worse, the identity of the nation has been moulded by these forces over the centuries. But for the sustained struggle for independence in medieval times Scotland would have been conquered and colonized and it is no coincidence that two of the nation's most famous hero figures, William Wallace and Robert the Bruce, are forever associated with that remarkable period, which still has resonance to the present day. It was not simply a question, however, of removing the threat of subjugation. Essentially, the Wars of Independence helped to fuse the confused mix of kindreds, clans, and tribes into a nation. There is therefore much truth in the saying that Scotland was born fighting.

The place of the Highland regiments in national identity was based on this age-old tradition of the Scots as a martial people. Within the Union they were seen to be the military spearhead of empire, confirming the Anglo-Scottish relationship as a partnership in which the Scots contributed more than their fair share, quite literally in blood. Contrasts were drawn in the late Victorian era with the Irish, who contributed many more men to the imperial effort than the Scots but whose absolute loyalty to the Union and empire could be questioned at a time of increasing nationalism and movement to home rule in Ireland. Scots, on the other hand, were not only willing, they were also loyal. It was probably entirely apposite, therefore, that, when the sun finally set on the greatest territorial empire the world had ever seen, with the handover of the colony of Hong Kong to China in June 1997, the pipes and drums of the Black Watch ended the ceremonial with 'Auld Lang Syne'. Yet the regiments not only helped to cement the Anglo-Scottish relationship between 1750 and 1914, but they also sustained a strong sense of Scottish identity within the Union state. They were imperial units but their soldiers, distinctive in dress and appearance, were recognizably and unambiguously Scottish, martial champions of the nation.

---

[52] Quoted in MacKenzie, 'Introduction', 17.

From the end of the Napoleonic Wars the number of Scotsmen joining
the regular army had declined in proportion to the Scottish share of the
national population. Yet in 1914, with the outbreak of the Great War, all that
seemed to change. Scots in fact joined up during the volunteering phase of
the conflict in 1914–15 in significantly greater numbers than the other three
nations of the United Kingdom. By July 1915 the average rate of enlistment
for men in Britain was 20 per cent, but 24 per cent in Scotland. A third of a
million Scots enlisted voluntarily before conscription was introduced in
January 1916.[53] So great was the response that in some parts of the country
recruitment had to be temporarily suspended as the agencies could not cope
with the flood of numbers. The fact that most Scottish regiments had a local
base of recruitment meant that towns and districts, enthusiastically encouraged by the press, vied with one another to stay ahead of the competition as
the number of volunteers reached levels never seen before in any previous
conflict.[54]

Historians have speculated on the reasons for this new popularity of the
profession of arms. Some of the theories advanced include the attractions of a
secure income and employment in a period of economic instability; an
alternative to emigration which had been taking place on a very significant
scale in the years before the outbreak of war; the lure of adventure in lives
which were often dull and humdrum.[55] But the influence of the martial
history of the Scots was also crucial. It is striking how the rhetoric of
recruiting drew heavily on the traditional beliefs of distinctive Scottish fighting prowess in the age-old defence of the empire.[56] Posters, press comment,
public statements, and political speeches were all carefully created to appeal to
a generation of young men bred on a diet of militarism. The most popular
youth organization in Scotland, the Boys' Brigade (founded in Glasgow in
1883), was organized in a quasi-military style and gave its vast membership a
taste of the qualities of duty, obedience, loyalty, and love of country associated
with good soldiering. Adventure stories, school history books, and the cigar-
ette cards which many youngsters collected presented war as an adventure,

[53] E. Dewey, 'Military Recruiting and the British Labour Force during the First World War',
Historical Journal, 27 (1984), 199–223; D. R. Young, 'Voluntary Recruitment in Scotland,
1914–1916' (unpublished Ph.D. thesis, University of Glasgow, 2001).

[54] Richard Finlay, *Modern Scotland, 1914–2000* (London, 2003), 6–7.

[55] Ibid.

[56] E. W. McFarland, 'Introduction: "A Coronach in Stone"', in Catriona M. M. Macdonald
and E. W. McFarland (eds), *Scotland and the Great War* (East Linton, 1999), 6.

an opportunity to rise above the mundane and engage in heroic deeds. And always at the forefront of the visual images was the iconography of the Highland soldier uniformed magnificently and colourfully in kilt and tartan. An examination of the columns of *The Scotsman* and the *Glasgow Herald* for the first year of the war conveys the strong impression that only Highland regiments represented Scotland in the conflict. The amateur poetry printed in the press consistently made reference to the glens and crofts of the north which had produced Scotland's crack troops. The Black Watch, Cameronians, Gordon Highlanders, and others had their 'skirmishes' at the front picked over in minute journalistic detail. Emphasis was placed on the fact that the Germans feared above all the ferocity and dash of Scotland's kilted regiments. The great battles of the imperial past where the Highlands had distinguished themselves, such as Waterloo, the Alma, Lucknow, and Dargai, were also a common point of reference in many reports. Not all commentators were impressed. One, A. G. Macdonnel, responded acidly in his *My Scotland* some years after the war:

... The Lowlander was to be allowed to wear the coveted panoply, to stand in the ranks of the regiments that bore historic names, to be called a Highlander, and no questions asked. In return he was to do nine-tenths of the fighting, and nine-tenths of the dying, and all the credit was to go to the Highlander, and no stones thrown. Each side made a contribution, the one putting their lives into the common pool, the one an undeserved name and the other an unearned fame.[57]

Indeed, in the generation or two before the Great War, interest in militarism in Scotland reached a peak unprecedented since the Crimea and Indian Mutiny in the middle decades of the nineteenth century. In 1859, the volunteer corps which had been raised during the Napoleonic Wars were resurrected. These part-time amateur soldiers, drawn mainly from the urban areas and the artisan classes, proved to be remarkably popular in Scotland. The nation raised twice as many per head of the male population as the rest of the United Kingdom. The county in Britain which generated most volunteer units was industrial Lanarkshire, with no fewer than 107 formations.[58] Even there, Highlandism had its effect: 'the simple grey uniforms characteristic of the volunteers throughout the county were enlivened by tartan flourishes and by the presence of designated "highland companies" wearing full highland military

---

[57] Quoted in Strachan, 'Scotland's Military Identity', 329.
[58] Ibid. 328.

dress and consisting of a core of volunteers who ostensibly considered themselves to be of highland origin'.[59] By 1914, the volunteers had been reformed into the Territorial Force, which was the key engine of mobilization during the first eighteen months of the conflict.

The volunteers had also made their mark during the Boer Wars, when around 5,000 of them saw active service in South Africa. They served with considerable distinction and these citizen soldiers attracted much attention from the local press at home in the areas from which they were recruited. Even pro-Boer newspapers, such as the *Edinburgh Evening News*, were supportive and took a keen interest in their exploits. They were lauded not simply for maintaining the martial tradition of Scotland but for volunteering precisely at the time when the military situation in South Africa was at its most critical. The volunteers, together with the Scottish regiments of the time, were given an emotional welcome on their return as the 'saviours of the Empire'. Marching behind pipe bands through crowded streets, they were applauded in countless villages and towns up and down the land before being royally entertained by grateful communities at numerous formal receptions and civic lunches.[60] The age-old bond between the identity of the Scottish nation, empire, and the military tradition was once again consolidated and became the foundation for the mass recruitment of 1914.

Select Bibliography

Stuart Allan and Allan Carswell, *The Thin Red Line: War, Empire and Visions of Scotland* (Edinburgh, n.d.).

T. M. Devine, *To the Ends of the Earth: Scotland's Global Diaspora 1750–2010* (London, 2011).

J. A. Cookson, *The British Armed Nation 1793–1815* (Oxford, 1997).

Diana Henderson, *Highland Soldier: A Social Study of the Highland Regiments 1820–1920* (Edinburgh, 1989).

John M. MacKenzie (ed.), *Popular Imperialism and the Military* (Manchester, 1992).

Andrew Mackillop, 'More Fruitful than the Soil': Army, Empire and the Scottish Highlands 1715–1815 (Edinburgh, 2000).

Steve Murdoch and Andrew Mackillop (eds), *Fighting for Identity: Scottish Military Experience* c.1550–1900 (Leiden, 2002).

Edward M. Spiers, *The Scottish Soldier and Empire 1845–1902* (Edinburgh, 2006).

Heather Streets, *Martial Races: The Military, Race and Masculinity in British Imperial Culture, 1857–1914* (Manchester, 2004).

[59] Allan and Carswell, *Thin Red Line*, 34.
[60] Spiers, *Scottish Soldier*, 182–97.

8

Scots Churches and Missions

Esther Breitenbach

Throughout the period of the rise, expansion, and decline of the British Empire, Scottish churches took part in religious endeavours arising from the experience of empire itself, participating in evangelizing movements among colonists, developing Presbyterian churches in Scottish emigrant communities, and establishing foreign missions in many colonial territories. This chapter aims to outline the development of Scots colonial churches and foreign missions, and to ask how they shaped Scots' understanding of their place in empire.

Colonial Churches

Like all migrant communities, Scots took with them their religious beliefs and practices. In the eighteenth century emigration from Scotland, as for England, was characterized by denominational diversity, and thus among Scots settlers were found Catholics, Episcopalians, Presbyterians, and members of dissenting churches. The climate of greater religious freedom and tolerance in North America, facilitated by the failure of the Anglican Church to become the established church of the American colonies, provided for some a motive for emigration. For others, such as Jacobite supporters forced into political exile, religious affiliation was integral to their political sympathies. Many Scots emigrants belonged to dissenting and secessionist churches, who cooperated in inter-denominational ventures, such as the work of the Society in Scotland for the Propagation of Christian Knowledge (SSPCK) in North America.

The established Church of Scotland was—like the Anglican Church—slow to address the religious needs of emigrants, whether 'sojourners' or settlers, and it was not until the 1820s that organized support for this was initiated in Scotland by the formation of the Glasgow Colonial Society.[1] By this time, however, a number of Presbyterian churches had already been built in colonial territories for expatriate Scots. Outside British North America, where Scots Presbyterians had been arriving since the mid-eighteenth century—for example, there had been a 'Scotch Congregation' in Quebec since 1763, though they did not have a church building, St Andrew's, till 1810[2]—the earliest of these appears to have been the St Andrew's Presbyterian Church in Bombay, established by 1814. Around the same time moves were also afoot to found Presbyterian churches in Madras, Calcutta, and Kingston, Jamaica.

In eighteenth-century India, the majority of British residents were in the employ of the East India Company (EIC), whether in military or civil service. Although Scots were disproportionately employed by the EIC through a highly efficacious system of patronage,[3] one of the consequences of the English origins of the company was that religious provision was confined to Anglicanism. Thus the Church of England founded churches in India earlier than did the Church of Scotland, while the soldiers of the EIC were ministered to by Anglican chaplains.[4] Regiments of the king's troops, however, might be served by chaplains of different denominations. For Scots soldiers, commanding officers could make application to the Church of Scotland for a minister, hence some regiments were served by ordained Presbyterian ministers.[5] Such provision was a matter of concern for the Church of Scotland, which wished its claims as a national church to be recognized through the provision of Presbyterian clergymen as army chaplains, and which convened a committee in 1812 to address this.[6] In 1840

---

[1] The Society (in connection with the Established Church of Scotland) for Promoting the Religious Interests of Scottish Settlers in British North America, usually known as the Glasgow Colonial Society, was formed in 1825. See Elizabeth Ann Kerr McDougall and John S. Moir (eds), *Selected Correspondence of the Glasgow Colonial Society, 1825–1840* (Toronto, 1994).

[2] http://www.standrewsquebec.ca/ (accessed 27 September 2010).

[3] See, for example, George McGilvary, *East India Patronage and the British State: The Scottish Elite and Politics in the Eighteenth Century* (London, 2008) and chapter 3 above.

[4] Andrew Mackillop, 'Europeans, Britons, and Scots: Scottish Sojourning Networks and Identities in Asia, c.1700–1815', in Angela McCarthy (ed.), *A Global Clan: Scottish Migrant Networks and Identities since the Eighteenth Century* (London, 2006), 19–47.

[5] I am grateful to Andrew Mackillop for confirming this with an example of a Presbyterian minister serving with a Highland regiment in India in the 1770s and 1780s.

[6] Revd John Wilson, *Index to the Acts and Proceedings of the General Assembly of the Church of Scotland* (Edinburgh, 1863).

a further committee was convened specifically in relation to India, 'to procure an increase in chaplains...corresponding to the proposed increase of Episcopalian chaplains',[7] a demand given vocal support by Church of Scotland missionary Alexander Duff.[8]

The initiative for founding Presbyterian churches in India came from Scots within the EIC, and the renewals of EIC charters were crucial moments in the development of the Church of Scotland's presence in India. Subsequent to the 1813 charter, the General Assembly passed an Act in May 1814 'for the establishment of a branch of the church in India', as the EIC directors had agreed to the endowment of three churches in the presidencies of Bengal, Madras, and Bombay.[9] The position of the Church in India was further enhanced through the 1833 charter by which 'the Church of Scotland was fairly established in India, the Government having made it imperative that there should be a minister of the Church of Scotland settled at each of the Presidencies'.[10]

Bombay had a St Andrew's Presbyterian church by 1814, while St Andrew's Church in Calcutta dates from 1818. In Madras, it was publicly notified in 1815 'that the East India Company wished to build a Scotch Church for the benefit of their Caledonian employees'.[11] The Church of Scotland sent out the Revd Dr Allan to India with authority to form a congregation, and the church was founded, at a site described as 'the finest in Madras', in 1818. It is clear that religious services took place prior to churches being built, as was also the case with Anglicans,[12] though it is not clear how significant religion was to late eighteenth-century 'sojourners' in India. On the one hand, there was a high turnover of young men, some of whom were interested in Indian religions and culture, others who may have been religious Moderates, or not particularly engaged by religion at all. Yet, above a certain rank and social scale, some show of religious observance was an expectation. Support for the foundation of Presbyterian churches in India may have reflected not just

---

[7] Ibid. 147.

[8] Alexander Duff, *Bombay in April 1840: With Special Reference to the Church of Scotland's Mission There* (Edinburgh, 1840).

[9] Walter Steuart, *A Compendium of the Laws of the Church of Scotland* (4th edn Edinburgh, 1830), 459.

[10] Wilson, *Index to Acts*, 46.

[11] Somerset Playne, J. W. Boyd, and Arnold Wright, *Southern India: Its History, People, Commerce and Industrial Resources* (New Delhi, 2004), 118.

[12] See Stephen Neill, *A History of Christianity in India: 1807–1858* (Cambridge, 1985).

the proportion of Scots in EIC employment and their status, but also the changing character of the resident communities in India, with a growing number of officials being accompanied by wives and families. It may also have reflected rivalry with the Anglican Church, exhibited particularly in the choice of sites and imposing character of the Presbyterian churches in the presidency cities.

The timing of the foundation of a Scots kirk in Jamaica was also influenced by patterns of migration. The majority of Scots emigrants to the Caribbean in the eighteenth century were young single men, seeking to make fortunes and then to return home, although there were also phases of emigration of Jacobite exiles and of loyalists from the USA following the War of Independence. The degree of decadence of Caribbean societies perhaps also did not favour the development of religious institutions. It was in response to their perception that the 'religious tide' was 'at low ebb' that a group of Scots came together in 1813 to 'establish the church of Scotland in Jamaica'.[13] The first Scots kirk there, described in 1821 as 'the handsomest building in Jamaica', opened in 1819. According to Douglas Hamilton, the late arrival of the Church of Scotland in the Caribbean can be explained by the fact that in the British West Indies 'religious fervour seems only to become animated when Catholicism confronted Protestantism', and also by the resistance of planters to Christianization of slaves.[14] However, by the late eighteenth century there was some Scottish interest in the Christianization of slaves, and while Scots were not among the first missionaries working with slaves—Quakers, Moravians, and Wesleyan Methodists having got there earlier—by 1800 the Scottish Missionary Society (SMS) had sent three missionaries to Jamaica.

In South Africa, the first Scottish Presbyterian church was founded in the late 1820s—St Andrew's Presbyterian Church in Cape Town.[15] Scots missionaries were then already operating in South Africa, the Congregationalist John Philip, employed by the London Missionary Society (LMS), and the SMS missionaries in Kaffraria in the Eastern Cape. St Andrew's played a role in abolitionist activities in the Cape, and ran a mission for former slaves.

[13] Velma Pollard, 'The Scots in Jamaica', in Giovanna Covi, Joan Anim-Addo, Velma Pollard, and Carla Sassi, *Caribbean–Scottish Relations* (London, 2007), 93–130, 113.

[14] Douglas Hamilton, 'Transatlantic Ties: Scottish Migration Networks in the Caribbean, 1750–1800', in McCarthy, *Global Clan*, 48–66, 60.

[15] The following paragraph draws on John M. MacKenzie with Nigel R. Dalziel, *The Scots in South Africa* (Manchester, 2007).

Over time, numerous Presbyterian churches were founded in South Africa, and by 1898 there were 37 Presbyterian congregations, plus 'ten native congregations' and 18 mission stations.[16] In the 1890s, Presbyterian congregations were also established in the future Southern Rhodesia. Compared to other communities of Scots emigrants, South African Presbyterians were less affected by the 1843 Disruption, although both tendencies were represented. However, as with other colonies, Scots of many denominations could be found—Catholics, Episcopalians, Methodists, Baptists, and Congregationalists. A distinctive feature of the South African experience was the Scottish contribution to the Dutch Reformed Church (DRC). The Calvinist DRC of the Dutch colonists, finding it impossible to recruit sufficient ministers from the Netherlands, turned to Scotland to assist. In the 1820s and again in the 1860s Scotland supplied ministers to meet the DRC's needs, and consequently many of the main DRC churches in the Cape had Scots ministers for much of the nineteenth century. MacKenzie has argued that these Scots became over time 'assimilated Boers', but also that the DRC was a Dutch/Scots hybrid, which, like the Scots Presbyterian Church, placed strong emphasis on education.[17]

Timing and patterns of settlement also shaped the experiences of Canada, Australia, and New Zealand. Canada, having had the longest period of settlement, was most affected by the divisions of the 1843 Disruption in Scotland, but, having endured some decades of disputes, also achieved the earliest unification of Presbyterian churches.[18] There were several factors which contributed to the export of the Disruption to Canada: a number of ministers who had come to Canada had suffered from the system of patronage in Scotland; others returned home to meet the Church of Scotland's staffing crisis, which resulted from the secession, provoking their abandoned congregations into support for the Free Church; and emigration in this period brought with it from Scotland many evangelicals and Free Church supporters. Thus, while some churches in Canada remained loyal to the Church of Scotland, there was considerable enthusiasm for the Free Church. Divisions between the churches also crystallized around the issue of state support. The Church of Scotland, in rivalry to the established Church of

---

[16] MacKenzie, *Scots in South Africa*, 181.

[17] Ibid. 173.

[18] Barbara Murison, 'The Disruption and the Colonies of Scottish Settlement', in Stewart J. Brown and Michael Fry (eds), *Scotland in the Age of Disruption* (Edinburgh, 1993), 135–50.

England, had waged a campaign to gain access to the state-funded clergy reserves (land set aside for the support of Protestant clergy),[19] but Free Church supporters were critical of the desire to hold on to such state benefits. This shifted them into the voluntarist camp, and contributed to the move against church establishment in Canada. After three decades of separation, the Presbyterian churches united in 1875.

In Australia, there had been small numbers of Scots settlers from the late eighteenth century, and the first Presbyterian church in Australia was built in 1809.[20] Emigration from Scotland was actively encouraged by prominent Scots in Australia in the 1820s, Governors Macquarie and Brisbane and the Reverend John Dunmore Lang. The latter, who was to have a long and controversial career both as a churchman and a politician, was an active promoter of emigration of Presbyterian Scots, whom he saw as helping to keep the continent Protestant, in the face of Irish Catholic immigration.[21] Despite some protests in Australia that the Disruption was a purely Scottish affair, the churches at home forced the Australian churches to take sides over the issue of financial aid from the state. Thus, as in Canada, the issue of the relationship between church and state was at the heart of Presbyterian divisions. Reunifications were effected in most states by 1870, a process made easier by the withdrawal of state aid to religion.[22] However, it was not until the turn of the century that reunifications took place throughout the Australian states.

As New Zealand was only beginning to be settled at the time of the Disruption, it was less affected by its divisiveness, although, as elsewhere, Presbyterianism was marked by disputatiousness. The Presbyterian Church in New Zealand dates from 1840, and was to an unusual extent 'a planned process', a 'conscious attempt to yoke together Edward Gibbon Wakefield's ideal of a class settlement and evangelical mission, as part of a world-wide strategy to defeat Popish ignorance by Protestant truth'.[23] Settlement driven by such religious motivations is perhaps best illustrated by the Free Church

---

[19] See John Moir, '"Loyalty and Respectability": The Campaign for Co-establishment of the Church of Scotland in Canada', *International Review of Scottish Studies*, 10 (1980).

[20] Malcolm Prentis, *The Scots in Australia* (Sydney, 2008).

[21] Eric Richards, 'Scottish Voices and Networks in Colonial Australia', in McCarthy (ed.), *Global Clan*, 150–82, 164.

[22] Prentis, *Scots in Australia*.

[23] Peter Matheson, '1840–1870: The Settler Church', in Dennis McEldowney (ed.), *Presbyterians in Aotearoa 1840–1990* (Wellington, 1990), 21.

colony established in Otago in 1848, an outcome of the formation in 1845 of a lay association of Free Church members in Glasgow. Presbyterian churches also grew up elsewhere in New Zealand, and while some splits occurred, congregations were aware that 'in a "young colony" there was no marked distinction of denominational identity and that a flexible approach was required'—on the whole, cooperation between churches was the norm.[24] Unification of the Presbyterian churches in New Zealand took place in 1901.

In discussing Scottish colonial churches, the focus has inevitably been on the main Presbyterian churches, and especially the Church of Scotland and the Free Church. Historians of colonial churches of Scots origin have frequently concentrated on the Disruption, subsequent divisions and re-unifications. The emphasis on the main Presbyterian churches also reflects the fact that among Scots emigrants these religious affiliations dominated. Nonetheless, it is important to emphasize the denominational diversity of Scots emigrants—in all colonies, as well as adherents of mainstream Presbyterian churches, there were to be found members of many dissenting churches, as well as Episcopalians and Catholics. Even where their numbers were small, members of other denominations could make an impact in their new environment, such as Bishop Strachan in Canada. An emigrant from Aberdeen, who had first been a Presbyterian, Strachan became an Anglican priest in Canada and eventually Bishop of Toronto. Among other things, he was an ardent supporter of establishment status of the Church of England in Canada.[25] In Australia, 'Scottish Roman Catholics were to make a contribution to their church's schools out of all proportion to their tiny numbers'.[26] Mary MacKillop, of Highland origin, who founded the teaching order of the Sisters of St Joseph of the Sacred Heart, was beatified by Pope John Paul II in 1995 and canonized in October 2010 as the first Australian saint.

Not all Scots emigrants would have been religious either in faith or in practice, and church memberships in the colonies as well as at home tended to have a particular social composition. Presbyterian churches in the colonies were, as John MacKenzie has put in it relation to the Cape, a 'locus of "respectability"'.[27] Typically, Presbyterians were associated with

---

[24] Matheson, 'The Settler Church', 34.
[25] Michael Gavreau in *Oxford Dictionary of National Biography* online, http://www.oxford-dnb.com/view/article/26619 (accessed 28 September 2010).
[26] Prentis, *Scots in Australia*, 156.
[27] MacKenzie, *Scots in South Africa*, 175.

industriousness, sober living, and commercial and professional success within the new societies which they helped to build. A pronounced emphasis on education was characteristic of colonial Presbyterian churches, and everywhere they were active in founding schools, colleges, and higher education institutions—from Jamaica to New Zealand. This emphasis on education was similarly apparent in the foreign mission movement, which has also left a legacy of prominent educational institutions. Presbyterians were, like other denominations, practitioners of philanthropy in colonial societies, sometimes prominently so. Eric Richards has noted 'the conspicuous philanthropy of successful Scottish colonists' in founding churches and in charity networks.[28] However, such philanthropy does not seem on the whole to have been particularly radical, and some churches have been judged to have had little concern with the poor and the socially marginal, as Matheson has commented of New Zealand.[29] Nor, on the whole, do the Presbyterian colonial churches appear to have been in the forefront of mission or philanthropic work with indigenous peoples, though this is a topic that would merit more research. The Presbyterian church at the Cape in the earlier decades of the nineteenth century probably serves as the best instance of a more radical and egalitarian perspective, though this was eroded over time as the Scots community established itself among the elites of Cape society.[30] Colonial Presbyterian churches gave some support to foreign missions, both those of the Scottish churches, and their own, for example, the New Zealand-supported mission in the New Hebrides[31] and the Canadian Presbyterian missions in China and India,[32] which over time were to become part of an international network of Protestant missions.

The history of colonial churches of Scottish origin still has many gaps. Historical scholarship to date has provided more in-depth coverage of churches within the colonies of settlement, often by historians of Presbyterian churches and, as noted, with a frequent focus on the Disruption. Furthermore, the territorial location of such studies has not necessarily drawn out comparisons, or looked at the international links between

---

[28] Richards, 'Scottish Voices', 167.

[29] Matheson, 'The Settler Church', 9.

[30] See MacKenzie, *Scots in South Africa*.

[31] Matheson, 'The Settler Church'.

[32] See Ruth Compton Brouwer, 'Canadian Protestant Overseas Missions to the Mid-Twentieth Century: American Influences, Interwar Changes, Long-Term Legacies', in Hilary Carey (ed.), *Empires of Religion* (Basingstoke, 2008), 288–311.

churches, whether institutional or informal. Yet the churches in Scotland had colonial committees throughout the nineteenth and into the twentieth century, and while the nature of institutional arrangements changed over time, connections were maintained. In the earlier part of the twentieth century, the Church of Scotland had a Colonial and Continental Committee, which was responsible for overseas churches for Scottish residents, for army chaplains with regiments serving overseas, and for links with 'daughter' churches in the dominions, and the Church still provided some financial and ministerial support to Presbyterian churches in the dominions.[33] The committee also encouraged ministers in Scotland to inform their counterparts in colonies of emigrants' destinations, and it promoted specific settlement schemes. How these relationships were reformulated as the empire declined and was replaced by the Commonwealth is still a matter for investigation.

While religion played an integral role in all Scots migrant communities, there were different patterns of development of churches, depending on patterns of emigration and settlement. Like the established Church of England, the established Church of Scotland was relatively slow to respond to colonization—notwithstanding the early interest by some sections of the churches in needs of colonists and in missionary work, for example the Anglican Society for the Propagation of the Gospel in Foreign Parts and the SSPCK. Strong has argued that, following the loss of the American colonies, the Anglican Church evinced a renewed energy for imperialist expansion,[34] and it is an intriguing question whether the Church of Scotland's efforts to found colonial churches in the early nineteenth century were a response to this, and whether locally based Presbyterians, for example in India, were motivated by such rivalry.[35] It is also apparent that Presbyterianism remained wedded to anti-Catholic sentiment abroad as well as at home, and that this could be appealed to as a motivation for emigration and settlement.

[33] I owe this information about institutional links and arrangements to Lesley Orr, my co-researcher on an ESRC research project on 'Empire and Civil Society in 20th Century Scotland' (ESRC Award No: RES-062-23-1790).

[34] Rowan Strong, *Anglicanism and the British Empire c.1700–1850* (Oxford, 2007).

[35] For example, see Neill's account of the confrontation between Anglican Bishop Middleton and Presbyterian Revd James Bryce in Calcutta over which church should have the tallest steeple. See Neill, *History of Christianity in India*.

The Disruption had a considerable impact on some colonial churches—and none seems to have been untouched by it. One consequence of this was increased support for voluntarism, and thus Scots emigrants played their part in colonial societies in resisting the establishment of any particular church. The divided colonial churches had all reunited by the turn of the century, and over time had set up their own forms of church government and organization. Relations between the Presbyterian churches in Scotland, in the colonies of settlement, and in Scots communities in India and dependent colonies became formalized through Colonial Churches Committees within the main Presbyterian denominations. It is clear that Presbyterian churches in the colonies of settlement played an important role in sustaining the cultural values of their societies of origin, and in sustaining a Scottish emigrant identity. Scots communities appear to have made a major contribution to the development of educational institutions everywhere in the colonies of settlement, as Scottish foreign missions were also to do in India, Africa, and elsewhere.

The Foreign Mission Movement

There are a number of ways of writing the history of missions. Terence Ranger has summarized these as denominational histories, histories concerned with the relation of missions to imperialism and capitalism, and those focusing on the impact of Christianity on indigenous religions,[36] while John MacKenzie has stressed the importance of analysing missionary work in terms of interactive relationships of whites and colonized peoples.[37] Drawing on these approaches, this chapter aims to add a Scottish 'national' perspective to the history of missions, addressing the impact that missions had on Scots at home, and providing an assessment of their impact abroad and their relationship to the imperial project. This Scottish focus serves to emphasize the complexity of the religious landscape in Britain and throughout its empire, and the need to avoid over-generalizing on the basis of research evidence about any one church or missionary society. At the same time, it is

[36] Terence Ranger, 'Christian Mission, Capitalism and Empire: The State of the Debate', Oxford Centre for Mission Studies Lecture, 21 June 2005, http://www.ocms.ac.uk/lectures/ (accessed 16 July 2010).

[37] John M. MacKenzie, '"Making Black Scotsmen and Scotswomen?" Scottish Missionaries and the Eastern Cape Colony in the Nineteenth Century', in Carey (ed.), *Empires of Religion*, 113–36.

recognized that the main Presbyterian churches still dominate the historical picture, and that even within the Scottish context there is a need for more investigation of other denominations.

Eighteenth-century antecedents

The conventional narrative of the origins of the foreign mission movement in Scotland is that this arose at the very end of the eighteenth century with the foundation of the Scottish Missionary Society (SMS) and Glasgow Missionary Society (GMS) in the 1790s, in parallel with the rise of missionary societies in England. Rowan Strong has recently contested this dating of the origins of English foreign missions, arguing that 'an official and conscious Anglican concern for empire, and for missions by the Church of England, dates continuously from the foundation of the Society for the Propagation of the Gospel in Foreign Parts (SPG) in 1701'.[38] In line with this argument, it is clear that various aspects of eighteenth-century experience were directly connected to the emergence of the missionary societies in Scotland, although the emergence of late eighteenth-century societies marked a distinctive new phase. Prior to this, episodes of evangelical fervour had played a part in encouraging missionary enthusiasm: for example, the period of religious 'awakening' which manifested itself on both sides of the Atlantic, and in which Scotland played a notable part in the form of the Cambuslang revival. Probably most influential in developing missionary interest and support, however, was the SSPCK.

Founded at the beginning of the eighteenth century, the SSPCK had as its main aim the spread of education and Protestantism in the Highlands and Islands of Scotland. It aimed to tackle the 'ignorance and superstition' regarded as being prevalent in the Highlands,[39] and while instruction was also to be given to 'Papists',[40] Society reports provide evidence of the Society's anti-Catholic stance.[41] Initial steps to create the organization

---

[38] Strong, *Anglicanism and the British Empire*, 6.

[39] I. Graham Andrew, *A Brief Survey of the Society in Scotland for Propagating Christian Knowledge* (Edinburgh, 1957), 4.

[40] See Henry Hunter, *A Brief History of the Society in Scotland for Propagating Christian Knowledge in the Highlands and Islands; and of the Correspondent Board in London; from the establishment of the society in the year 1701, down to the present time* (London, 1795).

[41] See *A Summary Account of the Rise and Progress of the Society in Scotland for Propagating Christian Knowledge* (Edinburgh, 1783).

were taken in 1701, though these were not immediately successful.[42] After a lobby of the General Assembly of the Church of Scotland in 1706, the organization obtained formal approval in the form of a royal patent in 1709. Significantly, the organization's full designation as originally proposed was the Society for Propagating Christian Knowledge in the Highlands and Islands, and in Foreign Parts.[43] In the eighteenth century, the work that the SSPCK funded in 'Foreign Parts' was missionary work with Native Americans. Financial resources devoted to this were small compared to the overall outgoings of the organization, and initially depended on the legacies of individuals who had specifically stipulated that their donations should be dedicated to this purpose. Subsequently, the 'North American Indian Fund' was increased by collections made on the occasion of the preaching tour of Native American minister Samson Occom[44] in 1767, during which 'the good people of Scotland' turned out in large numbers 'to see and hear a copper-coloured man'.[45]

The first use of SSPCK funds for missionary work in America occurred in 1730, and between then and the end of the century a small number of missionaries enjoyed the support of the Society, most famously David Brainerd, who was to become an American evangelical icon.[46] In 1774, the Society received a request for support to send two freed slaves, who had converted to Christianity, on a mission to Africa to their country of origin in the Guinea coast, but it is not clear whether this came to fruition. By the end of the eighteenth century, missionary work with Native Americans was judged to have had variable success, and indeed the Society's Committee felt that 'the fruit upon the whole, has not corresponded with the labour bestowed'.[47]

The SSPCK's organization and work during the eighteenth century was a precursor to the work of the later foreign mission societies and of the

---

[42] Andrew, *Brief Survey.*

[43] Ibid. 4.

[44] Hunter names him as Sampson Occom. Hunter, *Brief History,* 35.

[45] Ibid. 36.

[46] John A. Grigg, *The Lives of David Brainerd: The Making of an American Evangelical Icon* (Oxford, 2009).

[47] The Society in Scotland for Propagating Christian Knowledge, *An Account of the Funds, Expenditure, and General Management of the Affairs of The Society in Scotland for Propagating Christian Knowledge: Contained in a Report drawn up by a Committee of their Number, appointed for that Purpose* (Edinburgh, 1796), 58.

subsequent foreign mission enterprise of the main Presbyterian denominations in the nineteenth century. While a small part of the Society's work, the aim of a mission to 'Heathen Nations' formed one of its fundamental objectives from the outset.[48] This was understood in Providentialist terms as a Christian goal, as a means of challenging Catholicism, and as a means of defending the British colonies from French and Spanish enemies. The missionary work supported by the SSPCK showed, according to Henry Hunter, 'that a righteous Providence demonstrates its constant attention to the affairs of this World', thereby making 'individuals and nations instruments of prosperity or of punishment to each other, according as they have acted well or ill'.[49] Thus religion and politics went hand in hand.

Work carried out in America paralleled what was being done at home in the Highlands and Islands, if on a much smaller scale. Typically, missions employed ministers and schoolmasters, aiming to teach literacy and the English language, and at the same time to offer instruction in settled agricultural practices which aimed to replace nomadic ways of life in which hunting played a crucial role. While not identical to practices in Scotland, it can be seen to be made up of the same component parts: instruction in Reformed Christianity, literacy, and particular forms of industry and labour—farming in North America, and fishing, agricultural improvement, and cottage industries such as spinning and weaving in the Highlands and Islands. Indeed, the SSPCK's modus operandi, deemed to have been successful in 'civilizing' the Highlands, continued to function as a powerful model for nineteenth-century missions, as evidenced, for example, by Alexander Duff's use of the Highland analogy in his support for English-language education in India. The Society's employees were designated as 'Missionary ministers', and information about their work was disseminated to the Scottish public, although this did not yet approach the scale and organization of the nineteenth-century foreign mission publishing enterprise. However, reporting of the business of the Society and occasional short histories played some role in informing the public about efforts to Christianize Native Americans. Further publicity was given to this by the highly successful tour by Occom, mentioned above, and also by publication of David Brainerd's journals, and those of other missionaries.

---

[48] Hunter, *Brief History*, 22.   [49] Ibid. 47.

The SSPCK was a non-denominational organization, even if its member-ship was dominated by the established Church, and this non-denominational model was adopted by both the LMS and the early Scottish missionary societies. Given that many supporters of the SSPCK were evangelicals, it seems likely that there would have been considerable overlap between SSPCK and missionary society members and supporters, although further research would be needed to establish the extent to which this was the case. Notably, however, one leading member of the SSPCK, the Revd Dr John Erskine, minister of Old Greyfriars Church in Edinburgh, was also a leading advocate for foreign missions in the 1796 General Assembly debate, at which it was first proposed the Church of Scotland should support them. Indeed, in the same year, it was Dr Erskine who gave the SSPCK report which expressed disappointment at the results of endeavours to Christianize Native Americans. This raises the question as to whether it was disillusionment with the North American experience that led at this time to a reorientation towards other potential converts, in the Caribbean, Africa, and India. Certainly, the work of the anti-slavery movement, which entered upon its first phase of activity in the late eighteenth century, had drawn attention both to the circumstances of enslaved Africans and to the countries from which they were abducted, leading to a growing enthusiasm for missionary efforts both in the Caribbean and in West Africa.

In the earlier period of colonization, the association of salvation with freedom produced ambivalent attitudes towards Christianization of slaves, since slave holders' interests were at stake, including those of Scots in the Caribbean.[50] However, by the late 1780s organized anti-slavery activity was emerging in Scotland, as elsewhere in Britain. Factors which contributed to this included several cases in Scotland concerning the legal status of black slaves, reports from the Caribbean about slave conditions, and speaking tours by abolitionists such as that by William Dickson in 1792.[51] Enlighten-ment thinking had helped to establish an intellectual case against slavery, though the views on slavery of key Enlightenment figures were often complex and ambiguous, and few were active abolitionists. In the emer-gence of abolitionist societies in Scotland in the early 1790s, an important

---

[50] See T. M. Devine, *Scotland's Empire* (London, 2003); Douglas Hamilton, *Scotland, the Caribbean and the Atlantic World, 1750–1820* (Manchester, 2005); and Iain Whyte, *Scotland and the Abolition of Black Slavery, 1756–1838* (Edinburgh, 2006).

[51] Whyte, *Scotland and the Abolition of Black Slavery.*

role was played by Church of Scotland evangelicals, and this movement was the immediate precursor to the emergence of foreign missions. Early missionary activity was directed to slaves in the Caribbean, and to initiatives such as the creation of a colony of freed slaves in Sierra Leone, of which Zachary Macaulay,[52] son of an Inveraray minister, was to become Governor in 1794. Dr Erskine, who supported sending 'black missionaries' to Sierra Leone, was a founder member of the Edinburgh Missionary Society and a member of the Edinburgh Society for the Abolition of the Slave Trade.[53] Similarly, Dr Robert Balfour, a founder member of the GMS, appealed to missionaries to challenge slavery. As Whyte has commented, 'The missionary impulse was a constant element in the anti-slavery movement,'[54] and, indeed the goal of eradicating slavery in Africa continued to animate the foreign mission movement throughout the nineteenth century.

THE GROWTH OF THE FOREIGN MISSION MOVEMENT IN SCOTLAND[55]

As noted, foreign mission societies were first formed in Scotland in 1796, following the example of the Baptist Missionary Society (founded 1792) and the LMS (founded 1795). Among the founders of the LMS (non-denominational but dominated by Congregationalists) were a number of Scots, and the Society recruited missionaries disproportionately from Scotland throughout the nineteenth and into the twentieth century.[56] This is illustrative of Scots links to British networks of missionary societies, and to other religious and philanthropic organizations, such as anti-slavery organizations or the temperance movement. Both the GMS and Edinburgh Missionary Society came into being in early 1796, with the latter almost immediately undergoing a name change to the Scottish Missionary Society (SMS). The Church of Scotland General Assembly was asked in 1796 to support the missionary societies, but declined to do so.[57] The view that 'heathens' needed to be

---

[52] Macaulay, a leading member of the Clapham Sect, was one of the London Scots with whom evangelicals in Scotland maintained close contact.

[53] Whyte, *Scotland and the Abolition of Black Slavery*, 72.

[54] Ibid. 71.

[55] The following section draws on Esther Breitenbach, *Empire and Scottish Society: The Impact of Foreign Missions at Home, c.1790 to c.1914* (Edinburgh, 2009), especially ch. 4, 54–89.

[56] James Calder, *Scotland's March Past: The Share of Scottish Churches in the London Missionary Society* (London, 1945).

[57] Church of Scotland, *Account of the Proceedings and Debate in the General Assembly of the Church of Scotland, 27th May 1796* (Edinburgh, 1796).

'civilized' before they could be Christianized prevailed, while leading Moderates were also nervous of the potential radicalism of this new type of voluntary society, viewed with suspicion in the atmosphere of reaction produced by the Revolution in France. By 1824, however, the Church of Scotland had been prevailed upon to endorse foreign missions, and in 1830 the first Church of Scotland missionary, Alexander Duff, commenced work in Calcutta in India. Meanwhile the non-denominational societies had supported missions in India, Africa, and the West Indies, with some reorganization of affiliations between the societies and the Church of Scotland occurring prior to the Disruption of 1843. The Disruption had a considerable impact on the developing foreign mission movement—all but one of the Church of Scotland missionaries went over to the Free Church, and the Church of Scotland had to build up its missionary workforce again. While this recovered over time, it never caught up with the Free Church in numerical strength, nor with the United Presbyterian Church, formed in 1847 by the union of the Secession and Relief Churches, and also active in promoting foreign missions. The remaining SMS and GMS missionaries were transferred to the Free Church and United Presbyterian Church.

It is a notable feature of foreign mission support that women were actively involved from an early stage, as supporters and as missionary employees, with their contribution as the latter growing markedly after women gained access to higher education. By the 1820s, there were several Ladies and Female Missionary Societies, such as the Lanark Ladies' Scottish Missionary Society and Dunfermline Ladies Association.[58] Women's organizations were put on a more permanent footing with the formation of the Edinburgh Ladies' Association for the Advancement of Female Education in India in 1837, and the Glasgow Ladies' Association for promoting Female Education in Kaffraria in 1839. The first female missionary agent was employed by the Edinburgh Association in 1838.[59] The Ladies' Associations also split on denominational lines in the aftermath of the Disruption.

Thus from 1843 onwards Scottish foreign missions were mostly organized on denominational lines, dominated by the three main Presbyterian churches. The non-denominational Edinburgh Medical Missionary Society,

---

[58] *Scottish Missionary and Philanthropic Register* (1826).

[59] Lesley Orr Macdonald, *A Unique and Glorious Mission: Women and Presbyterianism in Scotland* (Edinburgh, 2000).

established in 1841, was an exception to this. It supported directly few of the missionaries it trained, tending to place them with Church of Scotland, Free Church, or LMS missions. The LMS continued to derive active support from Scotland, both in the form of missionary recruits and in the work of locally based auxiliaries, such as those in Edinburgh, Glasgow, Dundee, and Aberdeen. Later in the century, the Scottish Episcopalian Church also established its own missions, around 1870—prior to this period it had channelled support to its sister Anglican Church. The Catholic Church only began to send missionaries from Scotland in the 1930s. Thus Scottish-supported foreign missions in the nineteenth and early twentieth centuries were a Protestant phenomenon, dominated by the main Presbyterian churches, although it was from the dissenting churches that some of the most famous Scottish missionaries emerged—Robert Moffat, David Livingstone, and James Chalmers, all Congregationalists who served with the LMS.

By the 1840s, then, foreign missions had become an established part of Presbyterian life, even if actual numbers of missionaries were relatively small. The splits in the Church had the effect of energizing religious life, and the foreign mission movement subsequently expanded at the same time as church extension programmes were carried out at home. Such expansion did not necessarily follow a smooth path, and there were frequent appeals both for money and missionary recruits.[60] Various episodes and events did, however, stimulate greater interest in foreign missions from time to time. For example, the Indian uprisings of 1857 and 1858 provoked widespread debate on the role of missionaries in India.[61] Evangelicals lobbied strenuously for greater access for missionary ventures, and were rewarded with an increase in support for missions in the period immediately following the uprising. Livingstone's explorations in Africa and his plea for people in Britain to follow his path in bringing 'Christianity and Commerce' also stimulated interest in missions, though it was not until after his death in 1873 that the Scottish Presbyterian churches acted on this appeal. The expedition to Nyasaland (Malawi), launched in 1875, resulted in the establishment of missions there by both the Church of Scotland and the Free

---

[60] See Andrew Ross, 'Scottish Missionary Concern 1874–1914: A Golden Era?', *Scottish Historical Review* (1972), 52–72.

[61] Esther Breitenbach, 'Scottish Presbyterian Missionaries and Public Opinion in Scotland', in Andrea Major and Crispin Bates (eds), *Mutiny at the Margins: New Perspectives on the Indian Uprising of 1857; Volume 2: Britain and the Indian Uprising* (Sage: New Delhi, 2013), ch. 4, pp. 74–94.

Church, with the United Presbyterian Church also contributing in the person of Dr Robert Laws. Defence of the interests of the Scottish missions became the subject of a popular campaign in the late 1880s, with the British government being urged to secure the territory from encroachments by the Portuguese.[62] Developments in Nyasaland continued to interest the Scottish 'mission public', as did missionary activities in South and West Africa. Missionary figures such as Robert Laws in Nyasaland, James Stewart in South Africa, and Mary Slessor in Nigeria became well known to the Scottish public. Earlier missionaries such as Alexander Duff and John Wilson were also revered as missionary and educational pioneers.

Developments at home also fed missionary enthusiasm, for example, the 1870s Moody and Sankey revival and the growth of the Student Volunteer Movement in the 1880s.[63] Arguably, imperialist expansion in the late nineteenth century additionally fuelled interest in the foreign mission movement, since this best exemplified the 'civilizing mission' which British rule claimed to embody. Women's role in missions, and the extension of this as they gained access to higher education, was another factor in stimulating interest, complemented by a parallel reorganization of women's participation in church life.[64] Thus support for the foreign mission movement in Scotland grew throughout the nineteenth and into the twentieth centuries. At the same time, the movement enjoyed a wider audience for its publicity in church circles, and a heightened public profile, as evidenced by public celebrations and press coverage of events such as the 1910 World Missionary Conference in Edinburgh, the Livingstone Centenary celebrations of 1913, and the establishment of the Livingstone National Memorial at Blantyre in the late 1920s. Foreign missions remained an integral part of Presbyterian religious life up until the period of decolonization of the 1960s. As churches in colonial territories acquired independent status along with political independence, foreign mission work became much reduced in scale, though a residual presence was maintained in Israel and Palestine for some years.

---

[62] See John McCracken, *Politics and Christianity in Malawi 1875–1940: The Impact of the Livingstonia Mission in the Northern Province* (Cambridge, 1977), and Andrew Ross, 'Scotland and Malawi, 1859–1964', in Stewart J. Brown and George Newlands (eds), *Scottish Christianity in the Modern World* (Edinburgh, 2000), 283–309.

[63] See Clifton J. Phillips, 'Changing Attitudes in the Student Volunteer Movement of Great Britain and North America, 1886–1928', in Torben Christensen and William R. Hutchison (eds), *Missionary Ideologies in the Imperialist Era: 1880–1920* (Aarhus, 1982).

[64] See Macdonald, *Unique and Glorious Mission.*

Over time, the relationships between the Church of Scotland and the Presbyterian churches which Scottish missionaries helped to establish were transformed in character, gradually becoming one of partners in an international network.

THE MISSIONARY WORKFORCE

Compared to other groups of Scots who played a role in imperial expansion, rule, or settlement, such as soldiers, colonial administrators, and emigrants to British colonies, missionaries were numerically a very small group. Prior to the Church of Scotland's endorsement of foreign missions, there were only a handful of Scottish missionary society employees, their work augmented by their wives. While there were occasional cases of married women being employed in missionary work, generally married women were not paid employees, and as the wives of male missionaries were expected to contribute to the work of the mission without pay. While this practice continued well into the twentieth century, over time there was a greater public acknowledgement of their role.

By the early 1870s, the three main Presbyterian denominations employed around 120 missionaries between them, and by the time of the union of the Free Church and the United Presbyterian Church in 1900, there were around 290 paid missionary employees working for the two main denominations, with over 80 missionaries' wives working unpaid.[65] By 1930, the Church of Scotland, following reunification with the Free Church, employed 702 missionaries, of which 193 were married women working without pay. While single women missionaries were first employed in the late 1830s, numbers remained few over some decades. As women gained access to higher education and professional training, as teachers and nurses, for example, numbers taking up a missionary vocation expanded considerably. Correspondingly, they became proportionately greater as part of the missionary workforce. Women, taking paid single women missionaries and unpaid married women together, made up 42 per cent of the Free Church missionary workforce by 1880; 60 per cent of Church of Scotland missionaries by 1890; and 64 per cent of the reunited Church of Scotland's missionaries in 1930.

---

[65] For more detailed discussion of numbers, see Breitenbach, *Empire and Scottish Society.*

Evidence exists that Scots contributed a disproportionate share to spheres of imperial activity such as colonial administration, the armed forces, and emigration, and this claim has also been advanced for missionaries. At the time of the World Missionary Conference of 1910, the *Scotsman* declared that: 'In proportion to its population Scotland has done more for missions than any country in the world. It has sent some of the best of its manhood to establish and to man the outposts of Christianity.'[66] However, figures compiled by Eugene Stock for missionaries of the principal British societies in 1900 indicated that Scots made up 9.7 per cent of the total,[67] at a time when the Scottish population was around 11.6 per cent of the total UK population (1901),[68] thus undercutting *The Scotsman*'s claim of a disproportionate Scottish contribution at that time. There is no doubt, however, that by the late nineteenth century the Scottish Presbyterian foreign mission movement had achieved both a high public profile in Scotland and an international reputation. Stock's *Handbook of Missions* applauded the pioneering efforts of several Scottish missionaries, and praised the 'Scotch Presbyterians' for their 'foremost' role in the development of educational missions and for also having led the way in medical missions.[69] The location of the 1910 conference in Edinburgh served as an endorsement of the Scots' leading role, as well as providing the opportunity for much public celebration of it.

If it undermines the claim of a disproportionate contribution, Stock's book, however, does emphasize the tendency for Scottish missionaries to be well educated and professionally qualified. In many ways, education was central to the success of the Scottish foreign mission movement. The relative openness to higher education for men, the level of education provided for girls, and access for women to higher education towards the end of the century all contributed to a well-educated missionary workforce, which in turn promoted the value of education for others. This was crucial not just to the calibre of recruits for Scottish missions, but also to the missionary practice which they instituted. Missionaries were essentially a professional middle-class group, notwithstanding iconic working-class figures such as

---

[66] *The Scotsman*, 14 June 1910.

[67] Eugene Stock, *A Short Handbook of Missions* (London, 1904).

[68] Ibid.; population figure quoted in *Twentieth Century Facts*, Research Paper 99/111, Office for National Statistics.

[69] Stock, *Handbook of Missions*.

Livingstone and Slessor, and thus attained a social and class position which provided links to powerful players both in Scottish society and abroad.

This professional middle-class character is likely to have continued to define the missionary workforce in the twentieth century, though it would have remained open to upwardly mobile individuals of working-class origin. Missionary numbers reached a peak in the inter-war years, with declining numbers in the post-Second World War period reflecting changes in the theory and practice of missionary work, as well as the increasing secularization of society.[70] In the 1950s and 1960s, missionaries tended to become more involved in administration, in management and training of local staff, and in working with partner churches such as the Church of Central Africa Presbyterian and Church of South India. Although not a numerically large group, the missionaries' location within middle-class networks in Scotland enabled them to be influential well into the twentieth century. Overlapping memberships and intersecting interests of church, university, civic, and business circles meant that the movement both enjoyed the endorsement of elites, and had the capacity to reach a wide audience through a variety of channels.

IMPACTS OF FOREIGN MISSION MOVEMENT

An element of the ongoing debate about whether or not foreign missions were essentially a tool of imperialist expansion and rule is the question of the impact which foreign missions had on the peoples whom they sought to convert. Some historians have downplayed the role of missions, arguing that they had contact only with small numbers of people, and that they often had little impact in terms of religious conversion. Others have argued that missionaries were often critics of empire, and that it was mission-educated groups who became central to nationalist and independence struggles. It is therefore pertinent to ask what is the evidence concerning the role of Scots missions. However, historical research on the impact of Scots missions is uneven in territorial coverage and varied in approach, ranging from the critical to the celebratory. The historian must often still have recourse to nineteenth- and early twentieth-century sources, or to hagiographic biographies, sources which, on the one hand, have been under-utilized and, on

---

[70] I owe this information about twentieth-century developments to my co-researcher, Lesley Orr.

the other, have not yet been subject to much critical reappraisal. There are some exceptions to this; for example, the literature on David Livingstone and on missions in Malawi has produced important critical re-evaluations.[71] More studies of the character of John McCracken's invaluable history of Scots missions in northern Malawi would do much to enhance understanding of the effects that missions had, economically, culturally, and politically, and it is perhaps surprising that no other study of such depth has emerged since its publication in 1977. There is nonetheless a growing literature on Scots missions, from which the following discussion of key themes draws.

Preaching and evangelization were, of course, central to missionary work. However, Scots missions also placed great emphasis on education, often playing a significant role in the development of educational institutions, from elementary schools to higher education. For example, Free Church missionaries Alexander Duff, John Wilson, and William Miller helped establish, respectively, the universities of Calcutta, Bombay, and Madras.[72] A notable feature of educational practice was its inclusion of 'female' education from the early decades of the nineteenth century[73]—supported by Ladies' Associations at home—while from the mid-century onwards 'zenana'[74] work in India was promoted as a Scots-led innovation in work with women.[75] Scots missionaries were also active in providing medical facilities, in applying technical and scientific methods within training institutions, in the development of physical infrastructure, and in the encouragement of various types of cultivation and other economic activities.

---

[71] See, for example, McCracken, *Politics and Christianity in Malawi*; John M. MacKenzie, 'David Livingstone: The Construction of the Myth', in Graham Walker and Tom Gallagher (eds), *Sermons and Battle Hymns: Protestant Culture in Modern Scotland* (Edinburgh, 1990), 24–42; John M. MacKenzie, 'Heroic Myths of Empire', in idem (ed.), *Popular Imperialism and the Military* (Manchester, 1992), 109–37; Andrew Ross, *David Livingstone: Mission and Empire* (London, 2002).

[72] See entries on Alexander Duff and William Miller in *ODNB*, http://www.oxforddnb.com (accessed 2 July 2010); Dr M. D. David, 'John Wilson—an Educationist', *Journal of the University of Bombay*, 43.79 (1974), 87–114.

[73] Laird comments that the initiation of education for girls was a complete innovation. See M. A. Laird, *Missionaries and Education in Bengal, 1793–1837* (Oxford, 1972).

[74] The 'zenana' was the name given to women's quarters, where women lived 'in seclusion'. This arrangement was by no means universal in India, though in missionary literature it came to typify the situation of Indian women.

[75] This approach was claimed to have originated with Church of Scotland missionary Dr Thomas Smith. See *Free Church of Scotland Record*, 11, 15 December 1861; and Minna Cowan, *The Education of Women in India* (Edinburgh, 1912).

Given that the numbers of missionaries were relatively small, particularly in relation to their ambitions for wholesale Christianization, a typical strategy was to enhance their impact by the training of 'native' Christians as catechists, Bible-women, and teachers. Above all, the ideal of missions was the ordination of converts as ministers, but the strict criteria imposed for admission to this rank placed severe limits on the numbers who succeeded. Much was made of any who did become ordained ministers, some of whom were trained in Scotland, such as South African Tiyo Soga.[76] In terms of Christianization in general, the impacts of missions were often limited, though Christian churches were, of course, established in territories where missions were active. Within India, Christian converts remained a small minority. In Africa, Christian churches saw more substantial growth over time, though there were occasional breakaways with the formation of hybrid forms of Christianity incorporating elements of indigenous religions, a phenomenon which had also occurred in the West Indies, and which missionaries invariably deplored.[77] Furthermore, despite a rhetoric of building up 'native' churches, which would eventually become autonomous, missionaries and the churches at home were slow to relinquish a paternalistic attitude towards the churches they had helped to establish.

However much missionaries saw themselves as acting benevolently in offering the 'gift' of Christianity to peoples typically characterized as 'heathens' or 'savages', their interactions with colonized peoples were often aggressively interventionist. In India, for example, Scots missionaries, alongside other Protestant missionaries, campaigned for the imperial state to outlaw practices such as 'sati', child marriage, and female infanticide.[78] In twentieth-century Kenya, Church of Scotland missionaries were prominent in attacking the practice of female circumcision, then described in rather more euphemistic terms.[79] Such practices were then controversial and

---

[76] See MacKenzie, *Scots in South Africa*.

[77] See, for example, discussion of secessions in South Africa in MacKenzie, *Scots in South Africa*.

[78] See, for example, G. A. Oddie, *Social Protest in India: British Protestant Missionaries and Social Reforms, 1850–1900* (New Delhi, 1979).

[79] Reports on this appeared in *Kikuyu News*, the newsletter of the Church of Scotland mission at Kikuyu. Missionary Dr John Arthur was a prominent advocate of action on this issue, and the Church of Scotland's publicity led the Duchess of Atholl, MP, to take it up in Parliament. Missionary attempts to change this practice provoked much hostility, and proved very divisive among the Kikuyu Christian community. See Kenneth Mufaka, 'Scottish Missionaries and the Circumcision Controversy in Kenya, 1900–1960', *International Review of Scottish Studies*, 28 (2003), 47–58.

remain so where they persist, continuing to generate campaigns for change or abolition. However, campaigns by missionaries and supporters at home have been subjected to critiques by historians, on the one hand because the emphasis on such practices served to create distorted stereotypes of the nature of Indian and African societies, and on the other because of the power relations articulated in such movements, in which colonizers acted on behalf of others whom they regarded as 'degraded' victims.[80] It is clear, nonetheless, that some campaigns for social reform also garnered support from indigenous, often elite, groups, and that missionaries worked in alliance with such groups, for example, William Miller's involvement in the anti-nautch ('nautch' girls were dancing girls, often associated with prostitution) movement, together with the Madras Hindu Social Reform Association in the 1890s.[81]

It can be argued that campaigns against social and cultural practices were a form of cultural imperialism, and there is a sense in which this cannot be gainsaid. Yet the complex sets of circumstances and social relationships within which missionaries operated could allow for solidaristic alliances to be established between missionaries and groups of colonized peoples, founded on humanitarian and egalitarian beliefs. At the same time, campaign rhetoric might consistently present pejorative stereotypes of the cultural practices of others. The humanitarian actions and campaigns of missionaries often suffered from such ambiguities—opposition to slavery, advocacy of the rights of indigenous peoples, defence of their rights or land from the depredations of white settlers, and so on, could simultaneously assert human equality, while suggesting cultural and/or racial inferiority. Furthermore, missionaries themselves were not a homogeneous group and did not all articulate the same views of colonized peoples. Scots missionaries who have been held up as the champions of egalitarianism, such as John Philip and David Livingstone, were no doubt representative of the least ambiguously stated humanitarian positions (though not wholly unambiguous), but many others shared the intolerant and racist attitudes to other cultures that were the hallmark of their times.

---

[80] See, for example, Antoinette Burton, *Burdens of History: British Feminists, Indian Women, and Imperial Culture, 1865–1915* (Chapel Hill, NC, 1994); Lata Mani, *Contentious Traditions: The Debate on Sati in Colonial India* (Berkeley, 1998); Andrea Major, *Pious Flames: European Encounters with Sati, 1500–1830* (New Delhi, 2006).

[81] Oddie, *Social Protest in India*.

Outcomes were not always what missionaries had hoped for, either in terms of conversion to Christianity or in terms of economic development. However, missions, in providing access to western education, often furnished a means for colonized peoples to adapt to the transformations occurring as the result of colonization and imperial rule. This might be in the form of access to particular types of employment, for example, lower-grade civil service posts in India. One impact in Malawi was that it enabled educated Malawians to migrate to South Africa to become part of the expanding industrial workforce there, rather than as missionaries had envisaged, as developing viable forms of economic activity as alternatives to slave trading in Malawi itself.[82] In the context of slave trading, a benefit that missions could offer was some form of protection from hostile attacks, particularly when the frontier missions became incorporated within the formal empire. Mission education was also to facilitate the rise of a growing nationalist consciousness across the empire, and many nationalist leaders were the product of mission education provided by Scottish and other missions.

Despite the stated aim of building up 'native' churches which would become self-sustaining, missionaries were slow to encourage the autonomy of such churches, and similarly they seem to have been relatively slow in coming to a recognition of the justice of nationalist or anti-colonial demands in the twentieth century. A well-documented aspect of twentieth-century experience has been the role of missionaries in opposing federation in Rhodesia and Nyasaland in the 1950s.[83] Missionaries in Malawi had a history of advocacy on behalf of Malawians, had given evidence to government commissions, and had represented Malawians on the Legislative Council. Their opposition to federation arose from its favouring white minority rule, and fear of the spread of apartheid from South Africa. The well-publicized success of missionaries in gaining the 1959 General Assembly's support for their anti-federation position has highlighted a moment of radicalism that may be atypical, however, of the attitudes of missionaries and of the membership of the Church of Scotland towards decolonization.

---

[82] See McCracken, *Politics and Christianity in Malawi*.

[83] See, for example, Ross, 'Scotland and Malawi, 1859–1964'; John Stuart, 'Scottish Missionaries and the End of Empire: The Case of Nyasaland', *Historical Research*, 76.193 (2003), 411–30; T. Jack Thompson, 'Presbyterians and Politics in Malawi: A Century of Interaction', *Round Table*, 94.382 (2005), 575–87.

Missionaries were not necessarily homogeneous as a group, and were by no means uniformly radical. In India, only a small minority of missionaries actively supported nationalist demands for independence, while the majority distanced themselves from politics and some were anti-nationalist.[84] In South Africa, where there was a tradition of radicalism among nineteenth-century Scottish missionaries, the twentieth century was to witness its erosion and the adoption of much more equivocal, not to say acquiescent, positions towards segregation and the apartheid regime.[85]

Was the practice or impact of Scottish missionaries any different from that of other British Protestant missionary societies? Broadly speaking, the ways in which Scottish missions provided an interface between colonizer and colonized that facilitated imperial expansion and imperial governance were similar to British missions generally. Any distinctiveness in their practice may have been one of degree rather than of kind. The emphasis within Scottish missionary practice on both education and medicine perhaps marked it out to some extent, particularly with respect to the place given to scientific and technical instruction. This contrasted with some English missionary societies, where far greater emphasis was placed on evangelization. A related distinction was the level of educational attainment typical of Scots missionaries, again providing a contrast with some English missionary societies. Scots' tendency to be better educated was a major reason for their disproportionate representation among LMS agents.[86] Clearly, Scottish missionaries were promulgating in Presbyterianism a particular theological and organizational form of Protestantism, and there is no doubt that they themselves perceived this as distinctive, and that this sustained their sense of Scottish identity. To what extent there was a 'nationalist' consciousness embodied in their religious and educational practices which particularly fostered the development of nationalist consciousness in their pupils and converts remains a matter for speculation. The perceived success of Scottish missionary approaches and work did, however, feed into national pride at home, with the foreign mission movement being acclaimed as a Scottish contribution to empire. Indeed, arguably, the most important impact of foreign missions was at home.

---

[84] J. H. Proctor, 'Scottish Missionaries in India: An Inquiry into Motivation', *South Asia*, 13.1 (1990), 43–61.

[85] MacKenzie, *Scots in South Africa*.

[86] Calder, *Scotland's March Past*.

Impact at home

The foreign mission movement was sustained by networks of local supporters, which typically operated on a Scotland-wide basis. This was true from the inception of missionary societies in the 1790s, while such networks became formalized within the organizational structures of the main Presbyterian churches in the post-Disruption period, and continued within the twentieth century, through the key phases of church reunification which took place in 1900 and 1929. Crucial functions of such networks and structures were fundraising in order to finance the employment of missionaries and to provide resources for the construction of churches, schools, hospitals, and so on, the recruitment of missionaries, and the dissemination of information. News of the progress of the missionary enterprise was disseminated by ministers in the pulpit, through literature, public meetings, and exhibitions, as well as receiving coverage in the secular press. Given the levels of church membership in Scotland throughout the period—rising to a high point of 50.5 per cent of the population in 1905, but remaining substantial until the late 1950s[87]—missionary literature of various kinds had the potential to reach a wide audience.[88] This literature was characterized on the one hand by humanitarian discourses, for example, in defence of the rights of indigenous peoples or in opposition to slavery, but competing with these were racialized discourses that placed Europeans at the apex of an evolutionary hierarchy. Indeed, up until the early decades of the twentieth century, missionary literature was characterized by representations of other societies which helped to foster both racist and imperialist world views.

Over time, the work of Scottish missionaries and missions came to be widely celebrated as a Scottish contribution to empire. The rise of the genre of missionary biographies in the later decades of the nineteenth century, and the creation of missionary celebrities such as David Livingstone and Mary Slessor, brought this idea to prominence. The exploits and achievements of well-known missionaries were typically situated within the traditions of the Reformed Church, and seen as a fulfilment of the spirit of John Knox, or later church luminaries, such as Thomas Chalmers, who had been a

---

[87] See Callum Brown, *Religion and Society in Scotland since 1707* (Edinburgh, 1997).

[88] See Breitenbach, *Empire and Scottish Society*; see also Esther Breitenbach, 'Religious Literature and Discourses of Empire: The Scottish Presbyterian Foreign Mission Movement', in Carey (ed.), *Empires of Religion*, 84–110.

supporter of foreign missions. Missions were deemed to represent a dimension of the imperial enterprise morally superior to acquisition of land or economic exploitation; in this way the 'colonization' of Nyasaland by Scots missions came to be represented as redemption for the failure of Darien.[89] In the creation and celebration of this Scottish missionary tradition and contribution to empire, the Scottish origins of missionaries allowed the incorporation of famous LMS missionaries, such as David Livingstone and Robert Moffat, alongside those directly funded by Scottish churches. Thus the missionary enterprise provided a prism through which Scots at home perceived the empire, colonial territories, and peoples, while at the same time it fostered national pride in the Scots role in empire. This popular endorsement of foreign missions as a significant contribution to empire continued to have wide circulation in the inter-war years of the twentieth century, when missionary activities continued to be widely publicized through literature, magic lantern shows, cinema, and regular visits to congregations by missionaries on furlough.[90]

After the First World War, there was a reappraisal of missionary approaches, with the idea of a temporary 'trusteeship' role becoming more prominent, in which the aim of self-sustaining churches paralleled the idea of a gradual acquisition of political autonomy, often envisaged as a very long-term process. The Church of Scotland Church and Nation Committee, established in 1919, through specific sub-committees, demonstrated a continued engagement with imperial affairs, subsequently redefined as 'Commonwealth Relations'. The changed nature of relationships with dependent colonies in the post-Second World War period of necessity engendered much debate within international missionary networks, with a changing conceptualization of 'mission' taking place in the 1950s and 1960s among the Presbyterian Churches in the dominions as well as at home.

---

[89] See, for example, George Smith, *Life of Alexander Duff* (London, 1899); W. P. Livingstone, *Laws of Livingstonia: A Narrative of Missionary Adventure and Achievement* (London, 1921). The rhetoric of Nyasaland as redemption for Darien was still being articulated in the 1950s at the time of the anti-federation campaign. Andrew Ross has noted that 'Professor Shepperson suggested to a class in the University of Edinburgh that for the Scottish people Nyasaland was the success that had made up for the failure of the late-seventeenth-century colonial venture at Darien, and London must not be allowed to do down Scotland again'. Ross, 'Scotland and Malawi, 1859–1964', 305.

[90] I owe the information about twentieth-century developments in this and the following paragraphs to my co-researcher, Lesley Orr.

Following a review of committee and departmental structures, an Overseas Council was created in 1964, with the relationship between the Church of Scotland and Presbyterian churches arising from foreign missions being designated one of partnership. The way in which such changes also modified popular representations of Scottish missionaries is a question still to be fully answered. It is possible to argue that the well-publicized episode of missionary and church support for the political autonomy of Africans in Nyasaland in the late 1950s has served to maintain a positive construction of Scottish missionaries as humanitarian and egalitarian, which has obscured the extent to which foreign missions were historically allied to the imperial project—both wittingly and unwittingly—and which has obscured the range of missionary and church responses to decolonization.

Again, the question arises of whether Scottish experience was distinctive. There do not appear to have been missionary practices that were unique to Scots, although Scots placed a higher value on education than some other missions, while the Presbyterian form of church organization was distinctive and Scottish in origin. As for mission supporters at home, there were many parallels with missionary societies elsewhere in Britain, and in the growing Protestant mission movement in North America and Australasia, both in terms of typical activities, circulation of literature, and the dominant discourses within these. Furthermore, missionary societies elsewhere in Britain had a similar role in bringing empire home and shaping understandings of empire and metropolitan identity, as, for example, Susan Thorne and Catherine Hall have shown.[91] Whether or not there were substantive differences either in Scots missionary practices or their impacts abroad, it is undeniably the case that in its communications with its support base at home the movement articulated a shared, and explicit, Scottish national identity. Thus, if there was little distinction in the English-speaking world in representations of colonized 'others', metropolitan identities were differentiated beyond a shared British imperial perspective or 'Britishness', which in the Scottish context had neither the same prominence nor the same status as a Scottish national identity.

---

[91] Susan Thorne, *Congregational Missions and the Making of an Imperial Culture in Nineteenth-Century England* (Stanford, Calif., 1999); Catherine Hall, *Civilising Subjects: Metropole and Colony in the English Imagination, 1830–1867* (Cambridge, 2002); Susan Thorne, 'Religion and Empire at Home', in Catherine Hall and Sonya O. Rose (eds), *At Home with the Empire: Metropolitan Culture and the Imperial World* (Cambridge, 2006).

Conclusion

Scottish churches played a varied and sometimes prominent role in imperial expansion and settlement—through meeting religious needs and providing cultural cohesion to settler communities of Scottish origin, through endorsing and encouraging emigration, through institution-building both in settler and colonized communities, and through providing a channel of communication between communities abroad and at home. Religious affiliations and church membership both themselves constituted associative networks of Scots and served as an entry point to further associative networks within the secular world, easing the transition from home to colony. Missionaries operated also within such associative networks to build support for their work at home and abroad, to gain access to colonial elites, such as administrators, military commanders, and leading dignitaries within civil society. Thus Scots churches used their networks to operate effectively within British, imperial, and trans-atlantic circles and, in this sense, they clearly saw themselves as embedded within the circuits of empire.

Within a society in which religion continued to occupy an important place, both the foreign mission movement and links to colonial churches were to become crucial in mediating an understanding of empire for Scots at home. The period of decolonization effectively brought an end to Scottish foreign missions, and resulted in a transformation in ways of working internationally with other Presbyterian and Protestant churches, and in-deed, within wider ecumenical networks. Decolonization also coincided with the decline of religion and growth of secularism in Scottish society, with a debunking of missionary heroes and heroines, and a distancing from the imperial past. Religious life had, however, played a central role in shaping understandings of empire and in articulating Scottish identity at home and throughout the empire. The churches' engagement in empire was thus a crucial dimension of Scotland's experience of empire, and deserves to be acknowledged as such.

Select Bibliography

Esther Breitenbach, *Empire and Scottish Society: The Impact of Foreign Missions at Home, c.1790 to c.1914* (Edinburgh, 2009).
Hilary Carey (ed.), *Empires of Religion* (Basingstoke, 2008).

Angela McCarthy (ed.), *A Global Clan: Scottish Migrant Networks and Identities since the Eighteenth Century* (London, 2006).

John McCracken, *Politics and Christianity in Malawi 1875–1940: The Impact of the Livingstonia Mission in the Northern Province* (Cambridge, 1977).

Lesley Orr Macdonald, *A Unique and Glorious Mission: Women and Presbyterianism in Scotland* (Edinburgh, 2000).

John M. MacKenzie, 'David Livingstone: The Construction of the Myth', in Graham Walker and Tom Gallagher (eds), *Sermons and Battle Hymns: Protestant Culture in Modern Scotland* (Edinburgh, 1990), 24–42.

——'Heroic Myths of Empire', in idem (ed.), *Popular Imperialism and the Military* (Manchester, 1992), 109–37.

——with Nigel R. Dalziel, *The Scots in South Africa* (Manchester, 2007).

Barbara Murison, 'The Disruption and the Colonies of Scottish Settlement', in Stewart J. Brown and Michael Fry (eds), *Scotland in the Age of Disruption* (Edinburgh, 1993).

Malcolm Prentis, *The Scots in Australia* (Sydney, 2008).

Andrew Ross, 'Scotland and Malawi, 1859–1964', in Stewart J. Brown and George Newlands (eds), *Scottish Christianity in the Modern World* (Edinburgh, 2000), 283–309.

——*David Livingstone: Mission and Empire* (London, 2002).

Iain Whyte, *Scotland and the Abolition of Black Slavery, 1756–1838* (Edinburgh, 2006).

9

Scots in the Imperial Economy

T. M. Devine and John M. MacKenzie

In the eighteenth century, post-Union Scotland established a remarkable dominance in several of the Atlantic trades. As we have seen in Chapter 2 the wealth derived from the major Scottish role as entrepôt in tobacco, sugar, and other imports and re-exports helped to finance the initial phase of the Scottish industrial revolution. Fortunes derived from Scottish penetration of the East India Company (Chapter 3) in the same period also fed into such reinvestment opportunities. Thus Scots enterprise, in somewhat different forms, had both western and eastern dimensions. However, even as the centre of gravity of the 'British World System'[1] shifted further from the North Atlantic and Caribbean towards Asia and the Middle East, later Latin America, Australasia, and, to a much lesser extent, Africa, the advantageous position developed by Scots in the eighteenth century was not lost. On the contrary, individual Scots and their enterprises were able to build upon the eighteenth-century foundations to a remarkable degree. Indeed, few regions of the United Kingdom developed such a strikingly symbiotic relationship with imperial territories, a mutual economic dependence which was, however, to have damaging consequences in the twentieth century. Still, between the late eighteenth and mid-twentieth centuries, Scotland became an integral part of the new global economic order at all levels: industry, trade, emigration, and overseas investment. Emigration is considered in the Introduction and in Chapter 5; industry, trade, and overseas investment in this chapter.

---

[1] As John Darwin calls it in his *The Empire Project: The Rise and Fall of the British World System 1839–1970* (Cambridge, 2009).

The New Economic Order

By the 1770s, the Caribbean plantations alone supplied one-quarter of Britain's imports and, with the American colonies, around one-fifth of her exports.[2] However, the West Indies, the great source of imperial riches in the eighteenth century, went into rapid decline after 1815. In that year, the Caribbean colonies still contributed over 17 per cent of Britain's trade, but within a century, this had dropped to less than 1 per cent of the total.[3] As global economic relationships were progressively reoriented from the 1780s, the British commercial system became as much non-imperial as colonial. By 1914, the trades with Argentina and China were more important than those of Canada and the West Indies.[4] Nevertheless, the empire's share of British total trade in the 1850s was 23 per cent for imports, 30 per cent for exports, and 14 per cent for re-exports. By the outbreak of the First World War, the empire's share of British imports stood at around 25 per cent, 35 per cent for exports, and 12 per cent for re-exports.[5] The empire thus remained significant, but only within a wider pattern of trading relationships.

But these trades were transformed in their character and their scale by the uniquely rapid industrialization of the United Kingdom, a phenomenon which gave the British a lead which was to continue throughout the nineteenth century. By 1840, Britain accounted for 45 per cent of world industrial production, holding its own at 30 per cent in 1880. Exports and shipping exhibited phenomenal growth in this period. For example, the tonnage of shipping leaving British ports increased fourfold between 1834 and 1860.[6] This was also reflected in British demographic trends. By 1881, 44 per cent of the labour force was employed in industry, still a considerably higher figure than the rival economies in the USA and Germany. Only 13 per cent of British workers were in the agricultural sector.[7] To a certain extent, this was represented in the classic imperial and wider world economic nexus

---

[2] S. B. Saul, *Studies in British Overseas Trade 1870–1913* (Liverpool, 1960), 7.

[3] Andrew Porter, 'Introduction: Britain and the Empire in the Nineteenth Century', in idem (ed.), *The Oxford History of the British Empire*, iii: *The Nineteenth Century* (Oxford, 1999), 4.

[4] Saul, *Studies*, 228.

[5] Werner Schlote, *British Overseas Trade from 1700 to the 1930s* (Oxford, 1952), 88.

[6] J. H. Clapham, *An Economic History of Modern Britain: The Early Railway Age 1820–1850* (Cambridge, 1939), 211.

[7] C. A. Bayly, *The Birth of the Modern World 1780–1914* (Oxford, 2004), 173.

in which the main weight of primary production was located overseas, with the industrial processing of raw materials taking place in Britain. These internal demographic shifts were matched by the remarkable re-location of European populations into other regions of the globe, which itself contributed to the re-formulation and growth of commercial relationships.

The nineteenth and early twentieth centuries were indeed the great era of migration. Between 1820 and 1930, 32.1 million Europeans migrated to the USA alone, with Britain (including Ireland) contributing disproportionately to this exodus.[8] While the scale of movement to other regions, including Canada, Australasia, and South Africa, might be smaller, the effect was the same. Productive capacity was expanded; trading networks grew further; and the opportunities for British merchants and manufacturers increased.

This revolution in production and trade was matched by dramatic developments in banking, finance houses, and investment companies, as well as by striking transport and infrastructural transformations, including the development of railways, increased sophistication in locomotives to power them, much improved sailing ships, steamships, deep water harbours, canals of global significance (notably that at Suez opened in 1869), and the development of the telegraph and undersea cables. Even the emergence of a world system of time zones served to emphasize a global system which was geared to the requirements of the new industrial commercial networks. It is striking that the global morphology of harbours, canals, and railways was universally designed to feed international trade rather than the local requirements of specific territories, generally channelling products from the interior of continents to their coasts, with industrial imports running in the opposite direction.

At the same time, the protectionist system of mercantilism, together with its shipping restrictions, tariffs, and regulatory controls, was swept away. The British instituted a new free trading economic order precisely because their initial and inherent dominance ensured that this would favour their almost universal global trading penetration. Moreover, the establishment of British naval mastery from the Napoleonic Wars ensured effective protection of British commercial shipping. Latin American countries were liberated from former Portuguese and Spanish power; the development of an independent United States demonstrated that economic relationships

---

[8] P. J. Cain and A. G. Hopkins, 'The Political Economy of British Expansion Overseas, 1750–1914', *Economic History Review*, 33.4 (November 1980), 479.

could continue and prosper even outside the imperial relationship; an isolationist China was forced open by the British in a sequence of wars and was compelled to be part of these global networks;[9] while worldwide botanical exchanges ensured that products such as tea, cinchona, coffee, cotton, and later rubber would be established in easily controlled regions of the colonial empire.[10] Moreover, the development of the geological understanding of the mineral composition of the earth (facilitated by geological surveys and related museums[11]) helped to promote mining enterprises concerned with extracting both precious and base metals, some of them (such as copper) increasingly important in what has been described as the second industrial revolution of the later nineteenth century. Scotland was to play a part in all these developments, though whether the mass of the nation's population benefited is much less certain.

Scotland and the Global and Imperial Economies

The Scottish seizure of the opportunities of the new world economic order is well illustrated by the extraordinary growth of the city of Glasgow. By the 1880s, Glasgow had become one of the most notable examples of urban expansion and civic power and pride in the British Empire, even arrogating to itself the title of the 'second city of the empire'. As the 1880s produced a new turning point, sometimes known as the development of the 'New Imperialism', so did Glasgow appear to have become one of the most notable exemplars of the great nineteenth-century burgeoning of trade, industry, and transportation. In 1888, the city held a major exhibition in Kelvingrove Park, an exhibition which was designed to showcase the city's dominance in engineering, shipbuilding, and related heavy industries, as well as notable imperial relationships such as that with India. This was the first of a sequence of exhibitions, which continued with those of 1901 and 1911, culminating in the British Empire exhibition in Bellahouston Park in 1938, the last of the great imperial shows before a different world order was

---

[9] Michael Greenberg, *British Trade and the Opening of China 1800–1842* (Cambridge, 1951), 196–215; Gerald S. Graham, *The China Station: War and Diplomacy 1830–1860* (Oxford, 1978).

[10] Lucille Brockway, *Science and Colonial Expansion: The Role of the British Botanic Gardens* (New York, 1979); Richard Drayton, *Nature's Government: Science, Imperial Britain, and the 'Improvement' of the World* (New Haven, 2000).

[11] John M. MacKenzie, *Museums and Empire: Natural History, Human Cultures and Colonial Identities* (Manchester, 2009).

generated by the Second World War.[12] In the same decade of the 1880s, Glasgow expressed its civic and economic might through the building of a massively opulent City Chambers (or Town Hall), fronting George Square, the city's civic heart, well to the west of the old medieval city at the cathedral and Glasgow Cross, and a little to the west of the merchant city which had been the architectural and social expression of the Atlantic trades. Although the city had been one of the prime stepping stones for migrants heading westwards across the Atlantic and indeed elsewhere in the British Empire, its citizens seemed aware of its significance in the world order. The foundation stone and opening ceremonies of the City Chambers were watched by a large proportion of the population and the exhibitions were visited by striking numbers of people from Glasgow and beyond (11.5 million in 1901).[13] The South African War at the same period also brought large numbers of Glaswegians onto the streets to celebrate such events as the Relief of Mafeking, for Glasgow's people had done well out of that war.[14]

This apparent civic pride (albeit combined with dismal social depriva-tion) reflected the fact that Glasgow's economy was strikingly connected with the British imperial and global networks. By 1914, Glasgow and its satellite towns produced one-half of British marine-engine horsepower, one-third of railway locomotives and rolling stock, one-third of the shipping tonnage, and about one-fifth of all steel. The city had developed an extraordinary dominance, reflected in the range of engineering special-isms in engines, pumps, hydraulic equipment, railway products, and a host of others. In civil engineering, too, the west of Scotland was a celebrated centre of excellence, symbolized by the career of Sir William Arrol (1839–1913), the builder of the Forth and Tay bridges, Tower Bridge in London, and many other prestigious projects around the globe. Scottish engineers were celebrated throughout the world.[15]

---

[12] Perilla Kinchin and Juliet Kinchin, *Glasgow's Great Exhibitions, 1888, 1901, 1911, 1938, 1988* (Wendlebury, 1988); John M. MacKenzie, '"The Second City of the Empire": Glasgow—Imperial Municipality', in Felix Driver and David Gilbert (eds), *Imperial Cities: Landscape, Display and Identity* (Manchester, 1999), 215–37; T. M. Devine, *The Scottish Nation, 1700–2000* (London, 2006), 249.

[13] Ibid.

[14] *Glasgow Herald*, 21 May 1900.

[15] M. S. Moss and J. R. Hume, *Workshop of the British Empire* (London, 1977); John Butt, 'The Industries of Glasgow', in W. H. Fraser and Irene Maver (eds), *Glasgow*, ii: *1839–1912* (Manche-ster, 1996), 96–140.

The development of the heavy industries of the west of Scotland helped to replace cotton as the former lead sector of the first industrial revolution. This industry declined rapidly after the 1830s, although cotton thread manufacture, notably by Coats of Paisley, expanded to become a global industry, controlling no less than 80 per cent of world thread-making capacity in the early twentieth century.[16] In the east of Scotland, jute manufacture replaced that of other textiles (see below). Other Scottish towns developed specializations, including Kirkcaldy for floor coverings and linoleum, Galashiels, Hawick, and Selkirk for tartans, tweeds, and high-quality knitted goods, Kilmarnock and Glasgow for carpets (Templetons in Glasgow was the largest carpet manufacturer in Britain by 1914), Darval and Galston in Ayrshire for fine lace curtain manufacture.[17] Further industrial diversification was indicated by the success of James 'Paraffin' Young in developing the shale oil industry. There were also sewing machines from the American Singer Company in Clydebank, optical instruments from Barr and Stroud, wringers from the Acme company, as well as automobile and aircraft manufacture of the engineering giant William Beardmore. Chemical manufacture, for example in the great works of James Tennant, James White, and James Stevenson, was also important.[18] Interestingly, many of these entrepreneurs became the patrons of Scottish missionary activity.[19] Moreover, while the cotton and linen sectors of the early nineteenth century rapidly declined, the coal, iron, and steel industries, relatively sluggish in the earlier period, took off after 1830 to become, yet again, vital in the global economy. All of these burgeoning industries linked the primary producing regions of America, Africa, Asia, and Australasia into the industrializing regions of Europe.

[16] William Knox, *Hanging by a Thread: The Scottish Cotton Industry 1850–1914* (Preston, 1995); Don-Woon Kim, 'The British Multinational Enterprise in the United States before 1914: The Case of J. and P. Coats', *Business History Review*, 72 (Winter 1998), 523–51.

[17] Devine, *Scottish Nation*, 251; C. Gulvin, *The Tweedmakers: A History of the Scottish Fancy Woollen Industry, 1600–1914* (Edinburgh, 1973).

[18] S. G. E. Lythe and J. Butt, *An Economic History of Scotland 1100–1939* (London, 1975), 168–80.

[19] James White and his son John Campbell White were major funders, to the tune of well over £50,000, of the Free Church of Scotland's mission in Nyasaland (Malawi). The conditions of their workers at their chemical works in Rutherglen were, however, appalling and were exposed by James Keir Hardie in 1899. Other donors included James Stevenson, James Young, and the shipbuilder Alexander Stephen. John McCracken, *Politics and Christianity in Malawi, 1875–1940* (2nd edn Zomba, 2000), 59–61.

A few examples of notable exports help to demonstrate the bilateral relationship between Scottish production and global consumption. For example, whisky continued to grow in importance, with 20 million gallons charged for duty in 1884. According to Magee and Thompson, the exported products of the three major producers, Buchanan's, Dewar's, and Walker's, 'tended to follow the flag'.[20] Thus there were major markets in Canada, South Africa, and Australia. Beverages as diverse as Camp Coffee and Tennent's India Pale Ale, both produced in Glasgow, developed considerable exports to the Indian Empire. Thomas Lipton's teas (the grocery chain started in Glasgow) established notable vertical integration with tea plantations which he owned in Ceylon (Sri Lanka), imperial connections which he extensively advertised. Iron products from Walter Macfarlane's Saracen Works in Glasgow, including band stands, fountains, and other decorative material, balconies, as well as complete buildings, were exported throughout the empire.[21] Linoleum from Kirkcaldy also had strong export markets, with 58 per cent of all floorings exported from Britain heading for the empire in 1913. These trends were encouraged by the opening of colonial branches and the circulation of catalogues overseas. For example, the Scottish decorating company Cottier and Lyon opened a branch in Sydney in 1873 and helped to ensure a certain amount of cultural and design uniformity across the 'British world'.[22]

All of these industrial developments and worldwide trading relationships had a dramatic effect on the nature and structure of Scottish society. There was a substantial increase in the Scottish population, rising by 88 per cent between the 1750s and 1831, reaching 2.374 million in the latter year. Between 1831 and 1911 the population doubled to 4.761 million. This growth was matched by a dramatic geographical redistribution of population. There was a considerable immigration from Ireland throughout the nineteenth century, especially during the Great Famine and its aftermath, with smaller numbers coming from Italy and Lithuania. The levels of internal migration were also unprecedented. The majority of the new city dwellers moved from the farms, villages, and small towns of the rural Lowland and the border countryside, but Gaels from the Highlands and Islands were also well

---

[20] Gary B. Magee and Andrew S. Thompson, *Empire and Globalisation: Networks of People, Goods and Capital in the British World*, c.1850–1914 (Cambridge, 2010), 156.

[21] MacKenzie, '"The First City of the Empire"', 223.

[22] Magee and Thompson, *Empire and Globalisation*, 158.

represented. There is evidence that the overwhelming majority of country parishes lost population in this period. The concentration of people in the central Lowlands of Scotland was striking, with a near-doubling of population in the Edinburgh region between 1830 and the end of the century and an even more dramatic growth in the west from over 628,000 in 1830 to nearly two million. By that year, the western central counties contained 44 per cent of the total population. At the same time, Scotland was contributing strongly to the migration flows of the period, with some two million people leaving the country between 1815 and 1914. The corollary of all of this was that as rural employment rapidly declined (partly as a result of agricultural improvements), mining, building, and manufacturing correspondingly grew in significance. By 1911, 60 per cent of the Scottish population lived in towns, making it the second most highly urbanized country in Europe, after only England and Wales. Glasgow had a quarter of a million inhabitants in the 1830s; by 1871 this had reached half a million; and by 1914 the milestone of one million had been reached (partly through boundary changes).[23]

This new industrial and urban society became highly dependent on overseas markets. The North British Locomotive Works, an amalgamation of three companies in 1903, could produce 800 locomotives every year and made Glasgow the largest locomotive-manufacturing centre in Europe, exporting engines from the Clyde to India, many other parts of the empire (almost half of its production went to the empire), South America, and elsewhere. A special heavy-lift crane was built at Finnieston on the Clyde to transfer these increasingly powerful and weighty engines onto the ships that would transport them around the world. Two-thirds of Scottish pig iron production was exported. In the later 1860s, around a half of total production was still being sent overseas. The destinations of shipping tonnage clearing from the Clyde between 1886 and 1911 reveal the global dimensions of Scottish trade. The cumulative percentages for 1886, 1891, 1896, and 1911 indicate that 61 per cent of all shipping headed for Europe, the United States, Latin America, and the Far East (though some colonial Pacific islands, presumably accounting for tiny numbers, were included

---

[23] M. Anderson and D. J. Morse, 'The People', in W. H. Fraser and R. J. Morris (eds), *People and Society in Scotland*, ii: *1830–1914* (Edinburgh, 1990); T. M. Devine, C. H. Lee, and G. C. Peden (eds), *The Transformation of Scotland* (Edinburgh, 2005), 92–8.

in the latter figure). Canada, India and the East Indies, Africa, Australasia, and the West Indies accounted for the remaining 39 per cent.[24] Imperial trade (that is to territories directly within the British colonial system) was thus very important, but was proportionately slighter than that to the non-imperial world. But the so-called non-imperial world covered many areas, such as Latin America and parts of the Far East, which can be regarded as part of the British 'informal empire', that is regions which the British virtually controlled economically, but did not rule directly. Imperial imports constitute a rather lower proportion, something like 31 per cent, but once more 'informal empire' accounts for at least some of the rest. It should, however, be remembered that the imperial markets were generally safe ones, tied in by force of sentiment and oiled by business networks in ways that 'foreign' markets were not.[25] Empire markets were therefore less prone to disturbance.

Class, Expertise, and Technology

Scotland had established a firm foundation for these developments in the eighteenth-century trades and in the earlier forms of industrialization. By the nineteenth century, a large and experienced business class had emerged, connected with a political and social elite committed to national economic growth, together with a labour force which had already developed skills in engineering, mining, and textiles. This class had already been inculcated with the work and time disciplines of industrial capitalism. Moreover, by the key take-off period after the 1830s, the country had already developed a sophisticated infrastructure of ports, roads, and canals and was poised for the extensive building of railways. Coal and iron ore resources ensured a ready supply of raw materials and energy. Railways were initially designed to exploit these resources, but later became significant in the development of more distant trading routes. An international trading network—complete with Scottish personnel established in many overseas ports—was already in existence. Indeed, Scottish entrepreneurship and skills were to appear throughout the world in this period. In addition, Scottish migrants to Canada, the USA, South Africa, and New Zealand seem

---

[24] Mitchell Library, Glasgow, Clyde Navigation Shipping Returns 1886–1911.
[25] Magee and Thompson, *Empire and Globalisation*.

to have been more skilled and literate than others from Ireland, Scandinavia, Italy, and eastern Europe.[26]

The interlocking nature of Scottish economic developments is neatly exemplified by the meteoric rise of Dundee jute manufacture. The city and its surrounding region already specialized in coarse textiles, including linen, and thus an entrepreneurial class existed eager to seize the new opportunities. Jute fibre was imported from Bengal and was manufactured into a coarse textile for use as bags and the backing of carpets. A number of wealthy jute barons, generally exploiting cheap female labour, dominated the industry. For example, the Cox Brothers' Camperdown Works employed in the 1880s no fewer than 14,000 workers, mainly women. Crucially, the city was Scotland's leading whaling centre. Whale oil was an important constituent of the process by which the brittle jute could be softened for processing. Scots also became significant at the Bengal end of this trade and were later active in establishing jute mills there. Bags manufactured from Dundee jute were used for a wide variety of international commodities, from coffee to Latin American guano, as well as contributing to the huge market for sandbags. But Dundee also reflected the negative aspects of Scottish industrialism. Wages for all workers in Scotland were always lower than those in England, and particularly so when female labour was significant, as in Dundee. This gave Scotland a competitive advantage, but it also helped to establish a deep-seated tradition of proletarian poverty and social deprivation which continued to modern times.[27]

Shipbuilding constituted another remarkable growth sector of the Scottish economy.[28] In 1835, the Clyde launched less than 5 per cent of British tonnage. But it was the steam revolution that transformed this picture. Steam enabled the long estuary of the Clyde to be a positive advantage. The dredging of the upper river placed the heart of shipbuilding nearer the centre of the city and closer to the necessary raw materials. Engineering experience associated with steam technology was readily available, not least

[26] Chapter on 'The Great Migration' in T. M. Devine, *To the Ends of the Earth: Scotland's Global Diaspora 1750–2010* (London, 2011). See also Jim McAloon, 'Scots in the Colonial Economy', in Tom Brooking and Jennie Coleman (eds), *The Heather and the Fern: Scottish Migration & New Zealand Settlement* (Dunedin, 2003), 87–102, particularly 101; John M. MacKenzie with Nigel R. Dalziel, *The Scots in South Africa: Ethnicity, Identity, Gender, and Race* (Manchester, 2007).

[27] Gordon T. Stewart, *Jute and Empire: The Calcutta Jute Wallahs and the Landscapes of Empire* (Manchester, 1998).

[28] Moss and Hume, *Workshop of the British Empire.*

because engineering shops were already turning out steam engines for mills and mines, reflecting the value of steam in the early phases of the industrial revolution. It was a relatively short step to turning these skills in precision engineering to marine use. Henry Bell's *Comet* was launched on the Clyde in 1812 and was able to sail on its sheltered waterways. The real advances came with solutions to the technical and performance problems of the steam engine (notably by the cousins David and Robert Napier) and to innovation in iron metal working, culminating in the development of steel production in the 1870s. Meanwhile, the speed and efficiency of steam ships was greatly enhanced by the rapid shift from the paddle wheel to the screw propeller, as well as by the appearance of the triple expansion engine and its derivatives. Two-thirds of all British iron-built tonnage was produced on the Clyde between 1851 and 1870. In 1914, Glasgow's yards built one-third of all British shipping tonnage, constituting one-fifth of that of the world, production which was greater by a considerable margin than all the German shipyards combined.

The striking growth of Scottish industry was more than matched by the emergence of Scottish shipping lines with international ramifications. These firms (some of which later moved to London) were often serviced by important agencies, established in many foreign ports, which handled the fleets of ships, their manifold cargoes, as well as their passengers, in colonial and foreign ports around the world. Until 1920, Glasgow ranked third after London and Liverpool in shipping tonnage registered in the city. These three ports were the only ones in Britain to boast a Lloyds committee, reflecting the importance of insurance services in the city. In 1910, there were no fewer than 182 management firms in Glasgow and Greenock alone, the most significant of which managed considerable numbers of ships.[29]

Examples of Scottish shipping enterprise included Sir William Mackinnon (1823–93), who has been described as possibly 'the greatest Scottish tycoon of all time'.[30] By 1889 he owned five shipping companies, including the massive British India Line, which together had a total fleet value of £3 million.[31] Mackinnon, a Puritan Scot from Kintyre, established this great

[29] J. Forbes Munro and Tony Slaven, 'Networks and Markets in Clyde Shipping', *Business History*, 43.2 (2001), 22–3; Gordon Jackson and Charles Munn, 'Trade, Commerce and Finance', in Fraser and Maver (eds), *Glasgow*, 62–70.

[30] Michael Fry, *The Scottish Empire* (Edinburgh, 2001), 265.

[31] J. Forbes Munro, *Maritime Enterprise and Empire: Sir William Mackinnon and his Business Network, 1823–1893* (Woodbridge, 2003).

shipping conglomerate from his humble beginnings as a shipping clerk in Glasgow and Calcutta. He founded his British India Line in India and created a vast web of routes linking India to other Indian Ocean territories, to South-East Asia, the Far East, and Australasia, as well as to the Mediterranean and Europe. Agencies connected to the Mackinnon enterprises included Mackinnon Mackenzie to be found in India and the East,[32] while he poured some of his fortune into the Imperial British East Africa Company, chartered by the British government in 1888 to attempt to corner significant parts of East Africa against the threat of German colonial ambitions.[33] Its directors were almost exclusively Scottish. British India subsequently became part of the P&O group, a company with a number of Scots, such as Arthur Anderson of Shetland and Thomas Sutherland from Aberdeen, among its founding fathers.[34] As late as 1900, half of this mighty company's fleet was registered at Greenock, even although the connections with Scotland had largely disappeared.[35] When the Inchcape group was formed in the twentieth century, its leading light was James Lyle Mackay (later Lord Inchcape), born in Arbroath (1852–1932), who believed that Scottish energy, initiative, and ambition were better expressed overseas than in Scotland.[36] Mackay built his career on a partnership in Mackinnon Mackenzie's agency in India. Yet another Scottish shipping tycoon was the Greenock-born Sir Donald Currie (1825–1909), who worked himself up to a significant position in the Cunard Line in Liverpool and later founded the Castle Line, which served South Africa, and was amalgamated with the Union Line in 1900.[37] He made a considerable fortune, played a role in Cape politics (his daughter married a Cape premier), and reinvested in

---

[32] There were Mackinnon Mackenzie agencies in Karachi, Bombay, Calcutta, Colombo, Chittagong, Rangoon, and Hong Kong, as well as in China and Japan. The headquarters building in Bombay (Mumbai) remains one of the grandest buildings on the waterfront near Ballard Pier.

[33] John S. Galbraith, *Mackinnon and East Africa, 1878–1895: A Study in the 'New Imperialism'* (Cambridge, 1972).

[34] Freda Harcourt, *Flagships of Imperialism: The P&O Company and the Politics of Empire from its Origins to 1867* (Manchester, 2006).

[35] P. L. Payne, *The Early Scottish Limited Companies 1856–1895* (Edinburgh, 1980), 66.

[36] Stephanie Jones, *Two Centuries of Overseas Trading: The Origins and Growth of the Inchcape Group* (London, 1986). Inchcape's advice that energetic young men should leave Scotland to make their way is quoted on 38.

[37] Andrew Porter, *Victorian Shipping, Business and Imperial Policy: Donald Currie, the Castle Line and Southern Africa* (London, 1986).

several estates in Glen Lyon in Perthshire. Other notable shipowners included Sir William Burrell (1861–1958), who became a celebrated art and antiques collector, and Sir James Caird (1864–1954), both of Glasgow, who became the principal donor (on a grand scale) to the National Maritime Museum in Greenwich. This Caird should not be confused with Sir James Key Caird (1837–1916), a Dundee jute baron, who became a major philanthropist, not least to his native city. In New Zealand, the Northern Steamship Company was strongly Scottish in its origins, while the Union and Shaw Savill Companies (the latter amalgamated with Henderson's Albion Line in 1882) chose Scots engineers, masters, and mates to run their ships.

The Cunard line also had significant Clyde connections during its first forty years, since its founding partnership included George and James Burns and David and Charles MacIver from Glasgow.[38] Its Scottish character was maintained until it relocated to Liverpool in 1880. Rivals such as the Allan Line (operating to North and South America) were founded in Glasgow, as were the Donaldson, Anchor,[39] Albion, Glen, Clan, Ben,[40] and Shire lines.[41] Others were founded elsewhere in Scotland, such as the Aberdeen line from its eponymous city. Most of these companies established close connections with Scottish shipbuilding firms. British India, for example, took many of its orders to the Connel yard in Glasgow and ordered a record quantity of tonnage from Scottish yards. Riverine and coastal companies followed a similar path. The Irrawaddy Flotilla Company, immortalized by Rudyard Kipling, was another enterprise of Patrick or Paddy Henderson. It became the greatest river fleet in the world, with no fewer than 600 vessels.[42] It had almost all its vessels built at Denny's of Dumbarton, a company which had close connections with nearly twenty shipping lines, building 770 vessels valued at more than £20 million between 1880 and 1913.[43] Burma indeed became almost a Scottish preserve in shipping, served both by British India and by Paddy Henderson's line founded in Glasgow in 1854 (from 1860 the

---

[38] F. E. Hyde, *Cunard and the North Atlantic 1840–1973* (London, 1975), 8–24.

[39] R. S. McLellan, *Anchor Line 1856–1956* (Glasgow, 1956).

[40] The Ben Line was associated with the port of Leith. George Blake, *Ben Line: The History of a Merchant Fleet 1825–1955* (Edinburgh, 1956).

[41] Anthony Slaven and Sydney Checkland (eds), *Dictionary of Scottish Business Biography 1860–1960*, vol. ii (Aberdeen, 1990).

[42] Alister McCrae and Alan Prentice, *Irrawaddy Flotilla* (Paisley, 1978).

[43] P. L. Robertson, 'Shipping and Shipbuilding: The Case of William Denny and Brothers', *Business History*, 16 (1974), 36–47.

Albion Line). Meanwhile the Straits Steamship Company (which operated in South-East Asia) took its orders to Robb and Caledon (later amalgamated) at Aberdeen.[44] Even locally founded companies within the empire had close Scottish connections. An excellent example is the important Burns Philp company of Sydney, New South Wales, which operated on the Australian coasts and the Pacific islands. Sir James Burns and Sir Robert Philp were born in Stirlingshire and Glasgow respectively, and both emigrated to Queensland in 1862, the latter as a child.[45] They represent the manner in which Scots tended to form partnerships with fellow countrymen. (Philp later became the premier of Queensland.)

Some of these lines became specialists in the emigration business, thereby promoting the flows of Scots overseas. This was true of the Allan Donaldson lines to Canada and the Albion Line to New Zealand. All of this activity can be seen as partly rooted in the long traditions of Scots as seafarers in northern Europe and in the Scottish role in the East India Company from the eighteenth century, but it was also related to Scottish expertise in both engineering and navigation (with training in both well established in Scottish port cities) and Scots prominence in agency houses in such ports as Montreal, Calcutta, Singapore, and Hong Kong. One historian has suggested that 'the Eastern trade was so largely developed by Scotsmen with family connections in every port east of the Cape, not to speak of relatives in the neighbourhood of Lombard Street',[46] while another has suggested that 'the expansion of Britain's Far Eastern trade was largely the work of family and clan groups among whom the Scots were particularly prominent'.[47] In all of this, it is apparent that Scots also used important connections in London, which Andrew Mackillop has demonstrated were significant in the eighteenth century, throughout the nineteenth and twentieth centuries.

Twelve of the first seventeen trading partnerships founded in Singapore after its foundation as a British colony in 1819 were Scots.[48] Guthrie and Co.,

[44] K. G. Tregonning, *Home Port Singapore: A History of the Straits Steamship Company Ltd., 1890–1965* (Singapore, 1967).

[45] See the entries on Burns and Philp in the *Australian Dictionary of Biography*.

[46] Greenberg, *British Trade*, 37–8.

[47] Stanley Chapman, *Merchant Enterprise in Britain* (Cambridge, 1992), 113. An example of an export business was George Martin of Glasgow, who traded with Batavia, Singapore, and Manila.

[48] Neal Ascherson, *Stone Voices: The Search for Scotland* (London, 2002), 233. In the 1950s, in Singapore, Ascherson found that Guthrie's retained its Scottish character, drawing on a network of friends and relations in Scotland, 233–4.

established in 1821 by Alexander Guthrie from Brechin (and remaining in family hands for over a century), dealt in sugar, spices, vegetable oil, and coffee, before investing massively in Malayan rubber from the 1890s. The Scottish textile firm of James Finlay and Co., which specialized in cotton, succeeded in diversifying into Indian tea and jute as cotton declined in importance.[49] Thomas Sutherland, chairman of the P&O line, headed a group of Scots who founded the Hong Kong and Shanghai Bank in 1864.[50] The Rangoon Oil Co., later Burmah Oil, emerged from the Scottish shipping companies Henderson's and the Irrawaddy Flotilla.[51] Perhaps the most notable of these companies was Jardine Matheson, established in Canton in 1852 (with earlier antecedents) and becoming the most powerful 'hong' or trading house in Hong Kong, all-powerful in the China trade.[52]

William Jardine (1800–74) came from Dumfriesshire, while James Matheson (1796–1878) was born in Lairg in Sutherland. Both studied at Edinburgh University, but went East following family connections. Once established in their partnership, they became notorious for their ruthlessness and for their role in the opium trade from India to China. This trade, which had its origins in the days of the East India Company, was designed to correct the imbalance of payments in the China trade, since China resisted, and had no need of, imports from elsewhere in the world. The huge success of Jardine Matheson and Co. in this trade was helped by their diversification into shipping, first in their impressive fleet of elegant opium clippers and later into steam. They also became politically prominent and benefited greatly from the wars prosecuted by the British to open Chinese ports to the opium and other trades. Both reinvested considerable fortunes in Scotland, though their notorious reputations followed them there, not least when Matheson became involved in eviction and clearance from the Isle of Lewis, which he owned. Famously, Disraeli in his novel *Sybil* satirized Matheson as 'a dreadful man. A Scotchman richer than Croesus, one Macdruggy, fresh from Canton with a million in each pocket, denouncing corruption and bellowing free trade.' Disraeli's view was no doubt influenced by the fact that

[49] [C. Brogan,] *James Finlay and Co. Ltd.* (Glasgow, 1951), chs. 1–6.

[50] P. J. Cain and A. G. Hopkins, *British Imperialism; Innovation and Expansion 1888–1914* (London, 1993), 433–9.

[51] Darwin, *Empire Project*, 57; Chapman, *Merchant Enterprise*, 26.

[52] Robert Blake, *Jardine Matheson: Traders of the Far East* (London, 1999); Maggie Keswick (ed.), *The Thistle and the Jade* (London, 1982), Greenberg, *British Trade*, chs. IV to VIII; Geoffrey Jones, *Merchants to Multinationals* (Oxford, 2000).

Matheson was MP for Ross and Cromarty in the Whig interest from 1847 to 1862.

In many of these companies, it is possible to chart the operations of family connections, a willingness to employ other Scots through networks of friends and relations. Most were canny, often Calvinistic and puritanical, emphasizing the virtues of hard work and thrift. The company founders and principals themselves often had relatively short careers overseas before retiring, sometimes to Scotland, to reinvest their fortunes. They were invariably influential in imperial politics both at the so-called periphery and in London. They handed over their companies to relatives who maintained their Scottish connections until takeovers in the later nineteenth and twentieth centuries. Their success was partly based on the long Scottish tradition of such enterprises, partly on the resources generated by the industrial revolution at home, partly through financial institutions and through the investment propensities of a rapidly growing Scottish professional and business elite.

Scottish Investment and Financial Institutions

Scots had a long tradition of furnishing credit and investing abroad. Both the commerce with Poland in the seventeenth century and the Atlantic tobacco trade had flourished on loans and credit arrangements with Polish merchants and American planters respectively. But by the nineteenth century, the Scots had come to invest to an unprecedented extent, a phenomenon which reached a great peak between the 1870s and the Great War. In 1884, an anonymous writer in *Blackwood's Edinburgh Magazine* already identified tens of millions of sterling invested by Scots overseas and regarded this, compared with the size of Scotland, as 'one of the most striking paradoxes in the history of commerce'.[53] Another commentator, writing in *The Statist*, remarked that investors and speculators formed 'so large a percentage of the well-to-do class as to be rather the rule than the exception'. He went on:

In Edinburgh, Dundee and Aberdeen it would be perfectly safe to bet on any man you pass in the street with an income of over three hundred a year being familiar with the fluctuation of Grand Turks, and having quite as much as he can afford

---

[53] Anon, 'Scottish Capital Abroad', *Blackwood's Edinburgh Magazine*, 136 (1884).

staked on prairies or some kindred gamble. A dividend of twenty per cent or more is to a Scotchman of this class a bait which he cannot resist.[54]

The *Blackwood's* article viewed Scotland as contributing disproportionately to the capital flows leaving Britain, and saw this activity as constituting something of a revolution in Scotland's history. With a chauvinistic exaggeration, the writer suggested that 'England gives sparingly and Ireland hardly any. *Scotland revels in foreign investment*.'[55] Scotland almost certainly provided more capital per head of population than England.

Scottish investors had, however, made a rather slow start. In 1824–5, an Aberdeenshire landowner, William Leslie, invested in the Australian Agricultural Company.[56] They had become involved in Australia, with the foundation in the 1820s of the Australian Company of Edinburgh and Leith. In the 1830s and 1840s, Aberdeen interests had also entered the Australian mortgage market.[57] But it was not until the final decades of the nineteenth century that Scottish overseas investment became a significant aspect of Scots economic activity. By the 1880s, Standard Life was investing heavily in Australian and New Zealand wool production, often using sureties provided by Scottish border woollen mills, which had switched to sourcing their wool in the antipodes.[58] In the same decade, the Commercial Bank of Australia opened a deposit agency in Edinburgh. The growth in such colonial investment had been partly stimulated by investments in American investment and mortgage companies and in railroads, which developed notably in the depression in the United States after 1873. The second phase of Scottish industrialization in mining, iron and steel-making, engineering, shipbuilding, and Scotland's own rail network absorbed a lot of capital, but soon a wave of investment in land reclamation and development, gold and silver mining, sheep and cattle farming, not to mention city building and expansion, spread out from North America to the other continents. In 1883, an Australian banker in London described Edinburgh

---

[54] 'Scottish Investors in the Dumps', *The Statist: A Weekly Journal for Economists and Men of Business*, 15 (10 January 1855), 36.

[55] 'Scottish Capital Abroad', 468. Italics added.

[56] Magee and Thompson, *Empire and Globalisation*, 206.

[57] David S. Macmillan, *Scotland and Australia, 1788–1850: Emigration, Commerce and Investment* (Oxford, 1967), 352. See also Geoffrey Bolton, 'Money, Trade, Investment, and Economic Nationalism', in Deryck M. Schreuder and Stuart Ward (eds), *Australia's Empire* (Oxford, 2010), 212–13.

[58] Magee and Thompson, *Empire and Globalisation*, 227.

as 'honeycombed with agencies for collecting money not for us in Australia alone, but for India, China, Canada, South America—everywhere almost and for all purposes, on the security of pastoral and agricultural lands in Texas, California, Queensland and Mexico'.[59] Another good example of a key figure establishing a significant Scottish network is Andrew McIlwraith from Ayr.[60] He (sometimes in association with his brothers John and Sir Thomas) became an influential promoter of numerous Australian shipping, pastoral, and mining enterprises between 1875 and 1913, forging valuable relationships between his Scottish connections and the investment needs of his adopted country. Such examples could readily be repeated across the British Empire.

There is an irony in the fact that this considerable success in the nineteenth century was based upon a national reputation for the founding of financial institutions which was generally combined with some of the most dramatic booms and busts in the history of capitalism. Famously, William Paterson (1658–1719) from Dumfriesshire, who made his first fortune in the West Indies trade, had been a leading light in the foundation of the Bank of England in 1694, while John Law (1671–1729), who was born near Edinburgh, founded the Banque Générale de France in 1716. Paterson's reputation was to be severely dented by the Company of Scotland trading to Africa and the Indies and more particularly its fateful Darien scheme at the end of the seventeenth century. Not surprisingly, he became one of the prime enthusiasts for the parliamentary Union of Scotland and England. Law was destroyed by the failure of the French Mississippi Company, as well as by his gambling and many dubious dealings. Yet banks became a notable feature of eighteenth-century Scotland, though some of the foundations were matched by apparently disastrous collapses. Adam Smith considered banks to be a crucial element in economic development, noting in *The Wealth of Nations* that the trade of Glasgow had greatly increased after the

[59] Quoted in J. D. Bailey, 'Australian Borrowing in Scotland in the Nineteenth Century', *Economic History Review*, NS 12.2 (1959), 272.

[60] D. B. Waterson, 'McIlwraith, Andrew (1844–1932)', *Australian Dictionary of Biography*, vol. x (Melbourne, 1986), 282–3. See also J. Ann Hone, 'McIlwraith, John (1828–1902)', *ADB*, vol. v (Melbourne, 1974), 160–1 and Don Dignan, 'McIlwraith, Sir Thomas (1835–1900)', *ADB*, v. 161–4. Sir Thomas became premier of Queensland. He developed railways in that colony and in 1883 tried to force the British government into the annexation of part of Samoa in order to frustrate the Germans. The relations among the three brothers were often acrimonious.

foundation of banks there.[61] Although bank collapses continued through-out the nineteenth century—a notable example was the collapse of the City of Glasgow Bank, founded in 1839, in 1878—recovery was often swifter than expected and Scots were certainly associated with the foundation of banks across the British Empire. Magee and Thompson have suggested that two-thirds of all bankers in Canada were from Scotland.[62] They were also significant in New Zealand, where William Larnach (born in New South Wales of Scottish parents) was the most visible, but not necessarily the most successful.[63] He manipulated Scots family connections and went into part-nership with Scots. An intending emigrant to Otago, John Ross from Caithness, was delighted to discover that the London branch of the National Bank of New Zealand was largely staffed by fellow Caithness men. He was able to draw on finance which helped him first to set up as a draper in Dunedin and then establish a large-scale woollen mill in Otago with a Scottish partner, Robert Glendining (from Dumfries).[64] Scots were often involved in similar enterprises to those characteristic of Scotland itself, like mills, mining, and metal work, helped by the Scots personnel in many banks. Moreover, Scots became particularly involved in 'mutual' companies, that is insurance and building societies which were theoretically owned by the entire body of their investing members, rather than stockholders and directors.

Cape Colony offers good examples of both a notable bank and a mutual society founded by a Scot. John Fairbairn (1794–1864), from Berwickshire and educated at Edinburgh University, emigrated to the Cape in 1823. He was subsequently involved in the founding of the Cape of Good Hope Bank, which he insisted should be created on what he regarded as Scottish joint stock banking principles. He claimed that in Scotland there was a bank for every 7,500 in the population, which went a considerable way to

---

[61] Quoted in James Buchan, *Adam Smith and the Pursuit of Perfect Liberty* (London, 2006), 41.

[62] Magee and Thompson, *Empire and Globalisation*, 202. For the over-production of Scottish bank clerks, the role of the Institute of Bankers in Scotland in providing qualifications, and the consequent migration of Scottish banking staff, see S. G. Checkland, *Scottish Banking: A History 1695–1973* (Glasgow, 1975), 492–3.

[63] Tom Brooking, 'Sharing out the Haggis: The Special Scottish Contribution to New Zealand History', in Brooking and Coleman, *The Heather and the Fern*, 51. F. R. T. Sinclair, 'Larnach, William James Mudie, 1833–1898', *Dictionary of New Zealand Biography*, update 22 June 2007.

[64] McAloon, 'Scots in the Colonial Economy', 93–4. See also S. R. H. Jones, *Doing Well and Doing Good: Scottish Enterprise in New Zealand* (Dunedin, 2010).

explaining the prosperity of the country.[65] After an abortive attempt in 1826, which was opposed by the colonial authorities, the bank was established in 1837. Even more significantly, Fairbairn founded the Mutual Life Assurance Society in 1847, which became exceptionally powerful in the insuring sector and remains significant to this day.[66] Scots were also significant in banking and mutual societies in Canada and in Australasia. They thus helped to unlock investment opportunities throughout the empire and beyond. It is perhaps not surprising that they subsequently became significant in the mining industries of the Cape and the Transvaal, as well as in the plantations of Natal in South Africa.[67]

Thus, Scots were operating within a pattern of overall British investment which was staggering in its growth and scale. Between 1870 and 1915, British capital holdings abroad grew from £1 billion to £4 billion, a phenomenon described by Darwin as 'this astonishing mountain of wealth'.[68] By 1913, the empire's share of this stood at 43 per cent, with the settlement colonies of Canada, Australia, New Zealand, and South Africa absorbing a third of the total. Such investment was highly diverse in its geographical spread and in the range of economic enterprises at which it was directed. British investment comprised 44 per cent of total world investments, with other countries (notably France and Germany) trailing well behind. Britain had become the world's banker.[69] Scotland was playing a major role in this. The scale is exceptionally difficult to estimate, but one suggestion is that it rose from £60 million in 1870 to £500 million in 1914.[70] If true, this would represent a rise from 7 per cent of all British overseas investment to 12 per cent over this period.[71] One calculation suggests that in 1914, overseas investment was equivalent to £110 for each Scot, compared with £90 across the UK.[72] But the true figure is very difficult to define

---

[65] MacKenzie with Dalziel, *Scots in South Africa*, 80.

[66] Ibid.

[67] Ibid., ch. 5.

[68] Darwin, *Empire Project*, 117.

[69] M. Edelstein, *Overseas Investment in the Age of High Imperialism* (London, 1982), 48; C. H. Feinstein, 'Britain's Overseas Investments in 1913', *Economic History Review*, 2nd series, 43.2 (1990), 288–95; R. C. Michie, *The City of London* (London, 1992), 72.

[70] Sydney Pollard, 'Capital Exports, 1870–1914: Harmful or Beneficial?', *Economic History Review*, 2nd series, 38.4 (1985), 492.

[71] B. Lenman, *An Economic History of Modern Scotland, 1660–1976* (London, 1977), 193.

[72] C. Harvie, *Scotland and Nationalism: Scottish Society and Politics 1707–1994* (2nd edn London, 1994), 70.

because private individuals invested outside financial institutions (and such investments are largely unrecorded), while some Scottish capitalists worked through the London Stock Exchange. Moreover, emigrant Scots will have taken unknown sums overseas with them. After all, not all emigrants were poverty-stricken. Many were 'elective' migrants who took capital with them in the hope of securing greater success in the British Empire.

The figures seem to suggest that most Scottish capital went to the USA, Canada, Australasia, India, and Ceylon (Sri Lanka) with limited outflows elsewhere. Half of the investment went to the British Empire, and the Scottish contribution seems to have been about 60 per cent above the British average.[73] Many Scots may have preferred the empire to other destinations, perhaps because the colonies offered safer, if sometimes less exciting, returns.[74] But they were also highly prominent as investors in American railroads, stock markets, and mortgage companies.[75] In the 1880s in Australia, at least one-third of pastoral mortgage and investment company securities, and an even higher proportion of deposit receipts issued by banks, were taken up in Scotland. Until the Australian collapse in 1893, Scotland was the dominant source for loan funds.[76] While English capital was pre-eminent in New Zealand, the Scots still accounted for one-fifth of the total in the period 1860s–1890s. The Scots seem to have had a specialist niche in pastoral development and were particularly significant in areas of Scottish settlement in the colony.[77]

Between 1885 and 1914, which may be regarded as the high point of imperialism, Scottish investment decisively swung to overseas rather than domestic destinations. This is well illustrated by the Scottish insurance companies. In 1900 Scottish Widows had £6 million in foreign assets.[78] In the same year, Standard Life had £7.5 million overseas, a considerable increase on its figure thirty years earlier.[79] It is possible that, extrapolating

---

[73] Ronald Michie, *Money, Mania and Markets: Investment Company Formation and the Stock Exchange in Nineteenth-Century Scotland* (Edinburgh, 1981), 248.

[74] Magee and Thompson, *Empire and Globalisation*, 179.

[75] Liza Giffen, *How Scots Financed the World: A History of Scottish Investment Trusts* (Edinburgh, 2009), 54.

[76] Bailey, 'Australian Borrowing in Scotland', 269.

[77] Tom Brooking, '"Tam McCanny and Kitty Clydeside": The Scots in New Zealand', in R. A. Cage (ed.), *The Scots Abroad* (London, 1985), 165–8.

[78] Michie, *Money, Mania and Markets*, 154.

[79] J. H. Treble, 'The Pattern of Investment of the Standard Life Assurance Company 1875–1914', *Business History*, 22 (1980), 170–88.

from Standard Life, the seven leading Scottish life assurance firms had
between £40 million and £50 million invested overseas.[80] This would constitute at least half of their total funds. Standard Life had offices around the
world and was particularly assiduous in offering financial support to Scottish expatriate communities.[81] Scottish industries were diversifying in the
same period. J. & P. Coats, the great thread manufacturer, invested in
Canada as well as outside the empire.[82] Dundee jute firms opened mills
in Bengal and sent out clerks and supervisors.[83] These investments were
made by those who had created considerable personal fortunes out of
Scottish industries, including Tennant of the chemical empire, the Coats
of thread, William Weir, coal and iron tycoon, and Bairds of the iron-
making dynasty.[84]

Yet such flows of funds were not confined to great *nouveaux riches* figures
of trade and industry; many members of the middle and professional classes
who could find a margin over subsistence for investment also participated.
Even lower down the social scale, among the ranks of printers, weavers,
mechanics, tradesmen, and domestic servants, we can find investors in the
savings banks and penny banks which had become such a characteristic of
the period. Many were women, married, single, widows, and spinsters. By
1907 no fewer than 500,000 such accounts had been opened in Scotland, one
for every nine of the population of the country.[85] Moreover, large numbers
of people had money placed with insurance companies such as Standard
Life, Scottish Widows, and Scottish Amicable. At the middle of the nineteenth century, such companies had deposits which nearly matched those of
the Scottish banks. They were poised to become even more significant later
in the century, not least through their branch offices throughout the empire.
Thus there was a 'democratization of foreign investment'. The numbers of

---

[80] Christopher Schmitz, 'Nature and Dimensions of Scottish Foreign Investment 1860–1914',
Business History, 39.2 (1997), 42–68, particularly 66 n. 48.

[81] Magee and Thompson, *Empire and Globalisation*, 226. M. Moss, *The Building of Europe's
Largest Mutual Life Company: Standard Life 1825–2000* (Edinburgh, 2000).

[82] Kim, 'British Multinational Enterprise', 523–51.

[83] Stewart, *Jute and Empire*, chs 3 and 4.

[84] Robert D. Corrins, 'The Scottish Business Elite in the Nineteenth Century: The Case of
William Baird and Company', in A. J. G. Cummings and T. M. Devine (eds), *Industry, Business
and Society in Scotland since 1700* (Edinburgh, 1994), 76.

[85] M. Moss and A. Slaven, *'From Ledger to Laser Beam': A History of the TSB in Scotland from
1870–1990* (Edinburgh, 1992), 28, 32, 52, 74; C. H. Lee, 'Economic Progress: Wealth and Poverty',
in Devine, Lee, and Peden (eds), *Transformation of Scotland*, 138.

people with financial interests abroad rose from 4,000 in 1867 to 80,000 in 1913, with the average amount of individual investment declining. Probated estates reveal the growth in numbers of those with foreign assets, rising from 6 per cent in 1867 to 20 per cent in 1890, with such people spread across the cities and towns of the entire country.[86] Yet we must be cautious in two respects: first, democratization had its limits, confined to the middle classes and, at the outside, a few of the 'aristocracy of labour'; second, the empire always remained a destination for less than half of the investment, despite the ties of sentiment, migration networks, and a relative sense of security. Nevertheless, it may still be the case, as suggested above, that Scotland was one of several regions of the British Isles where colonial securities were preferred.

Such sentiment was encouraged by various colonial booms in the period. In South Africa, the discovery of gold on the Witwatersrand led to a tremendous boom, the economic repercussions of which spread to the emergence of considerable urban growth, the provision of ports and railways, and the expansion of shipping lines. In the 1890s, South Africa was the most popular destination for Scots apart from the USA. In the first Union of South Africa Census of 1911, a clearly disproportionate 20 per cent of all those with British birth came from Scotland.[87] Scots became important in the mining industries, in transport and communications, in harbour building (Scotland offered an ideal source of stonemasons and carpenters, often causing English migrants to feel aggrieved at what they saw as preferential treatment), and in many of the professions.[88] For example, Scots were key figures in the railways of Natal, as well as in engineering, metal working, and other skilled occupations which had their counterparts in Scotland.[89] The South African experience was accompanied by a considerable boom in Australia and New Zealand in the 1890s, with the export to Britain of wool, canned and frozen mutton and beef, together with butter and cheese (later fruit). By 1913, Australia and New Zealand were contributing 260,000 tons of mutton and lamb to Britain, about one-third of total consumption.[90] Indeed, consignments of frozen mutton from New Zealand were pioneered

---

[86] Schmitz, 'Nature and Dimensions of Scottish Foreign Investment', 56.

[87] MacKenzie with Dalziel, *Scots in South Africa*, 160.

[88] Ibid. 154.

[89] Ibid., ch. 7.

[90] James Belich, *Replenishing the Earth: The Settler Revolution and the Rise of the Anglo-World 1783–1939* (Oxford, 2001), 366.

in 1882 by the Albion Line. Scots were indeed heavily involved in all these activities, as shippers, agents, producers, and bankers. The first decade of the twentieth century saw a considerable boom in Canada. The rise of global agricultural and raw material prices helped to open vast expanses of land by then tied into the world economy through the railway system (and many of the leading lights of the Canadian Pacific Railway, including its engineers, were originally from Scotland). In the mining sector, nickel, copper, silver, and gold were exported in large quantities, creating an enormous demand for both labour and capital. Scotland and the Scots participated in this boom.[91]

Of course, the cyclical fluctuations in economies ensured that there were also depression periods, when losses could be incurred. Generally, however, Scots were well positioned to benefit from the boom times that often followed. Indeed, it has been suggested (in relation to American investment) that the stereotype of the 'canny Scot' does not apply to investment opportunities, when considerable excitement could be generated by reports in the British press of supposedly important developments overseas.[92] The creation of intelligence about such opportunities was encouraged by the emergence of a specialized capitalist press, both in Britain and in the colonies themselves, in which Scottish journalists were often active.[93] The rise of these intelligence networks was greatly facilitated by the speed of communication provided by the railways, steamships, and above all the electric telegraph. Journalists could gather information from the colonies with considerable speed.[94] The flow of letters between imperial territories and Britain grew dramatically.[95] Cables could broadcast opportunities in a matter of hours. Shipping companies and publishers began to issue guide books, often on an annual basis, which tended to contain a great deal of commercial and investment information. Another important source of

---

[91] A. K. Cairncross, 'Investment in Canada, 1900–13', in A. R. Hall (ed.), *The Export of Capital from Britain 1870–1914* (London, 1968), 153–86.

[92] W. Turrentine Jackson, *The Enterprising Scot: Investors in the American West after 1873* (Edinburgh, 1968), 4–5.

[93] Magee and Thompson, *Empire and Globalisation*, ch. 5.

[94] S. J. Potter, *News and the British World: The Emergence of an Imperial Press System 1876–1922* (Oxford, 2003).

[95] Belich, *Replenishing the Earth*, 122. Belich's examples are drawn from the United States, but the point applies equally to the British dominions.

intelligence was the establishment of personal networks.[96] Army officers, administrators, and other expatriate colonial sojourners were often able to transmit investment and commercial information back home to family members. Thus individuals linked colony to home.

Moreover, while such rapid communications could lead to inflated excitement and faulty as well as wise investment decisions, with much still to be lost as well as gained, investment decisions were partly helped by the fact that colonial busts did not always coincide. Booms in Canada occurred in the late 1870s and 1880s, were checked in the mid-1880s, and returned in the early 1890s and the years leading to the First World War. In Australia and New Zealand, the pattern was somewhat different, with good times in the 1870s and again from the late 1880s onwards, while in South Africa the booms (tightly allied to mineral discoveries) occurred in the 1870s (associated with diamonds) and the late 1880s and 1890s (with gold).[97]

If Scottish financial systems were already well developed and sophisticated in the Victorian era, they were always ready to benefit from new legislation and investment ideas. The Joint Stock Companies Acts of 1856 and 1862 reduced the risk for small investors in the event of company collapse.[98] An important new concept was the investment trust, invented in Belgium, but greatly developed in Scotland, where it became tremendously popular. Robert Fleming of Dundee helped to found an important trust in 1873, in this case concentrating on American investments.[99] The trust's principle, as it is today, was to diversify assets across a range of investments in order to minimize risk. Expert advisers could be employed for portfolio management, and therefore offered what seemed like a safer option for the small investor. By 1914, there were no fewer than 853 Edinburgh-registered general investment trusts, operating in a wide range of sectors across the world.[100] Through trusts and other investment forms, Scottish investors could hope for higher returns than they could secure on the domestic market.

[96] John M. MacKenzie, 'Empires of Travel: British Guide Books and Cultural Imperialism in the 19th and 20th Centuries', in John K. Walton (ed.), *Histories of Tourism: Representation, Identity and Conflict* (Clevedon, 2005), 19–38, particularly 33.

[97] Belish, *Replenishing the Earth*, 89.

[98] Michie, *Money, Mania and Markets*, 155; Payne, *The Early Scottish Limited Companies 1856–1895*.

[99] G. A. Stout, 'Robert Fleming and the Trustees of the First Scottish-American Investment Trust', *Friends of Dundee City Archives*, 1 (1999), 13–22; Bill Smith, *Robert Fleming, 1845–1933* (Haddington, 2000).

[100] Schmitz, 'Nature and Dimensions of Scottish Foreign Investment', 47–8.

The scale of the transformation of the Scottish economy enabling it to play such a role in the colonial and wider world can be readily established. Between 1798 and 1910, Scottish national wealth probably increased by a factor of at least twelve.[101] This wealth was grossly maldistributed: in 1867, Baxter estimated that 0.33 per cent of 'productive persons' controlled one-quarter of Scottish national income and a further tiny 8 per cent of this group absorbed almost half of the national income.[102] Thus the investment opportunities started out as being the preserve of a relatively small-scale elite. The question arises whether in pursuing these overseas ambitions, this elite starved domestic industry and other sectors of funds. There is perhaps little evidence for this. Rather, it would seem that investment opportunities in Scotland after the railway mania were far from abundant. Thus, much capital, often accumulated because of earlier Scottish manufacturing success, increasingly moved where returns were much greater. Nevertheless, some key areas remain to be researched. We know, for example, very little about what happened to returns on investments, whether they were reinvested in overseas opportunities, whether they contributed to conspicuous expenditure (at the upper end) at home, or whether they became an essential component of the income of elements of the middle classes. We also know little about remittances by migrants back to family at home. These must have occurred, particularly as easier forms of remitting money, through bank transfer, money orders, and later postal orders, became possible.[103]

Yet it remains possible that considerable flows overseas and social deprivation at home were two sides of the same coin. In 1904, the Cox jute family of Dundee, notorious for underpaying their workers, held investments in sixty-four companies, three-quarters of them transatlantic.[104] Meanwhile, housing conditions in Dundee, together with accompanying social deprivation, were

---

[101] Lee, 'Economic Progress: Wealth and Poverty', 155: E. Cramond, 'The Economic Position of Scotland and her Financial Relations with England and Ireland', *Journal of the Royal Statistical Society*, NS 75 (1912), 168–9.

[102] R. D. Baxter, *National Income of the United Kingdom* (London, 1867), 56.

[103] For remittances to Cornwall and elsewhere in England, see Gary B. Magee and Andrew S. Thompson, '"Lines of credit, debts of obligation": Migrant Remittances to Britain, c.1875–1913', *Economic History Review*, 59.7 (August 2006), 539–77. Such remittances must have been a widespread phenomenon throughout the country.

[104] Bruce Lenman and Kathleen Donaldson, 'Partners' Incomes: Investment and Diversification in the Scottish Linen Area 1850–1921', *Business History*, 21 (1971), 1–18, particularly 13–16; Michie, *Money, Mania and Markets*, 154.

among the worst in Britain, with cruelly high child mortality.[105] This situation was mirrored throughout Scotland. In 1914, nearly half of the population lived in one- or two-roomed dwellings compared with just over 7 per cent in England.[106] On the eve of the Great War, over two million Scots lived more than two to a room. This partly resulted from the fact that urban property was exceptionally unpopular for investors, large and small alike. Other negative effects of Scotland's relationship with empire were also soon apparent. The jute industry, the source of the Coxes' great wealth, went into rapid decline in the twentieth century, hit by competition from Bengal. The whaling industry, which had supplied the essential whale oil, was also disappearing. Elsewhere in Scotland, heavy industries often dependent on imperial markets were clearly vulnerable. Shipbuilding had artificial booms replacing lost tonnage after both the First and Second World Wars, but this merely masked under-investment and decline. Iron and steel faced foreign competition with which it often could not compete. It is tempting to suggest that J. A. Hobson's arguments in 1902 about low pay and the consequent economic brake upon working-class consumption may well work in the case of Scotland.[107] Scotland lagged behind in the 'new' consumer-based manufactures, such as household goods, electrical products, even cycles, and later motor cars, which were rapidly expanding in England. These did not take off in Scotland because of the levels of relative poverty among the mass of the population and the small size of the domestic market. The placing of capital elsewhere ensured that the country would miss out on the next great stage of economic development.

In Victorian times, however, the scale of Scots investment overseas was seen as a sign of great progress. In 1884, the writer in *Blackwood's* wrote that 'in the course of the first half of the present century Scotland was changed from one of the poorest to one of the most prosperous countries in Europe. From an unknown inaccessible corner of the world it has been transformed within the life of two generations into the favourite haunt of the tourist and the home of the merchant prince.'[108] From the perspective of the twenty-first century, these developments may seem much less benign.

---

[105] Sir D'Arcy Wentworth Thompson (speaking in 1938), quoted in Lenman and Donaldson, 'Partners' Incomes', 18.

[106] C. H. Lee, *Scotland and the United Kingdom* (Manchester, 1995), 40.

[107] J. A. Hobson, *Imperialism: A Study* (London, 1902).

[108] Anon, 'Scottish Capital Abroad', 468.

Select Bibliography

Neil Ascherson, *Stone Voices: The Search for Scotland* (London, 2002).

James Belich, *Replenishing the Earth: The Settler Revolution and the Rise of the Anglo-World 1783–1801* (Oxford, 2001).

A. J. G. Cummings and T. M. Devine (eds), *Industry, Business and Society in Scotland since 1700* (Edinburgh, 1994).

T. M. Devine, *The Scottish Nation 1700–2010* (London, 2006).

—— *To the Ends of the Earth: Scotland's Global Diaspora*, 1750–2010 (London, 2011).

—— C. H. Lee and G. C. Peden (eds), *The Transformation of Scotland* (Edinburgh, 2005).

W. H. Fraser and Irene Maver (eds), *Glasgow, ii: 1839–1912* (Manchester, 1996).

Freda Harcourt, *Flagships of Imperialism: The P&O Line and the Politics of Empire from its Origins to 1867* (Manchester, 2006).

Gary B. Magee and Andrew S. Thompson, *Empire and Globalization: Networks of People, Goods and Capital in the British World, c.1850–1914* (Cambridge, 2010).

M. S. Moss and J. R. Hume, *Workshop of the British Empire* (London, 1977).

J. Forbes Munro, *Maritime Enterprise and Empire: Sir William Mackinnon and his Business Network, 1823–1893* (Woodbridge, 2003).

Andrew Porter, *Victorian Shipping, Business and Imperial Policy: Donald Currie, the Castle Line and Southern Africa* (London, 1986).

Gordon T. Stewart, *Jute and Empire: The Calcutta Jute Wallahs and the Landscapes of Empire* (Manchester, 1998).

10

Scottish Literature and the British Empire

Angela Smith

Alternative Strategies

In his essay 'The Bonnie Disproportion', the Australian poet Les Murray writes that 'Scotland is still the only overseas country in which I have never felt foreign'.[1] A consistent motif in his poetry is an awareness of diasporic experience. Writing and living still where his Scottish ancestors settled, in Bunyah, New South Wales, in 1870, Murray remembers:

> ...my great-great-grandfather here with his first sons,
> who would grow old, still speaking with his Scots accent,
> having never seen those highlands that they sang of.
> A hundred years. I stand and smoke in the silence.[2]

His ancestral relationship with Scotland is still potent for him, but his children 'in the four generations prior to their own...have no less than nine ancestral nationalities, nine ethnic traditions. The Scottish one probably won't emerge more strongly for them from that Babel of faint voices than, say, the Hungarian one or the Swiss one.'[3] Rather than nostalgia, Murray's poetry explores what Stuart Hall calls hybridity. I begin by sketching in alternative strategies for discussing Scottish literature in the context of the British Empire, such as a survey of homesickness in the writing of settlers and their descendants, or an account of cultural nationalism, and then use Hall's analysis to focus on the ability of a group of Scottish writers who engage with the politics of the British Empire to anticipate the concerns of postcolonial theory.

---

[1] Les A. Murray, *Persistence in Folly* (Sydney, 1984), 84.

[2] Les Murray, *Collected Poems* (Manchester, 1998), 4.

[3] Murray, *Persistence in Folly*, 84.

One trajectory for this chapter could be to concentrate on the works of writers who emigrated from Scotland to different parts of the British Empire whose sense of displacement is powerful, before the ancestral voices become faint, and on the work of the descendants of emigrants who still feel a strong affinity with Scotland, as Murray does. Some examples of early settler writing by Scottish emigrants and of the contemporary interaction in fiction between Scotland and settler colonies give an indication that even the tip of that iceberg cannot be revealed. Nineteenth-century emigrant writing comparing Scotland and the settler colonies abounds. For instance, 'The Emigrant' by Alexander McLachlan, published in Toronto in 1861, hankers for the homeland:

> Though lovely's this land of the lake and the tree,
> Yet the land of the scarred cliff and mountain for me,
> Each cairn has its story, each river its sang,
> And the burnies are wimplin' to music alang,
> But here nae auld ballad the young bosom thrills,
> Nae sang has made sacred thae forests and rills,
> And often I croon o'er some auld Scottish strain,
> 'Till I'm roving the hills of my country again;
> And O may she ever be upright and brave,
> And ne'er let her furrows be turned by a slave.[4]

As David Daiches tersely remarks, 'Nostalgia is not the most productive of literary emotions, and it has been the curse of much Scottish literature.'[5] A Scot who emigrated to New Zealand, John Barr, makes a more abrasive comparison in 1859:

> There's nae place like Otago yet,
> There's nae wee beggar weans,
> Or auld men shivering at our doors,
> To beg for scraps or banes.
> We never see puir working folk
> Wi' bauchles on their feet,
> Like perfect icicles wi' cauld,
> Gawn starving through the street.[6]

---

[4] http://www.uwo.ca/english/canadianpoetry/longpoems/emigrant_mclachlan/the_emigrant. htmlV.

[5] Jenni Calder (ed.), *Stevenson and Victorian Scotland* (Edinburgh, 1981), 28.

[6] Quoted in Alastair Niven, 'The Scottish Element in Commonwealth Literature', in C. D. Narasimhaiah (ed.), *Awakened Conscience: Studies in Commonwealth Literature* (New Delhi, 1978), 34.

This substitutes a relieved practicality for yearning but, in the immediacy of a migrant setting does not, of course, address the complexity of the diasporic situation that Murray's family experience.

To make the comparison between fiction that hankers for and conforms to the past, and writing that engages actively with the present, one could contrast work by two contemporary Canadian writers of Scottish descent, Alistair MacLeod and Alice Munro, both of whom address imperial history. MacLeod's novel *No Great Mischief*, first published in 1999, tells the story of the narrator's ancestors, MacDonalds, who leave Moidart in 1779; the title is taken from General Wolfe's comment at Quebec in 1759. As he sent the Highlanders into battle he remarked that it would be 'no great mischief if they fall'. The novel traces the MacDonald red- or black-haired brothers in their present in Canada; it is about yearning for a primal homeland to which the migrant might one day return. One brother visits Scotland and is standing in Queen Street Station in Glasgow when an unknown red-haired man approaches him, assumes he is a MacDonald, greets him in Gaelic, and asks him home to his fish farm in the Highlands, saying, 'Perhaps you're coming to the past... We'll talk about *Bliadhna Thearlaich*—Charlie's Year.'[7] Towards the end, the narrator says good-bye to his grandmother in an old people's home where the residents and the young staff all join in singing a Gaelic song celebrating the Macdonalds: 'The brown dog looks up from the floor, as if once again everything is right with the world.'[8] The book ends with the narrator driving his brother Calum to their boyhood home, where Calum dies: 'I reach for his cooling hand which lies on the seat beside him. I touch the Celtic ring.'[9]

Nostalgia for a lost way of life and yearning for the solidarity of the clan permeate *No Great Mischief*, whereas Alice Munro's *The View from Castle Rock*, published in 2006, is intrigued by the transformation of a Scottish heritage into postcolonial Canada. Munro is a descendant of James Hogg, who might be said to have invented the stream-of-consciousness novel in 1824 with his *The Private Memoirs and Confessions of a Justified Sinner*. Munro is an equally troubling writer, disorienting her reader into making unexpected connections. The book itself is neither autobiography, memoir, nor fiction, but a slippery combination of all three, covering, like *No Great Mischief*, about 200 years in the life of the Laidlaw family and told in

---

[7] Alistair MacLeod, *No Great Mischief* (London, 2001), 244.
[8] Ibid. 251.   [9] Ibid. 261.

separate stories. In one of the early stories, the view from castle rock of the
title is a drunken misapprehension. Early in the nineteenth century James
Laidlaw staggers up to the castle rock in Edinburgh and urges his small son
to look at:

... a pale green and grayish-blue land, part in sunlight and part in shadow, a land
as light as mist, sucked into the sky.
  'So did I not tell you?' Andrew's father said. 'America. It is only a little bit of it,
though, only the shore. This is where every man is sitting in the midst of his own
properties, and even the beggars is riding around in carriages.'[10]

The boy is surprised, as well he might be, as he is looking at Fife. With
potent images such as this, Munro suggests that the view from Scotland of
the New World and the perspective on Scotland of the emigrants are
unstable, distorted by a range of aspirations and emotions. In a bizarre
but potent trope the narrator, writing in our present, asserts something
comparable to Les Murray's summary of his children's nine ethnic traditions. Murray writes: 'Their only real option is to be Australians... They are
unlikely to suffer possession by the spirits of the restless dead.'[11] In the
penultimate story called 'What do you want to know for?' Munro's narrator
links her discovery of a crypt in a country churchyard in Ontario with her
own discovery that she has a lump in her breast. The crypt is like a pre-
Christian burial mound in Central Europe, and the inoperable and probably
benign lump seems to represent that Scottish past which is part of the
narrator's being in a present where the traditionally farmed landscape
with fences and byres for cattle has been transformed into unbroken and
almost industrial featureless acres of crop-raising. As the narrator, who is a
writer, creates the present for the reader she critiques her own interest in
diaspora: 'We can't resist this rifling around in the past, sifting the untrust-
worthy evidence, linking stray names and questionable dates and anecdotes
together, hanging on to threads, insisting on being joined to dead people
and therefore to life.'[12]
  Another possible approach to the structure of this essay is suggested by
Vera Kreilkamp's chapter 'Fiction and Empire: The Irish Novel' in *Ireland
and the British Empire*, which identifies a relationship between form and

---

[10] Alice Munro, *The View from Castle Rock* (London, 2006), 30.
[11] Murray, *Persistence in Folly*, 84–5.
[12] Munro, *The View from Castle Rock*, 347.

ideology in nineteenth-century fictional depictions of the unresolved state of Ireland with 'their insistent focus on Irish national identity within an imperial context'.[13] Douglas Mack's *Scottish Fiction and the British Empire* also focuses on national identity and argues that the experience of the 'subaltern classes'[14] in Scotland can be compared with that of the subalterns in India or Africa: 'It was the duty of the Enlightened elite to secure the pacification of the lower orders at home, just as it was the Empire's task to secure the pacification of the primitive tribes of the lower Niger abroad.'[15] The phrasing echoes the final lines of Chinua Achebe's *Things Fall Apart*, drawing a parallel between the colonial powers and the social and political elite in Scotland. Achebe's assertion that colonized people must tell their own stories is equated with what Mack terms the 'subalterns' of British society, such writers as James Hogg, Robert Burns, and Lewis Grassic Gibbon, whose backgrounds and education were less privileged than those of Walter Scott, Robert Louis Stevenson, and John Buchan.

Diasporic Identities

My argument in this chapter will not focus, in the context of the British Empire, on nostalgia, nor on Scottish writers' engagement with the relationship between Scotland and England, nor on issues of class, but will concentrate on the significance of the Scottish diaspora, and specifically on the role of Scottish writers as interpreters of the dissolution of the British Empire; Robert Louis Stevenson and John Buchan both anticipated in their imaginative fiction the postcolonial theorists of the late twentieth century. Though some poets will be included, the emphasis will be on fiction, since the colonial process itself reiterated stories to inscribe its values and its heroes on the territories of empire, as Achebe understands and Jamaica Kincaid's scathing attack demonstrates: 'In the Antigua that I knew, we lived on a street named after an English maritime criminal, Horatio Nelson, and

---

[13] Vera Kreilkamp, 'Fiction and Empire: The Irish Novel', in Kevin Kenny (ed.), *Ireland and the British Empire* (Oxford, 2006), 155.

[14] The phrase is taken from Ranajit Guha's Subaltern Studies project, which sought to include the perspective of those who were traditionally marginalized by 'elite' history. Gayatri Spivak engages with this argument in her essay 'Can the Subaltern Speak?' in Cary Nelson and Lawrence Grossberg (eds), *Marxism and the Interpretation of Culture* (Basingstoke, 1988), 271–313.

[15] Douglas Mack, *Scottish Literature and the British Empire* (Edinburgh, 2006), 147.

all the other streets around us were named after some other English maritime criminals. There was Rodney Street, there was Hood Street, there was Hawkins Street, and there was Drake Street.'[16] The mimicry required of colonized indigenous people and slaves frequently pivots on the imposition of alien stories as Derek Walcott's 'red nigger', Shabine, laments:

> . . . but we live like our names and you would have
> to be colonial to know the difference,
> to know the pain of history words contain,
> to love those trees with an inferior love,
> and to believe: 'Those casuarinas bend
> like cypresses, their hair hangs down in rain
> like sailors' wives. They're classic trees, and we,
> if we live like the names our masters please,
> by careful mimicry might become men.'[17]

Stevenson's subtle depiction of the 'pain of history words contain' in his fiction about the fringes of the British Empire at the end of the nineteenth century anticipates the preoccupations of much postcolonial writing. Stuart Hall explores the antitheses:

[D]iaspora does not refer us to those scattered tribes whose identity can only be secured in relation to some sacred homeland to which they must at all costs return, even if it means pushing other people into the sea. This is the old, the imperialising, the hegemonising, form of 'ethnicity'. . . The diaspora experience as I intend it here is defined, not by essence or purity, but by the recognition of a necessary heterogeneity and diversity; by a conception of 'identity' which lives with and through, not despite, difference; by *hybridity*. Diaspora identities are those which are constantly producing and reproducing themselves anew, through transformation and difference.[18]

To clarify the distinction between diaspora as return to the sacred homeland and diaspora as a recognition of heterogeneity, I shall begin with two historical examples of Scots who used their expatriate experience to intervene in the imperial project in radically different ways, one of them

---

[16] Jamaica Kincaid, *A Small Place* (New York, 1988), 24.

[17] Derek Walcott, 'The Schooner *Flight*', in *The Star-Apple Kingdom* (London, 1980), 12.

[18] Stuart Hall, 'Cultural Identity and Diaspora', in Patrick Williams and Laura Chrisman (eds), *Colonial Discourse and Postcolonial Theory* (London, 1993), 401–2.

anticipating Hall's definition of diasporic diversity, and will then link their experience to what I take to be the two major Scottish writers who engage politically and philosophically with empire, Robert Louis Stevenson and John Buchan. The chapter will conclude with a discussion of two contemporary Scottish writers who offer retrospective readings of aspects of empire, James Robertson and Jackie Kay, enabling a contemporary audience to reassess their own assumptions about national identity. Both of them engage with Scottish involvement in the slave trade; as Catherine Hall writes, an exhibition was mounted at the Museum of Edinburgh in 2007, the bicentenary of the abolition of the trade, called 'It didn't happen here' which challenged 'the national orthodoxy that it was the English who were responsible for slavery while the Scots led the way on anti-slavery'.[19]

Paradigmatic Diasporic Scots

A Gaelic-speaking Scot, Lachlan Macquarie was sworn in as the fifth Governor of the colony of New South Wales 200 years ago, on New Year's Day 1810, replacing as Governor Captain Bligh whose term of office had resulted in him being deposed during the Rum Rebellion. Macquarie was a soldier who had seen service in the American War of Independence, in Jamaica, in Ceylon, in India for two separate tours of duty including participation in the battle against Tipu Sultan in Mysore, and in Egypt. Like my other paradigmatic Scot he bought a slave boy. The Indian-born 'George Jarvis' joined his household in Kerala; he sent him home to Scotland when George was about 12 so that he could be educated. George was with Macquarie for twenty-five years and was with him when he died. George and his wife, whom he met when she was a servant in the Macquarie household in Sydney, received an annuity and a house to live in on Mull after Macquarie's death. By 1815 George was described as a personal servant in Macquarie's will.[20] Macquarie's attitude to George is a marker of his ability to produce himself anew, in Stuart Hall's phrase. Vain as he undoubtedly was, he used his experience within the empire to implement in New South Wales experimental new policies designed to restore order and to integrate the

---

[19] Catherine Hall, 'Afterword: Britain 2007, Problematising Histories', in Cora Kaplan and John Oldfield (eds), *Imagining Transatlantic Slavery* (Basingstoke, 2010), 192.

[20] Robin Walsh, work in progress, 'Silent Witness: The Invisible Life and Lost Testament of "George Jarvis," Slave and Manservant to Lachland Macquarie'.

emancipists, who were often eschewed by free settlers, into a new concept of civil society against the wishes of the British government, which was obsessed with saving money. A convict remembered the arrival ceremony that awaited startled disembarking convicts in Sydney. The Governor greeted them:

The Governor addresses them, by saying what a fine fruiteful country they are come to, and what he will do for them if there conduct merits it; likewise tells them if they find themselves anyways dessatesfied with there employer, to go (immediately) to the madjestrate of the district, and he will see him righted.[21]

Evidence of Macquarie's programme of public buildings survives in modern Sydney. When the architect and forger Francis Greenway arrived in the colony Macquarie employed him to design buildings while he was still serving his sentence; the Barracks and St James's Church stand as evidence of Macquarie's vision of an urban community that was not simply a penal settlement: 'Macquarie was the first colonial official to refer to the continent as "Australia" in official despatches in the hope that it would become "the Name given to this Country in future".'[22] The botanic gardens were established during his governorship as a place of recreation for the citizens.

Macquarie's reforms are often seen as an example of the dissemination of Enlightenment ideas in Australia, though other historians, including Robin Walsh, the curator of the Lachlan Macquarie room in Macquarie University in Sydney, read the situation differently.[23] Macquarie was the son of a poor carpenter and he left school to join the army at 15; his education was paid for by his uncle, Murdoch Maclaine, the 19th laird of Lochbuie in Mull. His education enabled him to embark on a military career but, unlike his wife, he was not a reader. Walsh suggests that Macquarie's vision for New South Wales was based not on Enlightenment principles but on the clan system, and that he saw his role as that of the laird whose duty it was to enable less privileged members of his community to better themselves and improve the common good. In this instance, Scottish diasporic experience is used positively as Macquarie revised the model of patronage he had experienced in Scotland as a child and applied it to a situation of migrancy, both enforced and voluntary. His improvements made enemies of conservatives

---

[21] Quoted in Robert Hughes, *The Fatal Shore* (London, 1987), 295.
[22] T. M. Devine, *Scotland's Empire 1600–1815* (London, 2003), 283–4.
[23] Personal communication.

in Britain and Australia and eventually he returned to Scotland, but when he left he was said to have been cheered by a harbour full of people who had benefited from his liberal policies.

His counterpart, an example of a privileged Scot during the Enlightenment whose use of diasporic experience is retrogressive and whose life is reinterpreted in early twenty-first century Scottish fiction, is John Wedderburn. His father was Sir John Wedderburn, an excise collector for Prince Charles Edward Stuart, who was hanged, decapitated, and disembowelled in London on 28 November 1746, having been captured after the battle of Culloden Moor. He wrote to his wife from Southwark Gaol on the eve of his death asking her 'to instill into my Children male or female a just sense of what our country has suffered in Generall and I'm particular the eldest has it'.[24] John, the eldest, fled from Culloden in disguise and escaped to Jamaica. Though he had witnessed the carnage and cruelty at and after the battle he recouped the family fortunes by becoming a sugar planter in a system that depended on brutal exploitation. When he achieved his ambition of returning to his homeland to settle into his Perthshire estate, he took with him an African slave known as Joseph Knight, an intelligent boy whom he educated. Knight's ability to read enabled him to challenge Wedderburn in the Court of Session in 1774, claiming that slavery was not recognized in Scotland. Wedderburn blamed Knight's relationship with another servant, whom he married, as the cause of the conflict between himself and Knight, a marked contrast with the relationship between Macquarie and George. The verdict that 'the state of slavery is not recognised by the laws of this Kingdom' was greeted with satisfaction by the Edinburgh *Caledonian Mercury*, particularly because 'the freedom of Negroes has obtained its first *general determination* in the Supreme Civil Court of Scotland'.[25] Wedderburn's return to his 'sacred homeland' effected a change in it that he deplored, and Knight's and Wedderburn's memorials in the National Archives of Scotland[26] enabled James Robertson to unearth a forgotten story. Catherine Hall writes: 'New times, the time of globalization and migration, the time of supranational states and small nations, the time of ethnic conflict and racial belonging, all these require new forms of analysis and understanding and new histories

---

[24] http://pagesperso-orange.fr/euroleader/wedderburn/sirjohn.htm.
[25] Iain Whyte, *Scotland and the Abolition of Black Slavery, 1756–1838* (Edinburgh, 2007), 18.
[26] Court of Session records in the National Archives of Scotland CS235/K/2/2.

to help us grasp the past in the present.'[27] Robertson's imaginative detective story lays bare a willed collective amnesia about aspects of the Scottish diaspora relating to slavery.

Scott, Stevenson, and Buchan

There are, of course, Scottish novelists well before Stevenson and Buchan who set their fiction in territories of the British Empire, for instance Walter Scott's *The Surgeon's Daughter*. One of the *Chronicles of the Canongate*, it is a melodrama enacted on ethnic and racial lines set in the mid-eighteenth century onwards. The narrator, Chrystal Croftangry, is persuaded to write it by his friend Fairscribe, whose advice about Croftangry's concern for his Muse of Fiction is this:

Send her to India, to be sure. That is the true place for a Scot to thrive in; and if you carry your story fifty years back, as there is nothing to hinder you, you will find as much shooting and stabbing there as ever was in the wild Highlands. If you want rogues, as they are so much in fashion with you, you have that gallant caste of adventurers, who laid down their consciences at the Cape of Good Hope as they went out to India, and forgot to take them up again when they returned.[28]

The narrator replies enthusiastically, in that he has read a lot about India, but nervously as he has never been there, like Scott himself. Scott situates the story in south India, where British territorial expansion had been opposed; the novel is set just after the first war that the Muslim Haider (Hyder in the novel) Ali fought against the British, when Lachlan Macquarie was serving in the army. During the second Mysore War Haider Ali died and was succeeded by his son Tipu (Tippoo in the novel) Sultan. In setting the novel at this period Scott was reviving memories for his older readers. Claire Lamont explains that 'India was never out of the news in Scott's youth. Debates over the India Bill, finally passed in 1784 bringing the East India Company under Crown control, were important enough to bring down governments.'[29] Scott drew on his reading and on the experience of his friends and neighbours; Anglo-Indian vocabulary was in current use among Scott's acquaintances as ex-East India Company soldiers such as Colonel James Ferguson returned from service in India to settle in Scotland. As Scott

---

[27] Catherine Hall (ed.), *Cultures of Empire* (Manchester, 2000), 3.

[28] Walter Scott, *Chronicles of the Canongate* (London, 2003), 155.

[29] Ibid. 361.

said when he was writing the novel, 'I cannot go on with the tale without I could speak a little Hindhanee, a small seasoning of curry powder— Fergusson will do it if I can screw it out of him.'[30] The recruiting agent for the East India Company who entices young men in Scotland to enlist does so by painting an exotic picture of life in India: 'Palaces rose like mushrooms in his descriptions; groves of lofty trees, and aromatic shrubs unknown to the chilly soils of Europe, were tenanted by every object of the chase, from the royal tiger down to the jackall.'[31] Though the narrator's tone is wry here, he too depicts aspects of Indian life as exotically seductive, especially when women become objects of the chase. Unlike Stevenson and Buchan, Scott does not question the colonizing presence of the British, in this case in India, setting the novel safely in the past, and he focuses exclusively on the interaction between the British and the court of Hyder Ali rather than depicting the life of ordinary Indians. The plot pivots on the fact that Tippoo Sultan is inflamed with sexual desire for a young British woman. An Orientalist perception underpins the novel; the widow of a Scottish emigrant who machinates against Hyder Ali is known as the Queen of Sheba, is attended by a black slave, and wears exotic clothes including a turban 'decorated by a magnificent aigrette, from which a blue ostrich plume floated in one direction, and a red one in another'.[32]

Two young men who meet in Scotland at the beginning of the novel are compared throughout, one an earnest north Briton, Adam Hartley, and the other the illegitimate son of a Jacobite and a Spanish Jewess, Richard Middlemass. Both go to India, but the unscrupulous Richard betrays all the values his honest Scottish foster-father has tried to instil into him. His make-up and clothes reveal his decadence, which is by implication inherent in his Catholic/Jewish genes: 'His mustachoes were turned and curled, and his eyelids stained with antimony. The vest was of gold brocade, with a cummerband, or sash, around his waist, corresponding to his turban. He carried in his hand a large sword, sheathed in a scabbard of crimson velvet.'[33] There is a thematic insistence on his ancestry making him morally unstable. He gets his comeuppance when Hyder Ali has him crushed in public by an elephant, which Scott discovered was the practice in Tippoo Sultan's court. Hyder Ali comments, in faux-archaic foreign grammar, referring to himself in the third person to enhance his status, '"Do thou

---

[30] Ibid. 364.   [31] Ibid. 203.
[32] Ibid. 249–50.   [33] Ibid. 280.

say to thy nation, Hyder Ali acts justly." [34] Though the Muslim ruler does act justly, if brutally, unlike many of Scott's novels *The Surgeon's Daughter* conforms to clichés and stereotypes that are still current in British culture.

It was particularly Scott's historical fiction that engaged the imagination of Robert Louis Stevenson and John Buchan; as Murray Pittock observes, all three 'drew heavily on the period of Scottish history which can be characterised as the Fall of the House of Stewart: 1638–1788, the era which had seen Scotland's native dynasty and national independence lost, and the country riven by religious war'.[35] Certainly, Stevenson saw parallels between the loss of old Highland social and cultural values and the disruption of traditional norms in Samoa under the impact of the new 'civilizing' powers. Stevenson and Buchan were themselves, like Macquarie, actively engaged in imperial politics and wrote fiction that reached and influenced a wide public at the end of the nineteenth and the beginning of the twentieth centuries. Both of them broke the mould of fiction in their own time and both are widely read today. Buchan's novels are in the process of appearing in a new imprint from Polygon, and Stevenson's *South Sea Tales*, which were re-issued in 2008, have fulfilled a perceptive prediction that was made by Stephen Gwynn in the *Fortnightly Review* in 1894: 'What Mr Kipling has done for British India, Mr Stevenson is doing for the South Seas. He is peopling a definite field in our imaginations; there at least his work takes root in life; and, if I mistake not, to future generations his name and personality will suggest these islands of the Pacific.'[36] He was not mistaken; the number of Stevenson's critics and readers in the Pacific Islands increases and the editor of the World's Classics edition, Roslyn Jolly, writes that the stories' 'subject-matter places Stevenson as an important witness both to nineteenth-century imperialism and to the creation of the modern post-colonial world....to the transformation of nineteenth-century imperial culture into twentieth-century global culture'.[37] Both Stevenson and Buchan explore the complexity of colonial and class categories as subtly as Rudyard Kipling does, showing how race and status, and in Stevenson's case gender,

---

[34] Ibid. 284.

[35] Ian Brown and Alan Riach (eds), *The Edinburgh Companion to Twentieth-Century Scottish Literature* (Edinburgh, 2009), 33.

[36] Quoted in Robert Louis Stevenson, *South Sea Tales* (Oxford, 1999), pp. xxxi–xxxii.

[37] Ibid., p. xxxiii.

interact politically and make any kind of yearning for a homeland human but also irrelevant and anachronistic.

Stevenson himself was a migrant. He had suffered since childhood from a respiratory disease. His health became so precarious that he had to leave Europe, and in 1890 he bought the estate of Vailima on the island of Upolu, Samoa, and settled there. In *Treasure Island*, Stevenson's first novel published in 1882, the brutality of the treasure hunters on both sides is startling, but by the end conventional racial and class attitudes have been maintained. There are no indigenous islanders, and the masculinist ethos of the captain, the doctor, and the squire is endorsed, with the raffish Long John Silver escaping in South America, perhaps to his 'woman of colour', with an unfair share of the treasure. As Roslyn Jolly writes, by the time that Stevenson began to set his fiction in the South Seas, 'the anti-imperialistic and pro-native sentiments of all the stories clashed with the romance of imperialism being played out in English public consciousness and popular literature at the end of the century—a romance with which Stevenson could be assimilated only against the evidence of the stories themselves'.[38] Stevenson lived in Samoa from 1890 until his death in 1894; it was subject to joint German, British, and American control, which Stevenson opposed because he saw the heavy imperial presence as disempowering Samoans. He intervened in Samoan politics, supporting the native chief Mataafa, who declared war against a puppet king installed by German forces. Stevenson wrote to *The Times* protesting about repressive British legislation linked to tripartite control of the islands, specifically relating to the 'Regulation for the Maintenance of Peace and Good Order in Samoa'. *A Footnote to History* (1892) is Stevenson's account of imperial intervention in Samoa, caused by German anxiety to protect its commercial interests. Soon after he settled there he wrote to his friend Sidney Colvin, 'I feel it wretched to see this dance of folly and injustice and unconscious rapacity go forward from day to day, and to be impotent.'[39] His insight into the situation of the islanders came from the Highlands: 'In both cases . . . an alien authority enforced, the clans disarmed, the chiefs deposed, new customs introduced, and chiefly that fashion of regarding money as the means and object of existence.'[40]

---

[38] Ibid., p. xxx.

[39] *Selected Letters of Robert Louis Stevenson*, ed. E. Mehew (New Haven, 1997), 463.

[40] Quoted in William Gray, *Robert Louis Stevenson: A Literary Life* (Basingstoke, 2004), 115.

This politically engaged perspective was not what some of his readers wanted. Metropolitan responses were dismissive; Stevenson's friend Henry James wrote: 'Samoa was susceptible of no "style"... save the demonstration of its rightness for life; and this left the field abundantly clear for the border, the Great North Road and the eighteenth century.'[41] James, in his study of Stevenson, ignores Stevenson's South Sea stories and focuses only, in his discussion of the late work, on what was written in Samoa but set in Scotland. Stevenson explained 'The Beach of Falesá' to an uncomprehending Colvin: 'It is the first realistic South Sea story... everybody else who has tried, that I have seen, got carried away by the romance and ended in a kind of sugar candy sham epic... there was no etching, no human grin, consequently no conviction. Now I have got the smell and look of the thing.' He relishes the linguistic idiosyncrasy of the place: 'traders' talk, which is a strange conglomerate of literary expressions and English and American slang, and Beach de Mar [Polynesian pidgin], or native English'.[42] The story anticipates Conrad's *Heart of Darkness* in that its narrator, Wiltshire, is both critical of and complicit with imperialism without being able to analyse the contradictions of his position. His sense of intrinsic superiority is expressed clearly when he says of the Polynesians: 'They haven't any real government or any real law... and even if they had, it would be a good joke if it were to apply to a white man. It would be a strange thing if we came all this way and couldn't do as we pleased.'[43] This is increasingly complicated by his disgust at the exploitation of the islanders by his compatriots, his prejudice against missionaries, his fear of local spiritual practices, and his admiration of his wife's integrity.

Julia Reid places Stevenson's work in the context of *fin-de-siècle* social Darwinism, the belief that natural selection would ruthlessly exterminate those races assumed to be inferior. She argues that:

Stevenson deploys Darwinism precisely in order to censure the harmful effects of colonialism. Dissenting from the evolutionary progressivist interpretation of imperialism, he finds in the less optimistic aspects of Darwin's work grounds for believing that the colonial overthrow of an existing culture is not simply the natural or lawful assertion of the might of a more advanced party.[44]

---

[41] Quoted in Stevenson, *South Sea Tales*, p. xxxi.

[42] *Selected Letters*, ed. Mehew, 467–8.

[43] Stevenson, *South Sea Tales*, 24.

[44] Julia Reid, *Robert Louis Stevenson, Science, and the Fin de Siècle* (Basingstoke, 2009), 147.

Throughout the story, its beach setting is emblematic of its liminality, a culture perhaps on the edge of survival. In formal terms, the story itself is liminal, both romance and realism. What is evident to the reader from the opening paragraph of the story is the sensuous appeal the island holds for Wiltshire. He sees it first at an in-between moment, when he has been living 'near the line'. He arrives when it is 'neither night nor morning', when 'the land breeze blew in our faces, and smelt strong of wild lime and vanilla'.[45] He arrives to take over a store and to deal in copra, dried coconut, which is of considerable commercial value, and is immediately offered a 'wife' by Case, a trader who tricks and exploits him. The illiterate <u>Uma</u> values her marriage certificate which reads: 'This is to certify that Uma daughter of <u>Fa'avao</u> of Falesá island . . . is illegally married to <u>Mr John Wiltshire</u> for one night, and Mr John Wiltshire is at liberty to send her to hell next morning' (11). This is the moral, or immoral, pivot of the story, as Wiltshire feels increasingly repelled by his own subterfuge and falls deeply in love with his 'wife'. It was the passage about the marriage certificate that the publishers censored. When it appeared in the *Illustrated London News* in six instalments in 1892 the passage was omitted, making nonsense of the narrative. Stevenson insisted that Cassell's should reinstate it when the story appeared in book form, but there was further haggling that extended the one-night stand to a week. The interference attacks the realism Stevenson had crafted so carefully to reveal the commodification of the islanders by the riff-raff that drifted in the wake of the colonial administration.

This instance of using the mock marriage certificate to deceive the illiterate Uma is an indication of Stevenson's unravelling of colonial stereotypes. Far from bringing the natives education and enlightenment, the whites in the story use their erudition to cheat and exploit the island's inhabitants. When the islanders retaliate, their taboo seems to the reader a potent but non-violent expression of reproach: 'The rest were like graven images: they stared at me, dumb and sorrowful, with their bright eyes; and it came upon me things would look not much different if I were on the platform of the gallows' (15). At some level Wiltshire knows that he belongs, if not on the gallows, in the stocks, though he asserts his own superiority: '"I'm a white man, and a British subject, and no end of a big chief at home; and I've come here to do them good, and bring them civilization; and no

---

[45] Stevenson, *South Sea Tales*, 3.

sooner have I got my trade sorted than they go and taboo me"' (23). Stevenson's astute revelation of British class issues permeates the stories; people like Wiltshire, who has been bumming his way round the islands, try to pass themselves off as belonging to the educated upper classes. Similar inversions and deceptions happen with the white celebrant at the 'wedding', who is 'old Captain Randall, squatting on the floor native fashion, fat and pale, naked to the waist, grey as a badger, and his eyes set with drink. His body was covered with grey hair and crawled over by flies' (8). There is a macabre comedy about the depiction of this erstwhile member of the British Navy, who might be said to have 'gone native' except that the natives are clean and behave with dignity.

In 'The Beach of Falesá' Stevenson creates in Uma a character whose background and language are on the edge, as she is not a native of the island, but who rescues Wiltshire through her understanding of the cultural complexity that he wants to deny. When he explores the bush he finds 'a wall in front of me . . . there is no native alive today upon that island that could dream of such a piece of building' (54). Wiltshire may be right that no islanders could now create such a wall, but it may be another of his western prejudices, like the colonial assumption that only white men could have built Great Zimbabwe. Uma's charm for the reader lies in her ability to dismantle this pomposity. Her pidgin has a vitality that Wiltshire's clichés lack as she explains the source of the taboo:

'I 'shamed,' she said. 'I think you savvy. Ese he tell me you savvy, he tell me you no mind, tell me you love me too much. Taboo belong me,' she said, touching herself on the bosom, as she had done upon our wedding-night. 'Now I go 'way, taboo he go 'way too. Then you get too much copra. You like more better, I think. *Tofá, alii,*' says she in the native—'Farewell, chief!' (28)

This shows an amusing insight into Wiltshire's character that he is unaware of: her implication that he loves commercial gain more than her, and that he is pretending to be an aristocrat.

The final lines of the story pinpoint with extraordinary economy the cultural complexity explored in the tale, implying that the reader's attitudes confirm the narrator's own, another disjunctive moment. Wiltshire's son is being educated in Auckland but he worries about his daughters:

They're only half-castes, of course; I know that as well as you do, and there's nobody thinks less of half-castes than I do; but they're mine, and about all I've got. I can't reconcile my mind to their taking up with Kanakas, and I'd like to know where I'm to find the whites? (71)

The story places the reader in an insecure position by destabilizing the stereotypes of race, gender, and literary form.

Stevenson's novella *The Ebb-Tide*, written in conjunction with his stepson Lloyd Osbourne, is even more disruptive of the reader's narrative expectations than 'The Beach of Falesá'. The title may refer to the dregs left after the melancholy long withdrawing roar of empire, as the story is one of lawlessness under a veneer of authority in which American and British opportunists exploit each other and the islanders; there are references to French, Portuguese, British, and New Zealand colonialisms. Tides of stolen alcohol flow through the story:

Throughout the island world of the Pacific, scattered men of many European races and from almost every grade of society carry activity and disseminate disease. Some prosper, some vegetate. Some have mounted the steps of thrones and owned islands and navies. Others again must marry for a livelihood; a strapping, merry, chocolate-coloured dame supports them in sheer idleness; and, dressed like natives, but still retaining some foreign element of gait or attitude, still perhaps with some relic (such as a single eye-glass) of the officer and gentleman, they sprawl in leaf-palmed verandahs and entertain an island audience with memoirs of the music-hall. (123)

Unlike the opening of 'The Beach of Falesá', there is no romance here. The opening image of contamination, of Europeans disseminating disease, becomes part of the texture of the book. That the disease is as much moral and spiritual as physical is clear in the opening lines, with the commercial agenda of the emigrants becoming evident as they own navies and marry for a livelihood, using totemic objects such as an eye-glass to gesture towards their colonial status. Their own language is mimicked in the phrase 'chocolate-coloured dame'.

In a grotesque inversion of the norm, a dissolute trio of drunkards, two Englishmen, Herrick and Huish, and an American, Davis, shamble from a night on the beach in Tahiti past the Kanaka crew of a schooner. Davis entertains the crew, singing to a borrowed accordion and dancing, and the three are given breakfast by the islanders. When the Scottish captain of the vessel arrives, Davis breaks into 'Auld Lang Syne'. It fails to wring the captain's heart-strings: '"You set up any more of your gab to me," returned the Scotchman, "and I'll show ye the wrong side of a jyle"' (137). The fact that Herrick carries and dips into a copy of Virgil's *Aeneid* is an oblique irony. A text enshrining a foundational myth of patriotism and nationhood now 'speaks not so much of Mantua or Augustus, but of English places' (125) and of Herrick's lost youth. Stevenson's earlier fusion of romance and realism is abandoned for a much darker vision of empire.

The deliberate dislocations of the adventure genre in the plot gesture towards one of the themes of the novella, which concerns the failure of the imperial story. In Salman Rushdie's novel *Haroun and the Sea of Stories,* he envisages postcolonial narrative hybridity in the Ocean of Stories:

... because the stories were held here in fluid form, they retained the ability to change, to become new versions of themselves, to join up with other stories and so become yet other stories; so that unlike a library of books, the Ocean of the Streams of Story was much more than a storeroom of yarns. It was not dead but alive.[46]

In *The Ebb-Tide*, the stories of empire are dead, part of the flotsam left as it withdraws. The novella is full of quotation, sometimes in the narrator's voice. The echo of *Macbeth* in the narrator's comment that the 'clerk and Herrick stood not upon the order of their going' (137) is part of a texture of references that never adds up to a coherent world view. Quotations from the Bible rub shoulders with music-hall songs, and fragments from Goldsmith, Gray, Wordsworth, Henley, Swift, and Defoe pervade the text. An iconic moment from *Robinson Crusoe* is degraded by comparison, as the three con-men realize that the cargo on their stolen ship which they assumed to be champagne is water: 'The mug passed round; each sipped, each smelt of it; each stared at the bottle in its glory of gold paper as Crusoe may have stared at the footprint' (176). Herrick's attempt to inscribe his identity on the wall of the old calaboose is a grotesquely inappropriate rhetorical encomium from the *Aeneid* to the heroes who died beneath the walls of Troy. His classical education seems only to have equipped him with feelings of inadequacy in comparison with past empires.

This is part of the contagion that the Europeans and Americans bring to the islands. An even more sinister thread in the novella is its persistent reminders of slavery. Davis tries to sell his buccaneering ambitions to the others by comparing their plans with those of Hayes and Pease, notorious slave traders. Several of the ship's crew of islanders have, in the bizarre

---

[46] Salman Rushdie, *Haroun and the Sea of Stories* (London, 1991), 72.

colonial lottery, acquired ludicrous names such as Sally Day for 'a lean-flanked, clean-built fellow' (155), and one of them protests against it: '"Ah, no call me Uncle Ned no mo'!" cried the old man. "No my name! My name Taveeta, all-e-same Taveeta King of Islael"' (168). 'Taveeta' is a corruption of David, so a dignified Christian name has been replaced by 'Uncle Ned', a patronizing substitute. As the crew read their Bibles and sing hymns, '[s]hame ran in Herrick's blood to remember what employment he was on, and to see these poor souls—and even Sally Day, the child of cannibals, in all likelihood a cannibal himself—so faithful to what they knew of good' (169). It was, of course, the slavers' traditional practice to substitute western names for the African slaves' own names. In a darker version of diaspora than that in 'The Beach of Falesá', the reader observes Stevenson's insight into the disintegration of a very specific clan system caused by the intervention of empires and the rapacious predators that come in their wake.

John Buchan served as the private secretary to Lord Milner, the High Commissioner for South Africa, 1901–3, and his novel *Prester John*, set largely in South Africa, was first published in 1910. His last novel, *Sick Heart River*, published posthumously, was written when he was Governor-General of Canada. His long career as a public servant might suggest that his fiction would celebrate imperial values, perhaps with a dash of nostalgia, but even an apparently racist novel such as *Prester John* is complicated by the narrator's awareness of his own limitations in comparison with those of Laputa, the African freedom-fighter who tries to lead his people against the British. The narrator, David Crawfurd, is a young Scot who has an opportunity to go to South Africa, escaping from genteel Kirkcaple. As a boy he had to wear an Eton suit to church, but one night escaped with friends to the beach and discovered that the visiting African minister had done the same thing. He had 'shed his clerical garments, and was now practising some strange magic alone by the sea'.[47] He proves to be Laputa, and at some level he and David have the same impulses. David's sanctimonious diatribe at the end of the novel, when he has conspired with Captain Arcoll to defeat the insurgency, is often read as an expression of Buchan's racism:

I knew then the meaning of the white man's duty. He has to take all risks, recking nothing of his life or his fortunes, and well content to find his reward in the fulfilment of his task. That is the difference between white and black, the gift of

---

[47] John Buchan, *Prester John* (1910; Edinburgh, 2009), 7.

responsibility, the power of being in a little way a king; and so long as we know this and practise it, we will rule not in Africa alone but wherever there are dark men who live only for the day and their own bellies. (200)

This reads as a prose rendering of Kipling's 'The White Man's Burden' (1899), but the context of the novel undermines the imperial orthodoxy of Crawfurd's magisterial statement. He is consistently awed and intrigued by Laputa's charisma, by his noble figure, his mesmerizing eloquence, and his belief in himself as the heir of Prester John. The masculine bond between colonial servant and indigenous insurgent is strong; Laputa tells Crawfurd that '[y]our fate has been twisted with mine' (180) and Crawfurd feels a homoerotic respect for Laputa: 'As my eye fell on his splendid proportions I forgot all else in my admiration of the man' (80). The conflict within Crawfurd becomes explicit when he apologizes to the reader for it: 'God forgive me, but I think I said I hoped to see the day when Africa would belong once more to its rightful masters' (81).

This disjunction is most evident in the hauntingly disturbing *Sick Heart River*, in which a Scottish protagonist of Buchan's earlier novels, Edward Leithen, a pillar of the establishment and a survivor of the Great War, confronts his own imminent death. *Prester John*, whatever its paradoxes, is primarily an adventure story in the same vein as Rider Haggard's empire fiction. *Sick Heart River* purports at first to be an adventure quest, in which Leithen goes in search of a missing man. It proves to be a spiritual quest, more like *Pilgrim's Progress* than *King Solomon's Mines*. Leithen's lungs have been damaged in the Great War, but he has served as Attorney General, practised in the Inns of Court, and been an intimate friend of the rich and powerful in America as well as Europe. When his doctor tells him that he is dying of tuberculosis he has a moment of insight: 'Only now that his body was failing did he realise how little he had used it...'[48] This proves to be a rather arid discovery because he sets out to test his body to its physical limits rather than to enjoy it, but as he tracks a missing French-Canadian banker, Francis Galliard, he goes through a series of trials comparable to Christian's in *Pilgrim's Progress*. Leaving his London club and apartment and the New York smart set behind, he goes first to Quebec, then by air over the Barrens to the shores of the Arctic Ocean, and finally on foot into the Mackenzie Mountains. Though the novel is focalized through Leithen, it

---

[48] John Buchan, *Sick Heart River* (1941; Edinburgh, 2007), 14.

is not a first-person narrative; however, the reader sees only what Leithen sees. The narrative technique is both intimate and distancing as the narrator observes Leithen's wasting body and narrowing political interests: 'Here in Canada he did not care a jot about the present or future of a great British Dominion' (52). The voice modulates into an exploration of Leithen's inner life and emotional aridity:

He had had no wife, no child. Had his many friends been more, after all, than companions? In the retrospect his career seemed lonely, self-centred, and barren, and what was this last venture? A piece of dull stoicism at the best—or, more likely, a cheap bravado. (73)

The adventure plot should conclude with Leithen's discovery of Galliard, but that happens two-thirds of the way through the book. Using a series of parallels, Buchan traces the losses involved in diaspora. Leithen, Galliard, and Galliard's guide, Lew, have gone in search of a personal vision of Eden or redemption, and they have all failed to find the paradisal place of imagination or memory. The Holy City of the mind, the sick heart's destination, is destructively hideous when they reach it in its physical reality:

'I don't know what I'd expected. A land flowing with milk and honey, and angels to pass the time of day! What opened my eyes was when I found there was no living thing in that valley. That was uncanny, and gave me the horrors. And then I considered that that great hole in the earth was a grave, a place to die in but not to live in, and not a place either for an honest man to die in.' (134)

The beginning of the Second World War has already been signalled in the novel; ironically, at the point at which the British Empire is about to reach its dissolution, Leithen realizes what it could have given him if he had been less hidebound by convention. As the group returns from 'paradise' they find a real mission. Johnny and Lew are half Scots and half native Canadian, successful hybrids: Leithen admires Johnny's 'speech, which was a wonderful blend of the dialect of the outlands, the slang of America, and literary idioms, for Johnny was a great reader—all spoken in the voice of a Scots shepherd, and with a broad Scots accent' (44). Eventually Johnny and Lew, together with the French-Canadian Galliard, led by the dying Scot, Leithen, save a group of native Hare Canadians from their collective anomie. Leithen's Scottish heritage reasserts itself. When he first meets Father Paradis he says, 'I am an Englishman, as you see' (46), but later he says, 'I'm Scots, same as you' (121). He understands the Hare through his experience of the Highlands, without nostalgia. This is achieved, like Stevenson's depiction of the South Seas, with sensuous particularity:

The cold was more intense than anything he had ever imagined. Under its stress trees cracked with a sound like machine-guns. The big morning fire made only a narrow circle of heat. If for a second he turned his face from it the air stung his eyelids as if with an infinity of harsh particles. To draw breath rasped the throat. The sky was milk-pale, the sun a mere ghostly disc. (179)

Sick Heart River, a provocative title, ends with a masculinist vision of what empire might have been, in the collaboration of men of different ethnicities and religions to save the native Canadian Hares who have lost the will to live, partly because they are now afflicted by physical and psychological diseases imported from the old world.

Freeing History

I conclude with a coda which focuses on slavery and its aftermath in relation to diaspora. My examples are two contemporary Scottish writers who give readers in the twenty-first century imaginative insight into Scotland's involvement in the slave trade, and engage with the particularity of individual lives in the past. One of the epigraphs to James Robertson's *Joseph Knight*, from the Nigerian writer Ben Okri, echoes Achebe's insistence on the significance of the stories that nations and peoples tell themselves: 'If they tell themselves stories that face their own truths, they will free their histories for future flowerings.' Robertson's novel addresses the myth that 'it didn't happen here'. Moving between a present in 1802–3 and a past beginning in 1746, Robertson's detective story traces Archibald Jamieson's attempt to find out for John Wedderburn what happened to Joseph Knight after Knight's victory in 1778 at the Court of Session over his former master. Wedderburn's daughter Susan, at the family estate in Perthshire, notices a figure erased from a Wedderburn family portrait painted in Jamaica and realizes that 'Joseph Knight remained at Ballindean yet was always missing, visible yet invisible, present yet absent'.[49] Robertson's novel enacts that absent presence by making Knight a shadowy figure throughout the novel until the final twenty-five pages. The reader catches glimpses of him as a boy and later as a man, but his actions are always reported by others. Only at the end, after

---

[49] James Robertson, *Joseph Knight* (London, 2004), 25.

Wedderburn's death, does Robertson give the reader access to Knight's meditation on his enforced diaspora. Other slaves had told him that they looked forward to returning to Africa after death, but he has no distinct sense of his childhood home and remembers only the slave ship, though even here his memory dissociates him from himself, 'in the picture it was him and yet not him' (349). In Robertson's imaginative reconstruction of Knight's experience, he is enslaved by a Scottish master, freed by an Enlightenment court, and supported by other Scots: 'He was surrounded by the faces of men who had also once been slaves, near as damn it. They were all around him, and when they went down to the shore and into the earth together there was a joining of their souls that was like no other feeling' (353). They are the Fife colliers who earn almost nothing but contribute to a fund to enable him to contest his case. Robertson imagines Knight becoming a collier, in a situation where blackness is a routine part of all the miners' experience. The attempt at retrieval of his voice mirrors the initiatives in recent colonial history to rediscover the voices of the oppressed, the male and female subalterns, whether they be slaves, convicts, or working people.

Jackie Kay's *The Lamplighter*, at once an epic poem and a radio play, similarly imagines voices for four slave women in a fort, on the Middle Passage, and on a plantation, with Macbean as the voice of the *Zeitgeist* throughout. He explains that the trade cannot be carried out without chains: 'These are not cruelties; | They are matters of course.'[50] The success of the slave trade is inscribed on Glasgow's streets—Virginia, Tobago, Jamaica—and the popular song 'Glasgow belongs to me' is given an ironic perspective when it is sung by one of the exploited slave women. Macbean comments:

> In 1770 on the slave island of Jamaica
> There were one hundred Black people
> Called MacDonald;
> A quarter of the island's people
> Were Scottish. (81)

Black Harriot responds sardonically: 'My daughters have Scottish blood. | Scotland has my blood' (81), a comment on the sexual abuse of slave women by Scottish plantation owners, and on the brutality of the punishment inflicted on the women. Following this is the Lamplighter's refrain: 'My

---

[50] Jackie Kay, *The Lamplighter* (Tarset, 2008), 79.

story is the story of Great Britain | The United Kingdom, The British
Empire' (81). The play is permeated by phrases from the Shipping Forecast,
a reminder of the climatic hazards of the Middle Passage and of constant
enforced diaspora.

Kay herself, the child of a Scottish mother and a Nigerian father, who was
adopted as a baby by Scottish parents and brought up in Glasgow, constantly opens up new facets of experience in her work, probing diasporic and
national identity. In a tribute to Bessie Smith's blues music, she writes of the
need to memorialize for 'Everything that's happened once could happen
again'.[51] More positively, in 'In my country' in the same volume the speaker
encounters on the beach, another liminal space, a woman who sees her as:

> . . . the worst dregs of her imagination,
> so when she finally spoke
> her words spliced into bars
> of an old wheel. A segment of air.
> *Where do you come from?*
> 'Here,' I said, 'Here. These parts.' (24)

Kay and Robertson maintain the dynamic interaction between Scottish
identity and colonial or postcolonial involvement that is evident in the work
of Stevenson and Buchan. All these writers explore what Murray Pittock,
writing about Buchan, calls the conflict between an outward role and an
inner authenticity: 'Buchan writes par excellence of the experience of the
Scot in the British empire—outward conformity, inner longing, nostalgia,
rebellion, fear or simply the existential void of *mauvais[e] foi*, the Sartrean
bad faith which indicates that an outward role is compromising an inner
authenticity.'[52] In their work, some diasporic travellers in the empire are
fatally compromised, such as those in *The Ebb-Tide*, but others achieve, in
Stuart Hall's terms, a diaspora identity like Edward Leithen's which repro-
duces itself anew through transformation and difference.

In 'Elegy for Angus Macdonald of Cnoclinn', to return to Les Murray for a
final interpretation of diaspora within the British Empire, the poet laments
the death in Sydney of his Gaelic teacher, but speculates on the benefits of
leaving home. His image of exile as a rampart, a distiller of spirit from

---

[51] Jackie Kay, *Other Lovers* (Newcastle, 1993), 9.
[52] Brown and Riach (eds), *The Edinburgh Companion to Twentieth-Century Scottish Literature*, 29.

bruised grains, indicates that, like Macquarie, Scots or people of Scots descent who have had personal history of displacement and humiliation can understand the other's experience:

> ... but my fathers were Highlanders long ago
> then Borderers, before this landfall
> —'savages' once, now we are 'settlers'
> in the mouth of the deathless enemy—
> but I am seized of this future now.
> I am not European. Nor is my English.
> And perhaps you too were better served here
> than in Uist of the Sheldrakes and the tides
> watching the old life fade, the *toradh*,
> the good, go out of the island world.
> Exile's a rampart, sometimes, to the past,
> a distiller of spirit from bruised grains;
> this is a meaning of the New World.[53]

Select Bibliography

Literary works

John Buchan, *Sick Heart River* (1941; Edinburgh, 2007).
—— *Prester John* (1910; Edinburgh, 2009).
Jackie Kay, *Other Lovers* (Newcastle, 1993).
—— *The Lamplighter* (Tarset, 2008).
Alistair MacLeod, *No Great Mischief* (London, 2001).
Alice Munro, *The View from Castle Rock* (London, 2006).
Les Murray, *Collected Poems* (Manchester, 1998).
James Robertson, *Joseph Knight* (London, 2004).
Walter Scott, *Chronicles of the Canongate*, ed. Claire Lamont (1827; London, 2003).
Robert Louis Stevenson, *South Sea Tales*, ed. Roslyn Jolly (Oxford, 1999).

Secondary works

Stuart Hall, 'Cultural Identity and Diaspora', in Patrick Williams and Laura Chrisman (eds), *Colonial Discourse and Postcolonial Theory* (London, 1993).
Murray Pittock, 'Scotland, Empire and Apocalypse: From Stevenson to Buchan', in Ian Brown and Alan Riach (eds), *The Edinburgh Companion to Twentieth-Century Scottish Literature* (Edinburgh, 2009).
Julia Reid, *Robert Louis Stevenson, Science, and the Fin de Siècle* (Basingstoke, 2009).

---

[53] Murray, *Collected Poems*, 153.

National Identity, Union, and Empire, c.1850–c.1970

Richard J. Finlay

Writing just before the Union of 1707 came into effect, the Governor of St Christopher's in the West Indies, Daniel Clark, came up with a plan to secure British island possessions against the French:

Send me over ten thousand Scotch with oatmeal enough to keep them for 3 or 4 months, let me be provided with arms, we will make what men we can ... let us try our fortune, if we take it, we will have the plunder, the Scotch will have the land, in time the warm sun will exhale all those crudities that make them so troublesome, and 'tis not impossible but it may have the effect to make them more of a sociable religion; if we have not success if you choose out those that are so zealous to maintain the Kirk against the Union: if I get them all knocked on the head, I am of the opinion that the English nation will be no great losers by it. I think this no ill project, the Queen venturing nothing but a few arms and oatmeal.[1]

It was hardly complimentary. The Scots were clearly regarded as expendable and there was little glory attached to the footslogging associated with empire-building. Over a century-and-a-half later, this view was changed completely, with a number of English commentators noting with gratitude the Scottish contribution to Britain's imperial mission.[2] For later Scots, despite the evidence, the story of the British Empire began with the Union, and an irate petition complained that the Scottish regiments and soldiers that had acted so

---

[1] Governor Parke to Mr Secretary Hedges, 19 January 1707, National Archives, CO 239/1, 19, vol. 23 (1707–8), 723.

[2] Sir Charles Dilke, *Greater Britain: A Record of Travel in English Speaking Countries during 1886 and 1887* (London, 1887), 121, 353; J. A. Froude, *Oceana: Or England's Colonies Abroad* (London, 1887), 135. See also Introduction to this volume.

heroically in the acquisition and defence of the empire did not do so for the greater glory of 'England' but rather Britain:

Who built up this British Empire? What was its condition at the time of the Union? Save a few islands in the West Indies and the plantations in North America, which were afterwards lost through criminal folly, there were few possessions. The Rise of the Empire dates from the Union.[3]

By the 1930s, the Scottish role in the building of the British Empire was widely believed, in Scotland at any rate, to have been a greater proportionate role than any other constituent part of the United Kingdom. Andrew Dewar Gibb, a Conservative with strong Scottish nationalist leanings, praised his countrymen's effort in the British imperial project and detailed the role of Scots in each of the constituent continents of the empire.[4] What Gibb and his readers readily assumed was that the existence of a significant number of prominent Scots involved in imperial activity meant that there was an unproblematic relationship to Scotland, and, by implication, that Scottish characteristics, identity, and tradition overarched and bonded together these disparate actors over time and space to form the idea that there was a 'Scottish' contribution to British imperialism that was somehow more than the sum of activities of individual Scots. Historiographically speaking, in keeping with the changing Scottish political environment, the triumphalist version of Scottish involvement in empire was then replaced with a version that predominantly recast the Scots as victims of colonialism.[5] It has only been in the past few decades that scholars have begun to address the Scottish engagement with empire with reference to the wider historiographical debate regarding both imperialism and its British variant.[6]

---

[3] *Protest by the Scottish Home Rule Association against the misuse of the term 'England' and 'English' for 'Britain', 'the British Empire'. Its peoples and institutions* (Edinburgh, 1887).

[4] Andrew Dewar Gibb, *Scottish Empire* (Glasgow, 1937).

[5] In particular, Craig Beveridge and Ronald Turnbull, *The Eclipse of Scottish Culture: Inferiorism and the Intellectuals* (Edinburgh, 1981); Tom Nairn, *The Break-up of Britain: Crisis and Neo-nationalism* (London, 1981); Michael Hechter, *Internal Colonialism: The Celtic Fringe in British National Development* (Ann Arbor, Mich., 1998).

[6] In particular, John M. MacKenzie, 'Essay and Reflection: On Scotland and the Empire', *International History Review*, 15 (1993), 714–39; John M. MacKenzie, 'Empire and National Identities: The Case of Scotland', *Transactions of the Royal Historical Society*, 6th series, 8 (1998), 215–31; John M. MacKenzie, 'The Second City of Empire: Glasgow—Imperial Municipality', in Felix Driver and David Gilbert (eds), *Imperial Cities* (Manchester, 2003), 215–38; T. M. Devine,

One difficulty facing Scottish historians is to try to forge a place for their own contribution within an extensive historiography that will engage with the wider issues of the subject. A key problem is the issue of nationality, particularly the role of the 'nation-state'. As historians of the Third World are keen to point out, the European national variant of imperialism is of relatively minor significance. After all, is there little difference from the perspective of the indigenous population between, say, British and French imperialism? Second, national readings of imperialism have been challenged by the development of more sophisticated models of interpretation that focus on issues such as environmentalism, racial ideas, scientific and technological development, and the role of capital that tends to diminish the activities of individual nation states.[7] As Cain and Hopkins point out, whatever the claims of their detractors, South America was more important to British interests than parts of the world that were under formal imperial jurisdiction.[8] John Darwin has recently postulated a 'British world system' that locates the formal empire as one factor within a global web of British power and influence.[9] Perhaps a focus on global Scots rather than imperial Scots would be more appropriate in light of recent wider historiographical developments. Although the global Scots are easy to spot, what has remained elusive is the 'system' or 'systems' that connected them together.

While the role of the 'national' impetus has declined in significance in the wider debate on European imperialism, the Scottish case is made

---

Scotland's Empire, 1660–1815 (London, 2003) and idem, 'The Break-up of Britain? Scotland and the End of Empire', *Transactions of the Royal Historical Society*, 6th series, 16 (2006), 163–81.

[7] See, for example; Daniel R. Headrick, *The Tools of Empire: Technology and European Imperialism in the Nineteenth Century* (New York, 1981); idem, *The Tentacles of Progress: Technology Transfer in the Age of Imperialism* (New York, 1990); Richard H. Grove, *Green Imperialism: Colonial Expansion, Tropical Island Edens and the Origins of Environmentalism, 1660–1860* (Cambridge, 1996); John M. MacKenzie, *The Empire of Nature: Hunting, Conservation and British Imperialism* (Manchester, 1997); Raymond E. Durnett (ed.), *Gentlemanly Capitalism and British Imperialism: The New Debate on Empire* (London, 1999); Peter Cain and A. G. Hopkins, *British Imperialism, 1688–2000* (2nd edn London, 2001); C. A. Bayly, *The Birth of the Modern World, 1780–1914: Global Connections and Comparisons* (London, 2004); Alfred W. Crosby, *Ecological Imperialism: The Biological Expansion of Europe, 900–1900* (Cambridge, 2004); and John Darwin, *After Tamerlane: The Rise and Fall of Global Empires, 1400–2000* (London, 2007).

[8] Cain and Hopkins, *British Imperialism*, 243–75.

[9] John Darwin, *The Empire Project: The Rise and Fall of the British World-System, 1830–1970* (Cambridge, 2009).

problematic by the fact that while a nation, it was not a state. In many respects, highlighting the specifically Scottish dynamic of European imperialism is to swim against the historiographical tide. The danger is that the Scottish case will add little more than detail to the wider debate and the question can be asked; does it matter and should historians outside of Scotland be interested? Two further complicating factors emerge when examining the Scottish engagement with empire in the age of European imperialism. First, the state was central to imperial ambitions, but in the absence of a specific Scottish state, can the civil society which has been used as the principal explanatory model for the continuing existence of Scottish national identity be tailored, to borrow a phrase, to reconstruct the 'official mind' or 'civic mind' of Scottish imperialism. There is plenty of incidental evidence to show fairly extensive engagement with the empire, and hopefully a reconstruction of the civic mind of Scottish imperialism might provide the intellectual cohesion to tie them together into a more coherent model of understanding what might be described as 'civic imperialism'. This, however, relates to a second connected problem. Conventional historiographical wisdom has demonstrated that during the second half of the nineteenth century and throughout the twentieth century, Scottish politics were dominated by first the Liberal Party and then, after a Conservative interlude between the wars, the Labour Party, both of which were theoretically opposed to popular imperialism. So if there was widespread engagement with the empire, how do we square this with the existence of a political culture that was profoundly anti-imperialist?

The objective of this chapter is to explore the interaction between national identity and the relationship with British imperialism, and hopefully to demonstrate the complexities of the connections between regionalism or provincialism, Scottish national identity, and a wider British national and imperial identity. Furthermore, the chapter will show that these identities were in a state of flux and were not static over time and that at different times and in different contexts the relationship between regional, Scottish, British, and imperial identity varied. Broadly speaking, the era can be divided into three distinct phases. The first deals with the period before 1880, when provincialism was more dominant and there was little development of a specific 'Scottish' contribution. That was also marked by the propensity to define the nation as 'England' rather than 'Britain'. The second phase covers the period after 1880, when there emerged a clearer sense of a distinctive Scottish national role within the empire. Central to this development, it will be argued, was the importance of the redefinition of Unionism within the context of Ireland and the issue of home rule.[10] It will be argued that the rearticulation of Unionism allowed the Scots to recast their role within British imperialism within a specific *national* context. The survival of national institutions ante the Union of 1707 made for a more convincing case of national endeavour than Wales and helped funnel the direction of Scottish national identity in a different direction from Irish nationalism. Also, this development coincided with 'nation building' in the white dominions, of which maintaining the link with a wider British system of global government was central. The idea of multiple identities was not just confined to the British and Irish islands, but was mirrored throughout the white settler dominions. It will be argued that the reinvention of Unionism was fundamental in permitting a dovetailing of an increasingly populist engagement with empire that mirrored contemporary developments in Europe, where nationalism and imperialism seemed to go hand in hand. Unionism provided the necessary political language required to articulate Scottish activities within a *national* context. This redefinition of the Union was essential to the development of the 'civic mind' of Scottish imperialism. Furthermore, it can be suggested that 'civic imperialism' accounts for the disproportionate influence of the imperial engagement in Scottish political culture that was not necessarily reflected in electoral developments or party political support. Finally, the chapter will examine the decline of imperial sentiment and its relationship with changing ideas of Scottish and British identity.

Empire and Provincialism, c.1850–1880

By the mid-nineteenth century, Scots had a long history of engagement with the British Empire. From time to time, awareness that Scots made a *national* contribution surfaced and was reflected in the Scottish press and in other print media. Perhaps the best example of this is to be found in some of the statements of the National Association for the Vindication of Scottish Rights in the 1850s, which loudly proclaimed that Scotland was not a region of England.[11]

---

[10] Colin Kidd's latest offering on the Union has little to say on either Ireland or Empire; *Union and Unionism: Political Thought in Scotland, 1500–2000* (Cambridge, 2008).

[11] National Library of Scotland, NE 20, National Association for the Vindication of Scottish Rights, various pamphlets.

More often than not, however, attention tended to focus on the activities of individual Scots. One problem in assessing the Scottish contribution to British imperialism in the mid-nineteenth century is that it needs to be broken down into two component parts; what Scots did and how Scots perceived what they did. The danger of hindsight is a tendency to conflate the activity of individual Scots into a collective Scottish phenomenon, even though the ties that bind them were no more than the accidental place of birth of the actors.[12] The picture is further complicated when the perceptions of Scots within the empire are taken into account. While their sense of Scottishness shines through, predominantly the idea of the nation was 'England' and not Britain. Apart from the constitutionally minded, there was a tendency to see Scotland as 'incorporated' within the English state.[13] The Scottish press followed the English lead of using 'England' as the name for the state in international affairs.[14] Furthermore, the bulk of literature relating to imperial and international affairs produced south of the border referred to England, as did most members of Parliament.[15]

We have to go back to conventional wisdom in framing the Scottish intellectual response to empire in the mid-nineteenth century. Although a neglected subject, it is becoming apparent that most held that it was axiomatic that small nations were in decline and could contribute little to the development of international politics. Small nations, by their very nature, could not have a role to play on the global stage and, if anything, were regarded as a source of instability in the dominant British political discourse of the day. Ideas of state formation were increasingly influenced

[12] For a good example of the process of *post hoc* Scottification see John MacKenzie, 'David Livingstone: The Construction of a Myth', in G. Walker and T. Gallagher (eds), *Sermons and Battle Hymns: Protestant Popular Culture in Modern Scotland* (Edinburgh, 1990), 24–33.

[13] Although, as will be noted below, there was a campaign to stop the use of 'England' instead of Britain, it was only really effective in Scotland and the practice continued fairly unabated south of the border. Indeed, J. M. Robertson, a Scot sitting as an English Liberal MP, wrote about the English political system as late as 1912; *England: Her National and Political Evolution.*

[14] Numerous examples could be cited here, but see how in the aftermath of the 'Eastern Crisis' the Scottish press used England as the name of the nation. For example, see *Glasgow Herald*, 26 October 1876, 29 December 1879; *Dundee Courier and Argus*, 14 February 1879, and *Aberdeen Weekly Journal*, 4 April 1877. Indeed, the same newspaper reported a speech by the Tory West Aberdeenshire MP, Lord Douglas Gordon, who talked about 'England' and 'English interests'; 10 November 1877.

[15] Salisbury did it consciously, in spite of being asked not to. See Lady Frances Balfour, *Lord Balfour of Burleigh* (London, 1924), 83.

by social Darwinism, which held that the small nations of the world would be absorbed by the large.[16] Fears of turning into a 'Holland' were a constant *leitmotiv* among British imperialists. One major problem with articulating a distinctive Scottish role within the empire was that it went against current intellectual trends regarding state and imperial development. Furthermore, the intellectual current of British imperialism was based around the core of English state development that was by its nature expansive. This took little account of Scotland, other than to signal that it was one of the first areas to be absorbed by the 'expansion of England', as numerous English history books pointed out.[17] While the Scots may have claimed that the growth of empire started with the Union, the English view was that the incorporation of Scotland was the beginning of the 'expansion' of England. Small states were volatile, subject to competing claims of larger nations and a source of international instability. Ireland's turbulent relationship with the mainland seemed to bear this out.[18] In such circumstances, it was difficult to construct a distinctive Scottish *national* role within the empire. In any case, mid-century ideas of Scottish identity were a mass of contradictions, which, though making little sense to us today, were relatively unproblematic to contemporaries. This was the era when a campaign to create a monument to William Wallace coexisted with the propensity of the Scottish press to term the nation 'England'. That most bellicose of premiers, Lord Palmerston, illustrates this ambiguity during his visit to Glasgow to receive the freedom of the city in which he paid tribute to the abilities of the Scots, and then proceeded to talk about the foreign policy of England.[19] The era is replete

---

[16] See Lord Rosebery, 'Question of Empire: An Address Delivered as Lord Rector to the Students of Glasgow University, 16 November 1900', in John Buchan (ed.), *Lord Rosebery Miscellanies: Literary and Historical* (London, 1921).

[17] This is a theme that is fairly constant in English history books of the time. See, for example, J. R. Seeley, *The Expansion of England: Two Courses of Lectures* (1883), 131; J. R. Green, *A Short History of England* (London, 1876), 689: 'two peoples of common blood and common speech proclaimed to be one'; and for someone who did not like the idea of British see Fredric Harrison, *A Word for England*; 'As a real patriot, I grieve to see how the ancient and beloved name of my Fatherland is being driven out by the incessant advances of imperial ideas', quoted in Georgios Varouxakis, 'Great Versus Small Nations: Size and National Greatness in Victorian Political Though', in Duncan Bell (ed.), *Victorian Visions of Global Order: Empire and Relations in 19th Century Political Thought* (Cambridge, 2007), 136–59, 149.

[18] Varouxakis, 'Great Versus Small Nations'.

[19] *Glasgow Herald*, 29 September 1853.

with such incidents.[20] That most ardent defender of Scottish national dignity and imperial enthusiast, Lord Rosebery, referred to England's interest in the world with the reminder to his Glasgow audience that he did not mean 'just these two islands'.[21] Gladstone's critique of Disraeli's foreign policy in the Midlothian campaign, likewise, described the nation-state as England.[22]

It should come as no shock to discover that Scots within the empire, or engaged in empire-building, adopted the name England and English as their national nomenclature. David Livingstone is a good case in point. He dedicated his *Journey on the Zambesi* to the prime minister of England and called on the English navy to be more vigorous in the suppression of the slave trade.[23] John Philip in South Africa likewise differentiated between the English and the Dutch.[24] The Scottish churches, who ought to have known better, used the term 'English' to describe themselves to foreigners and indigenous people.[25] The distinctively Scottish enclave in Nyasaland (modern Malawi) used English, even when communicating to a home audience:

I am aware that it is almost necessary to make one remark for fear of misunderstanding. In speaking of our presence in Africa, and in several other ways, I use the term 'English', but in the general sense in which it seems natural to do so, moreover, it would lead to endless confusion if one had to teach the natives anew that the term 'British' had come to take up their quarters with them. From first to last it is plain that Scotland has paid noble tribute to her great countrymen, and

---

[20] See, for example, William Edward Foster, *Our Colonial Empire: An Address Delivered before the Philosophical Institution of Edinburgh* (Edinburgh, 1875), in which the terms 'England' and 'Britain' are virtually interchangeable.

[21] Speaking at Glasgow University Gladstone Club quoted in Lord Crewe, *Lord Rosebery*, vol. i (London, 1931), 139.

[22] W. E. Gladstone, *Political Speeches in Scotland* (London, 1884), in particular 94, 205, 217, 2080, 324, 352, 344.

[23] David and Charles Livingstone, *Narrative of an Expedition to the Zambesi and its Tributaries and the Discovery of Lakes Sharwa and Nayassa 1858–1864* (London, 1866), dedication.

[24] John Philip, *Researches in South Africa: Illustrations of the Civil, Moral and Religious Condition of the Native Tribes* (London, 1828), 1–87.

[25] See, for example, John Buchanan, *The Shire Highlands (East and Central Africa) as Colony and Mission* (London, 1885), 52–3: 'For the Shire Highlands and Lake Nyassa one may well claim that England should assume the protectorate. The Lake was discovered by an Englishman and English money, and the sum of English capital invested in the country at the present moment is not small.'

has infused her own determined spirit into the great undertaking which I had the honour to guide as pioneer.[26]

Other Scots were not even so self-conscious. In examining the use of 'English' by Scots in an imperial context, it becomes clear that it was used primarily to describe the state. Livingstone, for example, regularly invoked England in dealings of an international or diplomatic matter, such as the belief that the Portuguese turned a blind eye to slavery.[27] Kirk in his ambitions for Zanzibar talked of the advantages that would accrue to England.[28] At the same time, Scots would regularly partake in Burns Nights, St Andrew's societies, Scottish New Year's Day celebrations, and the like.[29] They were also well known, or notorious, for banding together and keeping close-knit communities. What is more difficult to discern is whether or not such activities were evidence of a provincial or a national community abroad. It might seem a moot point, but there is little to distinguish such kind of activity from, say, Yorkshire or Lancashire people in the empire, and few would argue that the latter evidenced aspects of *national* behaviour.

The predominance of a core–periphery model in explaining imperialism has tended to downplay the provincial in British imperial history.[30] This has not been helped by the strong London-centric bias that predominates in the writing of much British history. The absence of a major place for regional studies that exists in the historiography of continental Europe arguably has produced a lop-sided account of the British interaction with empire. This is all the more likely given the strong regional variations within the British economy, many of which had ties to empire. Just as Glasgow could be said to have its distinctive imperial identity, the same can equally be said of Liverpool and Birmingham.[31] The local dynamic of missionary endeavour, where

---

[26] E. D. Young, *Nyassa: A Journal of Adventures* (rev. edn by Revd Horace Walker, 2nd edn London, 1877), pp. viii–ix.

[27] Livingstone and Livingstone, *Narrative of an Expedition*, 7, 373, 631, 637, for example.

[28] Kirk to Salisbury, 19 January 1886, *British and Foreign State Papers*, vol. 77 (1893), 1110.

[29] Dilke, *Greater Britain*, 533.

[30] See Martin J. Daunton, 'Home and Colonial', *Twentieth Century British History*, 6.3 (1995), 344–58; B. R. Tomlinson, 'The Periphery and Imperial Economic History', in A. Porter (ed.), *The Oxford History of the British Empire*, iii: *The Nineteenth Century* (Oxford, 1999); and Andrew Thompson, 'Is Humpty Dumpty Together Again? Imperial History and the Oxford History of the British Empire', *Twentieth Century British History*, 12.4 (2001), 511–27.

[31] See MacKenzie, 'Glasgow: Second City'; Sheryllynne Haggarty, Anthony Webster, and Nicholas White (eds), *The Empire in One City? Liverpool's Inconvenient Imperial Past* (Manchester, 1986); on Birmingham see Catherine Hall, *Civilizing Subjects: Metropole and Colony in*

communities sent their own particular people, engaged in fund-raising, and maintained contact with individual churches was not confined to Scotland. As Simon Potter has shown, there emerged a common imperial information and dissemination process for the press, but this was refracted by the overwhelmingly regional basis of the British newspapers, where local imperial activities and people were highlighted.[32] The basis of recruitment to the military was at a local level, and certainly by the latter part of the nineteenth century strong bonds emerged in which particular places in Britain could claim ownership of their own specific regiments. Even warships were named after landlocked cities. Arguably, all this contributed to a profoundly regional dimension to the engagement with empire that has not had appropriate attention within the historiography. Scottish historians may have been first to highlight a phenomenon that was widespread through the British mainland. Furthermore, this regional factor is also evident in Scotland and, as already noted, the danger is that the regional phenomenon is packaged into a *national* endeavour retrospectively. A very good example of this can be found in emigration, where patterns of settlement and chain migration were heavily dependent on the local dimension.[33]

When Scottish identity in its national mould tends to surface in the mid-nineteenth century, it usually has to do with the residues of the national institutions that survived the Union of 1707. The treatment of the Scottish Kirk is a case in point, especially when it was denied parity of treatment with the Church of England in an imperial context.[34] This was a sore that grumbled on intermittently until the end of the nineteenth century. But again, it is worth emphasizing that collaboration with other churches and missionaries could transcend ecclesiastical and national boundaries. The Scots also had the habit of taking their educational practice and heritage

---

the English Imagination, 1830–67 (London, 2002) and Miles Taylor (ed.), *Southampton: Gateway to the British Empire* (London, 2007).

[32] Simon J. Potter, *News and the British World: The Emergence of an Imperial Press System, 1876–1922* (Oxford, 2003) and idem (ed.), *Newspapers and Empire in Ireland and Britain: Reporting the British Empire, 1837–1922* (Dublin, 2004).

[33] Marjory Harper, *Emigration from North East Scotland*, 2 vols (Aberdeen, 1988).

[34] See, for example, the *Presbyterian Magazine*, 2 (1852), 472; 'One fifth of the honourable East India Company servants belong to the Presbyterian communion, and yet are maintained by only six Presbyterian ministers; while for the four fifths, which belong chiefly to the Episcopal Church, 120 clergymen were paid.'

with them.[35] There is strong evidence that Scots used Scottish law for their last will and testament when serving in the empire.[36] The transplantation of 'Highlandism' was perhaps the most visible cultural manifestation of the Scots within the settlement colonies. One feature regarding this 'performance' of Scotland in the overseas colonies was that it was transmitted back, having the effect of reinforcing such images of Scottishness at home.[37] The widespread popularity of Walter Scott likewise reinforced the expectation of what Scots were supposed to be like, apparently obliging them to embrace those characteristics.

Although Graeme Morton has argued that there was a Unionist Nationalism in mid-nineteenth-century Scotland in which Scottish identity was used to reinforce British identity, we should be wary of anachronistic throwbacks.[38] Morton based his conclusions on the evidence of strong civic organizations in Edinburgh, yet how this was nationalist and not provincial is not really elucidated. The same argument could be made for any conurbation in mid-nineteenth-century Britain. Also, Unionism is largely taken as a given in a fairly unproblematic way without really elaborating on how this was evidence of a constitutional arrangement that had at its core the explicit recognition of a distinctive Scottish polity. While there is undoubtedly evidence of 'nationalist' bubbles emerging to the surface on occasion, this is not to say that it was part of a clearly articulated and understood set of political beliefs. Indeed, its core remained classic laissez-faire individualism in which the state, as a matter of political principle, was kept at arm's length, rather than a Scottish defensiveness of British governmental encroachment.

[35] For example, see D. H. Emmott, 'Alexander Duff and the Foundation of Modern Education in India', *British Journal for Education Studies*, 13.2 (1965), 160–9.

[36] I am grateful to Andrew Mackillop for this information relating to Scots in the East India Company. By the mid-nineteenth century, however, the legal position was such that Scottish law was not recognized in an imperial context. The *Oriental Herald*, 22 (1829), 219 makes the point that marriages officiated by the Church of Scotland outside of Scotland had no legal status and the *Law Journal Report*, 6 (1837), 572 makes the following point: 'where a Scotchman left his Scotch domicile and resided in India; he thereby acquired an English domicile; and that, as the deceased in that case died intestate, his property would be distributable according to the laws of England and not Scotland.'

[37] I am grateful to John MacKenzie for the idea of the 'performance' of Scotland in an imperial context.

[38] Graeme Morton, *Unionist Nationalism: Governing Urban Scotland, 1830–1860* (East Linton, 1999).

The New Unionism and the New Imperialism, c.1880–1914

Without the necessary language in which to articulate a distinctive *national* role within British imperialism, it is not surprising that Scots tended to use the appellation 'English' and accepted its widespread use for the name of the state. Events in Ireland, however, changed all this. Endeavours to make the Irish more 'English' had come to naught by the 1880s and it was increasingly recognized that Irish nationality was a fact of life which had to be accommodated.[39] There has been a tendency in Scottish historiography to assume the idea of Union as a somewhat static, changeless concept.[40] Unionism was rearticulated to take account of the legitimacy of Irish nationality, and while Unionists did not accept the legitimacy of Irish home rule, they did believe that Irish nationhood could be accommodated within the existing political structure of the British state. Gladstone's conversion to Home Rule in 1886 did have an impact on Scots and how they saw their role within the British state and empire.[41] The Scots were quick to adopt the language of nationality for their own purposes. This was crucial to Scottish engagement with empire because, without it, Scottish imperial endeavour would never be more than a local or provincial engagement. Comparisons were drawn between Scotland and Ireland, with the objective of highlighting the former's achievement and denigrating the latter's failure in a specifically national context. While the conversion to home rule pushed some Scots to demand an equal measure for Scotland, even among those who did not, Scottish nationhood became a political fact of life thanks to the reformulation of Unionism.[42]

[39] Jonathan S. Parry, *The Politics of Patriotism: English Liberals, National Identity and Europe, 1830–1886* (Cambridge, 2007), 86–120.

[40] Space does not allow much elaboration here, but the Union has been interpreted in different ways at different times. It hardly figured in political discourse before the 1880s, and as is argued below, was reinterpreted in the 1920s and 1930s in response to changed economic circumstances. Equally, the Union in post-devolution times is a different beast from that before 1997. James MacKinnon's *The Union of England and Scotland* (1896) was written according to the author to remind Scots that they too, like the Irish, had a Union with England.

[41] *Protest of the Scottish Home Rule Association against the Denial or Delay of Scottish Home Rule* (Edinburgh, 1980); 'The proposal to grant a legislature and executive government to Ireland, and withhold them from Scotland is unjust to a loyal, industrious and intelligent people, and appears to set a premium upon disorder.'

[42] Various Scottish Home Rule pamphlets, but see in particular T. D. Wanliss, *The Bars to British Unity or a Plea for National Sentiment* (Edinburgh, 1885) and *Scottish Home Rule: The Case in Sixty Points* (Glasgow, 1912), 1–4.

This reinvention of Unionism was essential to provide the Scots with an adequate political vocabulary that could recast previous imperial endeavours and current manifestations within a specific *national* context. This was especially the case in regard to comparisons with Ireland, and the fact that Scotland was not in a Union as a result of conquest was used to explain the difference between the two nations. The Scots had, as far as they were concerned, a genuine Union relationship with England, whereas the Irish could not shake off the fact of English conquest which coloured their perception of the Anglo-Irish Union.[43] Joseph Chamberlain used the Anglo-Scottish historical experience of conflict as a model which could accommodate different notions of nationality in time:

I had to think of how this new nation (South Africa) would stand, how these races would be concerned in the future of the Empire which belongs to both of them; Dutch and English—great people with many virtues in common, but still with great differences. Who would wish that the traditions of either should be forgotten or that their peculiarities disappear? And yet, we have to make of them a united nation. Here in the United Kingdom we have different races but one people. It would be rather difficult for an Englishman to feel exactly in the same regard, let us say, to Bannockburn, as a Scotsman would feel. Yet both Scotch and English are equally proud of having their full part in Waterloo or the Alma (applause). Why should it not be the same in South Africa? I ask of no Dutchman that he should forget his traditions, of which he may be justly proud, or abandon any peculiarities or prejudices of his race, any more than I would ask it of a Briton.[44]

Similar themes emerge in John Buchan's rabidly racist *Prester John* and the Anglo-Scottish model was still being cited in the 1930s as a model for South African Britannic nationalism.[45] Irish home rule helped make the Scots aware that they existed within the political framework of the Union, a fact that had received remarkably little attention before this. Unionism legitimized nationalism insofar as it posed no threat to the Union and was actively promoted as such. The arena in which the Scots could best articulate this unionist Scottish nationalism was within the empire. In retrospect, this seemed to provide a tailor-made outlet to articulate positive national

---

[43] Most followed the explanation used by Thomas Carlyle, *Essays*, vol. iv (1839), 137; see also *Fortnightly Review*, 22 (1874) and *Contemporary Review*, 61 (1892), 473–4.

[44] 15 May 1903 Birmingham Unionist Meeting, *Scotsman*, 17 May 1903.

[45] Darwin, *Empire Project*, 445. But see above, 273–4.

characteristics that worked towards strengthening the Union through the empire and it had the added advantage of allowing the Scots to accumulate previous achievements within this new reading of Scottish imperial endeavours.[46]

The connection of the Union to empire became part of Scottish political vocabulary after the 1880s and the period witnessed a nationalistic taint added to the activities of the Scots within the empire. Coming as it did in the period of European nationalism in the late nineteenth century, this allowed the Scots to assume the common characteristics of nationalism within the framework of the reinterpreted idea of the Union. Militarism was able to incorporate the local regiments within an increasingly national perspective and show that 'the old warlike spirit runs as high as ever in Scotland'.[47] The same phenomenon can be detected within the churches' missionary endeavours, and the local economic dynamic could be cast as a national enterprise. This is not to undermine the continued importance of the regional and local dimension, but it was increasingly fitted within a Scottish national perspective. The recasting of the Scottish economy as 'workshop' of empire pulled together the shipping interests of Glasgow with the Indian connections of Dundee. Glasgow was reinvented as 'second city of empire' because its imperial connections eclipsed those of Edinburgh.[48] The stipulation in 1881 that tartan be worn by all regiments, even Lowland ones, created a common perception of a Scottish military.[49] The Scottish missionary endeavour to Nyasaland was recast as the greatest Scottish imperial undertaking since Darien.[50] The period after the 1880s witnessed the growth of various organizations that were designed to

[46] A similar point is made by Bernard Porter in *Absent-Minded*, 18, that the cultural props of the New Imperialism of the 1880s have been retrospectively applied by some historians to past history to make Britain appear more imperialistically minded than it was.

[47] James Moncrieff Grierson, *Records of the Scottish Volunteer Force* (Edinburgh, 1907), pp. v–vi.

[48] In April 1867, a row broke out between Edinburgh and Dublin as to which was second city of the empire. The Irish case was that the Scots voluntarily transferred their capital to London in 1603 at the Union of the Crowns, leaving Dublin to become second city in 1801. *Scotsman*, April various dates, 1867.

[49] T. M. Devine, *Clanship to Crofters' War* (Manchester, 1994), 93.

[50] W. P. Livingstone, *Laws of Livingstonia: A Narrative of Missionary Adventure and Achievement* (London, 1921), 9.

promote this sense of Scottish national distinctiveness.[51] This was even extolled in the settler colonies. According to an Australian prime minister:

The Scotsmen who went out there remained ardent Scotsmen, but they became and continued most loyal and faithful Australians and they were ardent imperialists also to a man. And it was because they had this double or triple nationality and showed that they could be at the same time faithful to their Scottish memories and traditions, faithful to the obligations of the new land in which they lived, and faithful to the empire under the protection of whose flags were enabled to grow and prosper—it was because in their own persons of the Scotch united these three loyalties that they went so far to help them . . .[52]

Not only did the Scots use the case of Ireland to make the case that a nation could and should exist within the Union, but they also increasingly used the case of Scottish nationhood to make claims that the Scots were being neglected and ignored under the current arrangement, as well as using Scottish imperial achievement as added justification to have these abuses rectified.[53] Indeed, imperial over-achievement became a litany of Scottish self-perception in the period after 1880 and was used by politicians looking for an easy crowd-pleaser. Lord Rosebery was particularly adept at highlighting the Scottish contribution to the empire and moulding it into his description of Scottish national characteristics.[54] The *mythos* of a Scottish imperial destiny began to take shape as others added to a story that depicted the hardy Scots maintaining their independence until agreeing to the Union and then providing the cutting edge of British imperialism. In this version of the story, the empire only gets going once the Scots join the English. In this sense, the Union was transformed into a conduit for Scottish imperial ambitions and allowed the Scots to incorporate most of the typical characteristics associated with the growth of 'big nations' nationalism such as chauvinism, racism, providentialism, militarism, and the like. In part, this helps to explain why national identity in Scotland did not travel down the

---

[51] For geography, see Charles J. Withers, *Geography, Science and National Identity: Scotland since 1520* (Cambridge, 2001), 195–235, who argues that geography was more about 'knowing' Scotland rather than simply a promotion of imperial activities, and R. N. Rudmose Brown, J. H. Pirie, and R. C. Mossman, *The Voyage of the Scotia: The Story of Scotland's Forgotten Polar Heroes* (Edinburgh reprint of 1906 original, 2002).

[52] Quoted in Charles W. Thomson, *Scotland's Work and Worth* (London, n.d. [c.1909]), 790.

[53] William A. Hunter, *The Financial Relations between England and Scotland* (Edinburgh, 1892), 4.

[54] See, in particular, 'The Patriotism of a Scot', in Buchan (ed.), *Rosebery Miscellanies*.

road of small-nation nationalism, as was experienced in other European countries.

Scottish imperial self-perception is best shown when discussed in the context of how it repeatedly failed to dent English self-perception that the empire was predominantly an English national project and a reluctance to recognize that the Union theoretically entailed an equality of status in the imperial partnership. Wounded Scottish pride at being treated as a minor or insignificant entity increasingly brought howls of protest from the 1880s onwards. This could take place within the context of domestic politics, but it is worth noting how often the imperial dimension was used as the main vindication of the claim that the Union made for an equality of status. In South Africa, the careless use of England could provoke a politically out-raged Scottish response.[55] The following extract from a New Zealand newspaper about the coronation of the new King illustrates the point:

A second medal has been issued by the Scottish Patriotic Association, not only involving the same protest against the misuse of the term 'England' and 'English' in place of Britain and British. On the one side is the Union Jack, standing for Empire, and around it is the inscription 'Edward I of Britain and the British Empire, falsely styled Edward VII', while underneath the flag runs this inscription 'Our Empire is British, our Army, Navy, Flag, Parliament, and King—all are British, not English.' On the reverse side flies the Scottish flag with the inscription around it 'In defence of the honours of Scotland'.[56]

Coupled with the tendency to reinvent the past to show that there was a clear Scottish consciousness in past British imperial endeavour, the period before the First World War witnessed an increasing use of imperialism within the politics of Scottish national identity. Again, it is worth stressing how often the Scots would use the imperial stage as the best way to express national endeavours.

The creation of an imperial legacy in the period from 1870 to 1914 has cast a shadow down to the present. One problem with this legacy is that it has still to be subject to empirical investigation and, in particular, quantifica-tion. It was readily assumed by Scots (and still is) that they played a disproportionate role in the creation and maintenance of the British

---

[55] John M. MacKenzie with Nigel R. Dalziel, *The Scots in South Africa: Ethnicity, Identity, Gender and Race, 1772–1914* (Manchester, 2007), 260.

[56] *Fielding Star*, 29 August 1902.

Empire. It was also readily assumed that many Scottish 'characteristics' assisted in this process, whether as good businessmen or hardy soldiers or intrepid pioneers and adventurous explorers. While there is no doubt that this is what the Scots thought, it is an altogether different proposition to claim that numerically the Scots were over-represented within British imperialism. It is something that has yet to be fully tested, and perhaps Scottish historians should be wary about taking such claims at face value. The imperial legacy, it can be argued, was such an important aspect of both Unionism and Scottish self-perception that it led to exaggeration. Part of the strength of this idea was its elasticity and lack of development beyond a general and vague notion of the Scots as an 'imperial' race. Its pervasiveness was due to its acceptance by most of 'civic' or semi-official Scotland.[57] The churches, business, the military, scientific and learned institutions, the universities, the legal profession, and leading politicians—in short middle-class Scotland—could all acquiesce in their own particular way with the vision of Scottish imperial destiny. If we use Andrew Thompson's threefold definition of the imperial elites—the aristocracy, the professionals, and the entrepreneurs—we find powerful vested interests within Scottish society that bought into the imperial ideal.[58] The aristocracy, as John MacKenzie has pointed out, played an active role in imperial administration.[59] The Scottish professions, likewise, had a vested interest in connections with the empire. The opportunities of medical service and missionary work, it can be argued, provided an outlet for employment that was not always available at home. The Indian railways, through the auspices of the India Office, recognized the qualifications of eight institutions from Scotland compared with twelve from England.[60] West Coast shipping magnates found that the opportunities of empire brought together economic opportunity, religious convictions, and technological expertise.[61] It is also worth pointing out the considerable

---

[57] I have used the term 'civic imperialism' in the sense that it is related to civil society and provincialism and is founded on local connections. The tern 'civil imperialism' would sound ridiculous, hence the use of 'civic'. Duncan Bell has used the term in his *The Idea of Greater Britain: Britain, Empire and the Future of the World Order, 1860–1900* (Princeton, 2007), 137–49, which takes a much more robustly intellectually defined concept associated with civic republicanism.

[58] Andrew Thompson, *The Empire Strikes Back: The Impact of Imperialism on Britain from the Mid-Nineteenth Century* (2005), 10–37.

[59] MacKenzie, 'Scotland and Empire', 714.

[60] *Journal of the East India Association*, 4 (1873), 53.

[61] Crosbie Smith, *The Science of Energy: A Cultural History of Energy Physics in Victorian Britain* (London, 1998), 15–31, 150–2.

overlap that existed among these three categories. The aristocracy in Scotland patronized imperial organizations and learned societies, as well as lending their names to limited companies.[62] The business interests and commercial success of Scotland's foremost physicist, Lord Kelvin, did not impede his professional status, and medical ethics did not stop Dr Jamieson's notorious raid.[63] The semi-official nature of Scottish imperialism is not altogether different from its parent British version.[64]

Perhaps the best example of 'civic imperialism' is to be found in the largely Glaswegian engagement with Nyasaland (modern Malawi), although the activities and connections of the Dundee jute barons with Calcutta could also make a similar claim.[65] This brought together the Scottish churches, business, and humanitarian interest groups and initially had little involvement with the British state and government. Missionaries were inspired to carry the mantle of David Livingstone following his death and it is worth pointing out that the Free Church, which was the most avid in terms of missionary endeavours, was eager to emphasize its lack of connection with the state at the same time as the rise of the new imperialism.[66] The Glasgow African Lakes Company was formed with the express purpose of promoting 'legitimate' commerce as a means to circumvent the slave trade and made much of the fact that it would not sell guns or alcohol to the Africans.[67] In many respects, the enterprise was a classic embodiment of the 'Christianity and Commerce' slogan used by missionaries. It also highlighted the importance of classic laissez-faire values and a belief that overseas intervention need not rely on state support. The programme of missionary endeavour emphasizing 'industrial, commercial, educational, and evangelical' matters was basically an attempt to construct 'civil' society in Africa as the Scots understood it, with the interconnectedness of all these factors always highlighted.[68] Business leaders seemed

---

[62] See, for example, Forbes Munro, *Sir William Mackinnon and his Business Networks, 1823–1893* (London, 2003), 13–119.

[63] For Kelvin see Christine Macleod, *Heroes of Invention: Technology, Liberalism and British Identity, 1750–1914* (Cambridge, 2007), 365–7. Jamieson has yet to have a modern biographer.

[64] Darwin drives at the semi-official nature, or multi-layered development, of the British global system in which there was a suspicion of state involvement, 650–1.

[65] See Gordon Stewart, *Jute and Empire: Calcutta Jute Wallahs and the Landscapes of Empire* (Manchester, 1998).

[66] Stewart J. Brown, *Providence and Empire* (London, 2008), 266–7.

[67] *Glasgow Herald*, 13 January 1883.

[68] Ibid., 19 January 1883.

optimistic at the prospects.[69] Yet, the project soon began to run into the insurmountable problems of such overseas activity without state support. Missionaries ran into difficulties when working in an environment that had no European legal framework and were prevented from establishing their own.[70] The alternative of relying on native legal practice was believed to be too harsh. African hostility and slaving activity proved resilient and resistant to 'legitimate trade' and was blamed for the lack of commercial success. This failing was masked by increasingly emphasizing humanitarianism as the primary objective. Again, there was no recourse to state intervention, and the Company funded a war on slavery through private donations. It was only when there was the possibility of the territory being ceded to Portugal that a mass campaign was undertaken to secure Nyasaland as a British protectorate.[71] At the end of the day, formal imperialism was the preferred option only when 'civic imperialism' failed, and was probably the only time that Scottish public opinion changed British foreign policy in the nineteenth century. The missionary, business, and humanitarian interest groups have arguably had the effect of over-representing the role of the empire within Scottish society. Glasgow as 'second city of empire' also deserves a special mention. Its weight and preponderance within Scottish society and economy cast a greater shadow than that of London for England. Although presented as a Scottish endeavour, the Nyasa engagement was a predominantly Glasgow middle-class enterprise. The Scottish heroes of empire conformed to middle-class expectations of behaviour and those born lower down the social scale were promoted as examples of the 'lad' and 'lass' 'o' parts'. Interestingly, there was no Scottish equivalent of the English Tommy Atkins or Jack Tar. The Scottish imperial mission was strongly imbued with middle-class values, and while much work needs to be done

[69] Ibid., 13 January 1883; 29 March 1883. The Glasgow Philosophic Society meeting 'Water Communication in Africa' showed many were optimistic at a meeting held in the Glasgow Chambers of Commerce, *Glasgow Herald*, 27 July 1888: 'That in the interest of British and Colonial commerce, this chamber express their sense their sense of the importance of extending British influence and administration on trans-colonial territories in South Africa up to the Zambesi and of securing of its free navigation as an international river.'

[70] A. Chirnside, *The Blantyre Missionaries: Discreditable Disclosures* (London, 1880) and the defence by A. Riddel, *A Reply to the 'Blantyre Missionaries: Discreditable Disclosures' by Andrew Chirnside FRGS* (London, 1880).

[71] *Glasgow Herald*, 'The Nyassa Missions and the Portuguese', 26 February 1889.

on this, it did not seem to experience the 'democratization' of empire that was a feature of England in the latter part of the nineteenth century.

Moreover, we should be aware of the episodic nature of popular imperialism associated with specific events and issues such as Irish home rule, the death of Gordon, the anti-slavery campaign in East Africa, the Nyasaland protectorate and the quarrel with Portugal, and the Boer War. Irish home rule after 1906 was increasingly portrayed as a domestic issue rather than an imperial one.[72] We should also notice that the Liberal Party north of the border had a strong bias against further imperial expansion and was electorally dominant. Indeed, anti-expansionist sentiment was very much in evidence during Gladstone's Midlothian campaign and in the wake of the South African War.[73] Even militarism could be presented as representing Liberal civic qualities, as the high regard for the Volunteers demonstrated.[74] Although the Liberal imperialist wing of the party was represented in Scotland, it was relatively removed from the rank and file. Additionally, while historical attention has focused on the growth of the Scottish home rule movement and its assertion that it would strengthen rather than compromise the empire, it is worth pointing out that there were some anti-imperial voices.[75] Another factor to consider is the fact that many of the supposed qualities that made the Scots good imperialists or colonists were the same solid middle-class values of Liberal Scotland. According to the Liberal MP for Kirkcaldy and former administrator in India, George Campbell, 'the people of the United Kingdom are really unrivalled for adventure, enterprise and the development of the world. As a Scotchman, I need not speak vainly, for the testimony is universal that the Scotch are preeminent in these qualities.'[76] Finally, the Conservative Party and its

---

[72] Richard J. Finlay, 'The Scottish Press and Empire, 1850–1914', in Potter (ed.), *Newspapers and Empire*, 62–72.

[73] S. J. Brown, '"Echoes of Midlothian": Scottish Liberalism and the South African War', *Scottish Historical Review*, 71 (1992), 156–85.

[74] Grierson, *Scottish Volunteer Force* and Elaine McFarland, '"Empire Enlarging Genius": Scottish Imperial Yeomanry Volunteers in the Boer War', *War in History*, 13.3 (2006), 281–310, in particular 314 for the Citizen Soldier. It is also worth pointing out that although the Scots were proportionally over-represented in the Volunteers, they were under-represented in the regular army, with about 8% of the total; see Heather Streets, *Martial Races: The Military, Race and Masculinity in British Imperial Culture, 1857–1914* (Manchester, 2004), 176.

[75] See Thomas Shaw, *Patriotism and the Empire* (Edinburgh, 1901).

[76] George Campbell, *The British Empire* (London, 1887), 37. Campbell was elected MP in 1892 for Kirkcaldy.

Liberal Unionist bedfellows who were the keenest proponents of the imperial mission, with the exception of the 1900 general election, had a fairly dire electoral performance. Indeed, the widespread jingoism that accompanied the Boer War seemed to take the Scottish Liberal establishment by surprise. The party of empire found few electoral dividends north of the border; perhaps the most significant test of the appeal of imperial sentiment. This was particularly the case after the emergence of Tariff Reform and 'Imperial Free Trade'. It was comprehensively rejected by the Scots in the general elections of 1906 and 1910, when the values of Liberal Free Trade triumphed. Any sense of a contradiction between imperialism and laissez-faire was absent in Scotland, in part the legacy of Cobbett's Scottophobia, perhaps accounting for a lack of free trade purists in Scotland.[77]

In the period just before the outbreak of the First World War, the Scottish Unionists were increasingly bellicose in pushing their own particular reading of the Union and the imperial connection. The Liberals, on the other hand, although espousing either Imperial Federation or home rule all round, tended to focus on domestic issues. Although the empire was regularly invoked and the example of federalism in the dominions cited, there was little real engagement with imperial issues.[78] One of the keenest Unionist Imperialists, H. J. Mackinder, who sat for a Glasgow seat, accused the Liberal home rulers in Scotland as being under the influence of 'Irish' interests in their constituencies and not representative of Scottish sentiment.[79] Ireland and imperial loyalty did not go together. According to the Marquis of Tullibardine, the Union was fundamental to the Scottish imperial mission:

If you compare Scotland at the time of the Union with what it is now you will find that at that time we had not the help of England or the help of the Union or the help of the Empire as we have at the present moment. You will find that we were poor, that we were torn by faction, and that there was absolutely no scope for the inhabitants to get away to something better, and that we were absolutely at the mercy of every clique and every sort of faction. I say we were poorest at the time of

---

[77] For the importance of classic laissez-faire liberal ideas and the link to anti-imperialism see Bernard Porter, *Critics of Empire: British Radicals and the Imperial Challenge* (London, 2008).

[78] See, for example, the pamphlet *Scottish Home Rule: An Imperial Necessity* (London, 1911), which does not discuss the empire. Also, Liberal MPs often described Scottish home rule as an 'imperial' issue, but never elaborated why. House of Commons, Parliamentary Debates (*Parl. Deb.*), vol. xxix, 16 August 1911, Henry Dalziel 1930, Henry Cowan, 478–7.

[79] Ibid., 28 February 1912, xxxiv. 1446–7.

Union ... Whilst we had separate Parliaments there was always a conflict of political and commercial ideas, which absolutely throttled the whole colonising genius of our country. Then is it said that home rule would not deprive Scotland and its sons of their place in the Empire ... ? Are they prepared to say how in the Federal system, Scotsmen will fare in regard to positions in England and the Empire? How many do New Zealanders and Canadians get?[80]

His party leader, Andrew Bonar Law, as an Ulster Scots Canadian, kept a tactical silence. This exposition that the Union and empire went hand in hand was to become a commonplace in Scottish political discourse over the next forty years. Furthermore, it allowed civic imperialism to be repackaged as a national rather than a local endeavour. Scotland's claim to greatness rested on its imperial endeavours, which in turn rested on the foundation of the Union.

Imperialism, Unionism, and the British State, 1914–1970

The impact of the First World War undermined many of the nineteenth-century foundations of Scottish ideas concerning the Union relationship and its imperial connection. In explaining this phenomenon, it is not the case that the pro-imperial lobby in Scotland diminished; rather, they began to become outnumbered by those who were indifferent or hostile to the idea of an enthusiasm for a Scottish role in the empire. The voices of imperial scepticism began to be heard more loudly to challenge the monopoly of 'civic' Scotland when it came to representing the nation. The proponents of civic imperialism emerged from the war with fewer financial resources, more pressing domestic issues, and enemies that were closer to home. Also, it is worth commenting that in terms of the impact of the post-war dislocation and the regional impact of the economic downturn of the inter-war era, the Scots were disproportionately affected and this arguably helped to take the gloss off the pre-war global sheen of Britain's position in the world.[81] To counteract this development, the confidence of the pre-war era was increasingly replaced by greater pessimism, emphasizing Scottish dependence on, rather than partnership with, England.[82] The objective was

---

[80] Ibid. 1470.

[81] On the structural problems of the Scottish economy, see Richard J. Finlay, *Modern Scotland, 1914–2000* (London, 2004), 73–115.

[82] Richard J. Finlay, 'National Identity in Crisis? Politicians, Intellectuals and the "End of Scotland", 1920–1939', *History*, 79.256 (1994), 242–59.

clearly to increase the importance of the Union and empire as central to Scottish well-being. The argument went that if things were bad at the moment then it would be worse if it were not for the Union and that any future recovery was dependent on the re-establishment of the British world order, which was associated with the well-being of the empire.[83] It is remarkable to note the extent to which the Union was linked to empire and the assumption that the latter was of great importance to Scottish society. Defence of the empire was grouped into three areas, in which it was argued that the Scots did proportionately better than the rest of the United Kingdom and that any threat to the Union would undermine these important foundations. First, it was claimed that individual Scots did well out of imperial positions. Second, the economy was a prime beneficiary of imperial trade. Finally, the Union and empire were central to notions of national self-esteem and, without this, Scotland would become an insignificant nation. As will be argued below, such claims were more a psychological prop rather than a genuine need to construct a necessary defence of the Union, which was not in any real danger from a nationalist challenge.[84] As such, it can be argued that there was an underlying lack of confidence in the Scottish imperial mission in the inter-war era. While there has been a historiographical tendency to focus on the rise of the left and nationalism in this period, it is worth pointing out the remarkable resilience of the Conservative/Unionist Party which, by any measurement, was highly successful. Clearly, the heavy emphasis on the imperial connection did them little electoral harm at this time.

The prospect that positions within the imperial structure would be closed off to Scots as a result of devolution or separation was an alarming one for Unionists.[85] In essence, it was claimed that the influence and power of imperial posts was much greater than could be obtained at home and that the ambitious and talented would be denied opportunities. This was a powerful message to send to the Scottish professional classes, and although not yet empirically tested, there was certainly a belief that imperial service

---

[83] See the Unionists Association, *The Campaign Guide* (London, 1924), 829; Bob Boothby, *The Nation*, 9 March 1929; Sir James Lithgow, *Morning Post*, 19 November 1932; Lord McClay, *The Times*, 15 November 1932.

[84] Richard J. Finlay, *Independent and Free: Scottish Politics and the Origins of the Scottish National Party, 1918–1945* (Edinburgh, 1994), 162–206.

[85] For example, see *Parl. Deb.* 272, 313, 22 November 1932 for fears of exclusion from imperial posts.

soaked up a lot of surplus middle-class employment. Furthermore, there were plenty of imperial icons that could be called upon to back up the case that it was better to shine on a global stage than one nearer home.[86] The period also witnessed a fairly prolific outpouring of publications that continued to recast past Scottish imperial endeavours as a national enterprise. Missionary hagiography, the Scottish military tradition, the role of explorers, business leaders, colonial statesmen, and emigrants were all bundled together in a 'national' package.[87] The projection of the 'imperial nation' formed a key part of the Unionist vision of Scottish national identity, but it was closely associated with middle-class self-interest.[88] Arguably, the economic dislocation of the inter-war period placed an additional premium on imperial service as domestic professions were squeezed. The tendency of professionals to emigrate at a higher proportionate rate would certainly suggest that employment opportunities were limited. Also, the growing professionalization of imperial service with a greater demand for technological and scientific expertise provided new opportunities.[89] The other issue to take into account, though not necessarily an exclusive Scottish trait, was the importance of family ties and traditions forming a sort of inter-generational imperial service.[90]

[86] See MacKenzie, 'David Livingstone', 24–33.

[87] See, for example, C. R. Blake, *Scotland of the Scots* (London, 1918); Duke of Atholl *et al.*, *A Scotsman's Heritage* (London, 1932); Gibb, *Scottish Empire*; and the prolific outpouring of missionary biography by W. P. Livingstone.

[88] For a fictional account of the Scottish middle-class world view in the inter-war era and the centrality of empire, see George Malcolm Thomson, *The Re-discovery of Scotland* (London, 1932), part two.

[89] The Scottish professions and empire has not been studied, but given that there was a preponderance of Scots in the medical, scientific, and engineering professions, the fact that the imperial dimension increased in significance for Britain as a whole during the inter-war era must surely have been replicated in Scotland. According to the *Medical Directory*, the numbers of doctors working abroad or in the armed services increased from a fifth to a quarter between the wars; see Anne Digby, *The Evolution of British General Practices, 1850–1948* (London, 1999), 82. On colonial science, see MacKenzie, *Imperialism and the Natural World*, 185 and on the importance of science and technology professions in an imperial context in relation to the domestic population, see John M. MacKenzie, 'Popular Culture of Empire in Britain', in Judith Brown and Wm. Roger Louis (eds), *The Oxford History of the British Empire*, iv: *The Twentieth Century* (Oxford, 2001), 214 and Stuart Ward, *British Culture and the End of Empire* (Manchester, 2001), 29.

[90] For a good example of Scottish middle-class family connections with empire, see Niall Ferguson, *Empire: How Britain Made the Modern World* (London, 2004), pp. xiii–xvi.

The importance of empire to the economy was taken as axiomatic by many. In what might be described as popular political economy, 'imperial' trade was conflated with global trade and, given Scottish reliance on the international economy, it is not surprising that the 'imperial' connection was deemed to be so important.[91] The centrality of the empire to Scottish economic fortunes was promoted by two key factors. First, the conflation of global and imperial trade was fundamental to the traditional heavy industries that dominated the Scottish economy in the pre-war era, and there was no real attempt to engage in economic diversification; rather, there was an expectation that conditions would revert to their pre-war norm. Arguably, the preponderance of a 'global' or 'imperial' mentality was so fixed in the minds of the Scottish industrialists and business class that there was a reluctance to accept that the economic climate had fundamentally changed.[92] This conflation was so strong that it gripped the popular imagination to such an extent that it had a paralysing effect on economic and business strategy. While the promotion of economic orthodoxy might be expected from the business class, it is interesting to note how the empire also featured in Labour's economic thought. John Wheatley, for example, advocated 'socialism in one empire' and there was a recurring fear among the trade union movement that cheap native labour in the colonies would be used to undermine wages and conditions at home.[93] Second, after the impact of the Great Crash in 1929, there was a British-wide orientation towards greater economic ties with the empire.[94] This was especially popular in Scotland and the National Government made much of imperial

[91] Rightly, Porter in *Absent-Minded Imperialists*, 31, points out that the economic ties with empire in the formal sense were not as significant as with elsewhere and that care has to be taken in linking Britain's global economic interests with those of the empire as strictly defined. While semantically valid, the point remains, that as far as contemporaries were concerned, Britain's global position was *dependent* on having an empire, and as such, the two could not be separated.

[92] See R. H. Campbell, *The Rise and Fall of Scottish Industry 1707–1939* (London, 1980), 157.

[93] On Wheatley's thought see David Howell, *A Lost Left: Three Studies in Socialism and Nationalism* (Manchester, 1986), 229–65. I am grateful to my colleague Trish Barton for information on the cotton industry and trade union fears about the use of 'native' labour to undermine costs. See Patricia S. Collins, 'Brithers under the Sun: British Trade Unions and the Indian Labour Movement in the Inter-War Period', *Journal of Scottish Labour History*, 29 (1993), 30–46.

[94] See Philip Williamson, *National Crisis and National Government: British Politics, the Economy and Empire, 1926–1932* (Cambridge, 2003).

connections as a means of economic salvation.[95] The Empire Exhibition of 1938 was an endeavour to try and rekindle the former economic dynamism that had made the Scottish economy a world leader in previous times.[96] At the end of the day, however, little came from the imperial focus, and there is no evidence that this concentration on the empire had a major impact on the fortunes of the economy in the 1930s. Revival only came as a result of rearmament.[97]

The extent to which the Union and empire remained a focal point of national identity in the inter-war era was of great significance. At the immediate end of the war, before the full impact of the dislocation became fully known, there was arguably a heightened sense of imperial identity as a result of victory:

The importance of the colonial outposts has been most vigorously demonstrated by their practical loyalty since the grim autumn of 1914. In these years there has been a wider understanding and more intimate dealing between them and the mother country. Soldiers have travelled thousands of miles to fight in the European cockpit, and accompanying these warriors are their governmental representatives, their crown agents, their prime ministers, their delegates to Imperial Conferences. No names have achieved [greater?] familiarity in British ears—and it is no idle claim to state that a very large proportion of these are Scots. The colonising capabilities of the northern race need no vindication here; this adaptability is one of the chiefest qualities in the people.[98]

The social and economic turmoil which followed in the wake of the First World War could not help but impact on Scottish politics and culture. In time, one of the underlying themes regarding national identity to emerge—as was the case throughout Europe—was one of pessimism.[99] The dominant discourse by which the Scots measured their national self-esteem was based on past achievements, and consequently it was the failure to maintain the same level of nineteenth-century success that occupied most minds.[100] This

---

[95] See, for example, the annual Clydesdale Bank Survey on the Scottish Economy throughout the 1930s.

[96] Department of Overseas Trade, *Guide to the Pavilion of His Majesty's Government in the United Kingdom: Empire Exhibition, Scotland 1938* (London, 1938), 1–5.

[97] Campbell, *Rise and Fall*, 133–64.

[98] Blake, *Scotland of the Scots*, 61.

[99] For the British context, see Richard Overy, *The Morbid Age: Britain and the Crisis of Civilization, 1919–1939* (London, 2010), although it has little to say about Scotland.

[100] Finlay, 'National Identity in Crisis?', 254–5.

failure to live up to nineteenth-century expectations was complicated by changing cultural attitudes which no longer accepted many of these bench-marks uncritically: for example, popular militarism and mass emigration. In the assessment of the state of the nation, the global and imperial position loomed large: hence, Unionist fears that devolution or political separation would undermine the existing position as a 'mother nation' of Empire. The sense of decline in Scotland was contrasted with what, on the surface, seemed like an expansion in the territorial extent of the empire and a still reasonably prevailing confidence in the imperial destiny south of the border. A key aspect in the development of pessimism was the sense in which Scotland and the Scots were being marginalized, and this was best exempli-fied in the economy. The growing sense that the Scottish economy was becoming a 'branch' rather than an integral part of the whole was a major cause of concern among Scottish business leaders.[101] Also, the development of financial services in the south was not reflected to any great extent in Scotland. A litany of amalgamation, takeovers, closures, and contractions gave rise to the idea of the 'southward drift of industry' in which the life blood of the Scottish economy was being sucked out as the balance of economic power gravitated to the south-east.[102] The sense of hopelessness was exacerbated by the prevailing wisdom of the Scottish business commu-nity; according to one Unionist:

I know that businessmen and captains of industry tell us that the causes are economic. They say that legislation is of no avail and worse than useless. I cannot think so poorly of this High Court of parliament as to believe that it is powerless to arrest or at least to control the southward drift of industry.[103]

Yet, the faith in the broad tenets of laissez-faire remained undiminished, although the shipbuilding industry was quite happy to accept government subsidies. The failure to attract new industries related to the growing consumer economy kept the Scottish economy locked in its global/imperial orbit at a time when world trade was closing down. The collective mentality of the Scottish business class is best summed up in the outlook of its leading industrialist, Sir John Lithgow, who as leader of the Federation of British Industry, was one of the keenest proponents of imperial trade and was

---

[101] For example, *Glasgow Chamber of Commerce Journal*, September 1933.
[102] The classic account is G. M. Thomson, *Scotland: That Distressed Area* (Edinburgh, 1935).
[103] *Parl. Deb.*, 22 November 1932, vol. 272, 302.

appointed by the government to promote the viability of an empire trading block in the early 1930s. Lithgow argued that the loss of markets as a result of growing trade barriers could be compensated by directing all shipbuilding and heavy industrial orders in the empire to the mother country in the expectation that for the empire as a whole 'the bulk of merchant tonnage would be built in the United Kingdom'.[104] If nothing else, it demonstrates the remarkable degree of faith the Scottish industrial class had in the old imperial system's ability to adapt.

One major export that was noteworthy during the inter-war era was people. Emigration had been treated as either positive or neutral in the pre-war period, but by the 1920s it was regarded in a negative light and seen as another factor in the decline of Scotland.[105] Furthermore, it was coupled with widespread fears of unfettered Irish immigration, even though this was a fiction. As John Buchan put it:

Our population is declining. We are losing some of the best of our race stock by migration and their place is being taken by those who, whatever their merit, are not Scottish. I understand that every fifth child now born in Scotland is an Irish Roman Catholic...Britain, the Empire and the world cannot afford a denationalized Scotland.[106]

While the polemicists railed against emigration, the fact remains that some 400,000 Scots thought it preferable to staying at home, and it is not an unreasonable question to pose whether this reinforced imperial sentiment. Although information is patchy and most studies tend to focus on the 'Scottish' identity of the diaspora, less is known about its contribution to a 'Britannic' sentiment that has recently been identified as a fundamental

---

[104] Speech at the Canadian Club of Ottawa, 10 May 1931, quoted in *Canadian Transportation*, 49 (1946), 105. Lithgow's ideas are elaborated in *National Review*, 95 (1930), 874.

[105] See, for example, G. M. Thomson, *Caledonia: or the Future of the Scots* (Edinburgh, n.d.), Andrew Dewar Gibb, *Scotland in Eclipse* (Glasgow, 1932), and John Torrence, *Scotland's Dilemma* (Edinburgh, 1938). It is also worth pointing out that Canada was an important backdoor entry for the United States, which was probably the first choice destination of most emigrants, especially after immigration restrictions were introduced in the early 1920s. That said, the Scots-born population of the United States rose from 254,570 in 1920 to 354,323 in 1930, according to the US Census, which even accounting for a high death rate among Scots-Americans, shows that the empire of settlement was still vitally important as a first destination for Scottish emigrants.

[106] *Parl. Deb.*, 22 November 1932, vol. 272, 261–76.

aspect of Britain's world system in the nineteenth and twentieth centuries.[107] Although impossible to calculate with precision, the Scottish proportion of emigrants to the colonies of settlement in the period from 1900 to 1950 was higher than the respective share of the United Kingdom population. The fact that Scots were used to dual identities arguably made it easier to incorporate a further layer of colonial and Britannic identity. Indeed, the Union was used as a model to show that in spite of the growing sense of separation with the dominions, British sentiment was an effective bond to maintain unity. According to Arthur, Earl Balfour, the Statute of Westminster did not mean the disintegration of the empire:

If memory is to be the foundation of your future greatness, are your memories always so satisfactory that they will supply a solid foundation for the future? Well I am a Scotsman addressing Scotsmen, and I feel, therefore, peculiarly qualified to speak on this subject. I maintain, and I appeal to the history of my country to show that I am right, that these different traditions can well be united in one whole; that although these different streams which have met together to make our kingdom and empire, may have flowed from different sources, none of them need feel that the differences destroys the unity of the stream which has resulted in their coalescence. I absolutely will not allow any man, be he English or Scottish, to rob me of my share in Magna Charta and Shakespeare because of Bannockburn and Flodden.[108]

Sentiment and blood ties, it would appear, were more important than narrow economic interests or parochial concerns. In the absence of the economic dividends of the nineteenth century, it can be argued that the appeal of empire in Scotland became more emotional. One further point can be made regarding Britannic identity and Scottish emigration. In spite of the best efforts of the Scottish nationalist movement to recruit the diaspora to the cause, the Scots abroad remained committed to the Union and indifferent to a version of Scottishness that competed with or challenged Britishness. The contrast with the Irish could not have been greater. A final point is worth considering. Although the United States

---

[107] Darwin, *Empire Project*, 151–9, 497–8, 501–5, 540–52.

[108] Arthur James, Earl Balfour, speech in Edinburgh, 27 January 1927, in *Opinions and Arguments* (London, 1927), 198.

was not part of the imperial entity, there was a communal sense of 'Anglo-Saxon' identity, promoted among others by Andrew Carnegie.[109]

For many politicians and intellectuals, the imperial dimension of Scottish identity was fundamental and useful as a means to counteract the pessimism of the 1930s. As was mentioned earlier, the emphasis on past imperial glories became almost a fillip to counter contemporary problems, but what is more difficult to determine is how widespread imperial sentiment circulated in Scottish society and whether or not it increased or diminished. Although the growth of the Labour Party switched the focus of politics more towards domestic issues and the prevailing socio-economic circumstances definitely turned political attention inwards, it is not the case that imperial concerns disappeared entirely. The reunification of the Free and Established Churches in 1929 was the occasion for the first Moderator to call for renewed efforts in Africa to counter Catholic missionary efforts—no doubt this was influenced by the tide of anti-Catholic sentiment current in Scottish society. But it is worth pointing out that this most domestic of issues could still find an imperial dimension for its rallying call.[110]

Anti-imperialists had little impact north of the border. John Maclean is noteworthy for linking imperialism and capitalism and coming to similar conclusions as Lenin. His flirtation with Scottish nationalism was inspired by a desire to break up British imperialism from the centre and thus avoid the inevitable conflict for markets with the other great capitalist power: the United States. Maclean's ideas had little impact outside a small and fairly insignificant group of fellow travellers.[111] Closer to home, some nationalists were inspired by Irish Republicanism and constructed an ideology that was based on the belief that the Scots, as well as the Irish, were victims of Anglo-Saxon imperialism. Even then, criticism of the empire tended to be incidental and did not travel much beyond the confines of the British Isles, though reference was made from time to time to colonial nationalism.[112] Within mainstream Labour in Scotland, there was no real engagement with

[109] This is a subject that has yet to be explored, but see Carnegie's *Reunion of Britain and America: A Look Ahead* (Edinburgh, 1893) and *A Rectorial Address Delivered to the Students of St Andrews Delivered on 22nd of October 1902.*

[110] W. P. Livingstone, *Alexander Hetherwick: Prince of Missionaries* (London, 1934), 201.

[111] The best account is to be found in Brian Ripley and John McHugh, *John Maclean: Lives of the Left* (Manchester, 1989).

[112] R. J. Finlay, 'For or Against? Scottish Nationalism and the Empire, 1919–39', *Scottish Historical Review*, 71.191/2 (1992), 184–206.

the question of imperialism apart from fairly routine and vague notions that empire would be replaced by a socialist commonwealth. Surprisingly, little attention was paid to the cost of imperial upkeep; the moral dimension of holding down indigenous peoples barely registered among tender consciences and the benefits or otherwise of empire markets were not subject to much scrutiny. While Unionists waxed lyrical about the empire, socialists tended not to talk about it, but instead focused on matters closer to home, presumably because that is what they believed their voters thought was more important.[113]

The extent to which the Second World War acted as a fillip to popular imperialism in Scotland has yet to be studied.[114] While the enormous economic, financial, and political strains made the empire's survival unlikely, there was no real sense that that this filtered down to the popular consciousness. After all, Britain triumphed and the empire survived its severest test. The period witnessed an intensification of popular British consciousness that stressed the role of the empire. Arguably, if anything, the imperial dimension grew as a result of the war, and there was an intensification of the traditions of Britain as a global power. The old traditional industries boomed and the Scottish soldier played his and her part in the defeat of fascism across the globe. The extent to which the drift to the left focused attention away from the imperial to the domestic agenda was registered at a British level by the landslide victory for Labour in the 1945 general election. There has perhaps been a tendency to assume that the growth of a greater role for central government in social and economic policy is somehow at odds with maintaining a strong identification with empire. Just as is the case with Britain as a whole, there is no reason to assume that the Scots would have any less reason to show appreciation for

---

[113] Scottish Labour historiography has very little to say on the subject of imperialism; see I. G. C. Hutchison, *A Political History of Scotland: Parties, Elections, Issues, 1832–1924* (Edinburgh, 1986), 277–309; J. J. Smyth, *Labour in Glasgow 1896–1936: Socialism, Suffrage, Sectarianism* (East Linton, 2000), 70–125: John Holford, *Reshaping Labour: Organisation, Work and Politics—Edinburgh in the Great War and After* (Beckenham, 1988); I. Donnachie, C. Harvie, and I. S. Woods (eds), *Forward: Labour Politics in Scotland* (Edinburgh, 1989), 7–49; Alan McKinlay and R. J. Morris (eds), *The ILP on Clydeside 1893–1932: From Foundation to Disintegration* (Manchester, 1991), 123–77; and William Kenefick, *Red Scotland: The Rise and Fall of the Radical Left, c.1872–1932* (London, 2007), 159–84. The one exception is Gerald Douds, 'Tom Johnston in India', *Scottish Labour History,* 19 (1984), 6–21.

[114] For the British context, see Sonya O. Rose, *Which People's War? National Identity and Citizenship in Wartime Britain, 1939–1945* (Oxford, 2004), 197–285.

the imperial contribution during the war. Indeed, if it is the case that the Scots had a greater propensity to identify with the empire before the war, then arguably it should have been reinforced by the wartime experience. Although historians have drawn attention to the Welfare State as vital to reinforcing a sense of British identity and reinvigorating the Union, less has been said about the apparently successful outcome of the war and the vital role that empire played in securing it.

The Second World War was a turning point in Scottish history. As Tom Devine has pointed out, the period after 1945 witnessed a decline in the imperial dimension as it was replaced by an alternative British institution: the Welfare State. Indeed, it was to grow into the most popular British institution north of the border in the post-1945 era. What is more difficult to chart is how one replaced the other. It was certainly not the case that the imperial dimension suddenly evaporated after 1948; rather, it can be postulated that as the decline of imperial sentiment gathered pace, the importance of the Welfare State increased. Nor is it the case that there was necessarily a relationship between them; rather, as one declined another grew to fill the gap, possibly in an unrelated way. As empire declined, its sentiment would do so too, and as the importance of the Welfare State grew, so did popular support. That said, imperial sentiment proved remarkably resilient north of the border. Widespread Canadian and Australian emigration was hugely popular in the 1950s and 1960s, and Scotland continued its historic high rate of exporting people. Again, similar features were apparent that were in line with previous experience: both the propensity for skilled working class to leave together with an over-representation of middle-class professionals. The Canadian and Australian High Commissioners certainly thought Scotland was a worthwhile recruiting ground. If emigration is anything to go by, Britannic nationalism should have been reinforced after 1945. It is also to be remembered that Scotland experienced comparatively little New Commonwealth immigration in the post-war era, unlike England, and hence it is worth speculating on the extent to which the Scots were able to maintain a more positive view of the empire because they were insulated from its racial realities.[115] Furthermore, the Commonwealth ideal received enthusiastic support from the Church of Scotland, which was vigorous in its support for decolonization

[115] The figure on comparative rates of immigration were in 1966 2 per thousand for Scotland and 24 per thousand for England and Wales; Finlay, *Modern Scotland*, 305.

based on majority rule in Africa. Although the Commonwealth ideal tends
to get short shrift from historians as a means of bridging the change from
the reality of imperial retreat to the illusion of the continued existence of the
empire in a revised form, the continued links fostered by emigration to the
settler nations, support for the principle of African decolonization leading
to 'responsible' government, and the popular enthusiasm for the Commonwealth Games in Edinburgh in 1970 (the first to have the Queen in atten-
dance) may suggest that the ideal of the 'family' of British nations was not
totally moribund in Scotland in the post-war era. Finally, the fairly extensive
role of Scottish imperial professionals in the decolonization process ought to
be borne in mind.[116]

The economy changed little after 1945, as the traditional heavy industries
with their strong orientation towards the global market were buoyed up by
European and imperial reconstruction. Furthermore, the financial strain
following the war meant that the government had to earn as much export
cash as possible and two consequences followed. First, it meant that the
essential contours of the British inter-war economy remained unchanged,
with the south concentrating on consumer industries and the traditional
industries remaining in the north. Second, the pressing need to export
circumvented diversification, which lost its raison d'être in any case as
employment remained high. Although the traditional industries were orien-
ted towards the global export market, rather than a narrow imperial market,
the industries themselves did have a residue of association with empire.
Shipbuilding, textiles, and heavy engineering, for example, all had histories
that were closely associated with imperialism in the popular imagination.[117]
The projection of imperial grandeur, past and present, was frequently used
as a marketing ploy and as part of the strategy to justify the importance of
heavy industry to the future economic well-being of Scotland. Though
difficult to quantify empirically, because the jute industry in Dundee and
the shipbuilding and heavy engineering of the Clyde basin were so important to many people in the post-war period, it is hard to believe that their
imperial legacy could easily be forgotten. If anything, the former imperial
glory days remained the benchmark of success.

---

[116] See Trevor Royle, *Winds of Change: The End of Empire in Africa* (London, 1996), which
makes extensive use of the National Library of Scotland's *Scottish Decolonization Project*.

[117] At an exhibition in Glasgow in 1951 steam locomotives with an imperial connection were
given pride of place in the city centre; see Ward, *British Culture and the End of Empire*, 29.

The 1950s were a period of remarkable success for the Scottish Conservative and Unionist Party, which was the only political party to secure over 50 per cent of the popular vote in the twentieth century, achieved in 1955. Conventional wisdom has tended to focus on domestic affairs as the primary reason for Conservative success in this period, particularly in housing and social policy.[118] What has received less historical attention is the wider appeal of Conservative foreign and imperial policy in Scotland. Before 1951, the Tories had attacked Labour on its imperial policy and claimed that 'socialism would abandon the Empire'.[119] Arguably, the Empire Games in New Zealand in 1950, in which Scotland won two gold medals, and the impending coronation of the new Queen reinforced imperial notions in Scotland in the early 1950s. The furore that emerged over the use of the numeral 'II' in the coronation, if nothing else, showed that Scottish sensitivities regarding their understanding of the historic role of Scotland within the Union had not been blunted. In the era of the fourth British Empire, the Conservative governments mounted successful military campaigns in Malaya after 1951, dealt with the Mau Mau Uprising in 1952, as well as drawing the Korean War to a conclusion.[120] All of these witnessed Scots taking a military role, while the continuation of national service which posted them throughout the empire may well have fostered the survival of imperial sentiment. The Scottish economy did particularly well out of the wartime boom associated with the Korean War, and the defence industry grew as a result, with the expansion of Rolls Royce for aero engines and a tank factory at Dalmuir.[121] Along with the rest of the United Kingdom, public perception of the empire was given a new raison d'être during the Cold War, in which the process of decolonization was linked to geostrategic

---

[118] See James Mitchell, *Conservatives and the Union* (Edinburgh, 1990) and David Seawright and John Curtice, 'The Decline of the Scottish Conservative and Unionist Party 1950–92: Religion, Ideology or Economics?', *Contemporary British History*, 9.2 (1993), 319–42 neither of which pays much attention to foreign policy as a factor in Tory success.

[119] *Scotsman*, 7 February 1950.

[120] See John Darwin, 'Was There a Fourth British Empire', in Martin Lynn (ed.), *The British Empire in the 1950s: Retreat or Revival?* (London, 2005). For a useful summary of the six decolonization conflicts in which Scots served after 1945, see Sir John Baynes, Bt, 'Scottish Soldiers in the Last Years of Empire, 1901–1967', in Grant Simpson (ed.), *The Scots Soldier Abroad* (Edinburgh, 1992), 154–75.

[121] Till Geiger, *Britain and the Economic Problem of the Cold War: The Political Economy and the Impact of the British Defence Effort, 1945–55* (London, 2004), 283–92.

considerations regarding the spread of communism.[122] The Sterling area, likewise, was recognized as being vital to economic well-being and the importance of imperial ties.[123] The Suez campaign of 1956 received widespread press support in Scotland and John Stuart, the Scottish Secretary of State, was a hardliner in cabinet.[124] Although the campaign ended in disaster and signalled the end of Britain's ability to act independently on the world stage, the extent to which this was apparent to the Scottish public at the time is debatable.[125]

The military role which had been such a significant aspect of Scottish identification with empire was also slow to die out. The reintroduction of conscription during the Korean War and the fact that there was a continued global projection of British military power meant a reasonably high profile for the Scottish soldier well until the late 1960s. The action of the Argyll and Sutherland Highlanders in Aden in 1967, when the antics of their commander Lieutenant Colonel Colin Campbell Mitchell, 'Mad Mitch', gained a high public profile by sending in a bagpiper at the head of an occupation force to retake Crater, helped to confirm all the supposed attributes of the 'Fighting Scots' in the public imagination. Indeed, a comparison of the public engagement with two different high-profile military issues in Scotland in the 1960s—the resistance to basing the nuclear Polaris submarines in the Holy Loch and the campaign against the plan to disband the Argyll and Sutherland Highlanders Regiment—shows that the latter aroused far more

[122] The conflict in Malaya was portrayed as a straightforward fight against communism; see *Scotsman*, 7 February 1950, 'Resisting Communism in South East Asia' and 7 April, 9 June, 10 June 1950. Although the *Scotsman* was initially sceptical of the threat of the Mau Mau Rising in 20 September 1952, its attitude began to harden by 15 November, and on 2 December 1954 it gave widespread coverage of the atrocities committed against Europeans. Along with the rest of the United Kingdom, the Scottish press bought the idea that Kenyatta was a Communist. For the Church's attitude to communism in the immediate post-war era, see E. W. McFarland and R. J. Johnston, 'The Church of Scotland's Special Commission on Communism, 1949–1954: Tackling "Christianity's Most Serious Competitor"', *Contemporary British History*, 23.3 (2009), 337–61, and especially 350–1 for the colonial context.

[123] Both the *Glasgow Herald* and the *Scotsman* highlighted the significance of the sterling area throughout the early 1950s in their financial columns. On the sterling area and the importance that was attached to exports, see Catherine Schenk, *Britain and the Sterling Area: From Devaluation to Convertibility in the 1950s* (London, 1994). It was believed that the sterling area provided a 'soft' market for manufactured goods, although this was not necessarily the case.

[124] Keith Kyle, *Suez: Britain's End of Empire in the Middle East* (London, 2003), 204.

[125] With the exception of a student protest at Edinburgh against the invasion, there was little evidence of widespread discontent with the policy: *Glasgow Herald*, 4 November 1956.

interest and was able to mobilize greater public support. The 'Save the Argylls' campaign had the overwhelming support of the Scottish press, and even the Scottish National Party joined in.[126] While support for the Scottish military does not necessarily show that this was based on popular imperialism, it does, nevertheless demonstrate that the experience of empire had left a powerful residue in Scottish society. The amalgamation of the Scottish regiments into one unit in recent times likewise mobilized considerable popular support against it.

The reality, however, was that while the imperial legacy belonged to the past, the functions of the British state became more important in the present, especially as the economy got into more and more difficulties. The high point of the importance of state intervention coincided with the setting of the imperial sun, and by this time it was apparent to all that active state intervention could not be sustained at the same time as having widespread global commitments. By the late 1960s, a growth in Scottish nationalism that tended to equate the Scottish relationship within the Union as a form of imperialism, the circulation of ideas from the New Left that were more critical of empire, and a growing preoccupation with domestic standards of living and economic well-being, helped create a collective amnesia regarding Scotland's imperial past. The Continent became the main focus of Scottish business endeavours, and the booming economies of western Europe formed the template of aspiration and success. As Tom Devine rightly notes, the decline of the empire did not lead to a diminution in British identity north of the border, because the Union was reinforced in the public mind by the omnipresent agencies of the British state that touched the lives of more Scots and in more meaningful ways than ever was the case with the empire in its heyday.[127]

Select Bibliography

Judith M. Brown and Wm. Roger Louis (eds), *The Oxford History of the British Empire*, iv: *The Twentieth Century* (Oxford, 1999).

John Darwin, *The Empire Project: The Rise and Fall of the British World-System, 1830–1970* (Cambridge, 2009).

---

[126] See Douglas Sutherland, *The Argyll and Sutherland Highlanders* (London, 1969); the debate in the House of Commons, *Parl. Deb.*, vol. 778, 26 February 1969, 1718–19; Hew Strachan, *The Politics of the British Army* (London, 1997), 221; and the ambiguity of the Labour Party to Polaris is found in its *Report of the Annual Conference*, 60 (1961), 179.

[127] Devine, 'End of Empire?'

T. M. Devine, *Scotland's Empire, 1660–1815* (2003).

—— 'The Break-up of Britain? Scotland and the End of Empire', *Transactions of the Royal Historical Society*, 6th series, 16 (Cambridge, 2006), 163–81.

—— *To the Ends of the Earth: Scotland's Global Diaspora 1750–2010* (London, 2011).

R. Hyam, *Britain's Imperial Century, 1815–1914: A Study of Empire and Expansion* (London, 1993).

Colin Kidd, *Union and Unionism: Political Though in Scotland, 1500–2000* (Cambridge, 2008).

John M. MacKenzie, 'Essay and Reflection: On Scotland and the Empire', *International History Review*, 15 (1993), 714–39.

—— 'Empire and National Identities: The Case of Scotland', *Transactions of the Royal Historical Society*, 6th series, 8 (Cambridge, 1998), 215–31.

—— 'The Second City of Empire: Glasgow—Imperial Municipality', in Felix Driver and David Gilbert (eds), *Imperial Cities* (Manchester, 2003), 215–38.

A. Porter (ed.), *The Oxford History of the British Empire*, iii: *The Nineteenth Century* (Oxford, 1999).

B. Porter, *The Lion's Share: A Short History of British Imperialism* (various editions).

Andrew Thompson, *The Empire Strikes Back: The Impact of Imperialism on Britain from the Mid-Nineteenth Century* (London, 2005).

INDEX

Printed and bound by CPI Group (UK) Ltd, Croydon, CR0 4YY